Goodness Abounds
365 True Stories of Loving Kindness

Jodi Chapman, Dan Teck

& Over 275 Soulful Contributors

DandiLove Unlimited

This book comes from our hearts and is here to inspire you. Please know, though, that it is not a replacement for therapy or medical advice. If you are feeling like you could use some extra support, please seek out a professional in your area.

The views represented in this book are not necessarily a reflection of the publisher. Each author wrote their story in a way that they remembered the events happening. Please note that the publisher accepts no responsibility for any inaccurate information portrayed.

The authors who contributed to this book are from all corners of the world, and we have kept their native English spelling for each of their pieces. For this reason, you will see words like "color" and "colour" or "realized" and "realised" throughout the book – just depending on what part of the world the author is from. We also wanted to find a balance of maintaining consistency throughout the book while still honoring each author's belief system. For this reason, you will see that some words are capitalized in some pieces and not in others. For the most part, we capitalize words relating to God, Source, the Universe, and a Higher Power.

Ordering information available at:
www.goodnessabounds.com.
For wholesale inquiries, please write to: info@365bookseries.com.

Printed in the United States of America
ISBN: 13-978-0-9981251-2-1
Library of Congress Control Number: 2017946300

www.365bookseries.com

DEDICATION

We dedicate this book to two co-authors in our book series,
Sharon Rothstein and Vicky Mitchell, who passed away this year. They
were such loving souls who spread light everywhere they went and gave
so much of themselves during their time in this world.

They were part of our community, part of our lives, and part of our
hearts. They left us much too soon, and they will forever be missed by
those in this community, their families, and everyone they touched – in
person, online, and through their writing.

They exemplified what living a life of goodness looks like, and we will
forever be grateful to them for helping us see that goodness and love are
forever.

We love you, Sharon and Vicky.
Thank you for lighting up our world.

Contents

Introduction i

Chapter 1 – Helpful Strangers 1

A Rainbow in the Parking Lot – Michelle Radomski 2

The Amethyst Angel – Jodi Chapman 3

The Gift of Flight – Poppy Popowich 4

30 Minutes and a Blue Bucket – Marci Kobayashi 5

Winter Wonder – Judy Basaraba 6

Angel Dave – Danielle Pomerleau 7

The Road to Goodness – Anita D. Marshall 8

A Spiritual Encounter at McDonald's – Kimberly Brochu 9

Thank You for Being Beautiful – Lara Anderson 10

Unexpected Kindness from a Perfect Stranger – Lynn Spiro 11

Come, Let's Get You Home – Jamie Thomas 12

Grace and the Kindness of Strangers – Elizabeth R. Kipp 13

Concrete Kindness: There Are No Accidents – Kathy Damas 14

My Irish Angel – Cheryl Carrigan 15

A Memorable Encounter – Cornelia Merk 16

The Man in the Orange Suit – Alison M. Stokes 17

Christmas in August – Trish Mckinnley 18

Power Suit Angel – Victoria McGee 19

The Red Poppy Flower – Joelle Rose Szlosek 20

An Angel in Time – Marifran Korb 21

On the Road Again – Kimberly DuBoise 22

Heaven Sent – Meredith Fjelsted 23

Honeymooners with Heart – Jo Shepherd 24

The Angel in My Kitchen – Margaretta McIlvaine 25

Giving Me Wings to Succeed – Isabella Rose...26

Pay It Forward – Teresa Velardi...27

The Language of Kindness – Crystal M. Cathell..28

Heart of a Hometown – Diana L. Hooker..29

A Helping Hand – Ellouise Heather...30

The Energy of a Gift – Jenny McKaig..31

Our Very Own Bodyguard – Nora T. Barican...32

A Cup of Kindness – Isla Selupucin...33

California Earth Angels – Maureen Hollmeyer...34

With Hands Wide Open – Pooja Shende..35

A Bushel and a Peck – Lori Kilgour Martin...36

Sometimes God Cashiers at Walmart – Kathy DeFinis..37

The Best Flat Tire Ever – Katrina Ariel...38

An Angel Walking Among Us – Lisa "The Link" Rizzo..39

Sound to the Rescue – Sally M. Sutton..40

Ripples of a Prayer – Padma Gordon...41

The Goodbye Kiss – Patty Davis...42

Kindness Knows No Boundaries – Kathryn Shah...43

Magical Kindness Between Strangers – Alison Ellison..44

Hospital Room 222 – Kelly M. Spencer..45

Don't Judge a Book by Its Cover – Sharon Hickinbotham...46

Let Your Voice Be Heard – Joy T. Barican..47

Flowers from a Stranger – Sharyn Holmes...48

My Gracious Fairy Godmother – Denise Edelstein..49

The Answer...An Angel In Blue – Destrie Sweet Larrabee..50

The Power of Kindness – Diana L. Hooker..51

Cowboy to the Rescue – Karen Wythe...52

Thank You for Stopping – Anita D. Marshall..53

For the Love of Strangers – Isabella Rose...54

Golf Cart Man – Susan Bassett...55

Kindness in the Midst of Chaos – B. J. Garcia...56

Goodness Is a Global Affair – Keyra Conlinn...57

$5 Difference – Lydia Burchell..58

Chapter 2 – Family & Loving Relationships.............................. 59

I See You – Dan Teck... 60

My Sister, Sharon – A True Force of Nature – Ellyn Rothstein 61

A Valiant Act of Love – Isabella Rose.. 62

The Power of a Hug – Sonya L. Moore.. 63

Full Circle – Cathie Bliss.. 64

An Unexpected Invitation – Crysti Deusterman..................................... 65

My Father's Dignity – Lauren Bear.. 66

Breakfast with Jesus – Richard Saenz.. 67

The Gritty Goodness of Selfless Parenting – Alison Ellison.................... 68

Softly, as in a Morning Son Rise – Katie Keck Chenoweth..................... 69

Let's Help Each Other – Bevan Bird 70

Second Time Around – Marla David... 71

Wheels of Goodness – Kristy Carr McAdams 72

Satisfaction Beyond Words – Nancy Merrill Justice................................ 73

My Inspiration, Tony – Catherine Laub.. 74

The Power Is in You – Surabhi Kalsi.. 75

Unconditional Love and Kindness – Tahira Bharmal.............................. 76

The Healing Power of Unwavering Love – Gigi Florez........................... 77

Foster Father – Reema Sharma Nagwan 78

Saint Nana – Shayelee Johnson... 79

The Gifts of Love Tree – Jenna Kelland 80

Blessings Begin at Home - Tammy Gamester 81

A Father's Parting Gift – Salome Schori 82

Mom's Seeds Taking Root – Kaori Takada 83

Simply Indescribable – Kenneth I. Laws II.. 84

The Force of Brotherhood – Charissa May-Riley.................................... 85

My Angel Mom – Tere Moore... 86

A Summer Place – Barbara ("Bobbie") Carr 87

Reviving Our Hearts – Kim Brazier Flatland... 88

Accidental Kindness – Misty Proffitt-Thompson.................................... 89

Life Is Too Short to Be Small – Jody Wootton 90

With a Twinkle in Her Eye – Kathy Damas 91

The Gift of Time and Attention – Kelly Jenkins..................................... 92

The Greatest Joy Is Giving – Chadi Hemaidan 93

My Love Story – Carisa Montooth 94

Me Ke Aloha Pumehana – Katie Keck Chenoweth...95

A Grandpa's Love, Forever in My Heart – Vicki Ann Martinelli...........................96

Sacred Ground – Cindy Harpe Hively 97

A Ray of Light – Lisa R. Cohen..98

Walking with Ancestors – Lori Santo 99

The Little Shop – Neelam Patel... 100

The Matriarch – Lauren Bear 101

The Breath of Love – Jesse Hodgdon.. 102

Books, Empathy, and a Wonderful Memory – Shannon Townsend................... 103

My Mother's Love – Anne-Marie Hoyne.. 104

A Song for My Father – Gunhild Lorenzen.. 105

Coming Full Circle – Lori Thomas.. 106

The Beauties I Get to Behold – Kimberly A. Elliott... 107

Goodness Begins with Empathy – Valerie R. Vestal.. 108

A Life in Service to Love – B. J. Garcia 109

The Advent Calendar – Jodi Chapman.. 110

Chapter 3 – Friends & Neighbors... 111

The Tap Rats – Maureen Hollmeyer.. 112

Vicky Mitchell – Soul Sister Goodness – Giuliana Melo..................................... 113

Divine Timing – Kimberly Brochu 114

A Gesture That Left an Indelible Mark – Nora T. Barican 115

A Beautiful, Multifaceted Gift – Christine Callahan-Oke.................................. 116

Healing in Vietnam – Mauri Barnes 117

Angel in the Cold – Lisa Anna Palmer 118

Adventures in Motoring – Lori Thomas 119

Adopting a Jewish Mom – Joan Zietlow.. 120

The Power of Words – Michelle Evans.. 121

Neighborhood Helpers – Lori Thiessen.. 122

Footprints on My Heart – Keyon Bayani... 123

The Blessings of Friends – Helen Ferrara 124

Mary's Selfless Gift of Compassion – Ingrid Koivukangas 125

Three Seconds – Scott Fjelsted.. 126

Planting the Field of Dreams – Isabella Rose 127

The Power of the Word "Love" – Denny Long 128

My Angel on Earth – Catherine Laub 129

Love, Loss, and Fireworks – Sarah Lawrence... 130

Three Men Moved Me – Ray Goodenough 131

Circles of the Soul – Laura Garrett 132

The Neighbors – Kim Marks...133

When Others See the Goodness in You – Tanya Levy 134

So Grateful for the Unexpected – Karen Ceballos 135

Love as a North Star – J. Scott MacMillan 136

Forever in Our Hearts – Pauline Hosie Robinson......................................137

Special Delivery: Pennies from Heaven – Padma Gordon 138

Grateful to Be Alive – Kellie McGarry...139

It Is Always Possible – Leslie Sann 140

Starting to Live Again – Dianna Robinson Curren.....................................141

Because Someone Cared – Nora T. Barican..142

Earth Angels – Netta de Beer...143

A Simple Request – Diane L. Keyes..144

A Saint in the Storm – Beth Larsen 145

My Friend Frank – Ty Will 146

Graduating Together – Jamie Thomas 147

Love Conquers All – H. Michelle Spaulding...148

The Gift Bag – Robyn Dewar 149

A Heartfelt Moment for the Soul – Lynn Spiro 150

My Twin from Another Life – Maureen Hollmeyer....................................151

A Passion for Fashion…and Kindness – Cyvilstre Rio Olami....................152

I Live to Serve – Ruth Donald 153

Earth Angels Lighting My Path – Shirani M. Pathak 154

The Big Decision – Tanya Levy...155

One Precious Friend – Ray Goodenough 156

Someone to Watch Over Me – Joy T. Barican 157

Chapter 4 – Huge Hearts in Small Bodies 159

Little Heroes with Big Hearts – StacyLynn Rasmussen 160

Annie's Guardian Angel – Lynn Spiro..161

The Perfect "Rock" – Kimber Bowers...162

Petie – Lucy V. Nefstead...163

Never Too Young – Karen Ceballos 164

River Walk Rescue – Susan Elizabeth Schoemmell....................................165

The Creative Power of One Child – Nadene Joy Hagen 166

My Kind of Friend – Ella Wilson..167

Mammaw's Little Angel – Karen Hill 168

A Tiny Gesture Means So Much – Danielle Pomerleau 169

Voy's Tractorcade – Jamie Lynn Thompson 170

Bella's Dessert – Jacine Rilea 171

The Angelic Energy of Kindness – Wendyanne Pakulsky 172

My Son Has a BIG Heart – Donna H. Kater 173

No Goldfish for the Homeless – Haley Ryane Meushaw 174

The Power of Presence – Tamra Blankenship 175

Children Are Our Greatest Teachers – Nadene Joy Hagen 176

Love Beyond Language – Jenean Zunk 177

The Disappearing Gloves – Kelly Jenkins 178

A Grandmother's Miracle Healing – Debbie Labinski 179

The Wish List – Jenna Kelland 180

Chapter 5 – Animals & Nature 181

Paws, Breathe, Proceed – Michelle R. Griffith 182

The Gift of Bees – Kyra Schaefer 183

Freedom Ride – Mauri Barnes 184

Amelia's Chance at Life – Sharon G. Smith 185

Lost and Found: Joyful and Archie Bacon – Donna S. Priesmeyer 186

The Magic of Manali – John R. Fyfe 187

The Reebok Chicken – Kimberly Beer 188

Rescue and Relationship – Nora Rose 189

Passing Kindness – Michelle Smith Mufarreh 190

Rescue – Janet G. Nestor 191

Spring Green – Joy Harris 192

Max, the Generous Jack Russell – Veronica Mather 193

Becoming Free – John R. Fyfe 194

Puppy Love – Jena Brown 195

Sunflower Magic – Ruthie Lewis 196

Kiaora the Brave – Kris McLeod 197

Showered with Love – Lori Thomas 198

A Calico Named Ruby – Janet Womack 199

Doggone Goodness – Marla David 200

Rose Petals of Empowerment – Carrie Kondor 201

Dog Therapy – Nathalie Rivett 202

Goodness Soothed My Aching Heart – Nancy Merrill Justice 203

Experiencing Calm – Michelle R. Griffith 204

Furry Angels – Tiffany Andersen 205

The Deep Kindness of a Cat – Helen Ferrara...206

Grey and Bearded, Kind and Giving – Faye Rogers...207

Oreo the Cow – Tessa Shaffer 208

People Are a Problem – Marci Kobayashi 209

Tucker's Gift – Trena Anderson...210

From My Hands to My Heart – Nora Rose 211

Goodness Abounds, Even in Death – Claire Chew 212

An Autumn Walk – Joy Harris..213

Yoga Nidra Prayer Mascots – Cynthia Lee Horn...214

Be the Good – Davalynn Kim 215

An Angel for Our Animals – Alison Ellison..216

Gift of the Garden Light – Michelle Smith Mufarreh 217

Have Some of Both – Michelle R. Griffith 218

Blessed by a Butterfly   Pauline Hosie Robinson 219

Chapter 6 – Kindness at Work & School................................221

How Was Your Game? – Dan Teck...222

Help from a Generous Heart – Lori Thiessen 223

When the Client Becomes the Mentor – Maureen Hollmeyer...................................224

Flying on the Wings of Kindness – Eva Muserelli...225

God's Ace – Brian Monahan 226

Keys from the Heart – Kimberly Hutt...227

Pursue Your Passion – Robin Chellis..228

An Angel Named Joy – Irene E. Bradford..229

Public Display of Affection – Heather Wiest 230

Taking Time to Check In – Joanne Angel Barry Colon..231

Everyone Is Someone's Special Someone – Melisa Archer.......................................232

Compassion Blooms to So Much More – Jamie Lynn Thompson 233

A Moment Can Change Everything – Nicole Donovan-Wells.....................................234

Programming in Poetry – Cindy Smiczek...235

A Gentle Wall – Valerie R. Vestal...236

Praise Behind My Back – Lateefah Shaheed..237

The Art of Receiving – Daniel Nilon 238

Finding True Abundance – Ahana Lara...239

Positive Energy – Corina Y. Muro..240

The Greatest Gift – Anne Bradley..241

A Well-Respected Man – Catherine Laub..242

Love Always Wins – Michelle Goguen...243

Goodness of a Conscious Conversation – Carolyn McGee 244

My Students Are My Greatest Teachers – Tanya Levy.........................245

A Gift That Keeps on Giving – Joy T. Barican....................................246

Mr. Mickelson's Tall Girl – Marci Kobayashi 247

The Candy Man – Tiffany Clay..248

Joy Is in My Heart – Gunhild Lorenzen..249

Daydream Believer – Mike Monahan...250

A Final Wish – Marie Spencer-Rowland..251

All Things Connect with Love – Nadene Joy Hagen............................252

The Gift from Pastor S. – Diane L. Keyes...253

Hannelore, My Angel – Heather A. Dempsey.....................................254

Touching Lives – Vijaya Gowrisankar...255

Goodness Abounds in Mentorship – Nikki A. Creber.........................256

Beautiful, Spacious Gift – Joanne Angel Barry Colon........................257

Kindness to Self – Lola Pittenger..258

Courtney – Melisa Archer..259

An Unexpected Angel – Steph Walczak...260

Sarah's Story – Kimberly Brochu..261

Giving from the Heart – Felicia D'Haiti..262

Chapter 7 – Community...**263**

The Suncatcher – Tara Leduc 264

Unexpected Gifts – Kimberly Hutt..265

Welcome Home – Micheal Taylor..266

Ceara's Village – Annie Price..267

Unlocked – Diana L. Hooker...268

Beauty in Disaster – Leslie P. Felton...269

Grand Rapids of Love – Heather Wiest 270

The Grace of Giving and Receiving – Tandy R. Elisala.......................271

Meatballs Made Me Cry – Randy Bassett 272

Big Men, Big Hearts – Julie Jones 273

Breath of Gratitude – Chris Anderson...274

Tornado Strong – Jamie Lynn Thompson 275

Oh, Holey Sight – Sheila Jenkins..276

Praise You – Noelle Adamo...277

An American Dream – Hue Anh Nguyen...278

All Is Not Lost – Terry Corrao..279

Our Miracle Man – Tammy Foster...280

Just in Time – Mikaela Che'lean Hicks...281

Superheroes – Aphrodite Mirisis..282

Transitions – Charlene Williams...283

Dumela – Lauren Bear...284

Bubbly Blessings – Michael Brewer...285

Light Outshines the Darkness – Kelli Adkins...................................286

Opening to Receive Love – Erin Fritts..287

Goodness Abounds...Even on Facebook – Alisa Auger.....................288

Dancing in Istanbul – Sarah Atkinson..289

It Takes a Village – Shari Sorbo..290

Asking for Help – Taryn Pyle..291

Making Magic – Robin OK..292

Light a Lamp – Pratibha Badurkar..293

Generous Souls – Kimberly Hutt..294

Chapter 8 – Giving Back 295

Play Ball! – Mauri Barnes..296

With Tragedy Came Purpose – Farahana Surya Namaskar................297

Hugs and Haircuts – Cynthia Lee Horn..298

God Stepped In – Teresa Velardi...299

An Upward Spiral – Barbara Toller...300

The Kindness of an Unsung Hero – Tracey Swainson.......................301

Loving Choices – Linsey Fischer...302

An Earth Angel Among Us – Patricia LeBlanc.................................303

A Fighting Chance – Rev. Shelia Prance...304

People Helping People – Shannon L. Brokaw...................................305

Philanthropy – Carly Melnick...306

Divine Communion – Charlene Kussner...307

Seva – Ayeesha S. Kanji...308

Miracle from Heaven – Ruby Mabry...309

Sweet Nectar to My Soul – Courtney Long......................................310

Hungering to Make a Difference – Nicole Schiener Manary.............311

Kindness in Tragedy – Niki Meadows...312

Holy Chaos – Patricia Downing..313

I'll Stand by You – Danielle Redmond..314

When the Beatitudes Came to Life – Thomas E. Uharriet...................................... 315

Volunteering Makes a Difference – Teresa Velardi 316

The Power of One – Pass It On – Nora Rose 317

A Reason to Smile – Mauri Barnes 318

The Miracle of the Multiplying Food – Rhonda Lee... 319

Chapter 9 – Goodness from Beyond 321

A Flock of Angels – Annalene Hart.. 322

French Toast Ghost – Sarah Huffer 323

Parking Lot Miracle – Gretchen Oehler Hogg... 324

Peter's Gaze – John R. Fyfe 325

Goodness from Beyond the Veil – Nancy Merrill Justice..................................... 326

When God Steps In, Miracles Happen – Rani St. Pucchi..................................... 327

A Team of Life-Saving Angels – Melisa Archer.. 328

Jesus Loves You – Lupe Ramirez Peterkin 329

God's Gift – Saundra Lee... 330

Kindness from the Other Side – Claire Chew 331

Angels on Earth – Suzanne Fortino... 332

Witnessing Divine Guidance – Phoebe Fazio 333

Manifesting the Holy Spirit – Tiffany Andersen 334

You Can See Me Now – Kimberly A. Elliott... 335

A Shifting of Consciousness – Cheryl Lawrence 336

Frere Andre and the Umbrella – Cydney Mar... 337

Butterflies from Heaven – Debby Spitzig.. 338

Birthing into the Beyond – Chireya K. Fox.. 339

Gifts from Heaven – Tessa Wuyts 340

Spirit Provides – Teresa Madrone Sinay 341

An Angel Watching Over Her – Darlene Gaetz.. 342

What You Give, You Receive – Manpreet Komal... 343

Growing Vines of Goodness – Amy Lloyd... 344

Bella Angel Cards – Angie Carter.. 345

His Divine Timing – Karen Ciran-Barnes... 346

The Universe Sends Nothing but Angels – Michelle Anne Gould.............................. 347

The Goodness of Everyday Life – Helen Ferrara 348

Fade to Black – Marla David... 349

Winks from God – Katie Cox Jackson 350

Angels Watching over Me – Cynthia Starborn... 351

Chapter 10 – Everyday Goodness **353**

My Refrigerator Door – Amanda Roggemann 354

The Baby and the Bus Driver – Jerri Eddington.............................355

All That Jazz – Rebekah Bernard 356

Simple Kindness – Fiona Louise 357

Kindness in Edgemere Park – Cara M. Rosch & Alex Biholar.............358

Finding Goodness – Karen Wythe 359

A Love Story – Benjamin Bush...360

Kindness Counts – Kim Wright 361

The Enchanted Hour – Tiffany Andersen 362

Sparks of Love – Sarah Auger 363

I'm Not Alone – Cynthia Lee Horn 364

Nothing But More Goodness – Rael Hall..365

Goodness Is Always Waiting for You – Jennifer Larkin 366

It's the "Little Things" – L. A. Reeves 367

A Fabric of Small Kindnesses – Sarah Atkinson...............................368

The Roller Coaster of Goodness – Sabinah Adewole 369

Goodness Abounds in Everyday Folk – Lisa Hawkins 370

An Abundance of Love – V. Krishna Lakkineni 371

Goodness Equals Rightful Living – Marihet Hammann....................372

High Vibrations of Unconditional Love – Mimi Quick.....................373

Open Your Heart to Joy – Moni Rodriguez.......................................374

Loving Kindness – Nikki Ackerman..375

The Art of Being Courageous – Shari Sorbo.....................................376

Seeing Goodness – Karen Wythe...377

The Power of Kindness – Pauline Hosie Robinson............................378

A Cloudy Day Filled with Sunshine – Kris Martin 379

Conclusion **381**

Contributor Biographies **383**

Contributor Index **433**

Acknowledgments..**439**

Other Books in This Series **441**

An Invitation **443**

Introduction

This book came about because we were feeling overwhelmed by all of the negativity and divisiveness in the news and on social media, especially after the 2016 election here in the United States. Scrolling through our Facebook feed was no longer enjoyable due to one contentious post or news story after another. We were angry and disheartened, and we found ourselves sinking lower and lower into a pit of powerlessness and despair. We began questioning everything we thought we knew about the inherent kindness in people and wondered what had happened to the light-filled, loving universe we thought we lived in.

Our first inclination was to bury our heads in the sand and come up only when the world seemed sane and peaceful again. But something deep inside our soul whispered that loving kindness was still out there, that the majority of people still had huge hearts and were still making a positive impact in our world, and that it was up to us to turn on our "goodness radar" to find it.

Being on the lookout for goodness felt empowering to us – we liked having something to focus on that made us feel good instead of bad. So we started thinking about our lives – starting with the present and working all the way back to childhood – looking for evidence of goodness that we had experienced from both strangers and loved ones. We wanted to remember all of the moments – the big ones and also the small ones. We wanted to surround ourselves with all of these happy and life-affirming memories because we knew that they would help us have more faith in humankind again. And it worked. We began feeling more hopeful, and the cloud of darkness that had been surrounding us seemed to lift a little bit. We could see a glimmer of light again.

We were so excited to be feeling hopeful again, and we wanted to invite others to join us in finding, focusing on, and celebrating goodness in their own lives, too. We knew that many others were still feeling disheartened and powerless, so we thought that it would be wonderfully uplifting if hundreds of us came together to share our stories of goodness in one book so we could all fill our hearts with the knowing that no matter how bleak things looked, people were still so helpful and giving. As the stories began pouring in, each one we read renewed our faith in humanity and opened our hearts just a bit more. While reading them, we cried tears of joy as we were reminded of just how giving and kind people truly can be. And now, we're so excited to share each of these stories of goodness with you!

The 365 true stories in this book vary greatly, but they all have one thing in common: they add to an ever-growing mountain of evidence that goodness abounds! It's our hope that while reading this book, you can flip to any page and find a story that will provide inspiration, upliftment, and encouragement to reflect on the kindness you've experienced in your own life, to turn on your "goodness radar" and be on the lookout for more, and to have faith that goodness truly is alive and well in our world!

We love the variety of stories shared throughout this book. Over 275 co-authors came together to create it – each of whom is unique. We are spread out all over the world, speak different languages, have different professions, follow different religions, are different races, have unique experiences and points of view...our list of differences goes on and on. Yet, no matter how different we are, these stories remind us that we each go through similar life experiences. What we continue to find throughout each of the books in our series is how much we have in common. We all want to feel loved and to offer love, to express our deepest truth, to be seen and understood, and to feel peace and happiness. We all want to embrace our time here on Earth. And we all want to believe and really know deep in our gut that goodness abounds in our world.

As you'll see while reading these stories of goodness, they cover many different life experiences, and because of that, we never could have written this book on our own. Because these are true stories, the authors really needed to show up from a space of authenticity to be able to share them. They needed to be honest and vulnerable, especially since some of their stories are deeply emotional. It takes bravery to share in such a heartfelt way, and we are inspired by each of the authors for doing so. Each of their stories was needed to create the depth and richness that you'll find throughout this collection, and we're truly grateful to everyone who is part of it.

Examples of Goodness

As we mentioned, when we began reading these stories, we found a wide range of experiences. Some of the stories told of life-changing moments that you never forget, such as when an entire community came together to help someone in need or when someone was given a helping hand that changed the trajectory of their life. We also read many stories that shared quieter moments of kindness – moments that aren't always as easy to remember because they may not be as flashy as the bigger moments, but moments that can be just as powerful. These moments, when added up, become the fabric of our lives: a smile from a stranger, a helpful hand from a neighbor, a kind comment from a teacher, a hug when it is most needed, a caring note from a co-worker, a random act of kindness from someone you'll never see again, or an "I love you" that stays in your heart forever. We're so happy that we get to share all of these moments with you – the entire range of goodness – to help show how prevalent loving kindness truly is in our lives, in our communities, and in our world. It's everywhere.

How to Read This Book

As we do with all of our books in this series, we gave each of the co-authors free rein with their pieces and trusted that the book would come together in a cohesive way once we received them all. And that's exactly what happened. The pieces fell into 10 categories, which became our chapter titles:

1. Helpful Strangers
2. Family & Loving Relationships
3. Friends & Neighbors

4. Huge Hearts in Small Bodies

5. Animals & Nature

6. Kindness at Work & School

7. Community

8. Giving Back

9. Goodness from Beyond

10. Everyday Goodness

There are many ways to enjoy this book: you can read each entry in order on the day it appears, or you can flip through at random and let your soul guide you. Perhaps you have a favorite day of the year (such as your birthday or an anniversary) and want to see which piece appears on that day. Or maybe a certain chapter's theme is calling to you. For example, if you're feeling like you could use a boost of goodness immediately, you could start with Chapter 1 and read about how perfect strangers gave so much of themselves without expecting anything in return. Or if you're wanting to read about ways that people are giving back to their communities through charity work, you could turn to Chapter 8. If you're wanting to be reminded of goodness in the classroom, you can read some truly inspiring stories in Chapter 6.

There is no right or wrong way to read this book. You can read one piece each morning or night as part of your spiritual practice. Or you can read it in the carpool lane while picking up your kids from school.

Another suggestion for reading this book is to keep a journal nearby to jot down any thoughts and inspirations that enter your heart as you read the pieces – even if they don't make sense to you at first. Chances are, they will when you most need them to.

You can also read this book with your friends as a way to deepen your relationships and share your own stories of goodness with each other. You can meet (in person or online) and go through the days, or you can pick and choose them at random and share what you learned about yourself after reading the stories and taking them into your heart.

However and wherever you choose to read it, know that it's a powerful book – one that we believe has the ability to help you feel more connected to our world and everyone in it than ever before. By reading this book, you're consciously opening your heart to finding evidence of goodness in your own life, and we believe that once you begin focusing on it, you'll find yourself surrounded by it!

Giving Back

Because we've both experienced so much goodness from being around animals and nature, we'll be donating 5% of all profits from sales of this book to the Jane Goodall Institute. (You can learn more about this charity by going to www.janegoodall.org.)

Thank You

Thank you for being part of this journey with us. We hope you enjoy each of the pieces in this special book. We felt our own hearts expand while compiling them, and we hope that you'll experience that while reading them. It's our hope and belief that as we shine a light on goodness, it will grow and grow until it makes up the overwhelming majority of our experience! We certainly feel that the stories in this book show time and time again that our world hasn't fallen apart and gone to the dark side. They show that the light still shines brightly in each of our hearts. And they show that loving kindness truly is all around us and goodness truly does abound.

Hugs, love, and gratitude,
Jodi and Dan

Chapter 1
Helpful Strangers

S hortly after we started dating in 2002, we took our first road trip: from Jodi's home in Albuquerque to the Red Rocks Amphitheatre, just outside of Denver. The trip made absolutely no sense: it was a 900-mile round trip, and we both had to be back for work the next day. But we wanted to go see a concert of two of our favorite singers (Chris Isaak and Natalie Merchant) – and besides, we were young and in love, and we just wanted to spend time together and have an adventure. It turned out to be a bit more of an adventure than we'd bargained for.

Everything went smoothly on the drive up, and the concert was great; but on the way home, we blew out a tire. Today, this wouldn't be such a big deal because we now have a cell phone, insurance that covers towing from anywhere at any time, and the ability to change our own tire. In 2002, though, we had none of this. What we did have was a couple of guardian angels…in the form of auto mechanics who just happened to be driving past (at 2 a.m.!), pulled over to help (within a minute of our tire blowing out!), and got our tire changed faster than an Indy-500 pit-stop crew (while guiding us through the process so we'd know how to do it in the future – training that came in handy on several subsequent occasions). They wouldn't accept money or anything beyond thanks, and within a few minutes they were on their way…and so were we!

As we read the stories in this chapter, we realized that these angel-mechanics are far from the only helpful strangers out there. In fact, the world is full of kind people willing to lend a helping hand…not because it's their job or because they're family, but simply because they're good people who want to help make the world a better place. And they do.

A Rainbow in the Parking Lot

By Michelle Radomski

The heat hit like a blaze as I stepped out of the grocery store. One glance at the digital thermometer above the bank confirmed it: 111 degrees! Thank goodness I had snagged a front-row parking spot.

As I got closer to my car, I noticed something on the windshield.

"Why do people do that?" I grumbled. "Why do they put crap on people's cars when 99% of it ends up in the trash?"

I grabbed the bright pink envelope from under the windshield wiper without even looking at it. My irritation level was rising as fast as the Arizona heat, so I got in the car, cranked up the AC, and threw the envelope onto the seat next to me.

It was then I noticed the message delicately inscribed on the outside of the envelope:

I wish you a bright and beautiful day, full of miracles and magic.

Irritation turned quickly to delight as I felt the attention – and *intention* – that the giver of this gift must have poured into every word.

I read the message again and held the envelope to my heart. Someone had taken the time to purchase this envelope, write this message, brave the heat, and place pure love under *my* windshield. Tears of hope for our world rolled down my cheek.

I gently opened the envelope and felt my breath catch when I saw a crisp $20 bill with another handwritten note tucked inside:

Use this to make your own kind of magic today.

My heart swelled with gratitude for the gorgeous human who extended this act of kindness to me, a perfect stranger. And then, it nearly burst as I looked around in wonder to see brightly colored envelopes adorning the windshields of nearly 100 cars – a rainbow of kindness, beaming in the Arizona sun.

In that moment I knew that, in spite of what sometimes feels like a hateful world, hope, kindness, generosity, and grace are very much alive.

The Amethyst Angel
By Jodi Chapman

Dan and I excitedly put our tandem kayak into the lake and climbed in. Based on the map, we would almost immediately turn onto a gently flowing river, which we were really looking forward to since the lake was extra choppy. Our boat crashed into each wave, and I started to feel sick to my stomach and a bit scared. We flew down the current and were barely able to steer into a calmer inlet. We thought we had reached the river, but it turned out to be just another part of the lake. Somehow, we had missed the opening, and I dreaded having to turn around and go against the current to reach it.

By then, the wind had really picked up, and the water was filled with whitecaps. We returned to the main part of the lake and paddled with all our might. Soaked from the spray and exhausted from the physical effort, I could feel my anxiety deepening.

We soon realized that we wouldn't be able to make it back to our starting point, but we saw a private dock in the distance and decided to head to that instead. Thankfully, we managed to reach it and (with difficulty) pull ourselves and the boat onto the wooden platform. With shaky legs on the moving dock, we somehow made it to solid ground.

We were pretty far from where we'd parked, so I sat with the boat and our gear while Dan walked to get the car. I was soaked, shivering, and in shock. A woman in a white gown walked toward me and asked if I was okay. I told her what had happened, and she held me while I cried. She asked me to come to her house (which was just a few steps away) to warm up while we waited for Dan. I gratefully accepted. While there, she handed me a towel, some hot tea, and a huge chunk of amethyst, which she said would soothe me. I instantly began to feel calm and safe.

When Dan returned and I felt strong enough to leave, the woman took my hand and said that she wanted me to keep the amethyst because I needed it more than she did. At first, I turned down her offer, saying that it was too much. But she insisted. Eventually, I accepted her generous gift, and we hugged each other before Dan and I drove away.

I will forever be grateful for this "amethyst angel" who appeared exactly when I most needed a comforting soul to ease my fears.

The Gift of Flight

By Poppy Popowich

Will was on his way to the job he loves. As a flight attendant, he is able to meet people, connect with them, and hopefully make their day a little brighter.

This particular day, a young family (mom, dad, and son) sat in the front row, and Will struck up a conversation with them during the flight. It turns out that the boy was the same age as his son and had the same name. Will asked the family if they were traveling for vacation. The mom said no. He guessed again: "Are you going to see family?" Again, no. After Will's third guess – "For business?" – the mom felt compelled to respond.

"Chemo."

Will's heart broke as the story unfolded. The young mother had been diagnosed with breast cancer, and they were flying to Chicago for her treatment – a treatment she needed every three weeks. The family usually did not accompany her due to the expense of travel.

Will was overcome with emotion. By the end of the flight, they had forged an incredible bond. Earlier that day, he had wished that he could bless someone with his companion pass (which allows one person to fly standby for free when space is available). He wanted to give it to someone who really needed it.

He took the family aside and explained, "I want to help make your journey a little easier." He offered the mother his companion pass so she wouldn't have to be alone during her treatments. It was a tender moment filled with tears of compassion and gratitude. They accepted his offer, which they knew was raw, authentic kindness from Will's heart.

That moment not only changed this young family's lives forever, Will's life became brighter and even more filled with joy by sharing his heart and soul.

30 Minutes and a Blue Bucket

By Marci Kobayashi

I was miserable and feeling sorry for myself. I smelled bad and felt gross. It was the third day after my hip surgery, and I had just gotten permission to stand on my new titanium hip. Though I could stand up and stretch, I wasn't allowed to walk yet. But I didn't care about walking anywhere. All I wanted was to take a shower. The intern promised I could take one as soon as I got permission from the surgeon. Unfortunately, it was Saturday and my surgeon wouldn't be back until Monday.

After breakfast, one of the nurses came by with a hot washcloth so I could freshen up. I tried to be friendly and chat, but she must have noticed that my effort was forced. She said she would be back in a few hours with a treat. Though it was nice of her to say, I didn't really expect much.

About two hours later, the nurse walked into my room wearing rubber boots and a rubber apron. She said she had 30 minutes and knew something that would make me feel better. I was skeptical but let her help me out of bed and into the wheelchair.

The nurse wheeled me into a large room with a tile floor, two sinks, several handheld showerheads, and a huge tub. Next to the tub, I saw a big blue bucket and several towels. She parked my wheelchair next to the bucket and laid one of the towels over my lap. I was confused. We both knew that the surgeon had not yet given me permission to bathe. That's when she told me she was giving me a foot bath.

The warm, soapy water was heaven, and I cried. Even though my hair was dirty and my back was itchy, I felt like a queen after that foot bath. I felt witnessed and loved. I couldn't believe that the nurse had taken the time to help me with something so frivolous. I couldn't stop smiling. While the surgeon fixed my hip, the nurse helped fix my heart.

Winter Wonder

By Judy Basaraba

I used to live in the north, where winters are harsh: the days are short, and -40°C isn't uncommon. By January or February, "cabin fever" sets in; symptoms include a desperate need to get out.

Once, in the middle of a particularly acute episode of cabin fever, I heard about a lodge an hour and a half away that made wonderful cinnamon buns. That was all the prodding I needed! I decided to check it out.

Along the way, I saw lots of trees, but no lights, houses, service stations, or traffic. When I reached the lodge, the windows were frosted on the edges; only a small part in the center was clear. But it was warm on the inside – a cozy log cabin with a fire burning in a potbellied stove. The people there treated me like a friend. I only ate a quarter of the massive cinnamon bun; with a smile, they wrapped what was left.

It was close to -40° and dark when I left. About 10 minutes later, it seemed that my car wasn't getting enough gas. It moved slower and slower until it stopped. Still running but not moving, the heater wasn't working well. I sat there, clueless. Five minutes later, it "cleared itself" and I continued. Only a couple of minutes later, though, it happened again. *If the car stalls, there's no heat*, I thought, with visions of turning into a popsicle.

Then I heard a knock on my window. I opened the door. (The window was frozen shut.) There stood a huge hooded parka. (I couldn't see a face.) He asked if I was okay. I explained what had happened and said that I should be fine. He invited me to warm up in his truck while we waited. I declined, reiterating that I would be fine. "I'm sure you will be," he said. "But I'll just wait for you."

He sat in his truck until my car moved again. Then he followed me. When my car stopped again, he pulled over behind me and waited. I went back and told him he needn't waste his time waiting. But he told me, "It's not a waste." He followed me, stopping and starting, for five hours.

A few blocks from home, I looked in my mirror. He was gone. I never got his name or said thank you, so I'll say it now.

Angel Dave

By Danielle Pomerleau

This past year, one of my dear elder friends had been going through intense emotional hardship. The culmination of enduring a longstanding chronic painful physical condition, along with her husband's recent decision to leave her for a younger woman, was almost too much for her to bear. Concerned for her fragile mental state, I checked in frequently and had many dinners and overnight stays. During one of these visits, she asked if I had heard her story of "Angel Dave." With curious ears, I listened as she recounted it.

Feeling lonely, deflated, and despondent, she walked through the produce section of the grocery store. While attempting to get a plastic bag from a roll, she dropped the entire roll, which unraveled in disarray on the floor. With one hand clutching a colorful bouquet of flowers, she crouched down to clean it up.

As she did, a tall young man with penetrating blue eyes walked over, jovially saying: "Making a mess here, I see?..." He knelt down in front of her to assist with the clean-up. Seeing the flowers in her hand, he brightly asked, "What's the occasion?"

Being a very private person, she surprised herself by blurting out that the "occasion" was *her* – and she proceeded to fill him in about her husband recently leaving and her needing something to make her feel good. She watched Dave's face darken and his eyes fill with compassion. He asked if he could give her a hug, and she again surprised herself by agreeing. The hug was a real, heartfelt embrace that made her feel connected and cared for.

She thanked him, and they parted ways. About 10 minutes later, Dave sought her out and handed her a folded piece of paper. On the front was a heart, hand-drawn in Sharpie, and the inside read:

You are a beautiful, brilliant, incredibly strong soul,
and it's not the end of your story. :) - Love, Dave

This touched her so deeply that she still carries that handmade card in her purse wherever she goes. Whenever she is feeling down, she pulls the card out to read the kind words of a stranger.

The Road to Goodness

By Anita D. Marshall

As I stood shaking on the side of a Vietnamese road, I wondered what had possessed me to think that just one week after learning to ride a scooter, I could ride the 25 miles along the coastal road to the city.

My travel companion tried to persuade me to get back onto my scooter, but with the descending dusk, strong sea winds, and seriously questionable "rules of the road," I had lost my nerve. I could ride pillion home, but that left us with the issue of what we could do with the hired scooter. We had been warned they had a habit of going missing if left unattended too long!

A short distance away, we could see a roadside fish restaurant, so we went there to see if there was anywhere safe we could leave the bike until the morning. A petite young Vietnamese lady with a big smile and even more smiley eyes greeted us as we came through the door. Her English was good enough to understand our predicament, but instead of saying we could leave the bike there until morning, she said, "We go now. I ride your scooter back for you. You follow, yes?" There was not a chance to even eat in her restaurant as she grabbed her own helmet and set off up the road to my abandoned scooter.

We just assumed that my friend would take her back to the restaurant. But when we got back to our hostel, she hopped off my scooter, smiled, and went to the road side to flag down a scooter taxi. My friend rushed to say he would take her back, but she shook her head and said it was fine. Taxi bikes cost money even for the locals, so we tried to give her some money instead, but she would not take it. She simply smiled and said, "People have been good to me; now I do good for others" and gave one more big smile before hopping on a taxi bike and disappearing down the road. Thank you for sharing the goodness forward to us.

A Spiritual Encounter at McDonald's

By Kimberly Brochu

'Twas a few nights before Christmas when all through the house, I'd been cleaning and decorating and needed an out.

"What's for dinner?"

Really, dinner? Every year for the holidays our home becomes a revolving door of family, laughter, games, and love. Dinner, however, I am not prepared for.

"McDonald's it is!" I proclaim, grabbing my keys and venturing out into the cold.

Impatiently waiting at the light just outside of McDonald's, I spot a car coming up behind me in the breakdown lane. It doesn't look like it's actually "breaking down." Instead, it creeps up next to me, preventing me from turning. Then, as the light turns green, it cuts in front of me and turns into the drive-through lane of the "golden arches." Not in the mood for illegal driving antics, I blow my horn and follow him in, where I'm left staring at the over-sized bumper sticker on his back window: "God is my co-pilot."

Okay, I grin. *Maybe it's a message for me to chill a little bit.*

I place my order and round the corner to wait in line to pay, and again, stare at the message on the back of his window.

Five minutes later, frustrated and quickly losing patience, I'm still waiting for the same car that cut me off to pull up!

When I *finally* pull up to pay, the cashier informs me that the car in front of me has paid for my entire order! I quickly pull up, waving in an attempt to thank him for his generosity, as guilt washes over me for being so impatient. Unfortunately, I am unable to get his attention.

I watch as he reaches out to grab the only thing he has ordered for himself: a single ice cream cone. And to top it off, as he drives away, I see that he's wearing a Santa Claus hat!

Wow, I think with amusement. *Santa and God just bought our dinner — the holidays really* are *a time for miracles!*

Thank You for Being Beautiful

By Lara Anderson

John was one of my best friends. We talked every day about everything, from the mysteries of the universe to what we had for lunch. When he died of heart failure, I didn't even know he was that sick. Suddenly, there was a major void in my life where his presence used to be.

The day he died, I decided to go to the zoo – a natural, beautiful sanctuary where I'd have a safe place to mourn and try to make sense of why he'd kept his illness from me. I wore big Jackie O. sunglasses to hide my pain. As I walked down the hill toward the pandas, a man in his mid-20s with long blond hair walked up the hill toward me.

"Did you lose something?" he said.

"Yes, I lost my best friend today," I said, stunned that he could see right through my bulbous glasses.

He stepped closer and hugged me. "I am so sorry," he said. It was a hug filled with unconditional love and the warmth of many suns. He held me up with his frame, which felt as strong as an ancient oak, and I accepted and took in his care.

"Thank you for being beautiful," I said as we disengaged.

"Thank *you* for being beautiful," he said, smiling. "God told me to walk this way, that there was a dear sister in need."

This stranger's care helped me to know that I was not alone, that a force beyond me is always there. I didn't know what else to say, so we parted.

I found an abandoned exhibit where no one goes, sat on the bench, and cried. As I sat there weeping, the tall bamboo beside me bent and swayed with the purr of the lazy afternoon wind, and a peacock walked up to me and spread his iridescent feathers across my fallen tears. The tears dried with each splayed feather's flutter.

Unexpected Kindness from a Perfect Stranger

By Lynn Spiro

I recently traveled to my home in New York for three weeks to pack the last of my family's belongings and sell the house I had lived in for 35 years. This would be the final visit there with my family before putting the house on the market. Completing this project had been an emotionally charged and physically exhausting experience.

On the return drive, I became unusually sick and stopped numerous times. A 13-hour trip turned into 18 by the time I pulled into the driveway and crawled into my bed.

It seemed I underestimated the enormous toll the trip had taken on my body. My head pain became so severe that I collapsed and couldn't speak intelligibly or move my extremities. It was absolutely terrifying! I was transported to the ER for evaluation of a stroke and sent home six hours later.

Unfortunately, the head pain did not subside, and the same scenario played out a few days later. This time, however, I chose to go to a different hospital. Nine hours later, with no concrete answers, I was exhausted, anxious, and fearful that the nightmare would continue.

However, an angel watched over me that day. She was a nurse on the floor where I was admitted. She told me that her sole job was to make me comfortable, and she did it so well that I wept with gratitude. It wasn't just that she kept the lights low or brought warm blankets to cover me and fluffy pillows to stuff under my achy body, it was her demeanor. She was warm and considerate and just oozed a kindness rarely found in hospitals. She turned a frightening nightmare into a tolerable situation.

Thankfully, I have recovered from that medical crisis and have even been able to erase some deep emotional scars left over from past hospital visits – all thanks to the kindness of that one stranger who left me feeling like I had been touched by an angel. I am forever grateful! It is indeed proof that goodness can come in the unexpected act from a perfect stranger.

Come, Let's Get You Home

By Jamie Thomas

Michael was out in the late hours of the evening, spending time with his son and dog in a small alleyway in the small town of Shasta, when he heard the truck stop, the squealing of a flatbed being raised, and the crunch of weighted rubber on pavement. He walked into the empty parking lot of the auto shop, where he saw the tow-truck driver and the owner of the little green Subaru – a young man with a disabled car and in need of help in an unfamiliar place.

Michael walked up to the stranger and asked what was going on. The young man told his story – how he had traveled down from near the Canadian border and was headed to family farther south; his car had made the trip up until overheating at the California/Oregon border, leaving him stranded 300 miles from his destination.

Michael offered the traveler help; he was a mechanic himself and recommended a place to stay the night. The young man was relieved, and thanked him after they moved the car to a safe location.

The two of them then spent many hours together. When Michael inspected the car the next morning and saw that it was totaled, he offered the young man a ride in exchange for the vehicle. Time after time, plans for getting the lad home fell through, and Michael ended up sharing food, taking him into his home, teaching him about automobiles, and even transporting him to and from motels and friends' places, all while doing his best to juggle this new factor in his already chaotic life of near poverty and raising a child.

Finally, a plan held. On a snowy Friday morning, the traveler headed south in a friend's truck, with all his belongings, and made it safely home.

I was that young man, that traveler. And I continue to thank Michael every day for taking in a stranger, off the highway and nervous as hell, and getting me home. It's a debt I can never repay, so I will instead pass on the goodwill he shared.

Grace and the Kindness of Strangers

By Elizabeth R. Kipp

On the six-hour flight from Hawaii to Los Angeles, I began feeling tired and feverish. As I walked into the terminal in LA, I was unsure of where to go, but an agent kindly directed me to the red-eye flight that would take me home to Kansas City. The gate was quite far away, so I looked for someone with an electric cart, but there was no one available. Seemingly left with no alternative, I began to walk.

The signs pointing to my destination were spotty and not obvious to me, so I stopped to ask directions from people along the way. Each time I needed help, there was someone there to guide me. They expected nothing in return for their simple acts of kindness and service to me.

I rounded the bend of one area, feeling like I really wanted to find a chair or bench and rest for a moment. As if on cue, a gentleman driving an empty electric cart appeared. He was heading in my direction and offered me a ride. His timing and kindness in getting me to the next gate was a perfect example to me of how grace holds us.

When I reached my gate, my spirits had been buoyed by the many acts of kindness I'd received along the way, but my fever had intensified. I hesitated to continue the trip, dreaming of how nice a soft bed would feel just about then. I sat for a moment, weighing the cost of canceling my ticket at the last minute and having to buy a new ticket for a morning flight versus the benefit of taking care of myself by spending the night in LA. I went to the ticket agent and made my case. He surprised me by happily switching my ticket for a flight leaving the next morning at no additional cost – and he even helped me get a hotel room for the night. He didn't have to extend such assistance, but his sense of service and kindness to his customers guided his work.

The next day, I made it back home, grateful for a trip repeatedly graced by the kindness of strangers offering help without expecting anything in return – and providing numerous examples of how goodness abounds.

Concrete Kindness: There Are No Accidents

By Kathy Damas

This could be a simple story about tripping and falling. Accidents happen all the time, right? Maybe. It's what transpired afterward that's noteworthy.

I was in a hurry on that warm summer evening, distracted and juggling multiple bags. At a busy intersection, my toe caught and I went down hard (in a skirt, of course!). I'm grateful I wasn't hurt worse, a true concern as a middle-aged woman. Depositing that piece of skin on the sidewalk was a small price to pay for the reminder to slow down and pay attention. I quickly pulled myself together and assessed the damage as I self-consciously scurried on my way.

Then, from the opposite corner and across three lanes of traffic, I heard a clear, loud voice ask sincerely, "Are you okay?!" It came from a ragtag young man, one of the street people who often hangs out in groups downtown.

Surprised, but grateful for the concern, I happily yelled back with a weak but big smile, "Yes, just embarrassed!" and received an enthusiastic thumbs up from him in return.

In the following moments, I experienced an indelible shift.

There were nicely dressed people around me when I tumbled, but they walked by. Yet from across the street, I was buoyed by a verbal helping hand from a person who lives in a way I don't understand. I became painfully aware that insidious assumptions had crept into my being; I was guilty of judging and viewing others with disdain. His three words of concern not only touched my heart, they burst it open and deeply challenged my perceptions.

The dime-sized wound on my hand has nearly healed, but the scar and lessons from this experience will stay with me forever. We all need to be seen, heard, and respected. It's not that difficult to practice compassion and to connect with joy, to spread light and love to those around us – alike or not. Thank you, kind sir, for reminding me of these things…and also reminding me to check my assumptions at the door (or curb!).

My Irish Angel

By Cheryl Carrigan

During the trip of a lifetime – touring Ireland with my mom – we visited a beautiful handmade-crystal shop. This shop stuck out because it was owned by a woman named Shannon who, at 90, was still telling her story and living her dream. I loved her commitment to live true to her passion, and I desperately wanted to purchase one of her beautiful pieces; however, they were expensive, and having it shipped to the States made it out of my budget. I said to my mom, "One day, I will own a piece of Shannon's crystal."

Fast-forward two years: I walked into an estate sale and couldn't believe my eyes – there were two pieces of the very crystal I'd admired so much in Ireland!

I heard a small voice say to me, "Aren't they beautiful?" Dolly introduced herself and shared that she and her late husband had gone to Ireland 12 years earlier, and he'd bought these crystal vases for their 50th anniversary. I showed Dolly pictures of my mom and me in Ireland, and we shared stories about how amazing Ireland is. We lost track of time until I realized I had to get to an appointment. I told Dolly I'd be back soon.

Upon returning, I walked straight to where the vases had been, only to have my heart drop and spirits crushed because they were gone. Dolly saw me and came over. I asked who the lucky person was, and she smiled broadly. "You!" she said.

Confusion spread over my face. "Dolly, I can't afford these pieces." I told her that I'd just moved and cash was short.

She said, "You helped me laugh again, and I know that my husband would love for you to have these because your eyes lit up like mine when you saw them." With tears in my eyes, I told her that I couldn't possibly accept such a generous gift, but she insisted. "I've had these vases for years. They've brought me so much joy, and I want you to take them and enjoy! One day, you'll pass them on as I did. Call me your angel."

Thank you, Angel!

A Memorable Encounter

By Cornelia Merk

In 2001, I attended a training course in Portland, Oregon. On our free day, five of us decided to take the bus to go shopping. I was the last one to get on the bus, and, being from Germany and therefore unfamiliar with the public transportation system in the U.S., I put a five-dollar bill into the ticket machine. The bus driver was very apologetic when he explained that these machines don't give change. He offered, though, that if anyone needed a ticket before I had to get off at our stop, he would tell them to give me the fare money instead of putting it into the machine.

When I joined my friends, I explained how I had expected that these ticket machines worked the same as in Germany but admitted that it was my mistake and not a big deal that I had overpaid. While I spoke, I noticed a man sitting a couple of rows away watching me. He looked like a homeless man – unkempt hair and beard, faded clothes, and a few plastic bags at his feet, which, I assumed, contained all his belongings.

During the 20-minute journey, only a handful of people got on the bus, each holding a permanent ticket. The five of us were talking animatedly about our training course, when two stops before we had to get off, the man collected his bags, got up, and walked over. He shoved something into my hand, saying, "I don't want you to leave this country with a bad memory." Before I could react, he turned around and got off the bus. When I opened my palm, I saw that he had placed three one-dollar bills into my hand.

I was moved to tears. He had obviously overheard the driver's offer, and with no passengers getting on the bus who needed a ticket, he felt bad for me. To this day, whenever I think of my time in Portland, I think of a man who gave from the little he had to make a German tourist forget her mishap.

The Man in the Orange Suit

By Alison M. Stokes

Eight years ago, I was in the hospital after a fall that left me paralysed from the neck down. My friend Carol, who ran a holistic centre, told me that she had arranged for a healer name Master Hwa Shin to visit me. Originally from Tibet, he was in Ireland to give a lecture about an ancient healing technique he had re-developed, involving chanting and sound, which causes the cells in the body to vibrate and release blocked energy.

So there I was in the hospital ward when this strange man appeared. He was over six feet tall, with long black hair tied in a ponytail, and he was wearing a bright orange suit with a matching hat made of a strange quilted fabric. His arrival caused quite a stir; staff and patients alike wondered who he was, and word quickly spread throughout the hospital about the mysterious Tibetan man in the bright orange suit!

My friends drew the curtains around my bed for privacy, and he began his healing therapy, which lasted about 20 minutes. The nurses seemed quite alarmed at the strange noises coming from my cubicle, and they kept popping their heads in to check if I was all right. After the healing session, he gave me a recording of his chanting therapy and instructed me to play it every night at 10 p.m., when he would tune in to my energy frequency for further healing. Then he left with my friends and continued on to his lecture, which was over three hours away.

As instructed, I played his recording every night at 10 p.m., and slowly, over time, the power began to return to my arms and legs.

I will always remember this exotic-looking stranger from a distant land who found the time to visit me in the hospital and facilitate a healing session. He never asked for payment; his generosity astounded me and left me in no doubt that goodness is still bountiful in our world today.

Christmas in August

By Trish Mckinnley

Thirty years ago, I participated in diaper surveys. One particular day, I found myself in a 12x18 room with moms, kids, and the star – the baby with the diaper – for about five hours…or until the test diaper drooped off the baby's bottom. Qualifying babies received $50 for the study plus a package of diapers. As a young mom with a husband living out of town, dodging credit collectors, and desperate for milk and essentials, it was a blessing to get called for such an occasion.

I was eight months pregnant and already had three children (who were four, three, and one year old at the time). Desperate, we waddled in. Things were bad, actually worse than I let on. I'm the Pollyanna girl, so why I unloaded and confided in the mom next to me, I truly don't know. What I do know is that day she changed our lives.

We shared laughter about our frantic and fabulous lives being stay-at-home moms, juggling life, family, and dreams. She questioned deeper and somehow had me opening up like a sinner to a priest. Sharing the depth of poverty, fear, anxiety, worry, and hopelessness, I unloaded it all. She didn't know my full name. She didn't know where I lived. Where was the harm in revealing the concerns torturing my soul? Such a relief.

Our kids played. We all laughed. And we parted ways. What a gift she had given me that day: peace.

But that wasn't the end.

The next day, my son noticed something at the back door. "Santa's been here!"

It was August.

Then I saw the presents. Bags of groceries, piles of diapers, and new puzzles and books for my children. Everything we desperately needed and more: an envelope addressed to me with cash that would tide us over for months plus a request that I keep half just for me. "Promise. Just for you."

I don't know how she found me. I don't know how she found the time to gather all of that with her kids and responsibilities. I don't know how she did it. I just know I'm so blessed she did.

Power Suit Angel

By Victoria McGee

I have never been in a major car accident (knock on wood), but the one time I came close, I encountered an angel in a power suit.

For a time, I lived in Los Angeles, land of roads, freeways, and cars. One day while delivering some paperwork connected to my job, I found myself in the lovely neighborhood of Brentwood. I rounded a corner and scanned the road ahead, noticing a woman in a power suit walking on the other side of the street toward some condos. Suddenly, a car pulled out from a driveway on the passenger side, right in front of me!

I became all instinct. I turned the wheel sharply to the left, away from the other car, sending my car into a full 360-degree spin. When the car had done a full circle, tires screeching all the way, I was able to get control, stop the car, and pull over to the side of the road. I had come very close to death or serious injury and was shaking all over, gripping the steering wheel, and trying to regain my composure. The other driver had sped off, unconcerned with my well-being.

Then I heard a gentle tap at my car window. It was power suit woman. I rolled the window down.

"Are you okay?" she asked.

"Yes," I said, "just shaken up."

She put a hand on my shoulder. "I just wanted to tell you, you did an amazing job of not hitting that car. Would you like me to stay with you a few minutes?"

I told her no, thank you, that I just had to collect myself. She smiled, said she hoped the rest of my day was better, and walked away.

I rolled up the window and began straightening out the things in my car that had been thrown about. When I looked up again, I noticed that the woman had disappeared. Was she even real? I'll never know. I only know that her words comforted me and helped ground me so I could move on. I've never forgotten her kindness.

The Red Poppy Flower

By Joelle Rose Szlosek

My grandfather only cried when talking about two things: his family and his time spent with the Marines during the Korean War. They were never tears of sadness, however, but rather heartfelt, happy tears that welled up during moments of reminiscing. This man, my hero, was forever faithful and proud of his rank as sergeant and his decision to return home to western Massachusetts to marry the love of his life, Lucille, and start a family. This choice was hard to come by, yet happily resulted in five children and five grandchildren after 59 years of marriage.

On a sunny spring day in May of 2015, it had only been 16 days since the ceremonial folding of his flag by his graveside. Only 16 days since the piercing sound of rifles had rung out as a military salute. Only 16 days since the ceremony of my chosen hero. But on that 16th day, I made a decision to embody strength instead of sadness, and in doing so, exchanged the murky feeling of mourning for faith.

To normalize things again, I decided to go to the supermarket for a few food supplies, completely unaware that a small but powerfully healing act of kindness lay ahead.

With my uncle by my side and my bag of groceries in hand, we stopped to talk with a Marine wearing a Korean War hat and assisting with a veterans' fundraiser by selling red poppies: the flower of remembrance. My eyes grew wide because my grandfather used to bring me one every May after he had donated to the cause.

On this day, my uncle decided to make a donation and asked if he could take a red poppy flower. Without hesitation, the gentleman pointed to me and said, "Take one for her, too! One man gave me extra money and told me to give out flowers to the prettiest girls who stopped by."

In that magical moment, my heart sang with joy again as the poppy represented much more than a flower, but the remembrance of the infinite power and presence of love and kindness!

An Angel in Time

By Marifran Korb

Decades ago near my hometown, a gigantic tent was erected for musical theater in summertime — live entertainment featuring famous actors and singers.

When summer came, every inch of me was lit up like the strings of lights inside the tent. Standing as tall as my short self could, I put my $20 on the high counter and asked for my ticket. The clerk said: "You did not pay." Feeling helpless, I protested that indeed I had paid. To my suggestion that he must have dropped it, the clerk insisted: "No, you didn't pay."

On my teacher's salary, $20 was a chunk of money. The clerk obviously thought I would put up another $20. With my throat getting tight, I was flummoxed as to what to do. Time stood still. There were restless people behind me, waiting impatiently.

Suddenly, a man approached the clerk on my right side. Speaking firmly, without menacing, he stated, "She paid in full, and you know it. I saw the money. Give her the ticket now."

Without any argument, the clerk put it on the counter. Not waiting for him to change his mind, I grabbed the ticket joyfully. With pure gratitude, I turned around to my right, ready to thank the kind man who had defended me. But there was no one next to me. Looking at the people behind me, the stranger was not in line. People were milling around and heading to the tent, but too many to distinguish which man had been my hero. Before the play and during intermission, I searched. The man had vanished.

That night, I could not focus on the stage drama. I have no memory of the famous actors or what musical it was. My night was about my good fortune. I marveled at the random justice and goodness that I had experienced.

Was he an angel? The stranger appeared at the perfect time, saw what occurred, stood up for me, and disappeared into the crowd. That was angel enough for me.

On the Road Again

By Kimberly DuBoise

I was almost halfway through the 500-mile drive to my mom's house when I noticed I was almost out of gas, so I pulled into the next station. Before I could start filling up, however, I looked over at the passenger seat and gasped. My purse wasn't there! I glanced at the back seat and didn't see it there either. Frantically, I searched the whole car but still didn't find it. Then I realized what must have happened: I'd left my purse at the McDonald's where I'd eaten earlier that morning. I had to go back for it, but how could I get there with no gas and no money? (I know, I know. I should have had some emergency cash on me. But I didn't.)

Stunned, I stood outside my car in the sun, surrounded by gasoline fumes. I'm afraid I didn't remain very calm. The thought of my purse being gone for good, with my credit cards and ID, upset me. I wanted to be on the way to my mom's! I'd been up since five o'clock so I could leave early for this 10- to 11-hour drive! How was I going to get to this McDonald's with no gas and no money? And even if I did have gas, should I bother driving back there, or should I just assume that someone had taken my purse and all was lost?

These thoughts raced through my mind as I paced back and forth outside my car. Taking a much-needed deep breath, I tried to calm myself through prayer. I said a prayer for calm, a prayer for safety, and a prayer for HELP! When I opened my eyes, still a bit shaky and tense but feeling slightly better, I saw a gentleman come out of the gas station and head toward me rather than going to his car. "Do you need help?" he asked. I nodded, not trusting my voice for a moment. Then I exhaled and explained my situation. Well, that gentleman gave me $10 for gas. I was so grateful – such a gift!

I put the gas in and headed back to McDonald's. All the way there, I kept saying *thank you* over and over. When I got there, my purse was waiting for me! A couple had found it and given it to the manager – nothing was taken. Two acts of kindness in one day! My nerves were still raw, but my heart was overwhelmed with gratitude – and I was on the road again!

Heaven Sent

By Meredith Fjelsted

It was the night before my surgery. I was nervous about it, knowing that every surgery carries a risk. This wasn't my first surgery, but it was going to be my most invasive. So, the day before, I was running around doing errands. It was getting late, and I was tired. I had one last errand to do before I would be out of commission for at least the next six weeks.

On the way to the grocery store, the "what if" thoughts that had been simmering at the back of my mind bubbled into the forefront: *What if something goes wrong during surgery? What if I'm not okay? What if...?* I succumbed to these thoughts and acknowledged I was scared, so I said out loud, "God, I ask you to send my angels to me right now. I need a sign from Heaven that you hear me."

I shoved those thoughts back to the recesses of my mind when I arrived at the grocery store. As I roamed the aisles, I decided to buy myself some flowers in hopes that they would brighten my spirit. I chose the smallest, least expensive potted plant with little yellow flowers. I got to the checkout and began talking with the cashier and quietly told her why I was buying groceries and a little about my upcoming surgery. She inquired if I was buying the yellow flowers for myself, and I admitted I was. She unobtrusively turned on her cashier's light and raised her hand while I paid. Suddenly, another worker appeared with the most amazingly huge potted purple flowers – the biggest and most expensive in the store! She said to me, "These are for you!" I was incredulous.

I asked her name, and she said, "Angelique."

"Of course you are!" I cried. God had heard me and had sent an angel to show me that I am worth the most expensive flowers in the store.

"You're going to be okay," Angelique said as she hugged me goodbye.

Honeymooners with Heart

By Jo Shepherd

The Camino de Santiago pilgrimage in Spain had attracted me for years, and recently I got the opportunity to walk the final section. After 24 hours of plane travel, I began my first day exhausted, cold, wet, and lacking confidence. My backpack was ridiculously heavy, and I just wanted to go home.

Cowering outside a café as confident-looking pilgrims strode by in the rain, I was relieved when I heard laughter, and Donna and Chris from Melbourne, Australia, introduced themselves. They had started walking in France and were on their honeymoon. They sensed my vulnerability and suggested we walk together. Chris insisted on carrying some of my load.

They slowed their pace for me, kept encouraging me, and ensured I was well hydrated and coping. Their ritual of saying a prayer and placing a pebble on all the wayside markers was an inspiration.

After 12 miles (20 km), I was so tired that my legs were trembling. When Chris and Donna suggested I join them for dinner, I was grateful but embarrassed. (After all, they were on their honeymoon!) They also asked me to walk with them the next day, and for as many days as I needed, until I "found my feet."

The next morning, I lightened my load by mailing my excess gear to a pick-up point in Santiago. Donna humorously named my backpack's front pouches "Estelle" and "Violetta." She and Chris continued to accompany me, and I realized that if I stayed in the moment of just walking, step by step, I would be okay.

By lunchtime, I felt ready to walk alone. We made our farewells, and I watched Donna and Chris speed up their walking pace. I immediately missed them but felt buoyed by their faith in my capabilities. I no longer wanted to return home! To my delight, I ran into them at the end of my pilgrimage, at the Cathedral in Santiago.

Since my Camino pilgrimage, my friends have described me as more confident, determined, focused, and optimistic – embracing life more fully than before. I now realize that Donna and Chris were inspirational spiritual masters of practical, loving care.

The Angel in My Kitchen

By Margaretta McIlvaine

Two years ago, I renovated the entire downstairs of my retreat center. It looked beautiful with a new kitchen, new flooring, and two new bathrooms. I was so happy to offer this new space to the wonderful teachers and clients who had been coming for years. The gardens looked magical, the patio was just completed, and things were ready for a whole new level of service.

A week later, everything changed. I turned on the faucet and there was no water. I called a plumber, and after a thorough investigation, he said that the pump had burned out. I tried not to panic, paid him, and replaced the pump. Still no water. I called a well specialist who came over and determined that the well had run dry.

I was now in shock but made plans to find a new site for a well. The area where I live does not have much ground water. No luck again. The expenses, fear, and worry were mounting.

I had a sense to try one more plumber, who a friend had highly recommended. I knew I could not run the center without water, and I needed a miracle.

The next day, the doorbell rang. I opened it and was surprised at the kind, gentle countenance of the man. I briefly shared what was happening. He listened intently, was very quiet, and slowly and mindfully began checking the water pump, the well site, and the pipes leading into and out of the house. He then paused and went straight to the kitchen sink, opened the cabinet, listened carefully, and reached way into the back and turned off a knob hidden by pipes that fed the outdoor shower.

"Try it now," he said.

"WATER!!!!" I nearly cried with relief. "Numerous plumbers have come to fix this issue, and no one could. I was about to dig a new well. I am so grateful! How much do I owe you?"

He was quiet and mindful again and looked at me and said, "Your joy at this outcome is all the payment I need."

He gently picked up his tools, smiled, and walked out the door. Angels do exist, and one had just been in my kitchen. I will always be grateful for this deep act of kindness.

Giving Me Wings to Succeed

By Isabella Rose

I was so excited! I had just signed up for my second World Ventures Regional Training Event (RTE), which was four days away. I could barely wait to see my other half later that night to tell him the news — and to celebrate his birthday! I was also going to buy him a ticket as part of his birthday gift; traveling the world together was one of our dreams.

A few hours later, my world came crashing down around me. Matt had passed away unexpectedly. Suddenly, everything I had been working so hard for — my individual goals and the goals we held together — lost all meaning. How was I going to continue to move forward? He was my rock, my strength.

The night before RTE, I didn't want to go; my heart wasn't in it. But I knew that Matt would still want me to go, so I set the goal to attend for at least half the day; if I still wasn't feeling it at that point, I could go home.

The following morning, I checked into the event. Everybody else was excited and in travel/party mode, having fun, but I just couldn't do it. As I sat there, overcome with sorrow, a woman walked up and asked, "Do you mind if I sit here?"

"Of course not," I responded. She sat down next to me, and we introduced ourselves and began talking about World Ventures. I told her this was my second RTE and although I had just arrived, I was about to go home. As I shared my story about Matt — the accident in December, how he changed my life for the better, and his recent passing — I began to cry.

We stood up, and Michelle gave me a hug to comfort and console me. As she did, the tears started flowing even more. A friend of hers saw us and came over to make sure everything was okay, and Michelle shared my story with him. Michelle and Brandon encouraged me to stay, lifted my spirits, and gave me the strength I needed. Together with Matt, they gave me the wings I needed to succeed. I met my goal of staying half the day.

In Loving Memory of Matthew J. Adams

Pay It Forward

By Teresa Velardi

I thought I put my purse in the car when I left the house. On my way back from an appointment, 35 miles from home, I was nearly out of gas. I had no cell phone, no cash, and no credit card. My purse was nowhere to be found. Sometimes I'd put my wallet in my briefcase, leaving my purse at home. Not this time. As I searched my mind, I could see it sitting on the counter in the kitchen.

There was definitely not enough gas to get me home; I was running on empty. I stopped at the nearest station. When I asked at the pay station if I could call someone to give a credit card over the phone, the guy immediately said, "No, we don't do that." Pleading didn't help.

I went back to the car and began the fruitless search for money that may have fallen between the seats, under the mats or in the trunk. A few coins, most of them pennies were the result. As I closed the door, I rested my forehead on my arm, saying out loud, "Now what am I going to do?"

Just then, a man came up to me, reaching out his hand with a five-dollar bill. I stood there with a puzzled look on my face. He said, "Go ahead, take it."

"Really?" I asked.

He nodded, "Yes." He'd heard me talking to the clerk; "Take the money, buy the gas, and go get your son."

I asked for his address so I could pay him back. He said, "No need – pay it forward." I thanked him immensely and promised to pay it forward. And I have – several times. The kindness of a stranger created a ripple effect of paying it forward.

Goodness and kindness truly abound.

The Language of Kindness

By Crystal M. Cathell

As the train slowed, a platform emerged from the blackness. I held my breath, hoping this wasn't my stop. My trepidation grew when the train came to a halt and the doors opened. Despite my growing uncertainty, I stepped off the train into the darkness.

My lodging should have been visible from the platform. Instead, shadowy visions of woods and weeds greeted me. Doubt and dread crept in with the shadows.

From an upper platform, I spied cars in a lot some distance away. Expecting to find help there, I made the 20-minute walk.

When I'd arrived in Italy a few hours earlier, I was undaunted by the significant language barrier. Approaching these strangers, that barrier felt more like a chasm I couldn't bridge.

An hour later, a lone woman walked toward me.

I asked, *"Lei capisce l'inglese?"* ("Do you understand English?")

She responded, *"Un po."* ("A little.")

Hopeful, I continued. Fortune smiled. The stranger was a kindhearted soul named Stefanie, whose English was almost as bad as my Italian. For about 10 minutes, we struggled to communicate through broken language and gestures. The wind picked up, and it started to rain. She signaled for me to get into her car. I didn't hesitate.

Once inside, she called a bilingual friend to look up the phone number for my lodging. She gave me fresh bread and cheese to eat while she talked to my host and got the directions. She pulled out a map, showed me the way, then gave me the map. Forty-five minutes later, she delivered me to the front door.

Humbled by her kindness and her generosity, I offered money for her efforts, but she refused. We said *"Ciao,"* hugged, and laughed – no longer strangers.

Lost and alone in an unfamiliar country, I learned to hold faith in the innate goodness of people, even in trying times. Stefanie reaffirmed this. She reminded me that kindness is a universal language, and it was one she spoke perfectly.

Heart of a Hometown

By Diana L. Hooker

While taking a break from her daily chores, Cora scrolls through Facebook. She reads a friend's response to a post of someone requesting prayers for their 17-year-old son who just discovered he needs a heart transplant. Cora does not know the family or their son, but she knows where they are from, her hometown, a small community nestled in the Appalachian Mountains in southeast Kentucky, where very little changes, especially hard times.

In the post, she notices that the family is in a hospital just around the corner. She sends a private message introducing herself and asking if there is anything they need. The teenager says he would really like some fruit roll-ups. On her way to visit them at the hospital, she buys him several boxes of his favorite snack. Even though they are essentially total strangers, they find a kindred spirit in each other since they are from the same neck of the woods.

The mother is distraught with worry for her son. He seemed to be a healthy young man until one day he collapsed and they learned that his heart was failing. The doctors managed to get him stable but want him to remain close to the hospital in case of any complications and to await a donor. Since home is three and a half hours away, they worry about how they can afford to stay in the area.

Cora, wanting to do more for the family, invites them to stay with her, so for six months her home becomes their home. She gives them her master bedroom so he can sleep restfully and have easy access to the connecting bathroom. She pulls another mattress into the room so that his mother can sleep nearby, and she sleeps on her couch in the living room. Far from their friends and family and forced to endure more than any family ever should, they find a piece of home in Cora's.

Her selfless compassion proves that no matter how long ago or how far away, sharing the heart of a hometown creates a friendship among strangers.

A Helping Hand

By Ellouise Heather

I hurriedly grabbed the jacket to match my pinstripe suit and dashed out of the door. This is how I lived most days, power-striding my way from one moment to the next. It was becoming harder as time went on, with less energy and more to forge through, but I pressed on. I paced through the local university campus. Suddenly (and with seemingly no explanation), my overworked behind found the ground. Had I slipped or tripped? I couldn't be sure. I was knocked out of my stride to the tarmac and immediately froze to the spot. I could feel an alarming pain in my tailbone and was too scared to move.

As the awareness of my surroundings slowly seeped in, I noticed that I'd fallen beside a construction worker's vehicle. I could hear talking nearby but couldn't see anyone; I concluded that they probably couldn't see me either. I remained rooted to the spot, still trying to wrap my head around the situation.

I don't know how long I was down there, whether it was seconds or minutes, when a hand reached down towards mine. It belonged to a young man in a red shirt, with a backpack on his shoulders that suggested he was a passing student. Gratefully, I took his hand and steadily rose to my feet. I don't remember anything more about this brief exchange except how thankful I was. As he marched onwards, I appreciated that he clearly needed to be somewhere. Yet he'd still taken the time to lend a hand.

As I slowly started to make my way down the street to the hospital, mud on my suit and tear-stained makeup on my face, I heard the construction workers starting to jeer. On a normal day, this might have gotten to me, but not today. It was akin to a rusty old tin rattling about while a melodious harp was playing. It made the kindhearted gesture of a stranger even more powerful. Although I don't remember his face, he reminded me of the depths one good deed can reach in a busy world.

The Energy of a Gift

By Jenny McKaig

My husband and I were beginning a move from one corner of the continent to another. It was the move to have our dream life in a location we love – with a lot of effort to get there.

My husband was driving – hauling a 13,000-pound trailer with all our household belongings – while I travelled by plane with our daughter: a smiley, silly, demanding, crawling, nearly walking 11-month-old. As a pregnant mom with fatigue, nausea, and a sore back that acted up almost daily, I was already exhausted from packing and was now physically feeling the constant care and attention required by our little one.

After loading and unloading bags, a baby, and a stroller through security, and walking what felt like a 20-mile jaunt, I arrived at the gate and started to dismantle the baby stroller. With wheels strewn amidst diaper bag, my carry-on, and our daughter (who I was trying to prevent from crawling away), I was sweating and out of breath.

A man stepped forward to ask, "Are you travelling with her on your lap?"

"I am," I said.

The next words he spoke brought tears to my eyes: "I've got a Plus seat. Do you want my seat so you can have more space with her? It'll make things easier."

I wriggled like our 11-month old but eventually accepted his generous offer – a random act of kindness that he couldn't have known meant so much. He couldn't have known how full the weeks leading up to that moment had been, and how my daughter had been awake the night before so I had little sleep. He had no idea I would be caring for her on my own for four days afterwards until my husband completed the drive.

I was still tired physically, but my heart was full and grateful. I thanked him infinitely.

I believe that you can feel the energy of a gift. I knew he wanted nothing in return, simply to do something that would brighten someone's day – which he did!

Our Very Own Bodyguard

By Nora T. Barican

Following the Sunday church service, my daughter and I decided to walk around the popular 150-year-old Sydney market, which boasts a wide variety of stalls: fashion, cosmetics, sporting goods, giftware, gadgets, crafts, souvenirs, and a small section for fresh fruit, vegetables, seafood, and plants. With such an extensive range, you can see what the attraction is that made us choose to spend a lazy afternoon in this environment.

Typical of window shoppers, we found ourselves checking out each aisle and stopping at any stalls that caught our fancy. Walking arm in arm, we engaged in light conversations and shared a few laughs.

After walking for quite some distance, we felt the need to sit down and rest our legs, so we searched for a good café. Not finding one, we decided to leave the marketplace. As we headed out, we heard a man's voice behind us. Not certain if he was talking to us, we looked at each other first, then turned around, only to come face-to-face with a solidly built man.

This man started to explain that he had been following us for the last 15 minutes. Unable to fathom why he would have done so, we patiently waited for him to continue. He told us that he was a plainclothes security guard and that he did not want us to be scared, but he felt it was his obligation to make us aware that we had stepped out of the market area, which is where his boundary ends. My daughter and I must have been thinking the same thing because we blurted out in unison: "What do we need to be aware of?"

The man cautioned us that we had been oblivious to the two men whom he noticed had been following us around. He could not confront them, as they had not done anything yet, but they seemed to be waiting for the perfect opportunity.

We thanked him profusely for having gone the extra mile, grateful that we had our own bodyguard keeping us safe. The man continued to keep us in his sights as we crossed the street.

A Cup of Kindness

By Isla Selupucin

My first pregnancy ended with the loss of our first child.

That evening and that rush to the hospital remains a blur of tangled emotions. I live in a foreign country, and everything seemed very alien and unfamiliar to me. I remember tears, pain, and incredible sadness. I felt, perhaps for the first time in my life, completely alone. My husband wasn't allowed to be with me all the time. Doctors breezed into my hospital room, telling me that I was young and had plenty time for more children. While my heart just hurt.

As my devastated husband was outside organising paperwork, someone briskly brought a breakfast tray into my hospital room. It lay untouched beside me. I had been sitting quietly in the darkness for a few minutes when a very cheerful cleaning lady came by to check the room. She quietly asked me why I hadn't eaten my breakfast; I told her that I only wanted tea and a slice of bread. She left the room, and I assumed she hadn't understood my Turkish (which, at the time, was quite limited). I was surprised when, two minutes later, she popped back with a plate of bread and jam and a cup of English tea. She opened the curtains, and the early morning sun burst into the room. The beauty and warmth of the sun's rays enveloped me. She sat with me while I ate and, once I'd finished, gently took my hand – again, just sitting with me. I don't remember her saying anything to me, but she quietly hummed the tune of what sounded like a Turkish ballad.

Sometime later, my husband returned and she disappeared, just as silently as she had appeared. That act of goodness, that pure kindness from a complete stranger, will always stay with me. A slice of bread, a cup of tea, rays of morning sunshine, and the presence of a stranger gave meaning to one of the saddest days of my life, and I will be eternally grateful.

In memory of Alex Selupucin – always loved, always missed
9/12/05

California Earth Angels

By Maureen Hollmeyer

It was another daily commute to work on a sunny morning in San Jose, California. I was in the middle lane on Highway 101 when all of a sudden, my car slowed down and eventually came to a complete halt. As cars drove by, I became terrified that I would get crushed. After about 30 minutes, I put my head in my hands and cried in frustration.

It was like watching Wonder Woman. She pulled to the side of the highway, put her hand up to stop traffic, walked over to my car, and single-handedly pushed my car to the side of the road. She asked me who she could call, and I gave her the number. An hour later, my ride came to help.

It had to be a divine intervention or a guardian angel that helped me; to this day, I don't know her name. Thank you, Miss Wonder Woman, Earth Angel.

About six months after that experience, my friend Danielle and I planned a day in San Francisco. We were looking forward to spending time at Fisherman's Wharf, where we could enjoy the cool air while rollerblading, watch the sea lions, and have some wonderful fresh fish.

I found an awesome parking spot right in front of the sidewalk at Fisherman's Wharf. We were about to go when Danielle said her door wouldn't close. I thought she was joking, but sure enough it wouldn't close. So for the next hour, I was on the phone with the car dealership with no resolution.

Just when we were about to call a tow truck, a stranger stopped and asked, "Your door won't close?"

"That's correct," I said.

"This is what I did all day at work today," he said and then proceeded to fix the door in about two seconds, after which he disappeared into the crowd.

I never got to thank him for coming to our rescue. I never even got his name or found out who he was. Did he work at a VW factory? Was he Superman? Was he just a kind, helpful man who happened to be in the right place at the right time?

Or was he another Earth Angel?

With Hands Wide Open

By Pooja Shende

As I write these words, I'm sitting in my home, sipping lovely hot vegetable soup, and enjoying the sound of heavy rainfall outside. (I just love the rain!) It is monsoon season here in Mumbai, India, as it is every year from June to October. Today's downpour takes me back to a beautiful experience I had when I was about 20 years old.

It was a similar time with heavy rainfall; my immediate family and a few cousins had decided to go for a three-day trip to a town called Lonavala, a popular destination during the rainy season. There are many beautiful places to trek around the area, as well as ancient caves, temples, and sites of historic importance.

On the second day of our trip, while it was pouring heavily, we went to enjoy a huge waterfall with lush green surroundings. It was in the jungle with hardly any people around. By late afternoon, we were all hungry. So, after freshening up, we went searching for a restaurant but couldn't find one.

After searching for some time, we approached some villagers who were living in huts and asked them if they knew of a place where we could eat. One of the villagers asked if we would like to come to their small eating joint, which was alongside their house. Happy to find food – and relief from the chilly environment outside – we gratefully accepted.

It was a lovely, cosy place with a campfire burning. It felt so homey. The moment we entered the eating area, I saw an old lady sitting next to the chula (a gas stove made out of mud for cooking purposes in villages) with a broad smile on her face, welcoming us with hands wide open. As soon as I saw her, something changed inside me. I admired her from the bottom of my heart. She prepared such simple food but with great love and affection. That was all she had.

This experience has stayed so fresh in my memory to this day because it offered a great lesson: You don't need anything to love people; all you need is an open heart to accept everyone in your world. With hands wide open and a charismatic smile, the world is yours.

A Bushel and a Peck

By Lori Kilgour Martin

After returning from a walk on a sunny afternoon, I noticed that the clock read 12:12. That was the time showing at the nursing station when I went for help, just minutes after my great-uncle Fred had returned home to God. This was a few years ago, and now Fred is guiding me to express the goodness that occurred then and blesses us still.

Fred had been living in a nursing home ever since his beloved Dorris passed, two years earlier. My daily visits with him there were always a bright spot in the day.

The night when his time on Earth was complete is forever etched in my heart. Taking turns with family members, my mother and I spent the entire day with him. At one point, we started singing, "I love you a bushel and a peck." He was aware – there was such joy.

As the day unfolded and flowed into the early evening, my parents became tired. The nurse working that night asked if I would stay with Fred. I accepted. It was an honor. I don't recall the name of this angelic caregiver, but the fact that she trusted me to stay meant so much and offered the courage needed to carry him through.

I held Fred's hand most of the evening. Nearing midnight, I stepped back and asked for all of the relatives who now reside in Heaven to please come. About 20 minutes later, he stopped breathing. I stood there in the gentle stillness as if held in God's arms. The nurse came back with me, checked his heart, then closed his eyes. After she left, this angel in our midst, the grieving began.

It was one of the most sacred days and nights of my life. The support from this nurse and everyone at the nursing home was simply amazing. Our family is grateful. And Uncle Fred continues to show us that he is fine. When we least expect them, the heavenly gifts appear in beautiful, radiant ways.

Sometimes God Cashiers at Walmart

By Kathy DeFinis

I often shop at Walmart late in the evening to avoid the busyness during the day. Over time, I noticed a particular cashier. She was efficient enough but was never friendly, never made eye contact or small talk. I decided that it was going to be my mission to make her smile. Every time I went there, I would make it a point to go through her line. I asked her how she was, whether she'd had a busy day, etc. Sometimes she grunted something back, but most of the time she really didn't respond, and she never smiled or acted friendly.

Fast-forward several months to an evening when I was in a terrible mood. Several personal problems were weighing heavily on me. I went for a drive to clear my head and eventually found myself stopping at Walmart for some household items. I saw my "friend" working that night and thought, *Great, I'll go to her line because I'm not in the mood to talk to anyone.*

So there I stood with my necessities in my basket and a big black cloud in my heart, feeling heavy and depressed. As I got to the front of the line, the cashier looked up, and as soon as her eyes connected with mine, she smiled the biggest, warmest, most beautiful smile. She actually said hello and asked how I was.

I was stunned!

All those months of me extending kindness and love to her now came back to me when I needed it. Overcome with emotion, I went to my car and cried. I no longer felt burdened. I had just experienced a beautiful connection. I understood that the light that was in her face was the light of God showing me that kindness does make a difference and is always appreciated, even if it isn't always acknowledged.

We don't always know the effect our smile or our kindness will have on another person, but sometimes it's gifted back to us and it is amazing!

The Best Flat Tire Ever

By Katrina Ariel

At the heart of our rural community is a hard-working woman named Lana-Michele who runs an equestrian club. Hanging out at her ranch one day, I had the pleasure of hearing this story.

Lana-Michele and a group of riders were on their way to a horse event, traveling the country road in a convoy of three trucks towing trailers with horses. As they passed through Native land, her trailer got a flat. She and her traveling companion told the others to go on to the event, and set to getting the tire fixed.

A First Nations man, John, pulled over to see if the women needed help. They did. The spare was flat, too. John had Lana-Michele pull onto the reserve land so she was off the road, and left her there while he took her tire to the gas station at the bottom of the hill, only to find that it wouldn't hold air. John returned to discuss what to do next, then proceeded to drive into town *again* to get another tire!

But the two friends couldn't have been stranded in a prettier place. They'd been invited past the No Trespassing signs onto land both had longed to visit for years. The sweeping green valley where the wild horses graze has trees on the hills above and water flowing through the field below. Delighted, the women walked their horses to the creek for a drink while they waited.

John, who Lana-Michele kept calling an angel, returned with a used tire that worked perfectly, and was able to secure two additional spares. Grateful, she gave him a hug and told him that his kindness had made her year. She saw the flat tire as a blessing, something that connected her with a good-hearted person and gave her a chance to set foot on sacred land.

As Lana-Michele shared this memory, she lit up with joy. My heart glowed as I listened, thrilled to see her receive the same generosity she puts into the world and grateful to be part of this small, caring community.

An Angel Walking Among Us

By Lisa "The Link" Rizzo

My husband and I were blessed to take a trip to Costa Rica. What an amazing country with great energy and tremendous natural beauty! But what touched my soul the most on this trip was a man named Rene, our personal tour guide. In addition to telling us about the places we visited, Rene talked about his life with his wife and daughter. With tears in his eyes, he described the great blessings and great losses in his life, telling us that, throughout it all, not once did he ever lose faith.

He then told us a story about a man who had stood in front of God and said, "God, I'm unhappy with my life." When God asked him how he could make his life better, the man said, "I want to be rich!"

God said, "Okay, I'll give you one million dollars, but you have to give me something in return: I want your legs."

The man said, "My legs?! I don't want to be without my legs!"

"Okay," God said. "I'll give you ten million dollars for your arms."

The man said, "My arms?! I don't want to live without my arms!"

So God said, "This is my last offer to you: I'll give you one hundred million dollars for your eyes."

The man couldn't believe that God was going to make him so rich. But then the man said, "No, I don't want to live without my eyes."

So God looked at the man and said, "So I have given you all you need to love your life: legs to get you where you want to go, arms to work hard with and create the life you want to build, and eyes to see the beauty all around you. All you ever need now is the faith to get you to a place of peace and love in this life."

Rene had been through so much, yet he'd never lost his faith in God – and God had never failed him. He put his daughter through school, and she became a teacher. He built a simple home for his family. And he made a good, honest living helping people like us enjoy our time in his beautiful country. All I could do is cry looking at this angel who reminded me that all I need to do is to have faith.

My husband and I gave him a big hug and said, "We never visit the same place twice, but we'll be back to see you and your tour bus again." He smiled and said that he would love to see us again. And he will.

Sound to the Rescue

By Sally M. Sutton

At a very young age, my daughter was prescribed an antibiotic. I had no idea what it would do to her body. Months later, she began having stomach cramps and uncontrollable bowel movements that had a horrific odor. After many doctors' appointments, we were referred to a specialist who performed many tests, then decided to run a tube down her throat that resulted in no diagnosis. Guessing, he prescribed a compound drug that had to be filled at a special pharmacy. The pharmacist was surprised that this drug was being given to such a young child. It was refilled twice, but because of the potency, they wouldn't refill it anymore. Once the medication was finished, her stool reverted to the way it had been before the prescription.

Just when I was beginning to lose hope, a friend and I attended a holistic health fair where we met a lady named Regina Murphy who had a sound bed that my friend wanted to experience. While waiting, I told Regina about my daughter. When I was finished, she handed me an iPod and speaker and said, "I want you to take this home and play it while she sleeps; lay it on or close to her stomach." She explained that the music had frequencies embedded in it that help the body to heal naturally.

We exchanged numbers, and as I left, I thought, *This woman just gave a total stranger her last iPod and speaker set – wow, what a generous and loving soul she is!* I wasn't sure if it would help, but at that point, I was ready to try anything, so I decided to give it a shot.

To my surprise, in less than a week, my daughter's stool was much better than it had been during the month of medication. I called Regina to report the results and to return the iPod and speaker, but she said, "I want you to keep it and call me in another week or so." We continued the therapy for another week and half, after which my daughter's stomach no longer cramped and her bowel movements were back to normal. She was cured, thanks to sound therapy…and Regina's generosity!

Ripples of a Prayer
By Padma Gordon

One warm spring evening before my daughter was born, her father and I were eating dinner out on the patio of a local Mexican restaurant. This tall, thin, German man whom I loved was also someone with whom I had a challenging dynamic. However, what drew us together was our commitment to the Divine, for it was here that our hearts aligned.

It was he who initiated me into the reverent practice of holding hands and offering a prayer of thanks before meals. I love this ritual and continue it even though he and I are no longer a couple.

I was raised as a Reformed Jew, and in my family, praying was something you did on holidays; this made his introduction to daily prayer especially meaningful. I discovered that prayer has the power to transform things instantly, and in a prayerful moment, life's sacredness reveals itself in all of its radiant splendor.

As was our practice, this evening we joined hands across the brightly colored floral tablecloth and said a prayer of gratitude over our fish tacos. Having enjoyed our meal, we asked our jovial, honey-skinned waiter for the check.

He looked at us and nodded across the way. "The gentleman over there has already paid your bill."

We glanced across the terracotta-tiled patio to see a white-haired gentleman sitting alone. Gazing at him, I inhaled the kindness of his gesture; and as we both broke out into wide grins, I felt my heart expand.

Nearing his table, we paused to thank him. Out of curiosity, I asked, "What inspired your generosity, sir?"

"I was touched by your prayer," he responded simply. "As I watched you both, I could feel your love of God."

I sensed magic in the air as we strolled back to our car on that warm summer night, and I reflected on how our blessing had inadvertently blessed a stranger. I sighed, gratefully acknowledging how a simple prayer can be like a stone tossed into a pond, creating ripples of goodness far beyond what we can even begin to imagine.

The Goodbye Kiss

By Patty Davis

On a beautiful Sunday afternoon a couple of years ago, I had the sudden urge to go to Whole Foods even though I had just finished my grocery shopping at another store. Once I found my way there, I went in and bought a few things.

After I returned to the parking lot and began putting my groceries away, I saw a man in his mid to late 30s and a young boy standing next to him near my car. The man was speaking gently with the boy, and it was apparent that they were father and son. The man knelt down in front of the boy right there in the parking lot and took the boy's face in his hands as he spoke. I will never forget the way that they looked at one another with such love and tenderness. The boy was beaming at the man and took in every word. The intimacy and vulnerability they shared in that moment was captivating. I couldn't move. The man then kissed the boy, and I heard him say that he loved him. The man, still on his knees, gave the boy a hug, then they both stood up.

The man noticed me at that point and looked in my direction. I placed my hand on my heart and mouthed the words, "That is love."

The man said slowly and quietly, "I'm saying goodbye." There was not a hint of sadness, anger, or resentment in his voice. His words hit me square in the chest and took my breath away. The man and the boy walked toward the store, and I got into my car.

As I drove away, I could not stop the flood of tears and cried all the way home. I could not help but wonder whether the boy's parents were divorced or whether he had just spent the weekend with his father. As I began to process the experience, I realized that I had been guided to Whole Foods to receive a precious gift – the gift of seeing the power of love, courage, and the goodness of the human heart in action.

Kindness Knows No Boundaries

By Kathryn Shah

Vivid neon lights flash brightly as dusk falls in Tokyo. I find myself wandering the streets by Shinjuku Station, exhausted after a 15-hour sleepless flight.

At the busy intersection ahead of me, I watch in amazement as thousands of people cross without bumping into each other. How do they do that? Then it dawns on me: they know exactly where they are going, and I have no idea.

Crossing the road, I hail a taxi. The door swings opens, and I place my map in the hands of the bewildered driver, who takes one look at it, shakes his head, and drives off. The next two taxis produce the same result. I wonder: *What is happening? Is it too far? Why won't they take me?*

As I walk along, I approach several passersby for directions; they all shift nervously away from me. I notice a petite Japanese lady at the information desk who smiles at me but cannot speak English. Feeling overwhelmed at my lack of progress, all I can think about is a warm bed.

Disoriented, I wander blindly down a back street, finding myself in a strangely quiet part of the metropolis. A traveler at heart, I unexpectedly begin to succumb to the fear that has been quietly building up inside me.

As I turn the corner, I notice a Japanese man with kind eyes at a newspaper kiosk. Hesitantly, I approach him, and he starts speaking in Japanese. Disheartened, I turn to leave. Suddenly, a large black umbrella appears over my head. The kiosk owner smiles, picks up my bag, and motions for me to follow. We walk in silence, in the pouring rain, to the lobby of my hotel. As we wave goodbye, I know I'll never see him again, but his kindness and compassion will remain in my heart forever.

The Japanese man with the kind eyes didn't know me and he didn't speak my language, yet he took the time to help me – reminding me that kindness knows no boundaries as it works its magic through the people of the world.

Magical Kindness Between Strangers

By Alison Ellison

Jeremy has worked at the local grocery store for most of his life, beginning when he was 16. He is now in his early 60s and is still a bright, shiny presence whenever someone needs help in finding an item or carrying their groceries out to the car.

One afternoon, there was a minor car accident in the parking lot, and Jeremy was right there when it happened. While the accident was small, there was an injury. The person injured was Bill, an elderly gentleman who used a walker. Bill saw the fender-bender and went to see if everyone was all right, but on his way over to the accident, he tripped and fell, scraping his face and arms.

Jeremy moved back and forth between Bill and the two people who were exchanging information in regard to the fender-bender. Bill kept shooing Jeremy away, telling him he must help the others first. It was sweetly comical to watch the lighthearted but determined exchange.

No sooner had Jeremy agreed to leave Bill to return to the accident when he saw that Bill was having difficulty breathing. Jeremy came right back and sat down next to Bill, letting him know that everything had been taken care of with the fender-bender.

The scene that unfolded will be with me forever. While Jeremy waited for the ambulance to arrive, he carefully wiped Bill's injuries and leaned Bill's upper body into his, and then he started to hum a simple little tune. Those of us still in the parking lot looked at one another with tears in our eyes, knowing that we had just witnessed the magical wonder of human kindness.

Hospital Room 222

By Kelly M. Spencer

Each year, I host "Choose Kindness Day." Several dozen folks go into the community, offering random acts of kindness. Quite simply, I adore this day, witnessing so much connection and love within a community

My group, which included my mother, headed into the hospital to hand out teddy bears to patients. The nurse told us, "I think the fellow in room 222 would really appreciate one."

My heart sank.

Three years ago, due to chemotherapy complications, my father passed suddenly in room 222. We received a call to come to the hospital quickly. Still in my baseball uniform, I told him we had won the finals He said, "Eh to go, kid."

Those were his last words to me.

But on Choose Kindness Day, I was given an opportunity for healing and new perspective. I believe there are no coincidences. As we walked toward 222, I looked at my mom to check in with her. Her glance and smile let me know she was okay.

Upon entering, we saw a man about the same age as my dad, surrounded by his wife, daughter, and grandchildren. The staff informed us of his dementia.

"Can we offer your husband and father a teddy bear?"

They graciously agreed.

I walked around to the other side of the bed and held out the bear. "This is for you." His hands shook as he took the bear and set it on his lap. He then held out his arms open, signifying he wanted a hug from me. His embrace was surprisingly strong. A huge smile came across his face, and his eyes lit up. It was as though he knew I needed a hug. He looked down at the small bear and then held out his arms again. We hugged once more.

This man perhaps was confused and seemingly non-verbal, but it felt to me that he completely understood the energy of kindness, which he received with pure gratitude and gave back with generosity.

Don't Judge a Book by Its Cover

By Sharon Hickinbotham

How often we pass people on the street and judge them based solely on appearances. When we learn more of their full story, however, it can change our view of them…and our view of life!

I recently had such an experience. It all started one sunny autumn day while I was shopping at a local health-food store. A scruffy-looking man entered the store, apparently under the influence of alcohol, wanting to buy a book. He seemed to have left his manners outside. Due to his impolite behavior, he was asked to leave the store, and he never bought the book.

I had seen this man sleeping on the footpath with a blanket in the streets before, and I assumed he was homeless. Curious about what kind of book he might want, I went back to the store a few days later, asked the owner, and learned that it was called *Footprints on the Path*. Intrigued, I bought it and found that it was a spiritual book about trusting in God, the universe, spirit, and love. This book and its goodness so blessed my life that I bought a second copy, hoping to give it to the scruffy-looking man who had unknowingly introduced me to it. Inside the book's cover, I wrote: "Blessings from the heart of a stranger. Love is all around you. Hope within is never lost. Stay strong. Don't give up."

I went to the spot where I had seen him many times and walked up and down the footpath, looking for him. When I finally found him sitting on the pavement, I gave him the book and a bag of food, water, and goodies. After I left, I prayed for him to be led back to his right path. Even though I often returned to that area, I never saw him again.

I know that God has a bigger plan for his life. Perhaps this man will change his situation by using the book he was guided to. Or perhaps he will gain faith through a small act of love from a stranger – opening him to a greater love that casts out all fear and provides hope when faith is covered by darkness. I feel so blessed that I was led to this man and this book, that I had the opportunity to "be somebody's angel" (as I often encourage others to do), and that this man was able to reinforce such an important lesson: *don't judge a book by its cover.*

Let Your Voice Be Heard

By Joy T. Barican

I have always been fascinated with being on the radio, but I never understood why until Mum surmised that it may have something to do with being exposed to it since birth – she used to hang a small radio on my crib, high chair, and baby walker!

While growing up, I developed many interests, but my love of broadcasting never waned. I pursued other professions but kept an eye out for a chance to get a foot in the industry. When the opportunity came, I wasted no time in answering the job advertisement for a radio host.

The application requirements included a 15-minute demo to be recorded on audio cassette tapes. Because I didn't have a home-recording studio (and this was before the era of CDs, MP3s, and digital recording on laptops), I had to find a recording studio that catered to my specific need. After looking through the directory and making some telephone inquiries, I found the right studio. I penned some commentary to use as a script and enjoyed the recording experience.

The final product was high quality, and I was pleased. As I was preparing to leave, however, the recording technician gently cautioned me. He said he could see that I had something to offer but, given that I was applying to the top radio station in the state, the competition would be cutthroat, especially since I didn't have any experience. I appreciated his candor but told him that I still wanted to give it a try.

Then he said something that I've never forgotten: "Let your voice be heard. No matter where or how." It was this encouragement and his suggestion to check out local radio stations that led me to a five-year stint as a Radio Northern Beaches broadcaster.

His job was already done, the payment for the recording services had been made, and he could have left things at that. Instead, he kindly offered unsolicited advice, which allowed me to live my dream and be heard. I bless him, his work, and his family, offering my ongoing thanks for those kind, encouraging words.

Flowers from a Stranger

By Sharyn Holmes

The week of my 40th birthday, I experienced a panic attack so severe that it caused me to take a week-long absence from work. When I returned, I was still shaky and scared, wondering how I would ever get out of the hole of that breakdown. Breathing deeply and taking things slow was all I could do. I felt so fragile, like an eggshell that could crack under the slightest pressure. I had already cracked open and spilled a waterfall of tears the week before. In that moment, I thought those tears would never end. I knew the wounding was deep, and it would take everything I had to recover and feel whole again.

As I sat on a bench outside the supermarket, speaking with my husband on the phone, a stranger approached, holding a big bunch of orange roses. I paused my phone conversation for a moment, and the stranger handed me the flowers saying, "These are for you."

My immediate response was, "Are you sure?"

He said, "Yes, I think you are really beautiful and you deserve them." I thanked him over and over before he walked away and disappeared out of the shopping centre.

My husband wondered why the stranger didn't hang around to speak with me. I guess I will never know. It truly was one of those random acts of kindness, and I was the recipient that day.

If I ever had the opportunity to meet that stranger again, I would tell him this: I wish you could know how much your gift meant to me that day. It was the first sign after a very difficult week that everything would eventually be okay. I will never forget what you did. I don't know why you chose to give me the flowers, but I'll be forever grateful for how you reminded me that kindness and magic exist. Your one positive act brightened my day and made all the difference. Thank you.

My Gracious Fairy Godmother

By Denise Edelstein

My life changed one sunny Friday afternoon as I was driving back to my office, having just dropped my daughter off at swimming training. Suddenly, a car travelling in the opposite direction cut in front of me while turning onto a side street.

Standing on the brake, I heard myself screaming. That blue Range Rover, now directly in front of me, belonged to a girlfriend. Thank goodness my daughter wasn't with me!

My car ploughed into the Range Rover, spun around, and hit a pole. Sitting there shell-shocked, relief swept over me when I saw the other driver – fortunately not my friend after all – walking over to me, safe and unharmed.

Women began emerging from their houses with kind and concerned faces. My car door opened, and two women took me, arm in arm, across the road and into the adjacent home of an amazing woman, my "Fairy Godmother," who had miraculously appeared just when I needed to be rescued. Efficiently and calmly, she laid me gently on her lounge, phoned the ambulance, then phoned my husband. At the time, I was unaware that her kindness and goodness was to change my life.

Her goodness and graciousness engulfed me, and it will always remain ingrained in my memory. Despite my long recovery and selling my accountancy practice, there was a silver lining. During that time, I learned to see life differently, and my heart filled with gratitude, awe, and wonder. I learned to appreciate the little things in life, which made my heart sing, and coined the phrase "Pockets of Joy" to describe them. Before long, I used my new perspective to show other people how to discover their own "Pockets of Joy."

Ultimately, I wrote and published my book *52 Pockets of Joy: A Guide to Discovering Your Life Purpose*, which I launched on World Happiness Day. I now help heart-centred women follow their passion and start the online businesses of their dreams, doing what they were born to do and helping others. None of this would have ever have happened without experiencing the goodness of my Fairy Godmother.

The Answer...An Angel In Blue

By Destrie Sweet Larrabee

I sat in the front seat as my brother-in-law left the Cancer Center and got into the car. Weakened from his treatment, he lost his energy and fell, getting lodged between the edge of the car seat and the wheelchair. He could neither pull himself up back onto the wheelchair nor slide himself up onto the car seat. His panic and fear were palpable. Our loving family members, both inside and outside the car, were frantically trying to help. But he was just too big, and we were unschooled in such transitioning skills. He could barely talk, as his oxygen had been removed before he got into the car. In the midst of the panic, it seemed as if time froze, and I heard myself utter a faint cry of "Help!"

Just then, a woman dressed all in blue walked out of the center. When her eyes glanced toward the car, she immediately spun around and asked if we needed help. We gratefully accepted, and she soon had my brother-in-law back in the car seat with his oxygen on.

Our whole family shed tears of gratitude, relief, and pure joy! We profoundly thanked this amazing stranger, who turned out to be an employee just getting off of work. She said it was nothing – just part of her job. But I could see that she was pretty surprised at being thanked, and she mentioned that nobody ever thanked her. It was nice!

The longer I am blessed to live, the more I bear witness to the absolute beauty of our fellow human beings and their limitless ability to love and help others. Looking back on this incident, I see it as continued proof of this goodness, and I see that this beautiful, loving woman in blue was the answer to my prayer...our angel.

The Power of Kindness

By Diana L. Hooker

My friend and I start out early on a hot July day in Washington, D.C. With a map of the city and our Big Red Bus tickets in hand, we have a plan to see the historical sites of the city. Sitting on top of the double-decker bus blows our hair to disarray, and the heat of the sun melts away our perfect make-up of the morning. After hours of sweat beading down from head to toe, we take a break in the shade of the Lincoln Memorial. Wiping the perspiration with a cool cloth and drinking cold water helps us recuperate from the roasting temperatures. We press forward, knowing we have limited time but much more to see.

Weaving our way through the crowds of people with the same agenda of taking in the history and the same struggles of dealing with the unbearable heat, we make our way to the Vietnam Memorial after snapping a picture by the Reflecting Pool.

Stepping onto the tree-covered path, I see a lady and her husband standing at a concession stand. I make eye contact with the lady and smile as she approaches me. Once she reaches me, she tells me that she thinks I am a very beautiful woman and the dress I am wearing is very becoming on me. I am stunned by her compliment because I know how disheveled I am. After thanking her, we talk for a few minutes and agree that as women we need to build each other up. We part with a hug, sweat and all.

The compliment made me smile from ear to ear for the rest of day; it improved my energy and interactions with others. I no longer was focused on the sweltering heat but on recognizing the beauty surrounding me. That simple compliment reminded me that one act of kindness can make a difference not only for the person receiving but potentially in the lives of many others on the path.

Cowboy to the Rescue

By Karen Wythe

One day when I was in my early 20s, I took my two-year-old daughter and my friend Shirl for a shopping venture to our local Kmart. I only needed to purchase a few things, including diapers, but we ended up having fun shopping every department. Back in those days, we didn't have all the conveniences of cell phones and plastic bank cards, so we counted up our purchases in our heads to make sure we had enough cash. When we had estimated that we'd spent everything we had, we headed to the cashier.

Shirl checked out in front of me and was waiting for me at the end of the counter. What? I was $1.89 short. I asked Shirl if I could borrow the money from her. Looking panicked, she said, "I spent all my money. I'm sorry, Karen, I don't have it. What are we going to do?"

I looked at the merchandise on the counter and grabbed a pair of bikini underwear while saying, "You can take this off" to the cashier.

Just then, a voice behind me said, "No, here." Simultaneously, I saw a hand with two dollars reaching across the counter. There behind me was a young man dressed in a white summer suit with a white cowboy hat and boots – a truly unusual site in western New York! He paid the amount I owed without hesitation. Stunned by his gesture, I thanked him.

This provided an indelible lesson. It showed me how a small act can really relieve stress and bring joy. This goodness and generosity of a total stranger has remained with me for life. I have never forgotten the day a stranger bought me underwear!

Thank You for Stopping

By Anita D. Marshall

Tears streamed down my cheeks. I willed the platform board to change, to show the train to be on time. There were only six minutes between this train and my connecting train in York. The connecting train was the last one of the night, so if I missed it then I would be stranded and might not make it to the bedside of my dying grandpapa.

I had tried pleading with the lady in the ticket office to see if there was any way that the connecting train would wait, but she had apologetically said that there was nothing she could do.

I was in the middle of Kings Cross train station, crying my eyes out. For the most part, people simply averted their eyes, obviously uncomfortable. The board showed my first train had gone from being three minutes to four minutes delayed. I was looking down at the ground in dismay when…

"It will be okay – you will get there in time." The voice was strong and calm and sounded like liquid gold. I slowly looked up, then up a bit more because in front of me was a very tall man with soft, dark velvet eyes and ebony skin. Yes, even in my distress, I could not help but notice his presence. He explained that he had overheard me in the ticket queue and then repeated with such confident assurance, "Don't worry; you will get there in time – it will be okay." In that moment, I felt calm and belief. "Your train is coming in now; you had better hurry so you get a seat." I started to walk away and realised I hadn't really thanked him for taking the time to stop, but when I turned he had already melted into the crowd.

To the Earth Angel who took the time to stop and care, to express words of comfort to a distraught stranger, I want to say thank you. You were right – I did make it in time. The calmness I felt in that moment of meeting you continued for the whole train journey and beyond.

For the Love of Strangers

By Isabella Rose

Not long ago, I had to choose between being a victim and being a survivor. I chose to be a survivor. In the process of escaping a terrible situation, however, I fell through the cracks due to the way the U.S. government and judicial systems are set up and the availability of funding through programs for domestic-violence victims. Even though I made countless attempts to prevent this from happening, I was left homeless.

I went to the career center to use the computer, and my career counselor happened to be at the front desk. I told her my situation, and she walked me down to her office where she offered a listening ear, her love and support, and some food she had on hand. She also referred me to a store in the same building run by Catholic Charities. I shared my story with the women there. I'd left with very little clothing, so they allowed me to pick out shoes, pajamas, and several outfits. They also gave me bags of food and a cardboard cross of Jesus that I liked. They were no longer accepting donations, so they referred a woman with several bags of clothing to me!

Afterward, I sat in my car, overcome with tears of gratitude for the kindness, love, compassion, and generosity shown by my career counselor, the women I had just met at the thrift store, and the Sister who posted on my behalf for prayers and support in our Facebook group. I wondered how someone I knew for a few short visits and complete strangers could care more about me and my well-being than those who said they loved me.

As I continued to learn not to accept being mistreated, I again found myself in a position of not knowing who to turn to for help. The day before my 40th birthday, scared and alone, I remembered a message from a sister willing to help. I reached out to her. A few hours later, putting complete faith and trust in God, Goddess, and the Universe that I was making the right decision, I set out on a six-hour drive to meet my sister Sandy, over 310 miles away. I am so thankful I did! Not only did I meet a lifelong friend, I had one of the most special birthdays of my life!

Golf Cart Man

By Susan Bassett

I departed my daughter's hospital room to finally go home to visit my husband and son. After weeks of being with her 24 hours a day, I was ecstatic about joining a world I once knew. I longed to have homemade meals, sleep in my bed, make my own coffee, grocery shop, and, if time allowed, mourn this birth in private.

After witnessing my child suffer through multiple tests, blood transfusions, and open-heart surgery at 13 days old – coupled with the realization that this was not going to end anytime soon – my once-optimistic worldview had turned jaded.

I went to the underground parking garage the morning of my departure a more weathered woman than I'd been three weeks prior. All I wanted was to go home, but the universe did not get my memo. I searched for 30 minutes but couldn't find my car.

I prayed for help as I stood frozen, unable to make sense out of anything, waves of tears gushing down my face. Then, a man in a golf cart arrived at my side. (I call him "Golf Cart Man" because I never got his name.) He offered to help me find my car. We drove through rows of cars for what seemed like hours, but none of them were mine. Surprisingly, Golf Cart Man was not leaving my side. He was in this for the duration, a stranger dedicated to helping me return home – which, with his help, I eventually did.

Three days later, I returned to the hospital for my next round of what would be a two-year stint. I had several conversations with hospital staff about my experience in the parking lot, but everyone assured me that there was no Golf Cart Man. Some staff had been employed there for years. Some looked at me as if I were unstable. However, I knew the truth, and I was not going to forget that life-changing experience.

We all have a Golf Cart Man in our life, we just need to open our eyes. We are truly never alone.

Kindness in the Midst of Chaos
By B. J. Garcia

I arrived in New York City on Sunday, September 9, 2001, feeling apprehensive about fulfilling all the responsibilities of my role as event coordinator for the next three weeks in a city I knew very little about.

My sister, living in Millbrook, NY, graciously offered to come into the city on Monday to show me around so that I would be familiar with my surroundings. After a full day of sharing her generous and enthusiastic spirit with me, covering the city from top to bottom, she caught the last train out that evening as it was beginning to storm. That night, the city was shaken with loud claps of thunder, lightning, and pouring rain unlike any storm I had ever experienced.

Tuesday morning, September 11, I awoke to the phone ringing and a panicked voice on the other end shouting, "Are you alright?" It was my daughter calling, relieved to hear my voice. I had no idea what was going on, and she told me to turn on the television. I could not believe what I was seeing! In shock and disbelief, we remained on the phone together, holding each other in love, as the Towers went down.

There was chaos in the streets as masses of people flocked north on foot. Braving the crowds, I set out to buy a few provisions. In the panic and chaos of the unknown, the local markets were wiped clean, and I found myself without food or water and only a few dollars in my pocket and no ATMs working. We were in a war zone. There was no way in and no way out of Manhattan. Feeling desperate and alone, I reached out to one of our local volunteers, whom I had never met before, and shared my situation with her. Within the hour she was at my door, bearing gifts of food, water, money, and friendship as she took me under her wing. Over the weeks, in the midst of chaos and devastation, acts of loving kindness prevailed.

Goodness Is a Global Affair

By Keyra Conlinn

I could give you tons of examples of goodness experienced in my travels and my life abroad, but that would take an entire chapter. So let me tell you about one specific case, a random act of kindness that nearly brought tears to my eyes when it happened.

I was living in Amsterdam and going through a bad breakup. My partner had been the main provider, while I had a modest income that covered my debts back home and some personal needs. It was summer. My (English) students were taking vacations, and classes were minimal; in other words, I didn't have much cash. In fact, I had just gotten 30 euros from a two-hour session with a student, which had to cover my groceries for the week until I saw my next student. As I rode my bike back from the lesson, towards the grocery store, over and over again I repeated the mantra, "My life is abundant; all my needs are taken care of." I said it in my mind, I said it out loud, and I said it with a fervor unlike ever before; I dreaded the thought of asking my partner for help.

I arrived, did my selective shopping, and went to the checkout while trying to calculate what my total would be – I was just under two euros short. I looked at my options and moved something aside, asking the cashier to take it off as I held in the pain of my situation, the feeling of helplessness. The woman behind me in line, a middle-aged Dutch woman with curly, blonde hair, handed the cashier a bill to cover what I was short. I looked at her (I'm pretty sure my lip was quivering), smiled, thanked her, and took my bags.

It was a little gesture that I'm sure I've done in the past, but never could I have imagined the impact that it could have. That simple reminder of goodness really touched me. There are many differences between cultures, but in that moment, there were none.

$5 Difference

By Lydia Burchell

She could have woken to the same typical day, but this day was different.

Sleeping in the doorway of a downtown business, tucked in the alcove was her usual spot to spend the night. Vehicles passing by, people rushing to their destination, she lay unnoticed. Who would care about a woman dressed in rags sleeping on the streets? Many would pass with a thought of *Doesn't she have any better place to be?* or *She must be crazy!*

How could she ever explain the river of fear that ran through her? With years of a successful career, never did she imagine she would end up in this place of despair. It was even difficult for her to comprehend. Deep down, she knew she had hit rock bottom.

This night, however, was unlike the others. Upon waking in the morning, she noticed a folded piece of paper sticking out of her sleeve. Curious, she reached for it. To her surprise, it was a $5 bill. A stir of emotion rose within her. There were so many things she could do with $5. So many things she needed.

Regardless of what could be done with the money, she thought, the most meaningful effect of the $5 was the realization that someone had cared enough to offer help. Someone in the night had recognized her as more than a human being in need. Some stranger had recognized her as a living, breathing person.

Change was happening – someone cared, and it made all the difference in the world.

She wondered if he often kept a spare $5 bill in his wallet for the occasion to give to someone in need – if his intention was for her to know that someone cared. As he sauntered off into the night, he would never know the deeper impact of his generosity. He would never know the difference his caring made to this one woman as she rode the bus to her daughter's house, knowing that it was time to go home, time to make amends with herself and her family.

Thank you, stranger in the night. You changed my life.

Chapter 2
Family & Loving Relationships

I n 2001, Jodi was taking a walk with her mom, Nita, when they met Nita's new neighbor, Dan. They struck up a pleasant conversation and developed an instant rapport. When they left, Nita invited Dan to come by any time if there was anything she could do to help him. About 10 minutes later, he took her up on the offer. (Living in a new, remote area where he didn't know anyone, he didn't know how to get online, so he went to ask Nita for help.) While Nita went inside to look for the local internet service provider's phone number, Dan and Jodi sat on the porch and began a conversation that still hasn't stopped.

Jodi's mom was one of the few people who actually supported our relationship right from the start. Amid a sea of judgment (because Jodi was going through a divorce at the time), Nita did more than just accept our love, she celebrated it and embraced us both. Over the years, she's played a huge part in our lives – officiating our wedding, helping us launch our business, and even moving to Oregon with us for a year. Most importantly, she's been a constant source of maternal love and friendship for us both.

We're not the only ones blessed with a loving relationship and loving family, and in this chapter we celebrate many examples of both. In the pages that follow, you'll find stories of family members, spouses, and partners who have inspired us with their goodness. You'll read tributes to loved ones still on Earth and those who have passed on. You'll learn the life lessons they've imparted, cherish the special moments they've celebrated, and feel the love they've shared.

We hope you enjoy these stories and welcome our shared "soul-family" members into your heart!

I See You

By Dan Teck

My father and I chose significantly different career paths. He was an economist who specialized in international currency fluctuations. After leaving the Federal Reserve, he worked for a large bank in Manhattan and then as a consultant to multinational corporations. I managed a new-age bookstore, wrote avant-garde spiritual-comedic novels, and made eco-friendly journals (which led to a line of *Soulful Journals* and, eventually, this book series!). Not exactly what my parents envisioned when they sent me to college.

When my dad heard I wanted to be a Religious Studies major, he told a friend of mine, "With this background, the only thing Daniel will be qualified for is to be a full-time guru!" While I'd never aspired to be a guru (full time or otherwise), I figured that, as jobs go, one could certainly do worse (and, with my Jesus-style hair and beard, I already looked the part!). But I don't think he'd meant it as a compliment.

So when he sat me down for a Serious Conversation one afternoon (when I was in my late 20s, still working at the bookstore, still sporting the Jesus look, and still lacking any professional ambitions befitting a young man of my background), I was pretty sure I knew the direction the chat would take. Sure enough, it wasn't long before he began to describe a tableau of successful professionals he'd encountered during a recent trip to New York City. He told me how he'd stood on the subway platform, watching the businessmen in their power suits and leather briefcases, presumably rushing off to do important work at their important jobs with other important people. And then he gave me his most penetrating look and said, "If I ever saw you like that..."

I thought I knew how this sentence would end (with some variation of "...my heart would swell with pride"), but it took an unexpected turn as he finished his thought: "...my heart would break."

These simple, unexpected words were a gift to me. They told me that I was loved and appreciated for who I really was — not based on someone else's vision of success but based on my own. They told me that my father only wanted for me what I wanted for myself. And they told me one of the most important messages in the world: *I see you.*

My Sister, Sharon – A True Force of Nature

By Ellyn Rothstein

My sister Sharon's recent, sudden passing left everyone who knew her in a total state of shock and disbelief. It has now been nearly five months since that tragic day, and my mother and I still cannot believe that she was taken from our lives so abruptly. Every day without her is a reminder of just how much she is missed and how deep a loss her absence is. It still doesn't seem possible or real.

Sharon passed away on her birthday, which makes me believe that there was something otherworldly happening. Historical Jewish writings say that when one leaves this world on the same day they entered it, it means they have fulfilled their earthly mission to true perfection. With her strong spiritual beliefs and desire to help everyone she came in contact with, I believe that this theory must certainly be true.

Sharon and I, both extremely strong-willed individuals, certainly had our share of disagreements. That's what happens when an Aries and a Leo are sisters and the best of friends! It took many years to accept the fact that we could agree to disagree, maintaining our convictions *and* our friendship.

We had the greatest of times together because, even though our personalities were opposite, we enjoyed the same things in life. The most important shared experiences usually involved music, food, health and natural healing, and, of course, family. We would know what the other was thinking by just a quick glance, when at a concert and the singer hit an amazing note or when sharing a great meal at a favorite restaurant.

Sharon truly loved people, had many cherished friends, and connected with people so easily and naturally. She was equally loved by all who had the good fortune to know her. She was so full of life and always excited by the possibilities that her new experiences would bring. She was especially proud to be part of this *365 Book Series*, which she contributed to so beautifully.

She was taken from us way too soon but gave so much in her short time on Earth. She made an impact on everyone by just being herself. She has taught us all to appreciate each day and live it to the fullest. I will always cherish memories of the good times we had together and know that she is now and forever happy, joyous, and free!

A Valiant Act of Love

By Isabella Rose

I tried taking three deep breaths but was unable to. "Matt, I can't breathe! You gotta call 911…the car is filling up with smoke!" I started to panic as I dialed 911, hanging up before the call even went through. I knew I wouldn't be able to talk; I could barely breathe!

It didn't dawn on me that Matt was already out of the car, making his way around the vehicle to get me out. I heard him yell, "Push! You gotta push the door open!" He was standing on a rock, wedged between two large tree limbs.

"I am," I responded. "I think I dislocated my shoulder."

It seemed like almost instantly he had made his way back around the vehicle and was inside the car trying to help me out. "Give me your hand. I'll help you."

"I can't." I responded. "My arm…I can't put weight on it. I am trying. I don't know what to do!" Somehow I was able to turn enough to put my knee on the console, but as I reached out to Matt, I went unconscious.

The next thing I remember, I was in an ambulance with an EMT who was cutting my pant leg. I began to panic again, even more this time. I began screaming for Matt, not knowing what was going on, where he was, or if he was okay.

Then I heard his voice behind me: "I'm right here. You're okay. I'm not going to leave you. I'm going to stay with you." As soon as I heard the comfort and reassurance of his voice, I slipped back into unconsciousness.

I wouldn't be alive today if it weren't for the grace of God and Matt's brave heart, courage, determination, and love for me, risking his own life to save mine. I am forever blessed and grateful for Matt and his powerful, valiant act of love.

The Power of a Hug

By Sonya L. Moore

The sterile smell. The walk down the hallway as sympathetic eyes follow me and my family. The high-pitched, endless beeping of machines. Doors constantly opening and closing, followed by soft whispers of instructions and the soft humming of monitors filling the air. Where am I? I'm at Cincinnati Children's Hospital...again. I find myself in this place often with my daughter, Shanoah, who lives with a chronic and painful blood disorder: sickle cell disease.

There is something different about this admittance. Something is wrong. I feel it. Shanoah's pain is more intense, and the usual IV medication isn't working. My husband and I are growing more concerned by the minute as panic builds in our chests. Shanoah's crying eyes look at us as she asks, "Why is this happening to me?" Feeling helpless, barely holding it together, our hearts breaking, we stand by her side and silently pray to God to direct the doctors to find the right medicine combination to control her pain.

It hurts my soul to see my daughter suffer. I wish I could take her pain away. I can only watch, pray, and comfort her, but because I am emotionally and mentally shattered, I am having trouble finding the right words. I begin to think: *What am I going to do? I am her mother. I have to be strong. I can't lose it.*

At that moment, there is a soft knock at the door. The door slowly opens, and I instantly know who it is without turning around. It's the one person who knows me better than I know myself. It's my dad. He immediately feels my sadness, and he offers me one of the purest forms of goodness we have on this earth: a hug. He holds me very tight. No words are spoken. The power in that hug is enough. The goodness that instantly fills my heart restores my hope, my faith, and my strength, allowing me once again to be strong for my daughter.

Full Circle

By Cathie Bliss

Now and then, someone makes a huge difference in another person's life and doesn't even know it. It's pure magic when it comes full circle.

Recently, I was working one of my two days a month at our local antique shop when a friendly, vivacious woman bounced in. We chatted at the checkout counter, and she mentioned that I looked familiar. Truth be told, she did too, but grief brain had put a fog over so many of my memories. My precious daughter, Cailen, had died almost four years earlier, and I'd been gloomy and off-balance as that anniversary approached.

Jennifer, the shopper, suddenly recalled where we'd met. "I know! You came to my garage sale a few years ago!" A few *years*? I had to laugh! I'd been to hundreds of sales in the last several years; it's an occupational hazard for an antique dealer.

"You and your daughter were at my sale. She was in a wheelchair, and so was I. Her visit was life changing for me." I remembered instantly! Jennifer had been in a near-fatal car accident and had sustained severe injuries to her body as well as her spirit. She was despondent over how she would live the rest of her life.

And then, she said that Cailen – with her incredibly huge smile, radiant joy in living, and severe cerebral palsy – had healed her and made her want to live again. "She saved my life! They told me I'd never walk again, and I believed it. But your daughter's spirit and resilience sparked something in me. Everything changed, and look at me now!"

Jennifer asked how Cailen was, and I gently told her that Cailen was now in Heaven. It still feels like magic that Jennifer appeared on my rare workday, recognized me, and shared her story. It helped me out of my gloom, and graces me daily with love and joy. Cailen brought healing to Jennifer, and now I'm the recipient. It means more than I can say, knowing that Cailen continues to make a huge difference in this world!

An Unexpected Invitation

By Crysti Deusterman

Many moons ago, my brother and I got into a horrid argument. Heated words were exchanged; F-bombs were dropped. We were adults, so I certainly wondered if this would damage our relationship. It wouldn't be long before I knew.

Over the next year or so, I went through many life-changing events. I got divorced. I decided to leave California and return to Arizona, where I had to look for a new job. And I decided to move in with my parents while I regrouped.

But when my brother arrived at my doorstep to help me move, he offered an alternative plan. He lightened my mood with humor, suggesting that a move into our parents' home would surely leave me feeling like George Costanza (*Seinfeld* humor). He suggested that I move in with him and his wife while I got settled.

I was shocked.

It's a big adjustment to bring someone into your home. This idea hadn't even crossed my mind, but he convinced me his house would be a better place to heal. He thought I needed to be around people my age. He expressed concern that living at our parents' house, which was on the outskirts of town, might lead to withdrawing from life.

Looking back, my brother knew me better than I knew myself. I had not yet discovered what an introvert I am, and he was right. I was in a dark place; left to my own devices, I would have worked all day, retreated to my parents' house at night, and wallowed in self-pity.

So I moved in with my brother and his wife for six months, in which time we had great conversations. My little brother picked me up, dusted me off, and refused to let me recoil from life. He dragged me to a few parties, gave me several pep talks, and stayed by my side as I closed one chapter of my life and began another.

My brother, the guy I had the ugliest argument with, was right there as if it had never happened.

My Father's Dignity

By Lauren Bear

Dad had always been an adventurer. He'd done some crazy stuff, such as flying his tiny, unreliable airplane through the Rocky Mountains because it couldn't fly high enough to go over them. This is just one example of why we never thought he'd die of natural causes, but sometimes life surprises you.

My dad had visited every state except Alaska. So when his health began declining quickly, we rallied and arranged for our family to take an Alaskan cruise for my dad's last trip.

Like most people with failing health, my dad was feeling like he'd lost his dignity. He needed help with so many things, which is hard for an independent spirit to accept. Given his situation, I wanted to do everything I could to make this last trip extra special for him.

By luck, I guessed the captain's email address and told him about my dad. I was so excited that the captain actually got my email, and I was hoping that maybe we'd get a photo op and he'd say hi to my dad in the halls. What that email triggered, however, was something much better than I could have expected.

The captain must have recognized the importance of my dad's journey more than I did because he came through in the most important way. He invited my dad and our family for dinner at the captain's table and gave us a tour of the bridge. Another time, when coming back onto the ship after a port visit, the captain was there to greet my dad like an old friend. We got ready to take a picture of the two of them on the bridge, but the captain stopped us. He helped my dad out of his wheelchair to get the picture standing side by side.

Even though my dad had dementia, he remembered the captain. After the trip, he loved to show everyone the picture of the two of them together, and he beamed with pride.

From that memorable experience, I learned that treating people with dignity is the most powerful gift you can give.

Breakfast with Jesus

By Richard Saenz

"Really?!" I yelled. "I have to get on that old bus?!" It looked like it was held together with Scotch tape and was ready to break down at any moment. We hadn't even left yet, and smoke was already billowing up from the engine. I was 13, and my road trip was about to begin. My mom and I were heading to Mexico to visit my grandparents. We usually drove, but this time it was the bus on a budget.

Who am I kidding? We were always on a budget. My mom was single with four kids, so money was always tight. The drive usually took six hours, but this time it took 10 because the bus made several stops. At each stop, my mom would give me a dollar or two and have me get off the bus and give the money to people in need. We didn't have money to give away, but it felt great to give it anyway.

After a while, I started asking my mom, "Who's next?" I loved it! My mom clearly enjoyed it too, because we literally ran out of cash. Next, we started handing out bags of Cheetos! I think they liked the Cheetos more than cash. I thought, *Boy, people in Mexico really love Cheetos.*

When we finally made it to my grandparents' house, I was so tired that I fell asleep on their couch. I awoke to the sound of the doorbell; it was a homeless man asking for money. I heard someone shoo the man away, but then I sat up and watched as my grandfather followed him outside and called him back. He treated him like a best friend, even though he didn't know the man. My grandfather ended up giving him money. I saw how happy this made my grandfather. I knew the feeling.

When I told my mom what had happened, she told me my grandfather believed that Jesus would come to us in the form of people in need. My mom also said that when she was younger, she would wake up to make breakfast and find strangers at the breakfast table. Her father would invite people off the street to eat breakfast with the family. Impressed, I thought to myself, *Wow! My mom had breakfast with Jesus!*

The Gritty Goodness of Selfless Parenting

By Alison Ellison

There are many words to describe parenting, one of them being *selflessness*. We put our children first because we believe that their needs come first. Witnessing many selfless parents over the years has strengthened my own belief that there is something greater than ourselves at work in the universe.

My friend Sarah is one such mother, and I am in awe of her strength, determination, and resilience as a single mother of three. What she has accomplished in the 15-plus years I've known her is absolutely stunning.

Goodness comes in so many forms, and while many of the descriptive words for goodness tend to be light, kind, and uplifting, goodness can also be gritty, tenacious, and strong. Sarah's parenting has been gritty, tenacious, and strong.

Standing by her son, helping him with daily activities and functions while he went through an addiction to pain medication after he had a car accident, Sarah never wavered. When her daughter gave birth to a son at 16, Sarah moved the family so her grandchild could have a more stable upbringing. Sarah opened her home to a niece and her two children after their father died and helped her niece get back on her feet financially. Currently, Sarah has spearheaded an effort with her siblings to help her parents repair and sell their home because they can no longer care for themselves.

Watching Sarah move through each selfless act year after year reminds me that the qualities of goodness can be earthy, strong, and practical. Thank you to all the gritty, earthy, strong, tenacious, and practical souls who just put one foot in front of the other without fanfare to help others, every day of their lives.

Softly, as in a Morning Son Rise

By Katie Keck Chenoweth

It was my nephew Georgie Benson's 40th birthday, but instead of marking another year with candles on a cake, my sister and I held a celebration of his life before taking him to his final resting place. *What a long, strange trip*, I thought as I looked down next to my sister's feet. Inside a plastic bag was a box of our loved one's unfulfilled hopes for the future. Georgie had contracted HIV when he was 25. He had lived a difficult lifestyle, some would say, but he had always tried to help those less fortunate than himself.

San Francisco's January rain was relentless as we journeyed to find his favorite places. First stop: Grace Cathedral, where he received his HIV results – positive. We meditated while walking the labyrinth; marveled at the legendary artistry of Keith Haring's altar triptych, "The Life of Christ," in the AIDS Chapel; and stopped at the AIDS Quilt display to pay homage to those who had lost the fight. Contemplating this gravity in the light-filled cathedral, it struck me – this stark contrast is how he lived his life: in light and dark.

Next on the journey: his ocean of tears. As we made our way to the surf, a surprise of dorsal fins circled close to shore – not sharks, as we feared, but porpoises, harbingers of change, freedom. Alone, we scattered a keepsake of Georgie Benson as the waves surged and spit back and forth. *May he be safe; may he be blessed*, we prayed.

Back in the car, seeking warmth, we experienced a "moment" – the sky cleared and sunrays burst through soft clouds while the radio monitor was transmitting this message: "Softly, as in a Morning Sunrise" by George Benson.

As the phoenix rose from ashes, the "son" rose. My nephew's final act of kindness was for us – his gift. He showed us that his life transcended meaning, and he lives on through the veil now, free.

Let's Help Each Other

By Bevan Bird

We awoke to the clanking of chains. The van shuddered. It was past midnight. My dad said, "Good God, we're being towed!" and called out, "Hey, stop! We're sleeping in here!" We weren't towed away but had to drive around awhile before returning to Jericho Park, where overnight parking is prohibited.

I was nine years old and visiting my dad, Dick (during a time when I lived mostly with my mom). He was living in his van because while guiding kayaking tours in Mexico he'd gotten hepatitis, which knocked him off his feet. At 60, he was living off his meager savings, and his future looked bleak.

He parked his van outside the house of a couple of friends he'd met years earlier while kayaking the Similkameen River. Lesley was upside down, and he rolled her up. She was a refugee defence lawyer, Sam a venture capitalist. They invited Dick in and discovered he could help raise their two-year-old son. He became part of the family as he recovered his health.

They moved into a bigger house near the ocean. When Lesley had a baby girl, she asked Dick if he'd live with them full time and help care for the kids, freeing her for her legal work. He agreed to help. It felt good to be useful and appreciated.

Fussy baby Chaya put a lot of stress on Lesley, who wanted to be at once a lawyer and a mother. Dick took Chaya for walks in the stroller around Jericho Park to give Lesley the peace and quiet she needed. This kept everyone happy.

But the job gradually became more onerous and stressful. At 65, getting his old-age pension, which he saved, he felt it was time to retire.

He moved in with me in Dunbar, working part time. In 2007, he moved out, homesteading on the bank of the Similkameen, a river he'd always loved.

In 2011, when I was unemployed and deep in debt, he gave me a place to stay. I felt loved unconditionally! I helped him start a garden and fix up his home. Now I'm a digital nomad, and we spend our summers together. Happiness!

Second Time Around

By Marla David

I had only seen her through pictures, so when I got off the plane and was greeted by my new granddaughter (along with my daughter), emotions ripped through my heart and shook my very being. Everyone had told me how being a grandparent is one of the best things in life — something really great to look forward to. Still, I hadn't realized just how powerful the emotions would be until I held my granddaughter.

She is the epitome of grace. It is like looking at perfection straight on. The miracle of life. I find myself in awe of her, staring at her little hands, her feet, the mouth, little nose, and the eyes. I touch her gently. What does she see? What does she know? Is she still between worlds, as Dr. Wayne Dyer suggested?

A squirm that's all it takes. Suddenly, she belts out that wonderful newborn cry…just another form of grace. It is remarkable how the second time around, so to speak, brings just as much joy as the first. Even as different as it is from when I had my three daughters, holding my granddaughter has brought the same joy. It has allowed my heart to expand.

What is most surprising to me, though, is the feeling I have when I see and hear my daughter interact with her baby. Witnessing her nurturing her own child, as I did her, brought out a new emotion I had never experienced. She is such a wonderful momma, and it makes my heart flutter with joy. With tears welling up in my eyes, I watch my daughter shower my granddaughter with a love I could never have imagined her garnering. It is very sweet. My daughter and son-in-law are fabulous parents, and it makes me proud.

Children grow so very fast. Each day is a new beginning, and I look forward to memories my mind cannot yet conceive. The mystery of it fascinates me. I have much to be grateful for. Life is good, and the bounty is rich…the second time around.

Wheels of Goodness

By Kristy Carr McAdams

*"We make a living by what we get,
but we make a life by what we give." - Winston Churchill*

We called it the Mazda-ratti. Dad bought the fun, pale blue, pre-owned Mazda RX-7, which represented joy and freedom to him. The purchase of this car was "living out loud" for my father, and my family was happy to see him enjoying life.

My father had always been a serious gent, working long, late hours as a certified public accountant. He gave everything to his job and his family, living frugally.

Tall in stature, with a deep voice and granite expression, to say that he left many of my former boyfriends terrified (at least initially) would be putting it mildly. He came off like a tough cookie, but really, he was more like an M&M: tough on the outside, sweet on the inside.

Dad had a good friend named Ron. Ron's health wasn't so good, his finances were low, and he always seemed down on his luck. When I was a teen, Ron went through a particularly rough patch. He was without a car and had no means to improve upon the situation.

What happened next still stands out to me, all these years later: my father gave Ron his Mazda-ratti. He didn't talk about it; he just did it. It was magical to witness this giving, and it made me see my dad in a new light, as more than a "tough cookie." As Ron drove away that day, I cried – in joy for him, with pride for my dad, yet also in wistfulness, knowing what my father had let go of. The car he gave away was truly a gift from the heart. Goodness on wheels.

As the years went by, dad ended up giving away about four cars – fitting for a man whose last name is Carr!

Satisfaction Beyond Words

By Nancy Merrill Justice

On June 14, 2014, I accompanied my sister, Carol, to Nelson's restaurant at the magnificent Terranea Resort, situated along the cliffs of the Pacific Ocean with Catalina Island as a backdrop. The sun had burned off the morning fog, and the view up and down the coastline was spectacular!

A few of Carol's Gray Whale Census Volunteer friends had said they wanted to take her to lunch to celebrate her 59th birthday, and in spite of her failing health, she was determined to attend. Carol took slow, deep breaths and journeyed down the long hillside path until we reached Nelson's. To our surprise, instead of being seated at a small table, we were taken to an expansive outdoor patio area where numerous picnic tables were pushed together – all decorated with balloons, beautiful flowers, and festive birthday decor. The restaurant chef had even made a huge, beautiful, ocean-blue birthday cake with whales painted on top.

Familiar faces began arriving – more and more, many from long distances. You could see they all genuinely wanted to be there to celebrate this special occasion. Carol socialized for hours, embracing every moment of the festivities. I had never seen her so happy.

After returning home, I caught a glimpse of Carol sitting alone in the living room admiring the stack of cards and fun gifts she had opened a few hours earlier. Within her expression was a look of satisfaction beyond words. My eyes welled with tears. My heart overflowed with love and appreciation for every thoughtful soul who so generously planned Carol's spectacular birthday party, and for all who had come to honor and celebrate her.

For the past five years, Carol had gazed out over the Pacific where she found solace counting gray whales – a needed distraction from her divorce and battles with the ravages of breast cancer. Little did she know she would also find a family of friends full of goodness – volunteers at the Pointe Vicente Interpretive Center. It was through those friendships that Carol would find a sense of completion – and bid us all farewell.

My Inspiration, Tony

By Catherine Laub

When I met Tony, I was new to the dating arena again after my first husband left me and my three small children.

After dating Tony for about six months, I learned how great he is. My children and I were being supported by the government on Social Services income and living with my parents in two small bedrooms. Tony had a rental home and invited us to move into it and pay him only the amount of rent money Social Services allowed us. After living there for about a year, we moved in with Tony in his three-bedroom home. I didn't have to pay him rent anymore, and he began to support me and my children without any expectations.

I was not the first woman to be supported by Tony. He already had a young daughter when his first wife left him. Shortly after that, he met his second wife, who was also living on Social Services with three small children. Tony invited them to live with him and eventually formally made them his family. When that marriage ended, he was torn apart and decided just to have fun instead of looking for another wife. But when we met, he realized that I am the final woman to settle down with.

We met in 1992 and were married in 1998. Tony never had any second thoughts about supporting my children. I did work to help support them by purchasing food and taking care of their personal needs. Aside from that, Tony paid for all of our living expenses.

Over the years, Tony invited many different people to live with us temporarily. There was his daughter and her husband when they were first married. My nephew lived with us for about a year, and Tony even hired him in his small business. He did the same for my daughter's high-school boyfriend. There were many more invitees over the years, and Tony always helped out where he could.

Tony is a very giving man and helps everyone as much as possible. He is now 72 and has slowed down a bit but still says yes to everyone. Just recently, he allowed one of our granddaughters to have a big graduation party at our house. He put in a lot of physical labor but loved putting it together for Jessica.

Everyone should have a person like Tony in their life.

The Power Is in You

By Surabhi Kalsi

When I was a little girl, my mother was a working woman, and I spent a lot of time with my grandmother. I was the center of her universe, and she brought me up with unconditional love until I was five, when she passed away.

Shortly after she passed, I woke up in the middle of the night and saw her sitting on the floor next to her bed. I felt scared, as I could sense that she wasn't real. She was dressed in white and had an ethereal quality about her. Throughout the night, she just kept staring at me with a smile.

This strange experience was a lot for a five-year-old to process alone, so I spoke about it to my mother. To this day, I remember her response: "Did you pay your respects to her?" She didn't dismiss it or judge me; she just asked me to honour my grandmother. My grandmother had been away from home when she passed, so she had come back to say goodbye to her favourite grandchild.

I was lucky to be brought up by my grandmother during my formative years. She taught me that love is the most powerful force, a lesson that has stayed with me into adulthood. And I am doubly blessed to have a mother who didn't instill fear in me but instead nurtured me and allowed me to stand in my power.

One day when I was deeply upset and feeling disempowered, my mother told me, "You have so much power in you that you can change the world." I no longer remember what upset me on that day, but I remember what my mother said. Over the years, these words have firmly put the reins of my life back into my hands and served as a constant reminder that the power is in me, not in the external circumstances or other people.

When I look back over our relationship, the goodness — *her* goodness — abounds! I am so grateful for her and my grandmother's love.

Unconditional Love and Kindness

By Tahira Bharmal

As a little girl, she was afraid of needles, doctors, and anything medical. Yet she grew up to be the most nurturing caretaker I know. At 21, she met a woman suffering from cancer, and what started with a simple hospital visit to say hello turned into a lifetime of caretaking and nurturing. She now spends a great deal of time in hospitals and has developed a newfound comfort level for all things medical.

This soul gives endlessly to all who cross her path. If she commits to be there for you, she is there for you through it all. If anyone in the family is ill or has a medical condition, she is the one they call. She comes and takes care of everything. She nurtures.

She doesn't see herself as a nurturer or a caretaker, but to the rest of us, she is one of the most kind, loving, and nurturing souls out there. At times, she risks her own emotional, mental, and physical well-being to be there for those who need her.

All this is done with no expectation whatsoever. It comes from the truth of her heart and soul, and that is what makes her service – and *her* – so beautiful. I don't tell her enough what an inspiration she is to me.

I am blessed to call this soul my sister and, most of all, my friend. My dear sister, you do what you do with such aplomb. You are always there in the role of a caretaker for all who need you (even the ones who don't treat you well!). You give your kindness and love unconditionally, a goal that I, along with many others, work towards.

To me, you are truly the epitome of "goodness abounds" because you are sowing a bed of goodness, and it is coming back your way only in goodness!

The Healing Power of Unwavering Love

By Gigi Florez

Shortly after their vacation, he was diagnosed with heart failure. At that moment, she realized her life was about to change.

After searching from one doctor to the next for the best one to oversee his care, he was admitted to the intensive-care unit. Then, before they even had time to blink, the surgeries began. She lost track after the 10th one.

She witnessed his struggle and saw new sides of him at his weakest points, but her faith and love remained unwavering. She stayed by his side and reassured him that he would get through this. There was so much more life they had to live together.

During the year he spent in the hospital, she made it as normal and comfortable as possible. She completely gave herself to him; not a minute went by when she wasn't thinking of him, visiting him, researching his condition, or praying for him.

Many people disagreed with her decision to stay with him, but she persevered. Her family tried to understand what she was going through, but it was unexplainable. She internalized her deepest fears and remained composed throughout this grave situation.

It was only after he was put on the heart-transplant list that she saw the end of this painful journey. What normally would have taken months or years to receive took only a few weeks – a true miracle.

Now, as they prepare for recovery, she knows that her work isn't done. This is just the beginning of regaining their sense of normalcy. Taking one day at a time and helping him gradually get stronger, she knows they will get through this together, and more happiness will come out of this.

As I watch my daughter, I am so proud of her – amazed by her tranquility, her beautiful soul, and her power to heal – and I feel blessed by all the goodness she exudes.

Foster Father

By Reema Sharma Nagwan

I'd just started high school, and all was well. I was content with my world, which included two older sisters who would do anything to bring a smile to my face and loving parents who considered me a child prodigy. All the pieces in my life's jigsaw puzzle were in place…until the afternoon when one of the most essential pieces was lost.

I happily hopped off the bus, still radiant from my team's victory in a school sports competition, and was on my way home when I noticed Dad's secretary approaching me. At that moment, I had an inkling of why he was there but didn't have the courage to acknowledge it. We walked home in silence.

Upon seeing our neighbours crowded around our front door, my last ray of hope disappeared. It was custom for neighbours and acquaintances to gather to bid farewell to a lost one. When I got through the crowd, I saw Mum grieving for Dad. She looked frail, trying to cope with a jarring loss. I didn't even realise how big the loss was. I was numb in disbelief.

Looking back, I realise that Mum is a strong woman, stronger than I could ever be. At the time, though, she was in intense pain and grief. She needed someone to talk to, someone to put her life back together; that someone happened to be her brother. He was the only one who could really understand. She had lost her soulmate; he had lost his best mate.

Pausing his own busy life, he came over to spend time with us, helping us put our lives back on track. I wonder how many people would be willing to give the most precious thing of their lives – time – to others without expecting anything in return.

We bounced back to our lives as Dad would have wanted us to.

My uncle's kindness will stay with me for the rest of my life. I will always be grateful to him and will always regard him as my foster father.

Saint Nana

By Shayelee Johnson

"Of course she can stay here!" my grandmother stated as I broke down to her about the eviction I had just received.

As I packed up my daughter's belongings and put them into the car, the reality began to sink in: stuck, scared, homeless, pregnant, and with an abusive boyfriend. I couldn't have my daughter like that, so I did what I felt was the safest choice for her: I took my grandmother up on her kind offer to have my daughter live with her.

My grandmother is the only person I could go to for help. She's one in a billion – a selfless woman who raised her own six children, as well as me, my sister, and now my daughter – at the age of 71!

Twenty-six days after my daughter moved in with my grandmother, I went into labor. My grandmother said I could come to her home as long as my boyfriend at the time was not with me. Being in the home where I was raised, I felt a huge weight lift off my shoulders. Watching my daughter and grandmother reminded me of being a kid and how affectionate and loving this woman was.

It's now been three years since my eviction, and my daughter still lives with my grandmother. Seeing their relationship every day melts my heart. They're like peanut butter and jelly – happiest when they're together. Who am I to take that kind of love, friendship, and affection from either of them?!

I'm okay having my daughter at my grandmother's home. Sometimes I think about her living with me, but that seven-year-old's voice plays in my head: "I love you, Mama, but I want to live with Nana."

These two are my complete world. I can't thank my grandmother enough for everything she has done for me and my daughter. She's simply a saint!

The Gifts of Love Tree

By Jenna Kelland

When my twin girls were four and my son was six, I wanted to teach them that Christmas is not just about making lists for Santa and opening presents. I wanted them to appreciate that December is a month of giving, sharing time with family, and creating traditions. And I wanted to encourage our family to find more ways to express love and gratitude. This idea became the Gifts of Love Tree.

A visit to the dollar store provided a large Christmas tree cut-out and a package of ornament-shaped gift tags. I hung the tree on the door to the playroom, right inside our front door where everyone could easily see it. I explained to the children that this was a tree to recognize the gifts of love we give to one another and the gifts of love we receive from family and friends. They were easily excited by the idea of gifts. I explained that these weren't gifts to open or keep; instead, these were gift actions and thoughts that were planned and carried out to show that we love one another.

We talked about how they could help out friends and people in the community every day by offering a compliment or helping a friend find her mitts. Each day, I noted on a gift tag each gift of love they shared and each gift of love they recognized in their siblings' actions. They were excited to decorate their gift tags and select a spot to hang their messages on the tree. The tree was soon covered with messages: *I found my sister's pajamas. I helped my friend make a snow fort. I cuddled my sister. Mommy made us dinner. I put the boots away. I gave my sister a crayon.*

The Gifts of Love Tree wasn't taken down after Christmas that first year. It hung throughout the year with its reminders of how we all helped, shared, and spread love around the holidays. We added more decorations the following Christmas, and the tree is still hanging on the door near our entryway. When I stop to read the messages, I am reminded of how much love my children have to offer and how, as a parent, I need to help them see that their actions can make a difference in how people feel – and to encourage them to continue offering their gifts of love throughout the year.

Blessings Begin at Home

By Tammy Gamester

I knew John was a good man when I met him; I just didn't know *how* good until March 2011. We had only been married one year when we got the call that my mom was in the hospital, diagnosed with lung cancer and only given a month or two to live.

Mom decided to go into hospice. She declined slowly but, with the pain medicine, had a very good quality of life. She was one of the strongest women I've ever known.

John was wonderful to my mom. No one catered to her like he did. We took her to Nashville for Mother's Day to visit my cousin. In July, she had a dream that we took the train to Washington DC, so we rented a motor home and headed east. I was so blessed to be able to take my mom to see the Tomb of the Unknown Soldier and the Statue of Liberty – two things on her bucket list. I never would have been able to do this without John. He drove and took care of the RV. He helped with Mom, cooked for her, and pushed her all around in the wheelchair – she wouldn't let anyone else, just him. He treated her like he would have treated his own mother. We were blessed to get seven months with her, not the one or two the doctor predicted.

You might ask why this is such an exceptional thing to do. John had only met my parents once before, yet he was willing to drop everything and put our life on hold to move to Illinois and take care of my mother. He was so supportive of me, which you would expect a husband to be, but what he did for my mom went above and beyond. He has a huge heart and is such a blessing. I am so grateful to have him in my life.

A Father's Parting Gift

By Salome Schori

I recently met with a friend whose father had been severely ill. As I asked how he was doing, she smiled at me warmly and informed me that he had passed away. The news was not unexpected, but I was startled. Yet she looked so happy; how was that even possible? At my inquiry, she shared how she experienced the last few weeks at her dad's side.

My friend is an energy healer who communicates with the non-physical just as easily as she communicates with people. So when it became clear that her father didn't have much time left, she asked for spiritual guidance. Every day, she would ask what she could do to support her father. She was advised that she must let go of him as a daughter because her feelings for him were holding him here. She was also guided to remind him that his life had meant something and that he had many personal and professional achievements to look back on. Her father had hidden away some things that were important to him, and she let him know they had found them all. She also assured him that she and her siblings would be there for his wife, their mother.

Little by little, he was able to relax into accepting the inevitable. And when the last moment came, his daughter was sitting by his side, encouraging him to turn towards the light. In the moment he made the transition, she was filled with an exhilarating feeling of love and ease. She knew that what she was experiencing was really how he was feeling in that very moment. She could still sense him on the other side, and she heard him say, "If I had known how wonderful it is here, I would have let go much sooner!"

At this point of the narration, her eyes were sparkling as she said, "You know, this was one of the most wonderful experiences of my life! If I had any fear left of dying, it vanished in that moment."

Mom's Seeds Taking Root

By Kaori Takada

In my mid-30s, I had a phone conversation with my mom that still sticks in my memory. I had been living in Tokyo nearly half my life, far away from my hometown. Our weekend phone calls were almost a ritual, and our conversations sometimes lasted hours.

Back then, my work was full of challenges and kept me fully occupied. I enjoyed working, but as my busy days went on, I was secretly aware that I had started to feel gloomy. Adding to that, I was one of very few singles among my friends. I was holding a vague uncertainty about my future.

On that day, while talking with Mom as usual, she must have sensed something in my voice. Very calmly, she stated, "Kaori, everything in life comes in by destiny – careers, friends, relationships. Sometimes things may happen quickly, and many times you may fret. Most of it is out of your control, so the important thing is to live in the moment. Don't rush or despair. Just keep focusing on your day-to-day life wholeheartedly. Then, at each right moment, you will be given what you need."

Her words didn't bring any immediate change to my situation. But they were inspiring and made a profound effect on my mind, like she was planting seeds. She had created space in my heart around the feelings of uncertainty about my future so something else could grow.

Two years after that phone call, I met up with an old friend from college. Though we hadn't seen each other in years, we got married within a few short months. It was a magically fast but natural transition for us. And that was when I remembered the conversation with Mom. Oh, Mama, you were right!

Thankfully and happily, our adventurous marriage celebrates its 10th anniversary this year. And even though I now live a completely different lifestyle with a different future ahead, Mom's message always keeps me rooted in the present. *Arigato*, Mama.

Simply Indescribable
By Kenneth I. Laws II

There I was, 43 years old and starting over again…but I was a changed man. Something had awakened deep inside my soul that I still look for words to describe. Everything was brighter and clearer, and I was grateful for all of it – the good and the bad. I was finally ready to allow life.

It was almost at that moment when she appeared – my first wife, Tara. It had been 17 years. When she came to me, she said, "I just needed to see your eyes." Right then and there, we both knew.

We spent the next nine months in gratitude and elation. She told me everything about herself, as if I just needed to know it, and I reciprocated. We had no concept of time; there was only Now. I was being given this absolute love and acceptance that I had never experienced before.

She shared with me all that she knew pertaining to matters of spirituality. Those discussions, and all others, were never brief. In one of our lengthier conversations, we determined that love could not be described. I was witnessing a woman who had arrived at a point of absolute peace in her heart, with no hatred or judgment for any living being. There was only the giving of love and kindness.

Early one morning, there was a moment when we turned and walked toward one another and embraced. There was only silence, tears, and a depth of connection that I still cannot explain. It was beyond beautiful.

Two days later, she shared with me a dream of her entire life and said, "It means something; I don't know what." That night, she transitioned from this earth and my presence just as quickly as she came.

I look at it now as a true gift from God. I was given the gift of pure love. I remain forever altered by this experience, which I will never forget. Although I miss her deeply, I am eternally grateful for her and the gifts that she gave so freely to me, especially that which is simply indescribable: love.

The Force of Brotherhood
By Charissa May-Riley

My boys are very different in some ways, but so similar in others. The 13-year-old has short, dark, wavy hair, while the nine-year-old has long, straight, blond locks. Both wear glasses – one has small, dark frames; the other, large and light. Do they fight? That would be an understatement! The younger one loves to be around his older brother. He thinks he is very cool.

"Come play with me," he begs.

With an eye roll and look of annoyance, big brother huffs, "No way. I'm tired."

Relentless, little brother whines, "Come ON! Come play with me. Let's play Star Wars," and he moves toward the pile of intergalactic toys in the living room.

My boys' love of Star Wars bonds them in play every day. Patient and intent, they join forces to bring plastic spaceships, Stormtroopers, and Jedi action figures to life. The kindness they demonstrate is in sharp contrast to their daily squabbles and incessant arguments. Words flow freely, and each listens with anticipation while the other moves the plot forward. Together, they weave imaginative adventures of devastation, heroics, and escape in a galaxy far, far away. Sometimes I struggle with character names, planets, and worlds, but the storyline is easy to follow. Good and evil. Darkness and light.

What I like best is watching their faces – huge smiles, eyes crinkled, mouths wide open with laughter. Their body language changes, too. Instead of whining and eye rolls, they manipulate their toys with gentle, purposeful movements. It fills my heart and helps me trust that the force of brotherhood runs strong and deep. They are truly connected – brothers, playmates, friends. Sometimes it can feel as if they are at war, yet when something good happens, each turns to the other – sharing as if "It is only real once I share it with him." They hold one another's triumphs with care, remembering the details of each story as if it were the most important thing in the entire galaxy.

My Angel Mom

By Tere Moore

In October 1972, I was out of town with no access to telephone service. I flew home on the designated day, and my boyfriend met me at the airport. We had been dating for four years at the time, and our relationship was beginning to falter. While driving away from the airport, he told me that my mother had died suddenly. As you can imagine, the ride home was intense.

At 20 years old, losing my mom was quite a blow. After the funeral, our home was filled with angst and depression. Mom had died a few days before Halloween, which meant that those exceptionally close family holidays were fast approaching, and Christmas was my mother's favorite.

My boyfriend's mom, Betty, had always been as kind as any mom could be to the girl her son was dating, but that year she made the gracious gesture of inviting my dad, my sister, and me over for Christmas dinner.

In spite of the fact that I broke up with her son six months later, she immediately took me under her wing and became my "adoptive" mom. She watched out for me and supported me when I needed it. When I took a break from college, she helped me get a great job where she worked. She stood by me through my nine-year marriage and was still there for me when I became a single parent. She was not only a mom to me but a grandmother to my two sons and then a great-grandmother to their children. If ever I needed anything, she was there as though she were my very own angel.

Betty is now 87 years old and still going strong, performing her angel duties for not only me and my children but almost everyone she knows. She has been an excellent role model for me. Experiencing her giving and loving ways has inspired me to perform my own angel duties whenever and wherever I can.

Thank you, Betty, for being my angel mom and for loving me unconditionally as your "adopted" daughter.

A Summer Place
By Barbara ("Bobbie") Carr

"Gratitude is the music of the heart when its chords are swept by the breeze of kindness." - Author Unknown

One early September evening a number of years ago as my family gathered for dinner, my father announced, "I've been transferred to California." We were all thunderstruck, for we had always lived in the mid-Atlantic region of the country. My high-school sweetheart and I were just about to be separated due to each of us starting college in different states, and now a move that would separate us by thousands of miles! We wondered how we would be able to see each other again; both of us came from modest-income families, and it was unlikely that we'd be able to fly across the country to visit.

Into this personal chaos, help came via my older sister, Bet, and her husband, George. They had remained in New Jersey with their young baby and had a two-bedroom apartment in the area where our family had lived. They generously offered me free room and board for the summers before my junior and senior years in college. With my parents' approval, I was able to take advantage of my sister and brother-in-law's kind offer. My brother-in-law also made a connection at the company where he worked and helped arrange for me to have a full-time job during those two summers.

As I did not have a car, I relied primarily on a co-worker to transport me to and from work. She would not accept any money from me for gasoline – another generous person in my life during that time!

All the kindness I received back then allowed my sweetheart and me to see each other nearly every day, which kept our connection with each other very strong. My gratitude for those kindnesses was, and is, enormous: my sweetheart and I would later become husband and wife!

Reviving Our Hearts

By Kim Brazier Flatland

The August heat and humidity weighed heavily on my body, but the words spoken by my brother sent a chill down my spine.

"Dad had a heart attack."

My father had already gone through one life-threatening heart attack 20 years earlier, so I knew that this one would be a challenge as well.

After sharing what was unfolding on social media, a community of hundreds gathered in virtual prayer. Isn't it amazing that with one tap of a computer button, we can click on the power of prayer?

As I spent time at my father's bedside in the ICU those first few days, I grew worried. When I stepped out for a quick bite to eat, I asked for a sign that all would be well.

At a gas station near the hospital, the aroma of fresh-baked bread filled the air. My father's mother was known for her homemade bread. I commented on the delicious smell, and even though it was not yet packaged for sale, the clerk kindly sold me some. It felt as if my grandmother was telling us she was there alongside us.

Our hopes were deflated by a surgeon who felt that my father's condition made it too risky to perform surgery. It occurred to me that maybe the situation required a fresh set of eyes — those of a surgeon who held a strong belief in his ability to return a damaged heart to optimal function. Sure enough, our request for another doctor's opinion led us to that surgeon.

Later that day, I noticed a small, white feather on the floor in the family lounge — a sign from the Divine, leaving me with a feeling that my dad was in good hands.

Over the next month — through surgery and recovery — my family and I were the recipients of an abundance of kindness and love.

That was last fall, and my father is still with us...and doing well. Reflecting back, his hospital experience revived our hearts to a world filled with compassion and connection.

Accidental Kindness
By Misty Proffitt-Thompson

In the late 1990s, my self-esteem was terrible. I looked at my life and realized that I hadn't even hit 30 yet, and I was a divorced, single mother of three. At that time, my oldest daughter was 12 years old, and my twin boys were seven years old. Having a full-time job and being a full-time mother left little time for me to be kind to myself. At the time, I didn't really grasp what self-care was about, much less understand the necessity of it. I was raised to believe that doing something extra for myself was not only selfish but also unnecessary.

Although I was very happy with my kids, there was a part of me that wanted companionship. I was constantly on the lookout for someone who would take care of me and call me their number one. I felt at the time that I was incomplete, and it didn't help that some women I knew told me that because I had three kids, no one would want to be with me. Just when I thought there was really no hope for me, I was introduced to a young, single man who worked at our local community college. I remember constantly laughing at his incredible sense of humor, which I picked up on even when others didn't.

He saw something in me that, at that time, I didn't see. He encouraged me and made me laugh, and the best part was that he took care of me and called me his number one. He not only accepted me, but he accepted my children as well. After dating for about two years, we got married. Now, 17 years later, we have a 15-year-old daughter, and we are still hanging in there. It hasn't always been easy, but over the years he has truly helped me build my self-esteem, and now I have the privilege of helping others. He didn't realize how much his accidental kindness helped me.

Life Is Too Short to Be Small

By Jody Wootton

"Life is too short to be small," said my Auntie Grace. I can still hear her sweet voice saying those words, which she would repeat every time I visited her at her well-kept home, filled with family, animals, and memories. My Auntie Grace was no ordinary Auntie. She was more like a "Super Auntie"!

My Auntie Grace loved life more than anyone else I knew. In return, life gave back to her an enlightened mind filled with knowledge and the ability to connect with everyone she met. She had super powers when it came to this. When she met someone new, she instantly became your friend. By the end of your conversation, she would even know your birthday – and she would remember it! If you were lucky enough to be in her presence on your birthday, she would even bake you a cake or cupcake and give you balloons while she sang "Happy Birthday."

My Auntie had another super power: She was an incredible healer and wisdom chief in her field. She seemed to know how to find the best treatments for every child she met who needed her help, and she gave her knowledge freely to make a difference in their lives. She even helped colleagues on research that still is being done.

As I have grown up over the years, having a small family of my own and meaningful work, I pause to remember my Auntie Grace, acknowledge her life motto – "Life is too short to be small" – and reflect on how I can help spread goodness like she did. For me, it is about taking notice of all the small, positive, and meaningful steps in life that can move mountains.

With a Twinkle in Her Eye
By Kathy Damas

The young man grew nervous as he waited for his check. The late June sun was beginning to set, which happened early behind the heights of Mt. Whitney. The woman realized that her plan had sputtered. While eating with her daughter, she noticed him dining alone and decided to anonymously pay for his meal...just because! But the waitress had disappeared without telling him. The woman reluctantly confessed. Stunned, he thanked her profusely. That selfless act likely made a lasting impression on the German backpacker. He left to make camp with a full belly and even fuller heart.

Mom's generosity should not have surprised me. My heart burst with love for her! She was deeply happy, and I was happy for her.

On the second evening of our rare and special road trip, we sipped cool drinks after a long day of driving. A young woman (who I'll call "Patience") sat nearby in the small restaurant, waiting for a very late friend. We had nearly finished eating when Patience's friend finally arrived. The friend proceeded to talk nonstop about her new boyfriend. Overhearing was unavoidable, and Patience looked like she was melting into a puddle of weariness.

Mom's eyes began to twinkle. Determined to remain anonymous this time, she whispered strict instructions to our server, paid, and we escaped unnoticed. Outside, Mom exclaimed, "That was so much fun!" She was giddy with happiness, and her joy was contagious. I admired her spunk, her playful and generous spirit.

We strolled through town, profoundly content. As we exited the local bookstore, we literally bumped into Patience and her friend on the sidewalk! Marveling at the unlikelihood of this encounter, Patience tearfully said, "Thank you. You have no idea what your thoughtfulness meant to me." After offering repayment, Patience instead embraced Mom's suggestion to pay it forward and do something nice for another sometime.

Mom – and these experiences – inspire me to be more generous and spontaneous. I love and honor her for observing something in another that touched her and, most importantly, for taking action...without ego, from her heart. With a twinkle in her eye.

The Gift of Time and Attention
By Kelly Jenkins

After my first marriage, I was diagnosed with a severe case of endometriosis. I was lucky enough to get pregnant twice; however, the pain was increasing with every passing day. I had several surgeries and received shots to put me through medical menopause, but still I felt no relief.

I clearly remember the day when the doctor told me the only alternative left was a complete hysterectomy. What? I was only 27 years old. There had to be an alternative.

Unfortunately, there was not.

I can't even describe all the emotions I went through; however, I do remember being mad. Really mad. Why hadn't they invented a drug or surgery to completely heal such a painful disease? It was hard on me, physically and emotionally. I thought that no one understood what I was feeling. I had two very young daughters, was in constant pain, and felt as though I had no say in what was about to happen to my body.

The surgery was scheduled for Valentine's Day. After surgery, I woke up briefly to find my husband in the room with me before falling right back to sleep. Several hours later, I woke up to find my beautiful bonus (step)mom sitting by my bedside. I asked her what she was doing there, as I knew she had come from work and was probably tired. She looked at me and said, "I didn't want you waking up alone and being afraid."

At that moment, I knew I wasn't alone and had permission to feel all the feelings I was experiencing. That night, she never left my side. She listened to me, let me cry, and attended to all my needs. She was my real-life angel. She left the next morning when my husband arrived so she could go back to work.

Throughout the years, when people have asked, "What's the greatest gift you have ever received?" my answer is always the same: the gift of time and attention. That was 24 years ago, and it is still the greatest gift I have ever received.

The Greatest Joy Is Giving

By Chadi Hemaidan

My dad had Alzheimer's for 10 years, but he didn't start going rapidly downhill until the last year of his life. During that time, we wanted him to stay at home, where his family could look after him, instead of going to live at a seniors' home. That way he would know that we cared for him and loved him.

We tried to make him feel at home – in his own home, where he once sat out on the porch with my mom, drinking coffee in the mornings and evenings – but he was forgetting so much: the names of people he knew, places he had been, and even how to perform certain everyday tasks. It got to the point where he needed constant supervision, so I left my job (working with seniors and kids with disabilities) to take care of him.

Still, even during this time of needing extra care, he gave our family so much. He was always giving us happiness and love, which is what builds great relationships in a family. Perhaps the greatest gift for me was spending time with him. When I was taking care of him, we got closer than ever. We hung out, went places, and had a great time together. This made me realize that in my younger years I hadn't really known who my dad was; he was a great guy! Although I hadn't seen it before, I now understood more of my dad's work, his love, and how he felt for us. He had a life of happiness, and that helped me fulfill my own journey of what was to come for me.

It was hard to see my dad ill, lying in bed. But I knew that he loved us completely. In that last year, I learned so much from him; he was my greatest teacher. He was divine love.

My dad passed away on April 6, 2013.

Despite the sadness, it was a great joy for me to have been able to take care of him. I feel that *I* was the one who received the greatest gift. Making time to take care of a loved one reconnected me to learning more about my divine self, and that joy I experienced is something I will never forget.

My Love Story

By Carisa Montooth

My first boyfriend and I met when I was 17. We dated for three years and then broke up on my 21st birthday. It was gut-wrenching...he was my first everything.

I'd been abused in my childhood, so when we broke up, not only was there the pain of losing this person I loved so deeply, but there was this feeling like, "Of course after he really knew me, he realized I wasn't worthy of love."

I spent the next year deeply depressed – sobbing in the shower, crying in the car, and just wanting to be by myself. I told my friend that I'd be alone and miserable forever, and I believed it. But she said, "You're going to be *really* happy someday, and I'll be right there to see it."

Around that time, I started praying and meditating a lot. I learned that praying is asking the questions, and meditating is when you shut up and listen for the answers. As I did this, I realized something that totally blew my mind open: this breakup was NOT personal. I realized that my ex-boyfriend was just as messed up as I was and that he had a journey and healing of his own to do.

In that exact instant, I was able to forgive him. Once I did, I felt my energy change. I felt my heart open up again. The pain and grief eased, and I stopped struggling. I could rest. I felt grace.

About a year after that, my ex moved back to where I lived, and we became friends. One morning, he asked me to have breakfast with him. Afterward, he turned to me and said, "Carisa, I still love you. I want to spend the rest of my life with you. But I need to understand what happened when we were together before. Will you go to counseling with me?"

Now we've been married for 14 years and have a beautiful little girl. And my friend who said she'd be right there to see it was my matron of honor.

Me Ke Aloha Pumehana

By Katie Keck Chenoweth

It happened at a retreat in Molokai, the sacred Hawaiian island that remains unhurried in the midst of modern life. I arrived at 9:00 p.m. from the southern Outer Banks of North Carolina and looked forward to a cool bed and balmy breezes through open windows. The group, however, had other plans: a breathing meditation was soon to begin.

As I started the quick, steady breathing, I just hoped I could stay awake. No one would know if I was faking it! But somehow in the process, my subconscious took over. A woman appeared in living color. I could see her from the waist up. It was my mom – not as she looked before her death at 84 years old, but a younger version of herself at my age. She spoke to me like we were close girlfriends.

Emboldened by the breathing exercise and the lack of sleep, I said to her, "I'm having a bit of a problem forgiving you for some things that happened between us."

Rather than defend herself, my mother asked, "Do you love yourself?"

Without hesitation, I replied, "Yes, I do."

She looked at me quizzically. "Then what's the problem?" she asked. "If I was not the mother I was to you, then you wouldn't be who you are today. When you love yourself, you love me and you love God. When you forgive me, you forgive yourself and you forgive God. We are all one and the same. You chose me to be your mother so you could be who you are. There is no need to forgive, for just who are you forgiving?"

Then I blinked, and the image of my mom disappeared. I was speechless. My heart chakra suddenly felt light and free. The cords of discontent were cut.

I have accepted my mom as one of my guides, although she only brings me messages when I'm in Hawaii (a place she always wanted to visit – now it's where her spirit stays). May you be at peace. Thank you for showing me loving kindness. *Me ke aloha pumehana* – with all the love and warmth in my heart – and with gratitude.

A Grandpa's Love, Forever in My Heart

By Vicki Ann Martinelli

I appeared on June 10, 1958. Hello, Mom…but what happened to Dad? He had left the hospital very disappointed that a girl had arrived.

I was the first born to my parents, and I was the first grandchild to my dad's parents. My two sisters arrived after me, so Mom was usually busy. Dad was never around, but my grandpa was always there for me. I grew up on my grandparents' dairy cattle ranch. My grandpa ("Pops") and I did everything together. He would pick me up, and we would drive to the dairy to feed the calves, the cows, and the dogs.

When I was eight, my parents divorced and we moved to another town. I felt abandoned without my grandpa. My dad would sometimes call, promising to take us three girls somewhere. I'd wait for hours in front of the window, glancing down the long driveway for his powder-blue Ford truck, always ending up in the same story: another no-show.

Again and again, I heard the same voice telling me: he wanted boys not girls. I tried to figure it out: *What do boys have that I don't? Why are they "better"?* To prove myself, I competed in all the sports I could; nothing held me back. I overachieved because, although we were so poor, when I excelled at sports, no one saw the holes in my clothes. They saw who I was and my talent. But it didn't change things for my dad.

My mom would still take us to the ranch to visit our grandparents. My grandpa and I maintained our incredible connection. He loved me and believed in me like I was his own. In 1987, when he was in the hospital, he told me, "I hope I was the grandpa you wanted, because you were everything in a granddaughter I wanted." I burst into tears.

At a holiday gathering after he passed, I mentioned to the other grandchildren, "Wasn't it nice what Pops said?" – but I learned that he hadn't spoken those words to anyone else.

A couple of days before my mom passed away, she told me that Grandpa and his daughter didn't get along, so she never came home. That's why he was so happy when I was born: I was the daughter he never had. I was the little country girl who he could take with him when he did chores. What my mom told me was an amazing gift, resonating with goodness that I still appreciate all these years later.

Sacred Ground

By Cindy Harpe Hively

I was a little blue-eyed, braided blonde-haired girl with freckles across my nose, always ready to explore. And one of my favorite magical places to visit was the log cabin where my great-grandma lived. I would get out of the huge bed in the morning, ready to play till dark. The walk to the corncrib and barn – arm in arm with my cousins, surrounded by cows and farm animals – meant another day of curiosity and exploration.

Great-Grandma didn't have electricity or running water until I was much older. As a little girl, I experienced family gatherings at dark, sharing our day on the front porch. I treasure the memories of using candles and oil lamps to illuminate the way. I loved these old-time traditions, but I'm not sure if I ever got used to using the outhouse – especially after being stung by a wasp during one visit!

Recently, on a hot June day in North Carolina, my parents and I drove down that same dirt driveway we'd been on so many times before. Now, however, we could barely see the cabin. This home with so many memories was now nearly covered with plants and vines, which climbed almost all the way up to the tin roof, as if keeping the precious memories from escaping.

As I walked up to the cabin, my heart was so saddened at its condition. I wondered: *Why hasn't my family taken care of this home I loved so much?* When I reached the steps, pulled back the vines, and saw the door, I was transported back in time. I breathed in the experience and felt the sensation running down my face into my feet, awakening every sense in my being. Once again, I experienced the feel of being scrubbed in a tin tub under the moon and stars, the smells of the yard, the taste of food from this earth, and all the sights and sounds as I journeyed into the house.

I was standing on the most sacred ground in these moments. It was permission to let the "Wild" cover me when I needed to hide. I received the enchanted message that I could still hold these beautiful experiences within, despite what I considered destruction. The Divine Creator always makes sense of what we can't. We just have to open our heart's door.

A Ray of Light

By Lisa R. Cohen

"Together you will far surpass the stance of survival
and become enraptured in the dance of revival."
(from Grace is Born *by Lisa R. Cohen)*

My mother, Sandy, received her first breath on April 16, 1931. Shortly thereafter, her mother, Ray, experienced asphyxiating depression, which intensified, rendering her incapable of caring for her beloved family. Desperate for relief, Ray's husband, Leon, relinquished the care of their three children to the Jewish Foster Home and Orphan Asylum of Philadelphia and entrusted his wife's custody to the Philadelphia State Hospital at Byberry.

The Jewish Foster Home and Orphan Asylum fulfilled their commitment to rescue, educate, and provide a loving home for orphans as well as children of indigent families. My mom and her siblings were graciously swaddled with compassion.

Conversely, my grandmother, sheathed in abuse, succumbed to Byberry's hall of horrors. Tragically, Ray's light was extinguished on January 18, 1942.

Amid her storm of sorrow, my mom found solace in kindhearted people. Blessed with their support, she persevered until darkness kissed the dew of dawn, and tears gave way to laughter.

Mom is a sparkler who cherishes her family, friends, and community. She is a forthright woman who fervently protects those in her charge, including her husband of 57 years and her two daughters, three granddaughters, great-granddaughter, and sister.

She honors her mother's sacred memory by talking to the forgotten ones, imparting unsolicited advice, nurturing those who hunger, gifting lottery tickets, sending the perfect greeting cards, and praying for people in need of celestial intercession. My mom is her mother's "good-deed emissary."

Mom's life is a living prayer, inspiring us to grace the world with loving acts of compassion.

Walking with Ancestors

By Lori Santo

As I turn my attention to my Inner Vision, I know that the Truth lies within. I sense the pulsing, rolling explosion of light gleaming off the ancient molten lava just beneath the dark shadowlands of suffering, caught in a glimpse of my full awareness. The torrent of madness running through me is a raging river with nowhere to go. But I'm ready now to feel it all – to reclaim my power, usurped by enduring abuse that defined my life for years. I've been forged in a crucible of fire, assigned the holy pilgrimage to discover the wisdom of my anger and rage.

My ancestors, who labored for millions of years, navigating their own intimate relationship with rage, have bequeathed their knowledge to me, downloaded only when I give them my full attention and take the time to commune with them.

I struggled against this formidable fate for most of my life, paralyzed by my shadows and the depths of my ancestral, spiritual, emotional, and psychic wounding. But the moment I surrendered to the raging currents beneath my greatest sense of torture and became entirely willing to trust my God and the accompanying Oversoul that was also bequeathed to me, was when the scorch of the lava beneath my unconsciousness began to torch away my falsity.

I have experienced many visitations from ancients who are thousands of years old, and to consider that I fought against them, denying their existence, is astonishing to me. They are the giants that walk with me, guide me, and whisper soul-stirring cries for evolution. Their love for me is so vast, my mind cannot conceive it.

It takes my devoted willingness to believe, to drop deeper into my embodiment, to invite and usher them close, to keep my ear on their pulse running through me, and to follow their Sacred Guidance. Miracles pour down on me each and every time I heed their direction.

The Little Shop

By Neelam Patel

My parents, Maheshchandra and Minaxiben Patel, purchased a newspaper shop in a residential area of Reigate, Surrey, in 1983 and were one of the first Asian families in the area. When they first took over the shop from the previous long-standing owners, there was a period of adjustment, and the customers were patient and understanding as my parents learned the ropes. This, I believe, was an act of kindness within itself.

As time went by, I witnessed many kind deeds in this shop, and I was often able to participate in them. I recall a customer named Susan who used to shop for her dad. She came in each week with their dog, Sunshine. When Susan broke her arm, my parents asked me to carry a shopping basket for her and add the items she required. Once everything had been paid for, I was asked to pack Susan's shopping trolley bag for her.

As I grew up, my dad took me with him to deliver groceries to customers' homes when they were unable to come to the shop themselves. (This was before online shopping came along!)

My mum paid special attention to things that customers requested and would go out of her way to carry them. My dad was particularly good at entertaining customers' children and was able to make them laugh, so they always left smiling.

By connecting with their customers, they were often able to help with whatever was required. For example, if someone was looking for a house, my parents were able to share who was putting their house on the market; if someone required a legal representative, my parents could put them in touch with one.

Some may say my parents ran a newspaper shop for 29 years, but to me, they became the hub of the community and brought people together. Their legacy is the ripple effect of their love and kindness in the community they served.

I feel blessed and privileged to have been brought up by great role models and to be able to call them my parents. Thank you for continuing to inspire me to be thoughtful and kind.

The Matriarch

By Lauren Bear

There were three generations living in the house, plus me. It was a fairly traditional Thai household, complete with a well-maintained Spirit House to keep the spirits from making mischief in the home.

The family – Grandma ("Khun Yaa"), Grandpa, and their two sons, along with their sons' wives and children – had a sort of timeshare arrangement in the kitchen. People ate and cooked at different times, and we each had our assigned places to store food. Being part of a generous family, Khun Yaa would offer me things to try. She taught me to cut dragonfruit and shared her favorite brand of soy milk. When she learned that I liked something, I would periodically find that item in with my other food. She knew I liked fruit, so I would find bananas and avocado left for me, along with other little treats.

When I got up in the morning, Khun Yaa would already be up, listening to her Buddhist chanting. We'd often spend mornings before I went off to school eating, listening to the chanting CD, and sitting quietly before more family came down to eat. I knew that, after I left, I would miss those mornings, so I asked about getting a copy of that CD Khun Yaa listened to. She did something even better: she took me straight to the source!

Khun Yaa arranged for her and her sisters to take me to meet her favorite Buddhist monk at her favorite temple. It was a beautiful temple with gorgeous woodwork and classical Thai architecture. During our visit, we had an audience with the abbot (who, as it turns out, is her favorite monk). He gave me a stack of Buddhist books, as well as a copy of the chanting CD.

Khun Yaa's daughter-in-law would call her "Super-Mom," and she's right! The entire family followed Khun Yaa's lead in treating people with kindness and generosity. I'll be doing pretty well if I can embody just part of what I saw in Khun Yaa and her family.

The Breath of Love

By Jesse Hodgdon

Our first granddaughter, Jaylin, was a surprise in our lives; from 2,767 miles away, I heard about this being who'd entered our family, and something in the universe shifted. I couldn't wait to meet her! Two weeks later, she fell asleep in my arms, and I couldn't – or *wouldn't* – lay her down. I lowered myself back onto the bed, held her on my belly, and watched her breathe…all night long! "Goodness gracious!" my grandmother would have said.

Our grandson Theo and I are close – we live three miles apart, and we have always shared an intangible connection. One time when he was a baby, I made this silly noise – inhaling with a sound not dissimilar to a seal's – and he turned his head and took notice. In making the sound every time I saw him, he thought it was my name! "Good grief!" as Charlie Brown says.

When our second granddaughter, Emma, was born, I headed east again to greet this sweet new arrival. Really, were the other two ever this small? The magic of holding one so fresh, so newly sent forth into physical form is very close to perfection. She and I shared a room on my visit – she in her bed (for the most part!) and I in mine…lying there, looking out the window at the brightest twinkling stars, listening to her breathe…all night long! "My goodness!" I say.

Two years ago, our Pennsylvania family came here to Oregon for a vacation – all three "grands" together! My husband and I live in the foothills of the Siskiyou Mountains, on acreage among the trees. As others settled into their cozy beds inside, those three snuggly, wiggly, "don't-let-me-fall-asleep-and-miss-one-minute-of-this" children and I climbed into one queen-size sleeping bag, on one air mattress, on our upstairs deck. As we counted the shooting stars crisscrossing the warm summer night sky, I heard the stars whisper under their collective breath, "Goodness abounds!"

Books, Empathy, and a Wonderful Memory

By Shannon Townsend

I adore reading. To me, there's nothing better than a long book series – preferably with talking animals, young adventurers, and magic. I see the characters as they plod along, I listen to their voices and speech patterns in real time, and I always have the perfect melodic and slow-paced narrator bringing each perfect scene to life. It makes me a slow reader, but I wouldn't trade it for the world.

This love runs deep. The confiscation of my books when I was three years old is the only punishment I vividly remember having before the age of seven – and still ranks as the worst thing that's ever happened to me.

During a recent phone call, I mentioned to my Mom, "I have no idea where my love of reading comes from."

She took a long beat of silence. I could picture her curled up with her feet tucked under her, a couch pillow tucked under her arm, as she flashed to my childhood. "You don't remember your dad reading to you all the time? Each character had its own voice!"

This tidbit of forgotten reality was the greatest gift I've ever been given. Suddenly, I could hear and see my dad reading to my youngest and quietest brother and then to my middle brother as he sat fidgeting, anxiously waiting to ask questions about the story. Without my mom, I never would have realized that the reason I love to read out loud at any and all opportunities – in school, as a big sister, and on stage – is because of my dad. He's the generator of all those voices that play out in a hundred universes only I can see.

My love of reading is the backbone of every successful interaction I've ever had – all because my dad made silly voices and gave me access to empathy, allowing me to be fully present with others. I never would have known that the cornerstone of my personality came from Dad without the loving kindness Mom gave me in just a few seconds, from 1,253 miles away.

My Mother's Love

By Anne-Marie Hoyne

My first child was born at home in the middle of a sweltering heat wave. Day after relentless day of baking dry heat and restless nights in our uninsulated old farmhouse made the summer seem very long that year. Thankfully, my sister-in-law lent us her portable air-cooler when my time came.

It was a long, slow labour, and the midwife was incredibly patient. The clammy night was infused with the serenade of a hundred cicadas and the distant hum of the freeway. My husband was beautiful, attentive, and resourceful, the perfect birthing support. My parents were in the kitchen, making cups of tea, murmuring soft words of encouragement, and holding a quiet vigil for us all.

Our baby was born underwater in a homemade birthing pool and was graciously guided straight to my breast like a tiny newborn animal. I was given the pleasure of seeing for myself that she was a girl, and the tears of joy flowed freely. My husband cradled us both in his arms, and it seemed like a miracle had just happened right there in our living room. My parents met their first grandchild just minutes after she was born and over the next couple of hours, the midwife worked her well-honed skills with a calm, satisfied air.

After a few hours of sleep with our little miracle bundle between us, my husband and I were feeling quietly humbled. It was a big thing we'd done, and now we had another human being to care for. It was a responsibility we were both ready to embrace, but it also felt quite daunting. My mum ran a bath for me, and as I lay in the water, she gently washed my hair. Her loving presence and soothing touch were the ultimate kind and nurturing gifts at a time when I felt so open and vulnerable. I wept soft tears of relief and gratitude. And in that moment, I knew that we would be okay and our beautiful girl would thrive in the loving care of her tribe.

A Song for My Father

By Gunhild Lorenzen

My childhood liveliness was difficult to bear in a family who had just survived the atrocities of WWII. I loved to sing and dance around the house, until my father screamed at the top of his lungs, "Silence!" Saddened that the man I loved made me shut up so fiercely, I ran out of the house to hide under the comforting trees in the nearby forest.

It was not any easier for either of us during my adolescence. I wanted to understand him and asked many times: "Tell me about the war, please." He stayed closed.

Some years ago, my mother called to say that my father could not find the right words anymore. A man who always needed to control through his words was suddenly unable to talk sense. Gestures only. Another person in that situation would have become hardened, maybe. Not so with my father. He began to smile when sunrays fell into the room or when we came to visit. He did not need to prove anything any longer; he just was who he was. Finally.

Stroking his hand made him close his eyes, and I could see how his body relaxed and peace entered into him. Sometimes I showed him photographs from old times. He would squeeze my hand and let his tears run down without any composure.

I felt warmth and tenderness inside my heart when I was with him, and made more time in my busy schedule for visits.

No meaningful word came across his lips, even though he tried hard. "The sky is cold," he told me. I agreed, and we smiled.

One day, I started to sing. A melody just popped into my head: "Twinkle, twinkle little star."

He opened his eyes and his mouth, and out came a broken voice: "How I wonder where you are." We looked at each other in awe.

What was not allowed for me as a child became our expression of love then. My father offered me this gift of wonder just before he passed away.

Coming Full Circle

By Lori Thomas

I'm four years old, and I love nothing more than being outside and exploring. I'm fast, so I can find and catch everything from lizards and toads to grasshoppers and caterpillars. I let the big animals go but love to keep some of the insects.

My mom is the best at helping me learn. She studied zoology in college, and she can tell me about each bug and how to keep it alive. I can't do that myself because I can't read yet. I have jars all over my dresser filled with caterpillars, grasshoppers, grubs, beetles, and more. She taught me how to make a little home in a jar that matches the insect's outdoor home as much as possible. That means stuffing whatever plant I found the bug on into the jar for food and making sure they eat. She used to punch holes in the jar lids for air, but now I'm big enough to do it myself.

My mom never complains when I get dirty, and she never says any of the bugs I bring into the house are icky or nasty. She always helps me if I have questions.

* * *

I'm in fourth grade and taking my first entomology class. I was excited at first, but all we do is learn how to catch and kill bugs. That doesn't feel right. I think I like dinosaurs better.

* * *

Fast-forward to today. After decades of working in the corporate world, I'm coming full circle back to my first love: insects. I have undertaken various spiritual studies that include interspecies communication, and the insects have called on me to assist in changing their reputation in this world where they have been vilified. They actually serve as powerful messengers, but you must be able to listen.

Without my mother's kind and patient tutoring, I would not be able to offer these little creatures the respect and reverence that allows me to greet them as equals and work with them to help people heal aspects of themselves by returning to right relationship with nature.

Thanks, Mom!

The Beauties I Get to Behold

By Kimberly A. Elliott

I remember the story in health class about the mad dash – millions of sperm with the same bold goal: to be the victor in the spectacular fusion that sparks life. Yet I don't believe that it was due to random selection or survival of the fittest that you became mine. Even when I reflect on childhood Bible stories where children were given names that indicated their purpose – and their lives became synonymous with those qualities: bravery, deception, destiny, faithfulness, or folly – for me, their stories all pale in comparison to yours.

Though there isn't an "official" book on parenthood (I could still embarrass you yet…), I've done nothing with more intention in life than learn to nurture you. From the first realization of you until now, I've carefully weighed every choice. Of course, there's not one I couldn't have possibly made better; I've considered the eternal value of them all. There are some days I would not trade for anything – the joy of your smile and the light in your eyes was truly worth anything – while others literally stole my breath away, and I felt incomparable agony, feeling that you were unsafe or, worse yet, your future was uncertain.

I once read that studies show that 90% of new moms are able to identify their newborns by scent alone after spending just 10 minutes with them. Personally, I remember how I could look at your little face and tell that you had a fever by the change in appearance of the tiniest pores. And now, I rejoice at our singleness of thought, such as in those moments when we finish each other's sentences.

As I reflect today over every meaningful relationship, the gift of parenting you is by far my most rewarding. I lovingly refer to you both as my Beauties because there's nothing more brilliant than the color of my gratitude for the opportunity to see you laugh, learn, and love.

Every child you love does not have to be born to you naturally; but for me, loving you is the epitome of God's most natural expression.

Goodness Begins with Empathy

By Valerie R. Vestal

It has taken me nearly 40 years to understand how to generate true goodness. For many years, I have been doing nice things. A wise woman once told me that our greatest strength can be our greatest weakness – and oh, how right she was. My mother had shaped me into a woman whose motto was, "Put on your big girl panties and get over it." As a result, I accomplished many things but lacked sensitivity to others who were not able to employ this same philosophy. My stubbornness and ego stole the goodness inside me and derailed many of my closest relationships.

The very person who taught me that I could do anything (my mom) was now the brunt of misunderstandings, frustrations, and judgments. For the life of me, I couldn't understand why she couldn't manage money, lose weight, and keep a neat house. Days developed into years and decades of disappointment because I was trying to change her. My attempts tended to backfire, and the situation spiraled increasingly out of control. She was now struggling with a weight of over 450 pounds, and a house that resembled an episode of *Hoarders*.

While working in a Partial Hospitalization Program for people with behavioral health issues, I started to pay attention to the therapy program they had developed for patients. A key theme of the program was that relationships can improve through compassion. I knew that I had evolved from a good teacher to a good student when I went to visit my mom. Feeling a bit worn after a 45-minute drive and a day's work, I was still hopeful that the visit would be a good one. I was barely in the door when she looked at me and said, "Would you go to the store and get me a candy bar?"

I could tell by the look on her face that it really wasn't a good day. I gently said, "I believe you need a hug." We locked eyes, and she agreed.

Goodness begins with empathy.

A Life in Service to Love

By B. J. Garcia

As a child, through the eyes of love, I saw my mother as a beautiful, loving, generous spirit. Her life was about charity and community giving. She taught catechism and organized various guilds at the church and hospital. She was a Brownie and Girl Scout leader. Before becoming a wife and mother, her life was in service as a control-tower operator in the Navy, where she was decorated as a WWII heroine when she prevented a mid-air collision at Hyannis. She had an enormous love of gourmet cooking, adventure, the outdoors, animals, and people. She laid a beautiful foundation for us of high principles and a feeling of love and respect for life.

In my teen years, our life started falling apart as my parents struggled with alcoholism and financial problems. I viewed my mother with a critical eye, and we seemed to be at war with each other. Even though my mother had great challenges ahead of her, she was able to move us children out of a dysfunctional environment into a safe place where we were lovingly cared for.

In my adult years, when my whole world felt like it was crashing in on me, the only person I could share my situation with was my mother. She was there for me with an open heart and a listening ear. I felt her unconditional love and support carry me through that time. She had a beautiful way of allowing, accepting, and embracing challenging situations and adding a humorous perspective to it. Her laughter was contagious!

She suffered from cancer the last two years of her life, and it was now my turn to be there for her. It was a beautiful healing time for us both, and on her death bed she said to me, "Don't wait until the last 20 minutes of your life to know what life is about." Since then, through many years of internal searching, I have come to realize that my life is in service to Love, as was my mother's.

The Advent Calendar

By Jodi Chapman

In August 2002, Dan and I had only been dating for a few months but were already just about inseparable. Before we became a couple, though, he'd made plans to take a road trip that included camping at national parks, visiting friends, and going to Burning Man. I was scheduled to be in a friend's wedding during the same chunk of time, and while we were dreading being apart for almost two weeks, I was grateful that I had so much to distract me from missing him so much.

The morning he left, we woke up feeling sick to our stomachs. We felt like two magnets that had been drawn together, and it physically hurt to rip ourselves apart. But this trip was important to him, and being there for my friend was important to me, so we tearfully said our goodbyes, and he drove away. Later that morning, I opened my bedroom closet and found it filled with cards and presents, one for each day we'd be apart. Dan's note explained that he'd created an "advent calendar" because being together felt like Christmas. Part of me wanted to open everything right away, but I forced myself to wait. I'm glad I did because I'd soon be badly in need of anything that could lift my spirits.

Later that day, I went to the salon before the rehearsal dinner. On the way home, a woman turned left directly in front of me, and my car crashed into her SUV. Amazing people stopped to help me, and an ambulance took me to the hospital. I couldn't call Dan because he didn't have a cell phone, and we'd planned for him to call in a couple of days, since he knew I'd be busy with the wedding. That night, I came home from the hospital injured and in pain. I didn't know it then, but my recovery would take many years. I wasn't able to be in the wedding. I ended up having to leave my job because of the injuries. And I experienced chronic pain for years. That accident changed just about every part of my life...except for my love for Dan and his love for me.

My mom came to stay and helped me open all of the presents, which cheered me up and brought me closer to Dan. When he heard what had happened, he drove home non-stop from Oregon to New Mexico, and we've hardly been apart since. Every day truly is like Christmas when we're together. I'm so grateful for him and our love.

Chapter 3
Friends & Neighbors

We weren't sure what to make of her, but we certainly did notice our new neighbor. She was hardly inconspicuous: a rail-thin woman well into her 80s blatantly staring at us from the edge of our driveway each time we came or went, chastising us for letting our dog pee in our shared back yard (which she said "burned the grass") and expressing her disapproval of our air-conditioning "grinding away" in the record-breaking Bay Area heat.

Despite her hardened exterior, however, Mary Kay became increasingly friendly each time we saw her. She shared that she had attended UC Berkeley ("before it became…what it *did* in the '60s"), had two grown daughters, and had lived alone in that same house since being widowed three decades earlier.

After we'd lived there several months, she began to invite us over for afternoon card games. An avid bridge player, she made a concession by allowing us to play hearts – a three-person game we enjoyed, although she tipped her hand by muttering "spiiiied" under her breath whenever she drew a spade. Although we rarely drank, she served us wine (which she said was okay to have as long as it was after 5 p.m.) – insisting on white rather than red, so we wouldn't stain her carpet.

Three years later, when we moved away from the area, one of the hardest parts of leaving was saying goodbye to Mary Kay. Before we left, she had us over for one last game of hearts…and even served us red wine. We were careful not to spill.

In this chapter, we celebrate Mary Kay and all the other kind, quirky, wise, and wonderful friends and neighbors who enrich our lives and remind us that goodness abounds.

The Tap Rats

By Maureen Hollmeyer

I grew up in the 1980s, when then-popular Brat Pack members starred in the movie *St. Elmo's Fire*. The movie's theme was, "What is the meaning of life?" As a college freshman, I was clueless.

I was fortunate enough to have my own pack of friends. We called ourselves the Tap Rats because our favorite bar was Tap, and they always played the "Love Theme from St. Elmo's Fire" at last call.

Fast-forward to senior year when my parents decided I was moving to California with them. My last night in town was going to be my 21st birthday. The Tap Rats threw a huge surprise farewell party, followed by a night at Tap and an overnight at MJ's apartment. At 5 a.m., we finally fell asleep.

An hour later, we woke up to a telephone call from my parents. I can still hear their words: "We're leaving without you!"

Yes, I was late. I begged them to pick me up at MJ's apartment, but they had other plans.

I had to meet my parents in Kansas City at the bus station. I had little choice – they had my car, money, and all my belongings.

While I was in shock, the Tap Rats took care of me. Debbie lent me money for my bus ticket ($80, which at the time felt like $800!), MJ found me a suitcase, and we all tried not to cry.

We drove together to the bus station and waved goodbye like the scene in *St. Elmo's Fire* when Billy left on a Greyhound bus. As I looked out the back window, my vision blurred from tears.

Thank you from the bottom of my heart, Debbie, MJ, Connie, Nella, and Mary, for your kindness, understanding, and emotional support during those 24 hours. Thank you for making my college years the best and supporting me through thick and thin. I'm grateful for all your friendships, our wonderful adventures, and so much laughter!

Ultimately, the Tap Rats taught me the answer to that central question from *St. Elmo's Fire*, "What is the meaning of life?": LOVE!

Vicky Mitchell – Soul Sister Goodness

By Giuliana Melo

My friend. My confidante. My mentor. My guide. My coach. My healing partner. My beautiful mirror. My true soul sister.

Vicky brought so much to my life. She was a gift from God. During my healing journey and transformation from a little girl to a woman, God knew I needed someone who needed love as much as I did.

I met Vicky in personal mentoring. When we needed accountability partners, she offered right away. She and I healed through worthiness issues, wanting to be liked, and giving our power away. We learned to eat healthfully, work through issues with our kids, and grow with our husbands. We wrote in books together and created cards and coloring sheets. We mirrored the best of each other and the worst of each other. We dealt with anger through unconditional love. We instantly forgave each other and often called each other crying.

During our four years of healing together, we chose to triumph over our challenges. We wanted to work hard because we knew we had each other. We knew that, as we healed, we would shine brighter.

Vicky called herself a "joy bunny," and she really was! She was funny, quirky, intuitive, and smart. She was wealthy but humble and generous. She donated blankets to KindnessCrewCalgary for our first mission. She bought my products and shared her energy and love.

She really is love, light, and joy – the epitome of goodness. I cherish the time I had with her.

All of us want to be seen, heard, validated, and told we matter. She mattered to me, and I mattered to her. My mom always told me that if you had one good friend, you were rich. I am a rich woman because I had Vicky Mitchell in my life.

Life is so short. There is no time to leave important words unsaid. Don't allow anger to steal your happiness. Say "I love you" as often as Vicky did and taught me to.

Rest well, Vicky, my sweet soul sister. I'll see you on the other side.

Divine Timing

By Kimberly Brochu

I'd been living on cereal and pasta (with pizza thrown in as an occasional treat) for quite some time, so when there was *finally* a deposit onto my food stamp card, it felt as though Christmas had come two days early.

Carefully walking the aisles, calculating as I went, I meticulously chose what we needed, plus a few treats we hadn't had in months. How many times in the past, I thought, had I simply "run to the store for a few things," always spending more than expected. Oh, how life had changed for us.

My fellow holiday shoppers seemed to grow increasingly grumpy as we waited in line, but I focused on surprising my children as I gratefully slid my EBT card through the machine. "It's declined," the cashier said.

No, this can't be, I thought with mounting panic and embarrassment. The clerk called over the manager, who impatiently instructed me to call the welfare office; however, the welfare office had closed for the holidays.

The grumblings and whispers behind me grew louder as people became aggravated that their holiday preparations were being held up by a woman unable to pay for her groceries. All I could think of was arriving home to my kids, empty handed. The joy that had so recently filled my heart was now consumed in a fog of despair.

I apologized and began to leave, but miraculously, through a sea of people, I spotted my best friend. Noticing the small commotion surrounding me, she immediately came over. Humiliated, I explained what had happened. Without a second of hesitation, she pulled out her wallet, paid for my groceries, and scolded the manager, telling him he should be ashamed of himself for turning away a woman who needed to feed her children!

Reeling from the anxiety of what had happened, we walked out into the parking lot and hugged. As I drove home with a trunk full of treasures for my three precious children, my tears flowed.

Nearly 15 years later, I was able to pay that favor forward to a stranger; the tears that flowed on *that* day were tears of tremendous joy and gratitude.

A Gesture That Left an Indelible Mark

By Nora T. Barican

I've never considered myself to be someone who lives on the edge, yet somehow that is how renting a place makes me feel. Although there is the tenancy agreement, there will always be a clause stating that, provided the agreed-upon notice period is given, either party can cut short the term. This, coupled with the uncertainty of tenure beyond the contract's expiration date, hangs heavily on my mind. In my younger years, I would not have minded the possibility of being uprooted, seeing it as an opportunity for new beginnings and new surroundings to explore. Nowadays, I long for permanency.

With this desire in mind, I said goodbye to my years of renting and finally purchased an apartment. I don't regret the decision, although the move itself was very strenuous. Already exhausted from the days leading up to the relocation, my daughter and I somehow found the strength to lift and carry numerous boxes and items to the top floor of the apartment building. (It's amazing how many *things* one can amass over the years!) As the day wore on, we grew bone weary, famished but no longer having the energy to prepare a meal.

Just as we were getting ready to turn in and go to bed, there was a knock on the door. Opening it revealed what to us was heaven sent. Our next-door neighbour introduced herself as Liz Stoker and, with outstretched arms, handed us a bowl of hot homemade soup with bread – perfect on so many levels, particularly on a cold winter night.

Although we were grateful beyond words, Liz saw the surprised look on our faces. Liz proceeded to explain that as soon as she saw us moving in, she thought to cook extra to ensure she could share it with us. Right then, we knew that with such a great neighbour, we had chosen the right place to call home.

Since that day we moved in, we have enjoyed many years of mutual support and genuine friendship with Liz and her family. Featuring her generous spirit in this book is my way of expressing thanks for a gesture that left an indelible mark on our lives.

A Beautiful, Multifaceted Gift

By Christine Callahan-Oke

In August 2016, I excitedly hopped into my car and journeyed to Camp Good Life Project, a summer camp for creative souls and change-makers. The experience was heart-opening and life-changing, so when emails started to arrive about Camp GLP 2017, there was no question I wanted to attend – but I didn't know if I could make it work, budget-wise.

Then a camp friend and beautiful soul, Susan, caught me by complete surprise. She emailed me, saying, "Christine, I bought two tickets to camp this year and would be honoured to gift my extra ticket to you."

My hands were shaking as I read (and reread) her email. Susan was offering to bring me to camp. And *she* was honoured.

I slowly processed her message – it was a lot to take in. I was deeply humbled by her kind heart and giving spirit. At the same time, this brought up a big question for me: how could I possibly accept such a generous gift?

My receiving muscle was being stretched beyond its normal dimensions.

We hopped on a call and talked it through, and Susan eased my concerns. She explained she's been well blessed. She finds joy in giving in meaningful ways to people who don't expect anything but are grateful to receive something they see value in. Through giving, she believes she starts a chain reaction of good in the world. And she's right.

I was amazed and, once again, humbled. Without realizing it, Susan had given me far more than a ticket to camp (which was incredible in itself). She helped me realize that in receiving her gift, I was giving *her* a gift as well – the joy of giving something meaningful to someone who deeply appreciates it. She also shared some wisdom from Brené Brown that shifted my perspective on giving and receiving: we can't fully give with an open heart if we're not able to receive with an open heart.

Thank you from the bottom of my heart, Susan, for this beautiful, multifaceted gift. You opened my eyes and expanded my heart, and I'm so grateful.

Healing in Vietnam

By Mauri Barnes

I first met Jim Whelpley on a heart-surgery mission in Peru. He was brash and irreverent with his silly antics and jokes because he liked making people laugh. He had been on several missions already and was loved wherever he went.

As the biomedical technician, he was responsible for troubleshooting and repairing all of the equipment needed during the mission. He also assisted the hospital's employees by making urgently needed repairs to their equipment. We shared a love for photography, wandering the ancient city streets of Arequipa while he searched for parts in the hardware stores.

We met again on a mission to Viet Duc Hospital in Hanoi. Jim was noticeably quiet after his arrival. He was returning for the first time since serving as a soldier in what is known there as "the American War in Vietnam." He immediately made friends with the local people and told war stories, expressing his regret. Tears welled up in his eyes more than once as memories of that experience flooded his emotions.

On one particularly emotional occasion, I was visiting our patient from the previous day's surgery – a young man whose autologous valve replacement had been performed for the first time in Vietnam. A human heart valve from an American organ donor had been used to repair his failing heart.

While Jim was speaking with the boy's father (through a translator), the two men realized that they had been stationed in Da Nang at the same time on opposite sides of the Hai Van Pass. Jim's unit was to destroy any troops and supplies coming through from the north. The father's job was to protect those troops and supplies. There had been a three-month period when they were shooting at each other.

"I am glad that you were not a better shot" the boy's father said. "I would not have had my family." Jim, laughing through his tears, asked for forgiveness. "There is no reason to forgive," the old man said. "We were young soldiers doing what we were told."

"Hear that?" Jim smiled. "Once we were enemies; now we are friends."

Angel in the Cold

By Lisa Anna Palmer

A few weeks before Christmas, while I was having lunch at my friend Kathie's house, a -30°F cold snap moved in and took hold of the village nestled in the hills of southwestern Quebec.

Getting my van past her driveway and up the icy hill was a challenge. The steep incline was too much, and I began to slide backward uncontrollably. Terrified, I prayed and stood with both feet on the brake pedal. Down I slid until the van came to a sudden halt – just two inches from a tree!

Grateful and relieved, I took a deep breath, got out, and approached Kathie's neighbour, a total stranger. I asked if he had any ideas of how I could get back to the top of the hill, and he offered to help. I said, "Thank you, sir."

He smiled and said, "You can call me Dr. John."

Dr. John assessed the situation, then retrieved two rectangular metal wedges from his garage and placed them under the van's tires to create traction.

Success! I was out of the groove and away from the tree. Still, I had to drive up the hill and clear the abandoned tracks next. Seeing the petrified look on my face, Dr. John offered, "I would love to back this thing up and drive it up and out of here." Relieved, I handed him my keys and said, "Go for it, Dr. John."

He exclaimed, "Hop in!" and jumped into the driver's seat like a cowboy. He backed it up and then drove full speed ahead. Airborne, we cleared the tracks! He grinned from ear-to-ear, beaming, and we both whooped and hollered all the way.

Dr. John drove me another mile to the cleared highway, despite my pleas that he disembark closer to home so he wouldn't freeze. Nonetheless, he continued and ended up walking back in the cold just to make sure I made it to the highway okay.

Thanks, Dr. John! And thank the Lord for the angel sent to help me on a cold December day.

Adventures in Motoring

By Lori Thomas

I've just finished eating dinner with Chris and Mike at Traveller's Rest Equine Elders Sanctuary in Virginia, a place where old horses go to thrive. I was there earlier in the day with other women, offering Reiki to the horses most in need. I started heading home, but my car broke down on the way. A series of synchronicities and acts of kindness landed me back here once again with Chris and Mike.

But it's getting late. So now, two hours from home, I have to figure out how to get back so I can go to work tomorrow. We're out in the country, and my family lives far away, so I call the one person I know I can count on: Debi. As I explain my situation, she doesn't hesitate; she just asks, "How do I get there?" And then she makes the two-hour drive over back roads, in the pouring rain – to pick me up.

Driving with Debi is always an adventure. She drives the way she lives: in command. She owns the road. She's the matriarch of her family at home; she's the Sarge-in-Charge at work. A former Marine, she's gruff and direct; but she's also everybody's mother, with a heart as big as the whole outdoors.

This evening, she handles her car the way she handles life: tailgating other cars, speeding along pitch-black roads with the windshield wipers at top speed, barely avoiding hitting the car ahead when it stops suddenly, slipping into a right-hand turn lane at the last second when another car veers off to the left to reveal a line of stopped vehicles directly in front of us.

It may be rather harrowing, but her reflexes are excellent, and I am endlessly grateful to her for driving me home – and I know I'm not alone in benefiting from her generosity.

Unfortunately, Debi was taken from us way too soon. Her family misses her dreadfully, as do her friends and colleagues.

So, to Debi Parson, the angel: thank you so much for all that you did for me and for everyone in your life.

Adopting a Jewish Mom
By Joan Zietlow

While preparing to take a test for my Functional Medicine Practitioner certification, I had a week of setbacks. I was feeling vulnerable and not at the top of my game. We had a short window of time in which to take the test and submit our case study. There were only four days left to take the test when a friend died, and I'd only had a few hours of sleep the night before. I was having a ton of self-doubt, and stories about not passing were having their way with me. My fear was unrealistic, but it was real at the time.

My fears were rampant, and I was so tired from not sleeping that I was not thinking straight. But one of my colleagues who was also taking the exam was there to encourage me to face my fear and pushed me to take the test. She told me she was practicing her "Jewish Mom skills" (LOL)! She kept telling me, "You got this. And if you don't get it this time, you can retake – no big deal."

I ended up finding the courage to start the test at 7:30 p.m. and submitted it within two minutes of the two-hour closing window. What a feeling of relief to have it done, no matter what the outcome.

Now I had to start the process of submitting my case study. Part of the case study was getting the lab work into a PDF that my computer didn't have the software for, and I'm not a technology wizard. Again, my Jewish Mom came to the rescue; she was able to put all my documents into one PDF for me! That was the final piece to my certification, and I submitted just minutes before the cutoff.

Eight days after my submission, I was notified that I had passed and had my certification!

I'm very thankful for my adoptive Jewish Mom's support and strong nudging to face my fears and just "take the darn test"! Thank you, Nina, for not letting me bail!

The Power of Words
By Michelle Evans

When I was growing up, secrecy was paramount. "What happens at home stays at home!" was a phrase that burned into my being.

As a child, I didn't have many friends outside of my parents' party circle – children whose parents were also drug dealers and dealt out the same physical abuse my father did. I didn't talk to kids at school because I didn't want to slip up and say something I shouldn't. I was afraid of my father. I already infuriated him and faced the consequences at home in ways I couldn't understand. I wasn't about to risk that in front of other people; that would be super embarrassing and even more shameful. I didn't know what I had done to make him dislike me so much.

By the time I was 16, my father had graduated from cocaine to heroine, and I no longer had contact with him. Even the thought of it frightened me. At 18, I heard that things had gotten so bad that he was living out of a cardboard box. Thankfully, it was in a city far away from me.

When I was 19, though, he somehow managed to find my phone number, even though I had moved multiple times to different cities. This spurred recurring nightmares, and after a while I opened up to a good friend of mine. I talked about my childhood and my father. She asked why I had never told her before. Through the tears and the shame, I sputtered, "People would think less of me if they knew where I came from."

I will never forget the love and compassion in her eyes when she looked at me and asked, "How could people not think MORE of you if they knew where you came from?"

I wasn't ready to process and accept this at the time. However, it planted the seed for who I would grow to be today. For that, I'm forever grateful!

We may never know the impact or reach of the seeds we plant. One kind moment can change generations.

Thank you, Teresa Bickert.

Neighborhood Helpers

By Lori Thiessen

The trees in my yard are beautiful, but as poplars do, they get old and slowly die. This was the case one summer a few years ago. One tree had not produced any leaves and was completely dead. A couple of others also looked like they were at the end of their lifespan. It was unsightly, but my bigger concern was whether the next big wind would blow one over, damaging cars and property.

I knew they needed to be cut down, but this was an overwhelming task for me. Most tree services were charging up to $1,000/tree for removal. I didn't have that kind of money! I also didn't have the manpower and tools to do it on my own. However, I happen to live in a neighborhood full of goodness.

Not long after I noticed the trees' condition, I was visiting with a group of neighbors. We sat talking around the firepit, and when the conversation got on to yardwork, I mentioned my trees. Several of the men said "no problem," and one of them started organizing the others – making plans for the following afternoon involving several neighbors and two chainsaws. I went to bed that night grateful for the people I live around but still skeptical that it could actually happen.

The next day, time ticked by. Early afternoon morphed into later afternoon. I knew I couldn't go knocking on doors bugging people about if/when they were going to come help me. So I waited. And waited. Why did I even think this would work out?

I determined to have faith, and I waited a bit longer.

Then it happened. In an instant, my yard was full of humming chainsaws and busy neighbors. Within a few hours, they had cut down and bucked up the trees, stacked the wood, and cleaned up the branches. A bit of sawdust on the lawn and a gaping hole where the trees used to be was all that was left when they were finished. It was magic.

At a time when I didn't have money or resources I needed, this group of neighbors took care of me with hearts full of goodness.

Footprints on My Heart

By Keyon Bayani

A dear friend of mine died two years ago, and there isn't a day that goes by that I don't talk to her and think of her.

She had such a massive personality; she was someone who sucked the marrow out of life. She laughed, she helped everyone she could, she tried her hand at anything she wanted, and there was nothing she couldn't do (or wouldn't at least *try* to do) if it was what she wanted to do. She was fearless in life; she really lived to the fullest.

She looked after me when my first marriage broke down. Each night after we put our kids to sleep, she would drive over and sit with me, help me pack up my old life, listen to me, guide me, laugh with me, and be my shoulder to cry on.

She was also one of my biggest cheerleaders.

She was a constant in my life when I moved out of state to study. She even sent me vitamins to make sure I was looking after myself.

I'm not saying our friendship was perfect; it wasn't. Life got in the way, egos got in the way, and we grew apart.

I was blessed that I got to spend some time with her before she passed. We reminisced about the old times, laughed a lot, and planned to meet in Paris. It was just like old times.

When I left, we hugged and vowed to keep in touch, but life got in the way again. I never expected her to die!

My brave, beautiful friend has shown me, through her life and death, that whatever is happening in my life is a gift – it's something to be grateful and excited about.

I have life. I have choices. I can feel. What a blessing.

To my darling Effe, what a woman you were, what a life you lived, what big footprints you have left. I am a better person for knowing you, and I will live every day to its fullest because of you and *for* you.

God chooses his angels well.

The Blessings of Friends

By Helen Ferrara

I hear a tap-tapping at the door…it's a friend dropping by; she lives in our neighbourhood, which is how she saw the poster of my daughter's cat some years ago when he went missing. Concerned, as she loves cats, too, she phoned us at the time to see if we'd found him. Since then, she's continued to come by every now and again for a chat and a cup of tea, always bearing little thoughtful gifts – from a yummy snack to the beanie (woollen cap) she's knitted and brought round for me now, after I said I must get one soon for winter.

I thank her and tell her of some other friends who I'm going to visit. They live about four hours away in a small, gorgeous town, close to the ocean and surrounded by forests. They've invited me over for a few days to rest, relax, and unwind from the busyness I've had. They knew I had some writing to do, so they said, "Come and write here. We'll cook for you, and you can come for walks with us." So I made arrangements, and I'll be going soon. The thought of this delightful treat waiting for me is such a motivator for me to finish some planning work on time.

This also makes me remember another time when I went on a short trip by myself. It was many years ago, before I was married and had a family. Finances were tight, so the only way I could afford a holiday was to look after the home of friends near the Barrier Reef while they visited family back in the USA. Another friend drove me to the airport; then, just as she was leaving, she handed me an envelope and said, "You don't need to give it back; just pass it on some time to someone else when you can afford it." Opening it on the plane, I found a lovely card and inside it a "big fat note" that was to really make a difference in how nice a time away I had.

I'm truly blessed to have such caring friends who fill my life with goodness.

Mary's Selfless Gift of Compassion

By Ingrid Koivukangas

I was 23 years old with an 18-month-old son, living in an abusive marriage. The thing about being in an abusive relationship is the way you hide the abuse from those around you. You make excuses for black eyes: "Oh, I just tripped and fell and hit a doorknob." (Yes, I really did use that one.) I was ashamed, embarrassed, and very scared.

On the outside, we were a successful young couple with good careers and many friends. We had a nice home; we hosted dinner parties; we looked normal and happy. But the truth was much darker, and I felt that no one would believe what was really happening.

In retrospect, the stress I was living under must have been clearly apparent to everyone at my workplace, to my family, and to my friends. They just didn't know what to say or do, and I never allowed them to ask because I was too afraid to involve them.

I was growing increasingly scared as my husband's rages became more erratic. One of the final straws was when I walked in on him watching a newscast about a man who had killed his whole family; I heard him whisper, "Maybe that's what I'll do." I experienced firsthand what it felt like to have my blood run cold with terror.

I could no longer allow my son to live in this dangerous environment. Somehow I had to find a way to leave, but I didn't have a car, a safe place to go, or money. I prayed for help.

I went to work the next morning, and my co-worker Mary dropped a miracle right into my hand. She had bought a new car and was gifting me her old Datsun B210. I was in tears. As she looked deep in my eyes, I knew that she knew she was handing my son and me a lifeline.

A week later, that car helped us make an early-morning escape to a transition house to start a new life. I might not be writing this if it weren't for Mary's selfless gift of compassion. For that, I will always be grateful to her.

Three Seconds

By Scott Fjelsted

Divorce ranks as the second most stressful event one can encounter in life, and I can see why. In 2008, I left a marriage that had been dead for years. With this decision came a barrage of emotions, changes in relationships, and challenges.

One of the unexpected challenges was the advice and judgment of those closest to me. The advice, well intentioned I'm sure, was all over the board, as people were essentially telling me *their* life experiences, which didn't necessarily align with my own. The advice just confused me and left me feeling that I was going about this divorce the wrong way.

The judgment typically came from the religious people in my life who looked down upon divorce like it was a plague, never taking into account all the hurt, dissatisfaction, and hopelessness I had while in that relationship. They didn't seem to care that I'd found my soulmate who I loved more deeply than I ever thought I could love another human being. This seemed to have been trumped by the idea of divorce, even though my marriage had been dead long before it ended and my soulmate was not the reason for me leaving.

Every time I told someone that I had left my wife and was getting a divorce, I did so with hesitation. This was especially true of a client and friend of mine who was a strong Christian and one who had always treated me with kindness and Godly love. When I told her my situation the same way as I had with dozens before, she saw the joy in my heart; she simply smiled, calmly looked me in the eyes, and sincerely said, "That's wonderful, Scott! I'm so happy for you!"

These words were like salve to my soul. I didn't even know this was a potential response. This doesn't mean that she was okay with divorce. However, the light in her cared enough to see the beauty of the joy in me. These three seconds of goodness far outshined the months of judgment and advice I had received.

Planting the Field of Dreams

By Isabella Rose

My passion for living an all-natural lifestyle began in my early 20s, when I saw a nutritionist, began reading books by Elson Haas, and participated in a weekly yoga class. Several years later, I started reading books on aromatherapy and was introduced to Reiki. In my mid-30s, I wanted to become more involved in the alternative-health field, and although I still had many doubts, I started to consider a career in it. I became Reiki-I certified and began attending occasional meditation classes. As I started learning more about myself and connecting to my soul, the Angelic realm, and my spirituality, I decided I wanted to go back to school.

I shared with Michael, a close friend of mine, that I was taking aromatherapy classes at an online career school. He was happy to hear this and said, "It sounds like it is up and coming in the health and wellness field." He also offered to pay for my classes. I was stunned! I thanked him but declined. I was already enrolled in a payment plan, and I felt uncomfortable accepting such a generous offer. No one had ever invested in me or my future like this before. I wondered how I would ever repay him or show my gratitude and appreciation. With further conversation, however, I graciously accepted the offer and agreed to complete the program and get good grades (which I did).

I took Angel-meditation and aromatherapy classes while continuing to study other holistic-health modalities independently. Again, Michael offered to help with my education, this time paying for half of one of my Angel Messenger courses. As I progressed further in my studies, we started talking about my plans for the future and what I wanted to do with my certification once I completed it. He shared with me his vision and hopes to one day see me with my own storefront and product line. This vision is already coming true, as I'm just starting to make my aromatherapy products available to others, am in the process of earning my Doctorate of Natural Medicine degree, and plan on opening a healing center in the future.

I see now that all these were seeds planting my field of dreams…and nurtured by a special, generous friend who always believed in me.

The Power of the Word "Love"

By Denny Long

As an avid golfer, I migrate to Florida every winter from Michigan. You guessed it. I am retired and very blessed. Over the last four years, the same 16-20 guys and I have been playing golf together. Each has their own personality and quirks.

After each round of golf, we gather together in the lounge for drinks and snacks and share our stories or excuses of what happened on the links that day. Each golfer tries to outdo the other with their story.

One day before golf, one of the guys made a negative comment about a lady golfer who occasionally plays with us. He is a nice guy but sometimes says things without thinking or realizing that his words can offend people.

Later, the leader of our group announced that this individual would no longer be allowed to play golf with us. Even though there was no harm intended by the comment, he would not let it go. He wanted support from the group. Some guys were in favor and some were totally against it. The arguing became more heated to the point where it almost sounded like the group was falling apart.

Then, one individual stood up and took control of the conversation. He let everyone know that we all have made comments and said things that we wish we could have said differently. Then he said to the leader, "I love you, and I love him, and I won't let this come between all of us."

Silence fell over the table. Remember, these are 16 guys all trying to be macho. We realized what was said – not that he *liked* them but that he *loved* them. Then apologies crossed the table, and all was good again.

It made me realize how powerful the word "love" actually is. It was time for me to let my friends know that I love them and not just save it for my wife and family. If we used the word "love" a lot more often, wouldn't the world be a better place?

My Angel on Earth

By Catherine Laub

Mary is my sister Mary's mother-in-law, so we call her "Mary's Mary." I also call her my Angel on Earth!

Soon after we met, Mary became my best friend and spiritual guide. She introduced me to Padre Pio (who became one of my patron saints) and brought me to a quaint prayer group that inspired me to begin a spiritual path. After prayers, we would gather for dessert and conversation. It was always a great time being around Mary with this group. Whatever any of us were stressing about, she would have a supportive answer.

After many years, this group dissolved, but Mary remained a wonderful support and guide with my faith, and her prayers were always welcomed. She was always there for me, and she always knew when something was bothering me. Whenever she felt like something was wrong, she would reach out and ask, "Cathy, is everything okay?" We would go on to discuss the situation, and she prayed with me to help it pass quickly.

Mary was also a tremendous comfort during my health challenges. Whenever I needed her, she would come to my home with her healing oils and pray with me. When I was temporarily incapacitated following several surgeries, she cooked full meals and brought them over for me and my husband, Tony.

Even when Mary had her own health setbacks, she made herself available to babysit and help her children and grandchildren, and she always seemed to have time for everyone. I don't know where she got her stamina from, but she has always been an inspiration to me.

I don't see Mary too often anymore because my life took a new path. When we do see each other, we agree to get together more often, but life always takes over.

Although I don't see her as much as I used to, I know that Mary is always praying for me, and I am confident she knows the exact times to increase those prayers! Just knowing that I'm in her thoughts and prayers is such a powerful blessing in my daily life.

Love, Loss, and Fireworks

By Sarah Lawrence

It's only been six weeks since my oldest daughter passed. Her younger sister has had a rough summer so far, but what can I do? I am struggling to get out of bed in the morning, heavy and bound down with grief and loss.

Any other year at this time, we'd be eating Krispy Kreme donuts, lighting off fireworks on the driveway, and watching them light up the sky – a happy, intact family in Kansas, where anything goes on July 4th. Yet this year, we are broken. Our oldest has left us and gone to spirit, and I don't know what to do. At the last minute, we are invited to join another family's fireworks tradition, which has been going on since their family can remember.

At first, I feel more broken than ever. We are at an unknown house with only three people we know out of a large family. We find out that the house owners are the local EMTs for their small town's hospital. Their eyes are kind and the connection immediate; it's as if we know each other. Suddenly I feel as if everything will be okay.

We are told to follow them to a ranch, and we find ourselves pulling up to an old barn on a beautiful spread with a wide horizon. As my feet touch the ground, I immediately feel warmed and grounded. We are greeted by the owner and his regular crowd. Eating, talking, and general banter commences, accompanied by the staccato pops of firecrackers under the hot sun. No one there has ever met us before, but everyone welcomes us kindly.

Two beautiful horses, a gray and a palomino, flow toward us like water across the green grass as the sun starts to lower.

My husband and I find ourselves drawn in by lighting fireworks and by the beauty of the sunset. We light fountains and rockets, watching the colorful flowers trace up into the sky, celebrating our family and remembering our loss, helped by the kindness of friends old and new.

Goodness truly abounds.

Three Men Moved Me

By Ray Goodenough

This gift of friendship began when my buddies chose to move our poker game to my home because I felt the need to stay near my wife, Carol, when she began showing symptoms of Alzheimer's. Carol graciously proclaimed that Monday was men's night and stayed in our bedroom watching TV while the guys joined me at the card table. Our games were always ultra-friendly – with wild cards and plenty of laughter. If someone won $10 or $12, it would be the best night of their life.

Fast-forward two years: Carol and I, like so many others, faced foreclosure. Carol had suffered a stroke and had been accepted into a Skilled Nursing Unit. Given her condition and the fact that, except for using a walker at home, I'm confined to an electric wheelchair, I didn't know how I was going to manage the move. I found myself faced with a two-story, two-bedroom home (including a home office and garage) full of 40 years' worth of life accumulations. Needless to say, the thought of moving was overwhelming.

At this point, the guys were coming to play twice a week, but my "poker buddies" quickly transformed into much more. The three of them – David, Mike, and Randy – showed 24/7 dedication as they organized and packed up my entire house, transported my belongings into storage units, and moved me into a wonderful apartment. During those seemingly endless two months, they not only took care of my move but also handled my banking, meals, and grocery shopping. Throughout all their hard work (and all of my indecision about what should go where), they never stopped or uttered a word of complaint.

Now, over a year later, I still find it hard to comprehend the love and caring that quietly took place right in front of me.

I now live in the same Skilled Nursing Unit that Carol moved to. David, Mike, and Randy still visit me several times a week and still show the same unbelievable kindness, care, love, and friendship that they did during my move. Being graced with these three guys has taught me the meaning of real friendship.

Circles of the Soul

By Laura Garrett

Friends are like circles. They bring us around. They remind us who we are. Friends are lights that shine by their mere presence in our times of need. Their very essence brings us back to our true self. One friend who has done this for me is Dr. Shari Sorbo.

I met Shari while studying to become a licensed Spiritual Practitioner. She was kind, compassionate, caring, and guiding. I grew under her teaching, and she became a friend. I was inspired by her movement in life. I read every book she recommended. I practiced the techniques she showed me. As I practiced, I grew.

Due to some pressing personal and health concerns, I took a leave of absence as a Practitioner. I had multiple surgeries and completed a liver transplant evaluation – a journey that was long, painful, and stressful. During this time, I often isolated myself in order to tend to my health (as well as some pressing legal issues that needed my attention), but I remained devoted to my spiritual practice.

One day, after a lengthy absence from friends, I had lunch with Shari. Sitting across from her, she handed me a small package. Tears welled up inside. I knew this would be a gift for my soul. I opened it and saw MY word, *gratitude*, printed on a circle, tied into a bracelet. My heart took a leap, and my soul did flips.

Gratitude had been the cornerstone of my practice for years. This word always brings me home, into the soul of my heart. This was my heart word. Somehow, I had become caught up in doing and moving so fast that my word had gotten lost. I had forgotten to be grateful in everything. My friend Shari had brought it all back full circle with the gift of my word in a bracelet.

Friends are like circles, infinitely singing to us and calling us home. I'm eternally grateful for my friend Dr. Shari Sorbo.

The Neighbors

By Kim Marks

The new neighbors would barely say hello to you. They complained to the neighborhood association about everything and everyone in the area. They left little signs out to make sure we didn't step over the property line and touch their yard.

Within a year, their yard looked like a garbage dump. Tumbleweeds would roll through our yard in the fall and seed in the spring. Their chickens came into our yard, agitating our dogs and leaving droppings everywhere. I went over to explain that my dogs might actually catch one of the chickens and harm it. The response was, "We cannot keep them in our yard, so they will just have to learn." Needless to say, that was not what I wanted to hear.

One particularly stormy weekend we went out of town, leaving our beloved dogs home. Our pet sitters assured us the pooches were fine and our property had survived the storm.

A few days later, I was out in the yard and noticed that the gate looked odd. It was clear to me that the fence had blown over and had been temporarily repaired. Attached to the latch was a note from the neighbors apologizing that they could not fix the fence any better, but they had done the best they could. I was utterly surprised.

When I went over to thank them for their help, they told me they were worried about my dogs getting and staying out. Often when we were gone, the dogs escaped and they would put the dogs back in our yard for us.

Not only did these people fix my fence, but they kept a lookout for our dogs! I am still utterly grateful for what they did for me (and my dogs). I am grateful for their goodness and for the lesson they unknowingly taught me.

Now, whenever I see someone who rubs me the wrong way or I feel judgmental toward, I remember those neighbors who showed me that goodness is in everyone – you just have to look for it.

When Others See the Goodness in You

By Tanya Levy

Being a single parent is not easy.

After my marriage broke up, my toddler son and I moved to Cape Breton, Nova Scotia. I felt lost and alone. The people of this small town took good care of my son and me. Little by little, the goodness of others healed me.

A longtime friend gave me a pullout couch since I had very little furniture. Someone from my old church donated a dresser to me, and an anonymous friend of my babysitter donated a dresser to my son. My babysitter took my son even when he was sick so I would not miss too much work.

I remember feeling unlovable and still really wishing for a husband. A friend at church, when she learned I wanted a husband, started praying for me. Another friend told me to keep working on myself, that when I was ready, the partner would appear. I tried to believe her.

One day, I won some beauty products and was going to give them to a friend. Two ladies at my church told me to keep them for myself, to be nice to myself and to remember that I deserved nice things, too. They kept telling me they loved me just the way I was.

It took time, but eventually I started believing I was lovable and started taking better care of myself. I made time in my schedule for "wing group," where some of us from work went out to a local pub the night chicken wings were on special. My colleagues made me laugh and feel happier.

One night, they set me up on a blind date. Paul came to wing group and sat down beside me. He took my phone number. He called me the next day, and over time, we fell in love. I was able to see that love was possible because I now saw the goodness in myself thanks to all those who helped me. We were married four years later. He always sees the goodness in me.

So Grateful for the Unexpected

By Karen Ceballos

He came into our lives unexpectedly. Little did I know how important he would be. A retired accountant working as a taxi driver, he didn't seem the perfect candidate as my husband's caretaker. As a favor, he came to fill in for his brother-in-law, who needed urgent surgery. My husband's illness was debilitating and progressive – not an easy situation for on-the-job training, especially by me.

To my surprise, however, Chucho (the nickname for Jesus here in Mexico) learned quickly and soon became an important part of the family. He had a special effect on all of us. He was calm and trustworthy and had a gentle manner. He never missed a day on the job. How were we to know that he would also have a way of connecting with us spiritually? This was exactly what we needed. Being the loving and present person he was, he made it easier to face one day at a time and the approaching experience of death.

That day finally came.

Why was Chucho an angel? He came to us at a perfect time. He was humble and grateful for being part of the family and enjoyed getting to know the incredible person my husband was. He felt our pain and gave us the gift of compassion with a smile on his face. He was realistic yet positive and always willing to learn. What better gift is there than to support a family in need of an "angel" and help us through such a difficult time? We knew that the Divine was looking out for us all.

Spirituality has many definitions. It has many faces. In this case, it was the face of Chucho. May he always be blessed in this life!

Love as a North Star
By J. Scott MacMillan

I met Chris at a networking event, and we quickly became good friends. We would meet weekly for coffee and would discuss business and technology for hours. Shortly after, he invited me to his home, where I met his wife, Rebecca, a charming woman with a smile that lights up the room. Chris and Rebecca both had the inner radiance of happy newlyweds. They shared their joy by hosting a monthly gathering where friends would socialize and sing karaoke late into the night.

One night they noticed that I seemed kind of down and wasn't being myself. Without knowing or asking why, they invited me over for dinner and to sing with them at their favorite karaoke joint. I love to sing and was glad to find others who liked it even more than I did. They knew that singing was good for the soul and figured it would cheer me up – which it did.

As I began to spend more time with them, I started to open up about a life-changing experience that was making me question who I was. These newlyweds just opened their arms and began to shower me with love. They didn't judge or try to "fix me," sometimes staying up late into the night helping me unload painful emotions. Along with some sound counsel, they continued to be there for me and listen, and I began to find myself healing.

Formal therapy is sometimes necessary to help unpack past emotional wounds and repair, but there is nothing like real friends willing to give their time and attention and really *listen* to ultimately help a person heal.

I can't tell you how important it is to have these amazing people in my life. They have supported me and modeled how unconditional love works, all while cultivating their beautiful relationship as newlyweds. It's not often you come across a couple who both fully engage in helping another person. By sharing their time, this dynamic duo affirmed their love for each other by exhibiting unconditional love for a friend – lucky me!

Forever in Our Hearts
By Pauline Hosie Robinson

An act of kindness can leave you speechless. Sometimes the true depth of a person's kindness can take time to comprehend, especially when expressed through an act that impacts not only those involved but also leaves behind a historical footprint that will imprint the hearts of future generations. Such kindness unfolded in my life because a dying man wished to express his deep respect for an officer he served with in Vietnam – Lieutenant Ian Hosie.

Corporal Jack Brad conceived the idea of a quilt to honour my late husband. With the support of his wonderful caretaker and gifted quilter, Amanda Lock, Jack's dream began. Although only able to communicate via a white board, Jack and Amanda established a way to bring about Jack's vision. Twelve months in the making, photographs and personal messages from the soldiers and officers who served with my husband in 5 RAR Vietnam were assembled one by one to form this unique gift. "Forever in Our Hearts" began to weave a story of the many lives bonded by war – a war that would tear open the fabric of numerous families, including my own, as PTSD ravaged the hearts and minds of the men we loved.

In April 2016, I learned about the quilt from my son. Although I was filled with wonderment at such dedication to my husband, the years of trauma returned to haunt me. In my heart, I knew that this act of kindness had the power to heal. Jack's gift was opened in the presence of my family, plus close friend and fellow soldier Andy McDougal. Patchwork images of fresh-faced young men in a warzone were placed alongside heartfelt messages and tributes.

The quilt came intensely alive to grandsons who never knew their grandfather, to children who had experienced their father's pain, and to soldiers who had served alongside their "skipper." Brothers shed grateful tears. Heartfelt messages, poems, and images quilted with love transcended time and filled each of our hearts with wonder, especially as we read Jack's dedication to my husband: "What was evident was the respect for this fine officer, the best I have ever served with."

As Jack's dream unfolded, he passed from this world.

Special Delivery: Pennies from Heaven
By Padma Gordon

As a self-employed single mother of a sassy 11-year-old daughter, I often say, "There but for the grace of God go I." I marvel at how I'm able to make a living as a spiritual counselor in a small Northern California town.

God's help often comes through "earth angels." One of my earth angels is a sweet-as-pie, knobby-kneed, utterly adorable older female friend. We met nearly 20 years ago, and for almost five years we worked closely for a non-profit foundation that supported our spiritual teacher. During that time, our hearts fell in love. We shared many rapturous moments of nearly falling out of our chairs from laughter – such was the ecstasy of meeting in Divine Love.

We've walked each other through the proverbial "dark night of the soul" and celebrated the bliss found in the innermost recesses of the heart. She is my soul sister whose effusive generosity is inspiring. We share an extraordinary mutuality. I initiated her into dance and showed her how to come out of her head and into her body, while she taught me how to access my gentle, refined sweetness.

A while ago, there was a month when my private practice was a bit thin; its nature is to breathe, and there are slow periods. Feeling humble, with my daughter to support, I thought, *I could use a little extra this month*, and it was as though she'd heard the whispers of my soul.

A few days later, I opened my rusty mailbox to see a card grinning up at me – elegantly penned in her swirling cursive hand. My heart fluttered as I read her note: *For no other reason than the other day I was walking along the river, and it came to me to send this to you! Plus, you are so special.*

Incredibly, the check was for the exact amount I needed in order to pay my bills. I bowed in gratitude for the mystical way that God employs smiling angels with long, French-manicured fingernails to deliver *pennies from Heaven* just when I most need them.

Grateful to Be Alive
By Kellie McGarry

My night started off like normal: I stayed up to watch a show while my husband slept. Within a few hours, however, the night would grow into something far from normal.

A month earlier, I had been diagnosed with severe OCD. I had been obsessing about germs, and my life was suffering. I began to hate myself and my life. It didn't help that I was working a job around sick kids. Anxiety attacks became a regular part of my day. No one knew how depressed I was, and I tried to mask this with drinking too much wine.

Around 2 a.m. on that fateful night, after two bottles of wine, I felt terrified, ashamed, and worthless, and I decided I could no longer live. I'd had suicidal thoughts before, but this time I was determined to end my life. I looked up at the sharp knives on top of the refrigerator and grabbed one. I proceeded to the counter and slowly started scraping the knife across my wrist.

Suddenly, I felt scared. I reached out and shared my thoughts privately with my friends online, not thinking they would take me seriously. When I put the knife on my wrist again, I heard a startling knock at the door. I did not want to open it, so I ran to the bedroom and cried in my husband's arms. The pounding at the door continued: *Knock! Knock!* My husband got up and answered it, and the police said, "We received a phone call from a concerned friend of yours." The policeman stayed and talked to make sure I would be okay.

I knew right away which friend had called. At first I was angry, but now I see it as a wonderful act of kindness. If not for her calling the police in the middle of the night, I may have hurt myself or worse: died.

Her loving act awakened me to my urgent need for treatment. I'm happy to report that I'm now managing my illness and am grateful to be alive. At a time when I did not know how to love myself, I'm thankful for friends who showed me loving kindness that night.

It Is Always Possible

By Leslie Sann

As I leave my Chicago office, my wipers work hard clearing large flakes of snow mixed with salt from the roads. Driving home, I see freshly plowed snow piled up along the roadsides. Ten miles from my home, the snow stops. As I round the corner, I see my driveway smooth with virgin snow. Pristine, brilliant white. Beautiful to behold and calling me to play. Alas, it is 10:45 at night. While tucking in at some point this evening is a priority, there is no way I can park in the garage until the drive is cleared.

Though it is 12 degrees out, my coat is warm, my hat is snug, my mittens toasty. I am happy. My manuscript has been sent for a final edit. My day was filled with wonderful clients. I'm full of energy, and I'm looking forward to burning some fuel by shoveling.

I'm clearing the entry to the front door when out of the darkness a man with a shovel appears. My hackles go up as I wonder who is approaching. It is late. Most folks are asleep by now.

Tentatively I call out, "Hello," to which a friendly voice replies.

"Oh, it's you, Jim," I say, realizing I had yet again frightened myself over nothing.

My neighbor, who had been tucked into his cozy house, saw me working, put his warm clothes on and grabbed his shovel to join me. Why? To help me out. To be kind.

We have a lovely chat while shoveling, and in no time the drive is clear. We pause to enjoy the almost-full moon in the pitch-black sky reflecting gentle winter light onto a few scattered clouds.

I share my gratitude. He returns to his home, and I go into mine.

Jim's kindness reminds me of a Dalai Lama quote that has always inspired me: "Be kind whenever possible. It is always possible."

Starting to Live Again

By Dianna Robinson Curren

I had lost my relationship with God as I blamed Him for the losses I had experienced in recent years. My life felt overwhelming, and the losses seemed impossible to overcome. Worse yet, the only solution I could come up with was to shut out the world. I was spiritually bankrupt and afraid I'd never truly live again.

Surprisingly, one day as I was looking at Facebook, I saw a "Facebook Live" video and was drawn to watch. I was immediately encouraged, and my faith was awakened as Shari shared her inspiration and hope. I began to look forward to her videos, and I would watch them repeatedly. I soaked up all the positive energy Shari continually emanated.

After simply watching for a few weeks, I decided to say hello; and from there, it wasn't long before we were chatting online and communicating through email. She encouraged me to step back into my life, and I responded to her encouragement. Thanks to Shari, I was starting to live again.

In one of Shari's videos, she mentioned "Diva Day," an event sponsored by The Wellness Universe. Although I had little faith that circumstances would align for me to attend, I secretly longed to be there and participate in the day. I was thrilled when a few weeks before the event, Shari sent a message offering me inexpensive tickets. I was overwhelmed with gratitude for her beautiful act of kindness.

Finally, we were off to "Diva Day." I tried to have no expectations as we drove to the event. When we arrived, I saw Shari right away, and I received a hug from my new friend. When I walked into the venue, the positive energy was palpable. Every person I met exuded the same energy I had first seen in Shari, especially Elizabeth. Elizabeth prayed for me, and I received healing. I knew I had found my tribe; I was at home with these beautiful, enlightened women. I was changed, and the change was born out of the heart of my beautiful friend Shari.

Because Someone Cared

By Nora T. Barican

Within a week of arriving in a new country, my daughter and I were introduced to our neighbours. This lovely couple made an effort to engage with us, and their genuineness provided a solid foundation for our friendship. It was, however, their relentless nudging for me to make an all-important appointment that connected us at a deeper level.

One afternoon over coffee with the wife, the subject of physical examinations came up, and I mentioned that I'd undergone breast operations to have lumps removed. Knowing that we didn't yet have a local doctor, she gave me contact details of their family physician.

With all the excitement of our recent move, however, I didn't get around to making an appointment right away. After taking some time to settle in, explore our new surroundings, and do a few touristy things, my daughter and I redirected our energies into finding full-time employment and studying part time. Before long, we got caught up with the busyness of life. Meanwhile, our neighbour would ever so gently remind me not to delay the check-up.

Arriving home from work one day, I found a card under the front door with details of my upcoming appointment, organised by our neighbours. Sure enough, the doctor found more cysts, and a date for a procedure was scheduled. Gripped with fear, we breathed a sigh of relief when informed that the cysts were benign.

We are forever grateful for this lovely couple. Other than wrapping them in my prayerful thoughts, one can never fully repay or reciprocate such kindness. However, one can always do the same thing for others. Hence, whenever I hear that someone is unwell or in the hospital, I make time to visit or provide support, as I can appreciate the roller coaster of emotions (and the physical pain) they are likely experiencing.

In addition to the peace of mind I gained by learning that my cysts were benign, my neighbour's kindness and concern also reminded me of two of life's most important lessons: "Caring for others is an expression of what it means to be fully human" and "never stop doing little things for others, because sometimes those little things occupy the biggest part of their hearts."

Earth Angels

By Netta de Beer

When my dear friend – my soul sister – gave birth to a beautiful blue-eyed baby boy, I experienced such joy. That moment is forever engraved upon my heart. Three months later, however, I could tell that something serious was wrong with my friend. Her doctor referred her to a neurologist who, after many scans, found a large tumor on her brain stem. Late that evening, she was operated on, but the surgeon couldn't remove the whole tumor; it would have been way too dangerous. There was not much left to do, and the doctor told me she had three months to live. I was so shocked and told him he had no right to give her a life sentence. He suggested chemotherapy, saying that it could extend her life for a few months. It was heartbreaking for me, but my friend believed that she would get better. "God needs angels here on Earth," she told me with a smile.

I took her for chemo every morning. Afterwards, she always wanted to go for breakfast. Oh, how she enjoyed that! Through our talks and laughter, she forgot all about her sickness. Although she was in a wheelchair, we often went shopping. She always picked the most beautiful dresses, saying, "Life is too short to wear ugly dresses!" She amazed me more and more each day.

"Let's go on holiday," she said one day. "I want to feel the sand and sea between my toes." Although her doctor didn't think this was a good idea, we went anyway, knowing that it might be her last holiday. We had the time of our lives. Everywhere we went, we took pictures. We sat for hours watching the waves and making a photo album together.

Once we were back home, I could see she was tired. I wanted to say so many things to her, but she silenced me. This brought me to my knees, and tears flowed. She dried my tears and told me to be brave. Never once did she question God. Instead, she would praise Him and ask me to read to her from the Bible. After readings, she would cross her arms over her heart to show me that God is love.

Sadly, she died, but before closing her eyes for the last time, she drew something in the air: the wings of an angel. And then one angel came for another.

A Simple Request

By Diane L. Keyes

Once, while cleaning the house and listening to the Metropolitan Opera, I stopped and prayed: "Dear God, please find a way for me to attend the opera, the ballet, and the symphony. Thank you. Amen." Not an eloquent prayer, just a simple request. I have always been fascinated by the operatic voice, which my family did not appreciate; and at that time, a $200 opera ticket was not in my budget.

Two weeks later, the request nearly forgotten, a call from a friend informed me of a terrible flood in his friend Bill's home. Would I help? Of course! I made an appointment to view the damage. The insurance company's representatives had already cleaned up and were waiting for Bill to choose new paint, flooring, fabrics, etc. Furnishings needed to be refinished and works of art restored.

Six weeks later, with the restoration completed, I met with Bill for what I thought would be the last time to review the work and invoices. As I was about to leave, Bill said, "I would like you to consider something. I have season tickets to everything – the opera, ballet, symphony, and theater – and would enjoy your company."

For over 15 years, Bill and I attended magnificent operas, exquisite ballets, superb musical performances, and hilarious theatrical plays. Each event was preceded by fine dining and wonderful conversations, over which we formed a lasting friendship. Bill was a fascinating, complex man: a world traveler and philanthropist, the co-founder of a university that made education affordable for anyone who wanted to learn, an advocate for civil rights and equality for women, and someone who contributed to hospitals and bet on horse races. Occasionally, he shared some of the trials of his life, yet I don't recall a bitter word. He let go of the past, accepted the present, and was always hopeful for the future.

Bill and I remained friends until he made his transition. I remember him fondly and still feel such gratitude for his friendship, for the world of art and beauty he introduced me to, and for the miraculous way he entered my life: when God answered my little prayer, "tamped down and overflowing" abundantly!

A Saint in the Storm

By Beth Larsen

Living in NYC for the past eight years, I've really come to appreciate the dichotomy of the people here. There's a toughness, resilience, and determination. There's also caring and community, especially in times of need. This was never more apparent to me than in 2012 when Hurricane Sandy blew through and had a devastating impact on my lower-Manhattan neighborhood.

When the pre-storm warnings came in, I debated whether or not to grab my dog and cat and leave town. Having weathered the anticlimactic Hurricane Irene the previous year, I decided to take the gamble. I stocked up on candles, dry goods, and pee pads for the dog and filled the bathtub with water in the unlikely event that I'd be without power for a day.

Luckily, my building's management took things more seriously. Days without power turned into a week and then two. The staff took turns camping out onsite to ensure that all the tenants were safe and taken care of, checking in regularly to make sure we had flashlights, food, and water. They were there 24/7, and they did it all with a smile.

But one particular act of kindness stood out for me. I lived on the 12th floor, and our elevators went out with the power. After a couple of days, I needed to take my dog, Jake, out to get some exercise. At 12 years and 50 pounds, he was starting to suffer from arthritis. We slowly made it down the steps, but getting back up was a problem. One of the doormen, Josh, saw me struggling. Without a word, he walked over, picked Jake up, and proceeded up the 12 flights. He continued to do this for days until I could get into a hotel.

That gesture meant the world to me and allowed me to focus on finding a solution instead of being traumatized by the problem.

Luckily, dramatic events like hurricanes do not happen every day, but I have never forgotten Josh's gesture in my time of need. He truly was my saint in the storm.

My Friend Frank

By Ty Will

I met Frank at the Veterans Administration (VA) hospital. Frank was a Vietnam veteran, a Marine, and an all-around nice guy. We were both in the VA for the same reason: Post-Traumatic Stress Disorder (PTSD) – his from combat, mine from Military Sexual Trauma.

A psychiatric hospital may not seem like the ideal place to form a friendship, but that's where it happened with me and Frank. He was charismatic, outgoing, and very friendly, and he had impeccable taste in clothes. He always wore shorts, black-and-white shoes, a Hawaiian shirt, and an oversized gold cross around his neck. He was awesome!

I came into the hospital scared, frightened, and lonely. The PTSD had taken control, and I didn't know how to deal with the simplest decisions. I was admitted into Unit 8, where I met Frank at lunch time. He sat across from me and asked if I wanted to play cards. My first reaction was to say no and go lie down, but something told me to stay.

Every day after lunch, Frank would ask me to play cards, and I always obliged. He was fun to hang out with, and before I knew it, my depression began to lift. Frank and I both were released to go home, but Frank's home was the veterans' home.

Every Saturday night, I would go see Frank and play cards. Frank was my Saturday night date. We had fun talking and laughing over cards. I knew that Frank was sick, but I didn't know he had Agent Orange poisoning.

Frank died that year. It broke my heart to see him leave this earth, but the friendship and kindness he'd shown me at the most horrible time in my life gave me hope and joy. I wasn't with him when he passed, but I hope his spirit knew I cared for him and loved him.

Frank's kindness has resonated with me and has inspired me to finish college and become a social worker for veterans like me and him.

Graduating Together

By Jamie Thomas

I sat in my best friend's room on his recliner, absent-mindedly watching him play a video game. We had just discussed, for the umpteenth time, our high-school situations, and my mind was spinning with all sorts of thoughts. I was depressed, having dropped two elective classes and switched my college-level English class for an easier one. He was livid at his counselor, who had failed to inform him that he was missing necessary credits to fulfill diploma requirements and had recently told him that he'd have to repeat the entire year.

I looked at him. We had already talked about dropping out to pave our own paths. We were frustrated and tired of dealing with the superfluous nature of it all; we wanted to live life instead of being stuck in a classroom. It sounded freeing.

But how free would that be, really?

I thought about him: What he could do? What doors would be open (or closed) to him? Would it be worth it, or would it make things more difficult in the long run? I saw him suffering now. At some point, he'd have to face that again if he dumped school. I didn't want him to go through that. I wanted him to succeed.

I opened my mouth and was about to tell him as much. I stopped. What about me? I certainly didn't want to suffer like this again either. I hated every minute of it, but if I did it now, if we got it over with...

I spoke: "How about we make an agreement: If you work to get your diploma now, I will too, and we'll graduate together."

He looked at me and nodded. "Whatever gets us out of here."

Knowing that we were in it together changed everything for me.

Six months later, I shook hands with the principal, took my diploma, and proudly walked down the aisle between the rest of my classmates. I will forever remember walking into the sun with my best friend, standing next to each other for our final school photo.

Love Conquers All

By H. Michelle Spaulding

An adversary contacted me last night. We had been fighting a legal battle for 14 years. We had only met three times, always with lawyers involved. It was a messy circumstance; neither one of us was at fault. The human conduit to us had passed on to the other side. The frustration of no communication or miscommunication hindered the resolution of the problem.

A few years ago, I intuitively recognized that there were past-life and spiritual entanglements to uncover. I did my forgiving-and-releasing healing techniques over this situation. I prayed about it, wrote about it, and cried out in frustration. I asked myself: *What is the lesson here? Why won't this situation end? What is the tie that binds us together?* And I asked God and the angels to release whatever bad karma I had with this adversary.

Over a year ago, this person popped up on social media. I was able to see what they were doing, where they worked, and their current interests. Through this awareness, I realized that this person was just like me. We had so many things in common. How could I harbor hard feelings toward someone whose goals, dreams, and desires were so similar to mine? From that moment on, every time I prayed, I threw love at the situation.

Yesterday was my emotional bottom. I had to let go of my pride and reach out for financial help. I was spent – emotionally, physically, and spiritually. As I processed my day, I received a text from this adversary. I was like, *WTF – could my day get any worse?* I called her back, and the hard work that I had put into forgiveness and love came back to me multiplied. We shared our stories and our pain. We resolved misunderstandings and took responsibility for our actions. And we finished with a truce of unconditional love and acceptance of each other. It was a miraculous ending to 14 years of pain and suffering.

Love and forgiveness is the answer to all our human problems.

The Gift Bag

By Robyn Dewar

When we are lovingly aligned with our highest self, tremendous gifts are revealed.

Early this spring, I had a lovely visit from a new friend. While we chatted about life, she disclosed a heartbreaking story of broken trust. A distinctive satchel had been taken from her. With a heavy heart, she expressed that after many attempts to locate a similar bag, she was unable to find another like it.

When I asked her what her satchel looked like, she offered a detailed description. My eyes widened, and I smiled. I got up from my seat and walked into my office. I reached into the closet and returned to the living room and exclaimed, "You mean a satchel like this?" A huge smile stretched across her face. With glee, she exclaimed that it was the exact bag that had been taken from her.

I giggled with delight and lovingly said, "Bag found!" and I gave it to her. We were both so happy and celebrated the joy in the gift of a bag that gave back.

Not long afterward, I took a road trip to meet a dear friend. It had been a while since we had seen each other, and when we hugged, she excitedly said, "I have something for you." She handed me the most stunning tote bag. It was such a surprise. I had seen totes like this one before, but it was something I would not have purchased for myself.

"Wow!" I said, "I just saw this tote bag, and here you are giving it to me." Tears filled my eyes with gratitude.

"I have a surprise for you, too," I said to my friend. I handed her a package that I had been asked to deliver. The package, incredibly, was also a beautiful tote bag. She expressed that she would not have purchased it for herself. I suddenly saw the connections of the gift bags.

Today we celebrate in awe of the three separate gift exchanges. The "gift bag" offers new meaning to us now in our friendship circle.

A Heartfelt Moment for the Soul

By Lynn Spiro

Driving through the winding roads of her old hometown, Laney marveled at the brightly shining sun and clear blue sky spreading before her on that late spring day. She hadn't expected to be out and about, but a longtime friend had called asking to meet with her. Since it had been such a long time since their last visit and they probably wouldn't get a chance to do it again soon, she decided at the last minute to go.

She almost hadn't, though. She was only in town for a few weeks and had tons to do before she left. Plus, she was emotionally drained from dealing with family issues. Now that she was on the road, she was glad she had pushed through the excuses.

Soon, Laney pulled into the agreed-upon meeting place and saw her friend. She looked great, and it was comforting to see she hadn't changed much – she still had her bright smile and twinkling eyes, albeit a bit softer now. Linking arms, they walked into the restaurant, happily chatting away.

Having known her friend for 30 years, there was never a shortage of things to talk about: families, jobs, health, and now their newfound interest in spirituality. But Laney was holding something back; she was deeply unhappy in her marriage. When Laney eventually shared this, her friend understood, for she was divorced herself. Her friend covered Laney's hands, looked deeply into her eyes, and said, "I'm here, I've always been here, and I'm listening."

In that moment, the wall that encased Laney's bruised heart melted. Laney experienced a moment of clarity and thought, *This is TRUE friendship*. Within the heartfelt declaration, she found the unconditional love and acceptance that comes through true friendship, and in that moment, her heart began to mend.

Watching the glow of the setting sun on her drive homeward, Laney felt a peacefulness long forgotten. She knew that she would never again miss an opportunity to visit with her friend, for the heartfelt moment they shared was forever etched in her soul.

My Twin from Another Life

By Maureen Hollmeyer

On an ordinary day, I was taken on an extraordinary journey with my guardian angels. They presented me with visions of my past, present, and future related to my career, reminding me of how precious a friendship can be.

My first home visit that day was with a grandmother I had helped gain custody of her four grandchildren 15 years earlier. It took us several years to accomplish this, and it was a rare opportunity for me to see my past efforts lead to such a positive outcome. Also, it was a delight that I could help her again in another aspect of social work.

I immediately thought, *My twin from another life would be very proud.*

For my second home visit, I was there to help someone with their long-term goals as a senior citizen. Interestingly, the home was just across the street from where my "twin" and I used to live as roommates. Everything went into slow motion as a flood of memories came to me and made me realize the effects she still has on me in the present.

My angels also reminded me that my twin influenced my future, too, when she guided me to the idea of being a life coach. You see, if it weren't for my twin from another life, I never would have been able to help these families or individuals. When I was a victim of theft, my twin provided financial support, allowing me to graduate college as a social worker. She had been saving half of my rent money to give to me as a graduation gift, but she realized I needed it sooner. All she wanted in return was to see me provide support, comfort, and love to others as a social worker. She knew it would make both of our hearts happy!

I've never experienced such generosity or kindness. As I look back on that day, I realize that my angels brought my twin and me together in order for me to reach my life's purpose: to teach others about their angels.

Thank you, Jill, *my twin from another life* and forever soul sister.

A Passion for Fashion…and Kindness

By Cyvilstre Rio Olami

I recently witnessed a beautiful expression of kindness. It all began in March 2017. At that time, Oluwafunmilola was a petite, young Nigerian woman in her 20s who had recently finished her senior year of secondary school. She excelled at desktop publishing and other areas, but her true passion was for fashion. She had already passed an apprentice training for handcraft and was ready to take a job as a tailor while working toward becoming a professional fashion designer. Her dreams of working in the fashion industry seemed to be coming true.

However, due to the financial inconsistency of this line of work, she chose to take a job at a local café, where she earned a meager salary, but at least it was guaranteed.

Things were hard for Oluwafunmilola until a relative of hers talked about her situation with Ayobami, a young, vibrant friend of mine. Ayobami was working for a fashion-designing company in the heart of Lagos, Nigeria. Oluwafunmilola's relative knew that she would love to work in this industry, so he discussed her passion for this area at length with Ayobami and asked if he might be able to help Oluwafunmilola in any way.

About a week later, a friend of Ayobami's boss mentioned that she was looking for a new employee who could work with her. Ayobami took a chance, putting his own job at risk, and told his boss's friend that he could recommend a reliable, professional employee who could boost her business.

Within a week, Oluwafunmilola began working for this fashion-designing company, doing what she loved and earning two and a half times what she'd made at her previous job!

Witnessing these acts of kindness – from Oluwafunmilola's relative (who wanted to see her succeed in the field she loves) and from Ayobami (who put his own job at risk to help a stranger) – has really inspired me to open my heart and to help others whenever I can.

I Live to Serve

By Ruth Donald

I relocated from a place where I'd lived for more than 20 years to a place 4,000 kilometres away where I know no one.

The move had been ordained, and the magnetism that had drawn me to this place was indisputable; however, moving that distance alone had its physical challenges.

My son loaded the trailer and tied it down, but I had no plan for unloading on my arrival beyond "let's see what happens." It was as though this thought had an effect of reaching out into the field that perpetually flows and ebbs around me. I eased into the stream of goodness and willingness. Neighbours I didn't know had arrived at the door asking what they could do to help.

I sensed that the simple but explicit thought of reaching out – intending connection – is the "on" switch for the person best suited to my needs to present themselves. In a surge of realisation, I saw that I had a responsibility to consciously intend so that the connections could be made more readily within the flow of the field. I saw that it is not solely others who are serving me when I ask for help, but I who am also serving them. In a flash of inspiration, I saw that it is my task to assist the flow of goodness by the simple but crucial act of reaching out, of asking of others, of being willing to connect. By giving through requesting, I receive – and so the cycle continues to generate love and opportunities for love in action.

For decades, my response when thanked has been "I live to serve." I now see more clearly than ever that the service is magnified when I ask for help and allow others to serve.

Earth Angels Lighting My Path

By Shirani M. Pathak

It was the midnight hour before my 30th birthday, and I had an important decision to make: return to a job that was sucking the life out of me or take a leap of faith into the unfamiliar world of private practice?

Returning to my job felt like a terrible contraction, filling my body with dread. Taking a leap of faith and going out on my own felt like a big, open expansion, yet one that filled me with fear of the unknown.

As a single woman in Silicon Valley, would I be able to survive on my own? How would I pay the rent? How would I eat? These thoughts kept running through my mind. Turn back and slowly die inside, or leap into a new, mysterious world?

Finally, the message came through crystal clear: "Jump, and the net will appear."

And appear it did.

Ever since the moment I made the decision to quit my job and follow my divine calling, Earth Angels have lit my path. At every step of the way, an Earth Angel was there. In every moment of doubt or despair, another one appeared. Some were people who knew me, and some were complete strangers when we met. Some volunteered their time and expertise. Some generously donated their space.

When my path got dark and I felt I couldn't find God in my life, another Earth Angel appeared. They shared words of encouragement and reflected me back to my light. When my path felt unclear, another Earth Angel appeared, their gentle glow lighting the way.

As I was lost and confused, walking through the shadowy depths of my healership journey, they were all there, lighting the way. All of them seeing in me what I could not yet see within myself. Each of them giving me the strength and courage to forge through.

These are the men and women who lit the way as I walked through every dark nook and cranny of my soul. These are the Earth Angels who lit my path. For each of them, I am so truly grateful.

The Big Decision

By Tanya Levy

I was talking to God. My marriage had ended, and I had applied for a dream job that I hoped would work out back home in Nova Scotia, closer to family. I was worried, though. How would I get there driving alone with a toddler? Who might help me? I did not know how it would fit into place. I asked for Divine help.

Two nights later, my son and I went out to supper with my friend. When I told her I had applied for a job, she said, "If you get the job and arrange daycare and a place to live, I will drive you and your son to Nova Scotia." I started to cry. I felt so overwhelmed by her support, and I knew it was an answer to prayer.

After a telephone interview and two in-person interviews, I got the job. I arranged daycare through family connections and a place to live. I had two weeks to finish work, pack, and travel to Nova Scotia. My friend was able to free her schedule to drive me. It was a busy time, yet everything fit into place.

During our trip, there were challenging moments. My son developed an ear infection and was hard to settle. We managed to keep him occupied with toys, singing, stops to walk, and ice cream. Then 9/11 happened and the airport was closed, so my friend's return home was delayed. This meant she had time to explore Cape Breton and more time to help us settle, but it gave her little time to relax on the return end of her journey.

Good things happened on the journey, too. Most importantly, I learned that sometimes when we ask for help, we receive life-changing assistance. My friend and I have kept in touch. I will never forget the gift she gave me. This year my son graduates from high school. How fast the years have passed from that big decision 16 years ago.

One Precious Friend

By Ray Goodenough

One of my very first memories is of my drunken father chasing my mother around our house, accusing her of sleeping with the doctors she worked with and yelling that I was not his child. The ongoing script was: "You little bastard! You'll never amount to anything!"

That script held on. I lived it into adulthood through alcoholism, crime, and jail. My path of recovery led me to become a therapist. That training acted as therapy not only for my clients but for myself as well, and it resulted in a 180-degree turnaround. I found the belief that I was a decent, productive human being.

This transformation was, as they say, an "inside job." Once I'd made this change, however, I found my newfound self-respect reflected back to me from the outside as well.

One person who has illustrated this, again and again, is my friend "Kris" (as I'll call her). She shows a real interest in me and visits me often. She's provided me with some wonderful opportunities, such as when she paid for me to attend a weeklong silent retreat with a teacher we had both worked with. She's also the one who invited me to become a part of *Goodness Abounds*.

To me, these gifts are about much more than just money. They show me that I have, indeed, brought my life to a valuable place. These signs of validation from a respected peer bring up emotions that I've rarely felt in my life – emotions that transcend even kindness and goodness. The acknowledgment I feel from her is the very essence of *goodness abounds*.

My experiences with Kris have shown me how valuable even the smallest acts of kindness are – to me and to each member of humanity. I look forward to being a part of the ongoing affirmation of goodness in our world.

Someone to Watch Over Me

By Joy T. Barican

During the global economic downturn, hardly anyone was immune from its crippling grip. Employers were forced to implement cost-cutting measures. Employees who managed to keep their jobs had to work twice as hard to make up for the reduction in manpower. I was one of those employees, glad to have retained my position but having to compensate for staff shortage.

Maintaining a work-life balance became even more challenging. Working excessive hours, seven days a week, quickly became the norm. With over an hour travel time from home to office, I had little time to sleep or do anything else at home. It sometimes felt like I went home only to change clothes!

The main door of the building complex where I live is adjacent to the window of the first apartment on the ground floor. As I began working later hours, I noticed that no matter when I came home, the lights in that apartment were always on. I knew the elderly man who lived there, but only in passing. My mum and I had seen him before, shared smiles, and exchanged some pleasantries, but that was the extent of our connection. I didn't know anything about his life...or why he kept such late hours.

One late evening, as I quietly turned the key to get into the main building, I heard the man making some noise as he approached and spoke with me from the window of his apartment. Although I was always respectful and entered the building in silence, I greeted him with an apology, not certain if I had woken him up. He assured me he was awake and that he did not want to startle me as he approached. What he said next made my jaw drop: He said that he could go to bed now that he was sure I had gotten home safely. He went on to say that he usually stayed up so he could check that I had arrived from work.

Tears welled up in my eyes as I expressed my deep gratitude. After that encounter, we formed a friendship that lasted many years but was cut short when he transitioned. His passing made me miss his presence, but Joseph Toby Ellard's caring spirit forged a close bond between us that can never be severed.

Chapter 4
Huge Hearts in Small Bodies

We live just a few minutes away from the ocean, and spending time at the beach is one of our favorite things to do. Last summer, we were lying back in our chairs, basking in the sun, when we saw a boy who looked to be about 10 years old walk by us, juggling cans and bottles and other types of trash in his hands. His parents mentioned that they had forgotten a bag to put everything in, and we gave him ours that we had brought our lunch in. He literally skipped away from us and was so happy that he would now be able to pick up even more trash that he found on the beach! We were so inspired by his initiative to make the world a better place, starting right where he was: at the beach.

And this isn't the only child we've met who had a huge heart. When we taught middle-school journalism, one student always asked if he could wipe the chalkboard or clean our desk drawer. He was so happy to help us in whatever way we needed, and we were always grateful for him. Another student surprised us by helping us move, carrying one heavy box after another for hours on end. We couldn't help but reward his efforts by ordering a pizza! And so many of our students always greeted us with large grins and kind words, making us feel amazing.

So many children have such huge hearts in their small bodies. We've seen this time and time again in our own lives, and the stories that follow offer more examples, too. From the big things (such as starting a charity and giving back to an entire community) to the smaller but equally meaningful things (such as pushing a fellow classmate in a wheelchair or standing up for someone at school), children prove again and again how much goodness truly abounds in them. And we're so happy to share their big hearts here with you.

Little Heroes with Big Hearts

By StacyLynn Rasmussen

It was 8 p.m. when my family arrived at a local diner. I requested a booth far enough from the bathroom and the kitchen to ensure that we wouldn't be disturbed by swinging doors or clanking dishes.

The hostess directed our party of four to what used to be the smoking section but was now just a small partitioned area. I liked it because it was a little cozier than the rest of the open floor plan. We took our spots on the cold, cracked, red seats. My husband sat across from me, with a child sitting next to each of us as usual. He grabbed my hands, smiled, and gazed into my eyes while our boys decided between hamburgers and steak coins.

It wasn't long before a group of rowdy high-school boys gathered into the booth beside us in the otherwise empty room. They pulled up chairs from nearby tables and packed them into a cramped seating space. Our waitress was young and appeared to know them. She played along as they flirted, but her demeanor shifted when she detected a threatening undertone. She politely avoided them as much as possible, which seemed to bother them.

With bruised egos, they began verbally harassing her and throwing things at her so she'd be forced to bend over. We didn't want our children witnessing or overhearing them, so we requested our check. Before we could leave, however, our nine-year-old son, Ashton, jumped up from his seat to help her clean the trash. The waitress was touched by his kindness and was brought to tears. His six-year-old brother, Aidan, got up and helped, too. The teens were so humiliated that they immediately stopped, and instead commended them for being gentlemen. They apologized to her and left!

The kindhearted act and maturity of two young boys shifted the environment and dispelled the hostility of boys (who were almost adults) twice their age.

The waitress bought them milkshakes to thank them for being heroes!

Annie's Guardian Angel

By Lynn Spiro

Mikey sat up in bed, yawned, and stretched as he woke to the day. It was his first day as a third grader, and he was excited for it to begin! He dressed quickly and hurried down to breakfast. His mom reached in for a hug, but he wiggled away saying, "Aww, Mom, I'm too big for that." (Secretly, though, he still loved these hugs!)

When he heard the school bus, he grabbed his Batman backpack and lunchbox and turned to go. "Wait, Mikey. Just one more, okay?" she asked.

Sighing, he thought, *She's always taking pictures!* Since it made her happy, he just smiled and agreed to one more, then off he went.

He quickly found his classroom and took his assigned seat. A few minutes later, the special-education teacher walked in, holding the hand of a little girl named Annie. She was pushing something Mikey had never seen before – a walker – which helped her get around school. When Annie looked up, Mikey felt a flutter as he marveled at her pretty smile.

Mikey soon found many ways to help Annie. He held her walker as she stood, shadowed her down the hallway, carried her lunch tray, and even championed her when she was teased. It made him feel good to help Annie, and he was quickly dubbed "Annie's Guardian Angel."

When the school year ended, Mikey said goodbye to Annie. On that last day, his mother asked him why he looked so glum. He replied, "Because I won't see Annie anymore; she's moving." His mother reached to comfort him while he looked directly at her. "It's okay, Mom," he announced. "I'll be fine. I'm Annie's Guardian Angel, remember? I'll always be with her."

Mikey's Mom smiled to herself. She realized that the seeds of compassion and kindness had been sown deep within Mikey that year. She would watch those seeds bloom into many more acts of kindness and witness how he touched all those he met with the goodness of his heart. It had indeed been a good year.

The Perfect "Rock"

By Kimber Bowers

I was lost…in more ways than one. And I was beginning to think I could stay lost on this beach forever – just give up and be okay with that. Defeated and alone. Spirit had revealed many truths to me that I could not seem to align with my life. I longed for a deeper purpose to express the depth of connection I perceived, but I had no idea how to find it. I had received a call that I was not quite ready to answer.

After taking the wrong trolley in the wrong direction, I found myself adrift in a foreign country with no phone and no money for a return ticket. Now, instead of looking for a solution to this problem, I was getting lost in an intent search for the perfect rock along the lavishly decorated shore.

Sunset fell, and a young boy approached me. After helping me collect some rocks, he asked what I thought about God, and I began to cry. I cried for the pain of loss and growth and spiritual awakening and my inability to reconcile it with the world. I cried for the pain of trying to piece it all together in a way that honors the touch received and the guidance given. I cried for my inability to trust enough to answer that call.

This stranger – this homeless boy with his dark hair and bright soul – really listened to me. We talked about purpose and hope. I felt connected, understood. He told me his mission as a homeless youth, volunteering and setting an example for the boys who had given up. He described us both as soldiers in an army of light, assuring me that if I followed my heart, I would light the way for others. I felt this truth welling within me, inspired by his courage to embrace the call. Then, despite my resistance, he scrounged together change for my trolley ticket.

Spirit had indeed led me to the perfect "rock." His name was Michael, and through his light, I found the courage to embrace my own.

Petie

By Lucy V. Nefstead

To most, Petie was a nightmare: uncontrollable, loud, rough, sassy, and brash. Parents dreaded him, kids feared him, and teachers disliked him. At age 11, Petie fought, swore, smoked, skipped school, and was considered a failure, a trouble-maker on a downward spiral with little hope of redemption...in short: a loser.

I knew that Petie was trouble. He had always been naughty, except with me, his shy, timid nine-year-old first cousin. Petie was kind and protective of me. I assumed this soft side was only due to my being female and his younger cousin. He looked after me at school, defended me from bullies, sat with me on the bus, and kept me laughing at his jokes. Then, he was off to his next row.

I loved Petie and would watch him on the playground. If he saw me, he'd wave and continue fighting, smoking, or causing whatever trouble he'd been getting into. One spring day during recess, however, I saw a different side of Petie when I noticed him giving a boy his lunch money. I was shocked! It seemed so out of character. I kept watch. Each day, Petie gave money to the same little boy. One day, he brought treats for a scruffy cat. Another day, he fixed a pre-schooler's trike and tied his shoes. When classmates came around, Petie acted tough. But day after day, I watched Petie's acts of kindness before he went back to his expected bad behavior. Although he never saw me, I caught Petie being good. I witnessed a kind, caring boy give his time and money to others even if he had to do without.

Every day that spring, we rode the bus together, and as Petie put his protective arm around me or told me a joke, I'd envision him on the playground doing good and being kind. That was the real Petie! He gave me more than his affection and protection that year; he changed my life for the better...forever! He made me see that people and things aren't always as they appear to be, that there is good in all of us — we just have to look for it and catch a person in the act of being good...just as I caught Petie!

Dedicated to Peter (Petie) Whalen, who died serving his country.

Never Too Young

By Karen Ceballos

Back in the 1980s in Mexico, it was common to hear the doorbell ring and find someone waiting, exhausted from begging for money or anything else that one could spare. As I opened the door, I saw the desperate look of a woman who was accompanied by her glassy-eyed daughter, confirming to me once again how painful poverty is. I listened to her appeal and, feeling her pain, went to the kitchen for food, money, and anything else she could use.

I was walking back to the front door when I noticed that my six-year-old daughter, Cynthia, had followed me. She carried in her arms a special doll. It was not her prettiest doll, but it was still in very good shape and, more importantly, was the one she liked the most.

As I offered the money and food to the mother, she sighed with relief and said, "God bless you, *señora*!" Then, out of the corner of my eye, I saw my daughter step up to the little girl and place her doll in her arms. The little girl was so stunned she couldn't speak, but a tiny smile began to change her face. My heart stopped for a moment as I realized what a special gift this was in such a special moment. She was giving willingly and without hesitation. It was the purity and innocence of childhood.

Years later, Cynthia moved to the United States. To this day, she continues to give of herself to others. Her goodness of heart shows up in her work as a lawyer helping immigrants in all areas of need, in her passion for homeless and lost animals, as a loyal friend, and as a wonderful, loving mother. Years before any of this, though, she reminded me of an important truth: You're never too young to open your heart!

River Walk Rescue

By Susan Elizabeth Schoemmell

One day, I was feeling particularly stressed and decided that I needed to walk at a nearby park and commune with nature. I eagerly set out to enjoy a river trail walk under the canopy of tall and outstretched boughs of green.

Setting my foot upon the river trail, I noticed that the recent heavy rain had changed the usual dirt path into a muddy course. Deciding to continue anyway, I picked my steps carefully and kept my eyes focused on the trail ahead.

Suddenly, I became aware of the sound of footsteps moving at a rather fast pace on my left. A young teenage boy passed me by as his youthful stride quickly conquered the muddy path. He found a bench alongside the river bank, sat down, and opened a book to read.

I slowly walked past his riverside seat and found myself in a slippery patch that was no match for my weathered soles and suddenly found myself covered in a heap of mud. I expected to hear a snicker, if not an outright laugh from the nearby teen; instead, I heard a much-concerned voice asking if I needed help. I clearly felt helpless, as I could not gain my footing, and replied, "Yes, I need help!"

He quickly made his way to my side and offered his hand to help me up. He also tried to turn this humiliating situation into some humor, as he said he would blame me if he fell, too! After a slight chuckle, I felt his strength, and with his help, I stood up to survey the muddy mess. He turned, went back to his seat, and picked up his book as if nothing had transpired.

Walking back to the car with my whole left side caked with mud, I was very thankful for this stranger's goodness that came to my rescue. I realized that without his extended hand, I might not have gotten out of this predicament so gracefully.

The Creative Power of One Child

By Nadene Joy Hagen

Children have extraordinary imagination, creativity, and wonder. They are connected to Source and are blessed with the natural ability to create something from nothing.

This is a true story about a child who turned his dream into reality. From a young age, he could read hundreds of books, remembering every detail. He noticed things that the average person is not attuned to. He was putting together 2,000-piece Legos creations (at a 12-year-old level) by the time he was four!

This incredible boy (who is now eight years old) is my son. When he started kindergarten at a public school, he found out that there were limits put on learning. He could no longer explore and learn freely, and his love of learning began to wane. Every day, he would come home and tell me that kids need a fun school with hands-on learning instead of sitting at a boring desk doing worksheets. He said children need to use their imaginations and be treated as unique individuals.

One day, my son woke up early and started writing. He created a new hands-on camp called DEC (Discover, Explore, Create) Extravaganza Kids' Camp. He developed a different theme for each of the five days and planned each day to the very last detail. The sold-out camp was such a huge success that he planned a summer camp and several others that also filled up quickly.

He then turned his focus to starting a new educational system for children. He envisioned a school that would inspire individual thoughts about creating dreams and bringing a child's dream into reality – one that focuses on hands-on learning, life skills, and advanced learning techniques that children can apply to everyday life today and as our future leaders of the world. This amazing school is called Star Elite Academy.

At Star Elite Academy, kids begin their adventures of changing the world starting in the fall of 2018. Eventually, we will franchise worldwide! Thanks to my son's big heart, Star Elite Academy will create positive change and allow other children to live out their true purpose. If you believe in yourself and your dreams, anything is possible with God!

My Kind of Friend

By Ella Wilson

Pep rallies. What an unforgettable high-school experience. Hundreds of teenagers herded into a gymnasium in the name of school spirit. Being a strange mixture between wallflower, jock, and nerd, these assemblies were quite possibly the only thing that could make me yearn for math class.

One time, I found myself in a daydream halfway through a rally, only to be startled awake by the sound of booing. In the middle of the gym, there stood the basketball team. It didn't take long for me to realize that the booing was being directed at a single member of the team.

My heart sank. Why were they doing that? With every fiber in my being, I wanted to stand up and tell them to stop, but fear kept me in my seat. The booing finally died down, and the young man tried to brush it off, but I could tell it bothered him. It made me wonder what he must go through every day and how severely he must have been bullied throughout his years in school.

Driving home with my friend Jim, we discussed the events of the pep rally. Mostly, we were confused. Why such a strong negative reaction? Everyone was leaving school when we saw that very same boy walking on the sidewalk next to us. Then, to my surprise, Jim stopped the car and opened the door. He began having a very kind conversation with the boy and made plans to see him that weekend.

As we drove away, I remember feeling such love and admiration for my friend – for the strength of character he showed when he wasn't swayed by the majority of his peers, and for the amount of kindness he shared with someone he barely knew.

I only saw the boy a few more times before graduation. As he continued into adulthood, I hope he was able to turn his source of pain into feelings of empowerment. When I see him now in my mind, he is wildly successful and living the life of his dreams.

Mammaw's Little Angel

By Karen Hill

I struggled through a full year of breast cancer treatment. I resigned from a 13-year career because I lost my stamina, I became severely depressed, and I acquired additional health problems post chemotherapy. I lost relationships and material things and was unable to finish my education. I struggled to cook, clean, have fun, or even get out of bed. Throughout all these struggles and losses, however, I found happiness playing with my five-year-old granddaughter, Rebecca, God's little angel.

Rebecca stole my heart the moment she was born, and I have adored her ever since. She is so precious, loving, pretty, smart, fun, full of spirit, honest, and highly intelligent. She enjoys school, running, and riding her bike. Together, we enjoy singing, swimming, tea parties, playing in the sand, and much more. She has the kindest heart, the most beautiful smile, and a wonderful laugh.

During my darkest days, Rebecca stayed right by my side no matter where I was sitting or lying, encouraging me to wake up every day and play. Rebecca says, "Mammaw, I want to play a game," so I get up and play any game she wants. She says, "Mammaw, I want to read a story," so I get up and read to her. She says, "Mammaw, I want to play house," so we play house. She says, "Mammaw, I want to play the color game," so we play the color game. She says, "Mammaw, I can make you feel better," and I say, "Yes, you make me feel better every day."

When I am playing with Rebecca, I begin to forget about my insecurities, my fears, and my physical, mental, and emotional pain. She makes me feel good by asking me to play with her, and I enjoy playing with her. She never judges me. She spreads goodness to everyone she meets. She inspires me to be a better person. I am honored to be in her life.

I am so happy Rebecca loved me enough until I could learn to love myself. I smile every time I hear her say "Mammaw." Rebecca Lynn Cuneo, you are my angel!

Dedicated to Rebecca Lynn Cuneo

A Tiny Gesture Means So Much

By Danielle Pomerleau

In 2014 I finally made the very real steps to get out of my unhealthy 17-year relationship. It was a three-year ordeal that felt like a slow, painful death of my spirit. I was codependent, had little self-esteem left, couldn't fathom being without someone with whom I had spent half my life, and was straight-up scared to death. I didn't feel capable of "adulting" on my own. I spent every day in anxiety, trying my hardest not to cry every waking moment.

During this turbulent time, I had a handful of friends who did what they could to hold space for me and support me, most of whom were women in my belly-dance troupe. One day we had a new member – a young mother named Sarah who brought her four-year-old daughter, Riley. Sarah set up a blanket in the corner and told Riley that this was her area and she was not to leave it while in class. Out of my peripheral vision, I saw Sarah leaning over while her daughter whispered into her ear. Then I heard Sarah say, "Yes, you may go over," and I noticed little Riley making a beeline straight for me.

She locked eyes with me and was very intent on her approach. She was holding a flower she had picked on the way to class. When she got close, I knelt down to address her. She extended her hand with the flower and said, in a sweet little voice, "This is yours" – almost as if she knew she had picked it for me, although we'd never met. Then she simply turned around and went to her blanket, where she played quietly for the duration of our class. At the end of class, Sarah came up to me in wonderment, saying that Riley is extremely shy and doesn't ever approach people. She had no clue what had gotten into her.

Looking back, I know what got into her: *angels*, whispering to her, letting her know how much a small gesture of being gifted a flower from an innocent soul would bring happiness to my heart and make me feel seen and loved in that moment.

Sometimes, all it take is the tiniest of gestures to spark light into someone's life.

Voy's Tractorcade

By Jamie Lynn Thompson

The rumble of tractors can be heard coming down the road. The annual Voy's Tractorcade parade of tractors is on its way, with lots of tractors to see. Tractors from around the area join in the fun.

But this is no ordinary tractor parade. A 15-year-old boy started the Tractorcade as a service project through his church. With his interest in agriculture (his family runs a local 500 acre farm), putting tractors and service together seemed like the perfect fit. The whole idea is amazing! The Tractorcade is neighbors helping neighbors. It is a great time for the community to get together for fellowship and to help those in need.

The Voy's Tractorcade began in 2015 as a fundraiser, with proceeds going to the local food bank. The $25 entry fee includes the ride and a meal. The riders are not the only ones donating either. Area businesses also help out. The Tractorcade raised $1,500 in 2015, $1,700 in 2016, and $1,753 in 2017. That can really go a long way for much-needed food and supplies!

The entire Voy family is involved in the cause and even sells t-shirts to benefit the fundraiser. After the event, the family helps shop for items needed to fill the pantry that aren't covered by food stamps.

Voy is someone to be proud of for understanding the need of the food bank and taking the action steps to help so many people. His family roots of agriculture and tractors have led to feeding those in need. He was even voted Student of the Month on a local news channel by the viewers for all his innovation and hard work to help those who need it most.

Bella's Dessert

By Jacine Rilea

It had been a draining day. I had come home late, with shopping bags and dinner to prepare. I felt trapped. The dishes from breakfast were still there, and the house was a mess. Too many things. My two children had each gone to their rooms while I started dinner and caught up with the dishes.

Out came my seven-year-old daughter to socialise. This was her way. She loved to share stories and ideas. She had so many precious anecdotes from her day at school. What her friends had done. The things she had made. She wanted to help me with dinner and offered suggestions of what she could do. "What about dessert?" her sweet tooth started talking. So many new ideas and directions for our ordinary dinner I was preparing

I faltered. I couldn't concentrate. It was too much.

I looked down at her, realising I could barely absorb what she was saying. My empty promises of "later" just weren't cutting it. "I need some alone time, Bella." I said. She looked at me expectantly. "I need some time by myself," I repeated, to make sure I was understood. I felt my heart sink, seeing her spark fade as understanding set in.

She bent her head down, then gazed back up at me with soulful eyes. "Okay, I'll give you some alone time," she pronounced, and with a solemn smile, she walked quietly into her room.

My head cleared, but my heart was a blob in my gut. I finished preparing our plain dinner.

As usual, she complimented me on the meal and told me how much she enjoyed it. Then, as we took the dishes to the kitchen, she asked me if I had finished my alone time. I smiled at her and nodded and bent down to hug her. She squeezed me back. Together, we did the dishes and planned a dessert so elaborate it was never made, but I hold dear Bella's sweetness that day close to my heart.

The Angelic Energy of Kindness

By Wendyanne Pakulsky

There is nothing more beautiful in this world than kindness – that golden elixir of energy that hits the very core of our soul in angelic nourishment and ripples out into the world on so many levels. This energy can open up a soul and a heart in an instant. It can change our aura immediately to a brighter colour. It can touch human beings at a deep level, speaking to us in a profound language beyond words.

Perhaps nowhere have I experienced kindness more than in my interactions with children. As I work with them, I have had the blessing of them inspiring me and teaching me to let go, to laugh, to feel free in a moment, and to be gentler on myself. They have taught me the real meaning of life, the importance of being in the moment. They have brought me right back to a part of my life that I missed out on, reconnecting me to my inner child and helping me heal a big part of my own life.

In return, I have been able to share this healing and goodness by teaching others that it is really okay to let go, laugh, and create. There is value in appreciating the simple beauty of life – sunshine, butterflies, colours, rainbows, bubbles, and rain. And it is important to be okay with being yourself.

The goodness in a child's heart teaches us so much. Through my experiences with children, I've learned that their kind energy has felt like being with hundreds of angels teaching me and transforming me into an angel who can also ripple the energy of love and sunshine through and into others. I want to dedicate this writing to every single child in this world and, especially, to the many children who have touched my life.

My Son Has a BIG Heart

By Donna H. Kater

At a young age, my son Chris showed signs of empathy as well as friendliness. For his seventh birthday, he received a large Styrofoam glider plane. He really loved that plane, and we spent hours at the park. He would run, release it, and watch it soar with a big smile on his face. Then he would retrieve it and start all over again.

One day, Chris noticed a young boy, perhaps a year or so younger than him, watching the action. Chris invited him to take a turn. The boy was so taken with the plane and the fun he was having with his new friend Chris that he, too, had a big smile on his face.

When it came time to go home that day, Chris and I were packing up our things. Chris said, "Wait a minute." He walked over to the young boy and gave him the plane. They both had big smiles on their faces, and I noticed that my face got a big smile on it as well. My heart swelled with love and pride.

Chris, now an adult, works as a driver for an urban transportation service. Weekends will find him driving lots of people from place to place in San Diego. He just received his 1,000th five-star rating and forwarded me this message from one of his customers: "Thank you, Christopher, for picking me up at the Emergency Animal Clinic where my two puppies are in serious trouble because they ate two pieces of sugarless gum, which is deadly to dogs. My fault for not locking it up. You were especially kind when I told you I had no sleep or dinner last night, and you drove me to a drive-through so I could get a quick take-out breakfast. When you wished my puppies a speedy recovery, I knew you were a kind driver. You were kind, helpful, excellent, and quick! Great job!"

My heart swells again with love and pride. Chris is still a very kind and empathetic person. Goodness abounds in him. What more could a mom ask for?

No Goldfish for the Homeless

By Haley Ryane Meushaw

If you knew what we'd gone through with our daughter, you'd understand why it was hard to deny her any foods she wanted. So often she would become disinterested or angry around eating. Perhaps lunch with friends in first grade would positively influence her relationship with food.

By springtime, the volume of packaged snacks that had lost favor required a pantry purge, producing half a dozen bags for the homeless.

"Did you throw out the ones with ancient 'best-by' dates?" my daughter asked. "We got those goldfish before school even started." I explained that the food was still good. "Mom!" she protested, fists on her hips, "I wouldn't want any of them getting sick from expired food! Who would take care of them? How could they pay for a doctor?"

"No one's getting sick, and we are not wasting all this food," I argued.

Wait. I paused to consider, *How could she win this one?* Unconditional Love responded. I felt it dancing in my body. My own logic was no match for the power of my seven-year-old's love for humanity. I was proud that somehow she had it in her to rally for love.

I was astounded by the effects of her selflessness that day four years ago. In those few moments, something broke open within me. A necessary activation occurred, a spiritual upleveling, enlightenment on my journey of becoming a healer. Many times I had questioned, *Where does the healing come from?* I had not known how to "get there." My own unconditional love for others had been quietly unfolding and growing before then. But that moment with my daughter proved to be the key to enabling amazing healings for myself as well as many clients around the world. Plus, when they experienced relief, so did others near them.

My daughter did win big-time that day. She made the world a more loving, happy place, one person at a time, starting at home. Thank you, my darling. I love you forever.

The Power of Presence

By Tamra Blankenship

Everything is neutral, and our perceptions alter that neutrality into life's lessons.

While going through my divorce, I was struggling to find my footing and resentful about now becoming a "part-time parent" to my three children. In this divorce, I'd lost my best friend/soulmate and my business. The pain surrounding the altered direction of my reality had me clueless about what was next. I was about to turn 40 and had no real career. Starting from scratch, I was rediscovering myself while finding a means to support my children, who were each trying to find their own way.

My oldest became more disconnected than the others. Every day for a year, he would come home from school, finish his homework, and hide away in his room. With no financial assets available for professional help, one day I just decided to sit with him in silence. I thought unconditionally, loving thoughts from my deepest core, doing my best to help him feel supported and loved. I knew in my heart that words, no matter how supportive they might be, were not the way through this difficult situation. So, I sat…in silence, hoping for wisdom to navigate the situation. Setting aside my own feelings of being unsupported and derailed, fearing I was a total failure, I sat at the edge of his bed while he lay there, numb and disconnected. After an hour, I would say, "I love you so much," and then close the door as I left his room.

"Mom, do you know how many times you saved my life?" A sinking feeling of total fear that he was at the brink went through me.

"No, sweetie, would you like to talk about it?" At that very moment, I realized the value of being present to unconditional love, the power of presence, and how invaluable it is in letting people discover their own way.

My son discovered his voice, could express his truth, and found peace. Looking back on that time, I realize that, in him finding his way, I was given the unexpected gift of finding my way, too.

Children Are Our Greatest Teachers

By Nadene Joy Hagen

I have four children, and it never ceases to amaze me what absolute miracles they are. They're our best teachers, forcing us to look deep within ourselves and focus on the little things that matter.

Their hearts and souls are divinely connected before they reach a certain age where parents and society start to shut them down. If we're not committed to helping them be themselves, they can lose their identity and their purpose.

Most adults overlook the small things children do every day – making eye contact and giggling, saying "I love you" over and over, wanting to help in every way possible, and giving hugs just because.

My greatest wish is that my children (who are now eight, six, four, and two) grow up to be happy, kind, loving, and honourable; filled with divine grace; and surrounded by people who love them for themselves.

Children should be taught to give to others, especially those less fortunate. We sponsor two children – a boy in Africa my oldest son's age and a girl in South America my daughter's age. Watching them write letters to these children has been life changing.

My children donate their old clothes, books, and toys to families in need. We always donate food on Easter and Christmas. This year, we were given the privilege of attending an event where 600 homeless people were waiting for a free Easter meal.

Children can show us how to live with an infinite connection to the divine, living in the moment and following our hearts! They are our next generation of leaders. We must allow our children to be themselves and keep them free of any limiting beliefs.

Our thoughts become words, our words become actions, and our actions have the power to make the world a better place for all of humanity!

Love Beyond Language

By Jenean Zunk

Kristin was wheeling a patient out from the operating room when she noticed him. She had seen him earlier in the day but hadn't paid much attention, as the surgery schedule was full and the long day was spent focusing on the patient in front of her. Yet something about him drew her in. For a 10-year-old child who had been waiting all day for surgery, he was impressively calm and patient. He simply sat by his mother and played quietly with his teddy bear.

Earlier in the year, when a fellow doctor invited Kristin to participate in this medical mission, she had leapt at the chance. She had been feeling the call to get out of her normal routine, reconnect with why she had become a nurse in the first place, and volunteer. This past week in the Dominican Republic had been just what her soul had been calling for.

People waited all year to be seen by the mission, which usually only took adults; however, this child was in desperate need of a hernia repair, so they agreed to see him.

When it was the boy's turn for surgery, Kristin walked up to take him in. She did not speak his language, so she simply began playing with the teddy bear – hugging him and bouncing back and forth. As she reached out to the child, he looked up at her, smiled, and took her hand without hesitation. Kristin paused and drew in a breath. It felt almost as if this child could see straight through to her soul. The complete trust and openness he displayed was beyond anything she had ever witnessed before.

As they walked together into the operating room, tears began to form in her eyes as she realized that this child had given her a gift far beyond what she felt she was giving him. He had demonstrated for her love in its purest form: vulnerability and trust.

The Disappearing Gloves
By Kelly Jenkins

Many years ago, when my youngest daughter was in kindergarten, she would tell me that she needed new gloves every time we were shopping. Every week, I would end up buying her a new pair of gloves. The next week she would say, "Mom, I need another pair of gloves." After several months, I became so frustrated I told her she had to quit losing her gloves or I would not buy her anymore. Not deterred by my reaction, she continued to ask for more gloves. When I would fuss at her, she would just say, "I am sorry" and continue to ask for more.

It wasn't until I went to her parent-teacher conference that I found out the truth behind the gloves. The first thing her teacher said to me was, "You have the kindest daughter. Every day at recess she gives her gloves to any child on the playground who does not have them. I have never seen a child so kind and caring." I was stunned. I had no idea what to say. All I could think about was all the times I had fussed at her, telling her to stop losing her gloves!

When I got home that evening, I told her what her teacher had said. I asked her why she had not explained to me why she needed so many pairs of gloves. She just smiled and said, "Sometimes everyone just needs a friend." I never questioned her again about needing gloves. It just became a habit that every week we picked up more gloves for her to take to school.

This experience took place more than 20 years ago. Through the years, I have watched her be the same kind, loving, caring person that she was out on the playground. She is currently an elementary-school counselor and continues to show that same love and kindness to every child she comes in contact with at school. And yes, she is still giving gloves (and now coats) to the children on the playground.

A Grandmother's Miracle Healing

By Debbie Labinski

One time when I was sharing a story about angels and healing to a grandmother, she said, "Well, I need to share my story about a healing that I received." She proceeded to tell me that she had broken her wrist a few months earlier, and the healing process had been very slow. After her cast was removed, she went to physical therapy and did everything her doctors told her to do. She also did emotional work and prayed for help in dealing with the pain. But even after months of inner and outer work, the pain lingered.

The timing of this injury was interesting for two reasons: First, it came about just as she was writing a book about her experiences as a hospice chaplain. The fact that she broke the wrist on her writing hand felt like more than mere coincidence! Second, the injury occurred a few months before a family gathering, which proved to be the turning point in her recovery. It was also the day when she learned that her grandson is a natural healer.

The whole family was at the party, including her six-year-old grandson, who has down syndrome and a beautiful soul. The grandmother was talking about her wrist and the pain she still felt, even after all these months of medical help and pain medicine. Her grandson stopped, sat cross-legged, closed his eyes, and laid his hand on her wrist. She allowed this to happen, knowing how powerful prayer can be.

After the party ended, the grandmother went home and went to bed. To her surprise, she woke up the next morning to find that the pain had miraculously disappeared. What an amazing gift from a trusting little boy to his beautiful grandmother!

This wonderful example of trust, healing, and the power of prayer reminded me that there is goodness all around us; we just need to slow down and trust that God always sends an Earth Angel our way when we surrender our pain to Him.

The Wish List

By Jenna Kelland

When my son was seven, our family participated in a spring fundraising event for the local children's hospital. My perception was that he found the event noisy and overwhelming. However, about 10 months later, when we were talking about how to spend our Christmas charity money, I discovered that the fundraising event had had a significant impact on him.

Every year, we set aside some money to share Christmas with people in need. That year, my son suggested we donate our money to the Ronald McDonald House (RMH) to help families with a child in the local children's hospital. He remembered RMH from the fundraiser and wanted to help them with our Christmas charity money – as well as a contribution from his birthday money!

We agreed and checked the RMH website for their wish list. With list and budget in hand, I took my son shopping to choose items for RMH. His choices ranged from the practical (toothbrushes and toothpaste) to treats (juice boxes and granola bars). He selected each item carefully using his own criteria to decide what would be best for the family. Would they prefer blue or green toothbrushes? Should he get apple juice, orange juice, or both?

As he chose, we talked about helping the families, what it would be like to be in the hospital and away from home for Christmas, and making decisions about money. In the end, we had a cart full of shopping bags to take to RMH. He also decided to make a card for each family there. He counted the rooms the House had and got out his craft supplies. Each card offered holiday greetings or an encouraging message, such as "feel better soon," in his grade-one handwriting.

That was four years ago. Since then, we have contributed to RMH each Christmas; and each Christmas, my son has made his own contribution from his savings. Each year, my son reviews their wish list and selects items to donate. He is eagerly waiting until he is 13, so he can volunteer at RMH. Little did I know that the event, which seemed to be noisy and overwhelming to my son, had somehow motivated him to learn the truly valuable lesson of giving back.

Chapter 5
Animals & Nature

O ur lives are filled with so much laughter and joy, thanks in large part to always being surrounded by sweet and silly animals and a seemingly endless supply of natural beauty here on the Oregon coast.

When we walk on the beach or take our kayak out onto a lake, we can't help but feel the goodness that's all around us. The trees sway, the birds sing, the water glistens, and our hearts feel at peace. Anytime we feel overwhelmed by life and begin to question whether goodness is alive and well, we step into nature and instantly feel transformed and calmed.

Animals have this effect on us as well. Without even trying, they have the ability to ease our stress and calm us down simply by being near us. Our cats will pounce on a toy, which instantly makes us laugh. Or a seagull will sit right next to us on the beach, wishing that we would give him some of our sandwich. Or the harbor seals nearby will flop off a rock and playfully chase each other in the water. And each time, their antics fill us with joy and make everything feel right again.

Life can be hard sometimes, and being part of our always-changing world can feel unsettling to many of us. We sometimes feel surrounded by turmoil, hardship, and negativity. When that happens, we always go back to nature and back to animals – they are our safe haven. And they never fail to prove to us just how much goodness abounds within them and within our world. We focus on them until we feel strong and hopeful again. And we're both so grateful to share stories throughout this chapter of others who have found this same soothing salve and instant uplifter in their own lives.

Paws, Breathe, Proceed
By Michelle R. Griffith

Hooch sat among the ladies on the front porch, enjoying their monthly gathering for brunch. Hooch is a stocky, red, mixed-breed dog with a clear connection to pit bull in his lineage. He is a happy dog who loves his people and enjoys being included and recognized for his joyful contributions and contagious smile.

As the ladies were chatting, Hooch was distracted by squirrels in the yard and curious about individuals who were passing through the neighborhood, but he kept one eye on the porch ladies. He continued to work the group with his warm energy and contagious smile, intermittently offering his broad shoulders as an invitation to scratch his back.

Hooch was particularly interested in Cindy's report about her upcoming trip to Alaska. She shared her looming list of pending preparations, talking a bit about the destination and worrying about how she would be able navigate crazy schedules until the departure date — and the recent reports of bear attacks in the news!

Just as Cindy was fully consumed by the reality of pending tasks and organization, the careful planning of food, supplies, and bear spray...Hooch squared his shoulders, looked up at Cindy, and landed a big paw gently on her forearm resting on the chair.

Cindy immediately recognized how her imagination was on the verge of crazy making. Hooch sat still, smiling up at Cindy, inviting her to "paws." She glanced down at the big red paw on her arm with a smile, took a breath, and had a laugh. She thanked Hooch for his interruption and took a moment to accept his grounding influence. There was no need for worry. The packing and organizing is only a task to complete, and a healthy respect for bears in nature is part of the camping experience.

After Cindy expressed her gratitude to Hooch, we all took a moment to "paws," breathe, and honor the awareness of a big red dog who stepped in with a gentle paw to the arm — changing the energy of the exchange from overthinking to grounded awareness.

The Gift of Bees

By Kyra Schaefer

As a child, I had a particularly mischievous friend who would stretch my comfort zone. We would sneak off to "Big Rock," a large cluster of boulders at the end of my grandmother's road, where we'd kick off our shoes and play in the creek beds that stretched for miles.

One day, I was overly cautious about climbing a ladder of exposed tree roots that sank down to the creek bed from the above street nearby. My fearless friend went first. As she climbed, I remained in the creek bed.

Then, a swarm of bees (with obvious murderous intent) flew out from the roots. I screamed. They flew in my mouth and stung me around my head. I had nowhere to go. I couldn't run either way without them chasing me. I had no choice. In order to survive, I had to go toward my attackers' nest and climb the roots. My safety was lying within a few feet, so I braved the fog of bees and climbed.

Once I reached the street, I felt a deep calm settle over me. I had a clear mind, though I couldn't speak. The threat of bees no longer existed, and the world looked bright and easy, as if all the pain I would ever experience was over.

I found safety in the kindness of a neighbor as my friend ran up the hill to my grandmother's house. After I got shots at the hospital, my mother picked me up, brought me home, and laid me in the pool. She was gentle and kind as she swished the cool water across my hot, swollen, exhausted body while speaking an affirmation over me: "All the bees that will ever sting you have already stung you. You will never get stung again."

The bees gave me a gift that day: bravery. I withstood the most difficult and painful experience and survived. I am forever grateful for the kindness of others — including my mother, who spoke a spell over me that has lasted for more than 30 years.

Freedom Ride

By Mauri Barnes

Skimming through Facebook one morning, I noticed a post about a young black lab mix. He was scheduled for euthanasia when a woman from Buffalo, New York, posted that she wanted to adopt him and needed help to transport him from Tampa, Florida, 1,252 miles away. "Road Trip" someone posted. That was my sign; I'd yearned for a getaway, and helping to save this boy sounded like the perfect reason to take a road trip.

The shelter was nearly an hour away. I offered to visit, take pictures, and gather information. She was so appreciative, since a recent encounter with the caged pup had been met with fearful growling.

He was dirty and skeletal from neglect. Having been chained outdoors his entire life in hot, humid, and buggy rural Florida, he'd had minimal human contact. With an adopter interested, the staff had spent extra time with this gentle giant and gained his trust. I'd tucked treats in my pockets, wanting him to remember me when I returned. We took him outside, and tears filled my eyes as I watched him lean against his trainer, responding to the attention.

I completed the adoption papers and happily paid for his freedom. Tomorrow he would receive medical attention; on Saturday he would be ready to go. Sunday was Valentine's Day. Volunteer drivers were planning our exchange points on his freedom ride. Bobby Valentine's new life had begun.

Taking those first steps of freedom, he was smiling and easygoing, yet balked at getting into my car. Thankfully, a fresh bone enticed him to climb into the pillow- and blanket-lined space with his bone, a toy, and room to stretch out. As we drove away, he settled in, looking out windows, smiling.

He was a great passenger, enjoying rest stops, walks, and fast food along the way. I told him about the wonderful adventures ahead on this journey and the family with two doggie brothers waiting to welcome him into his forever home.

As the miles passed, Bobby moved closer and closer to me until his big head rested on my shoulder. "Happy Valentine's Day, Bobby!"

Amelia's Chance at Life

By Sharon G. Smith

An eight-week-old kitty arrived in a bucket at the community animal shelter. Her little malnourished body was deformed, and her infected eyes were crusted over. Unfortunately, she also had cerebellar hypoplasia (CH), a neurological condition that affects the part of the brain that controls physical coordination. Sadly, many kittens with CH are euthanized.

Our veterinarian, Dr. Mary, was on duty that day and chose to take her back to her own clinic. She sensed her strong will to live, and after the kitty survived a few more days, she could see that this little kitten might have a fighting chance. She named her "Amelia" and introduced her to Michelle, a woman who has taken care of many rescued cats. As members of Michelle's family, we have witnessed the magic of loving care for the homeless feline.

Amelia is seven months old now and weighs only five pounds. Because of CH, she may never be able to stand alone. However, she has an amazing appetite and, with help, eats all food offered. She has learned what the litter box is for but is still unable to negotiate the in and out process on her own. She is good at grooming parts of herself such as her right front paw, which she holds up in front of her face like a stop sign. Amelia seems to recognize us now and looks up at us with her beautiful turquoise eyes. At her own pace, she is growing stronger day by day. She purrs and cuddles in your arms the minute you pick her up.

Each member of the family has marveled at her determination. Taking care of her has been such a pleasure for all of us. We take turns carrying her around with us, making sure she is included in every way. Because of Dr. Mary's act of kindness and the loving help of Michelle and her family, the survival of this little kitty has become possible.

Lost and Found: Joyful and Archie Bacon

By Donna S. Priesmeyer

My husband, Tom, was gone for a few days. I was at home awaiting his return when I received a text from my friend who sent me a picture of a lost puppy who had come to the front door of her work, begging to come in out of the rain. I immediately told her he could come to our house. Later that afternoon, she arrived with a cute, frisky little Pomeranian. He leapt into my lap, gave me kisses, and instantly stole my heart.

When Tom got home, the puppy ran to greet him. It was as if he knew Tom and was happy to see him again. The puppy reminded us of our Pomeranian, Joyful, who had passed away the previous summer. Joyful had a long and happy life. She always lived up to her name, spreading joy to all in her presence. After she passed, we missed her terribly but couldn't imagine having another dog that could match her sweet energy and loving disposition.

Now, a year later, it took several days to locate the lost puppy's owner. There was no address or phone number on his collar, but we found the owner by tracing the rabies tag. By that time, we had fallen in love with the little guy. When I called the owner, he said it was his fault the puppy ran away because he was too busy to train him properly. My heart pounded, as I told him we had become quite attached and would love to keep his dog. He paused a moment and then kindly agreed. He said he would be happy to know that he would have a good home. He told me his name was Bacon and he was two years old. Tom preferred the name Archie, so he became Archie Bacon. He is precious, and every day of our lives, he touches our hearts and makes us smile!

I believe that it was no accident that Archie Bacon found us. I think he was guided to our home to bring more joy back into our lives by a little guardian angel named Joyful.

The Magic of Manali
By John R. Fyfe

As I wrap my wool poncho around me to keep out the wintry chill, I gaze in wonderment at the millions of glittering stars that light up the brilliant night sky. From my hill-house balcony, I await the rising of the full moon. In the utter stillness, I hear the jackals and wild dogs howling from the nearby hills.

A bright ivory crescent suddenly appears on the edge of the mountain peak. Mesmerized, I watch the moon expose her brightness, her fullness, illuminating the Himalayas. There are not many moments as wonderful as this. A sense of exhilaration engulfs me as I spot the Milky Way! It's a feeling I remember having as a child, and my heart flutters at the memory.

"Wake up, everyone!" I shout. "How can you forget this magnificence?"

Here in the Himalayas, I am not asleep anymore!

The next morning, I stroll down the muddy trail that heads toward old Manali. I pass tired-looking, old, wooden houses before arriving at a light-blue schoolhouse. There are children leaning out the windows, with happy, golden smiles on their light-brown faces.

"Hello, mister! Hello!"

I wave back, smiling, and continue walking up the twisting road that takes me to a narrow, wobbly bridge. Beneath it, the River Beas roars its way down the valley.

I follow a snowy path, forever climbing upward. My breathing is heavier due to the high altitude. At the plateau, I pause and spot an inviting cove. There I sit with my legs stretched out, my feet hanging over the cliff. I am awestruck from the breathtaking view.

The sharpness of the deep-blue sky stings my eyes, and I close them, feeling contented as the heat of the March sun warms my body. I think about the ferocity of the river, its source emanating from the glacier peaks, from the heavens. The river's tenacity and power smashes through rock and earth, forever going downward, forgetting where it came from, much like human consciousness. Hopefully, one day, our consciousness will rise again and we will remember our source!

The Reebok Chicken

By Kimberly Beer

She was waiting by my car when I got out of the gym.

A chicken. In a city parking lot.

To this country girl, it was obvious that this little red hen was not feeling well. She offered very little resistance to being picked up. She was not obviously broken; her limbs seemed connected in all the right places, and her wings moved easily under my examination. But she was cold, and her body felt thin and light. A quick feel of her crop told me she hadn't eaten.

I wrapped her in my gym towel, wondering how she'd gotten here, and tucked her into a safe spot in my car. I didn't hold out much hope, but I was willing to give her a chance.

We have an adage around our ranch that if an animal, no matter how sick, is willing to try to live, we will try with them. When I placed the hen in the warm coop with my hens, the sun was fading into a purple horizon. I said a small prayer that she would make it through the darkness.

When I did morning chores, the hen was up and around but still not looking healthy. She ate and drank, but she didn't leave the coop with the other chickens, staying instead in the warm straw a little longer.

As we sat down to watch TV the next night, a commercial came on for Reebok athletic shoes featuring a plucky red hen that breaks free from her life as a laying hen and learns to live free range. The hen in the commercial looked exactly – and I mean *exactly* – like the hen I'd found at the gym! She immediately earned the name "The Reebok Chicken."

Over the next few weeks, The Reebok Chicken continued to improve, each day a little brighter. Soon, she was venturing out of the chicken house, foraging for bugs and freshly budded clover. Today, she is a happy citizen of our flock, truly living free range and teaching visitors to the ranch what it means to overcome even the bleakest of circumstances and thrive.

Rescue and Relationship
By Nora Rose

When my kindhearted daughter, Lauren, graduated from college, she took a teaching job with a program in Mississippi. While there, she often visited the Humane Society to donate supplies and offer a little love where it was most needed.

After one year, Lauren was ready to return home. Two weeks before she left, she stopped at the Humane Society, where they had an abundance of dogs. She searched each area until she laid her eyes on a litter of five blond puppies who were covered in poop and living in appalling conditions. She was determined to rescue one of them! A frisky little pup with white markings jumped up on her arm. She picked him up and couldn't resist his sweet face and those captivating eyes – one green, one blue! He was the only one with two different-colored eyes.

This was the perfect gift to herself – a little make-a-difference remembrance of Mississippi in the form of a six-week-old Catahoula Leopard puppy. She paid the fees for shots and neutering. One week later, when she picked him up, he was sick (with what the veterinarian said was merely a cold) but healthy enough to be adopted.

Lauren took him with her and soon headed off on the 12-hour drive home with her new companion, Dane. She talked to him, listened to music, and thought about the friendship between a human and a dog, the unique chemistry of the relationship, that special bond, the love. She hoped someone would rescue the other puppies. They all deserved good homes.

When she pulled into the driveway, we were all ecstatic. It was hugs and kisses for everyone. But Dane was still sick. Our vet said he had the contagious parvovirus that dogs get from eating poop. He was given only a 20% chance of survival, but we nursed Dane back to health.

Eventually, they moved again, but Dane still remembers me. When he sees me, he gets crazy excited, sits next to me, and wants to sleep in my bed!

A short time later, Dane got a brother when Lauren adopted Buster.

Passing Kindness

By Michelle Smith Mufarreh

My dear friend Mitts died one morning just after I went to work. Then, my sweet Claire passed at the clinic. Prior to the loss of these two kitty loves, my cat Marlin departed on the basement floor while I was away. He died, likely and most hopefully, a sudden death. Each passing was unique, and for each, sadly, I wasn't present.

I believe that our spirit carries on after we die. Most days, I can be matter of fact about this. Still, experiencing the loss of a loved one calls forth so many questions. Should I have stayed with Mitts that day? Should I have picked up Claire earlier? How did I not know that Marlin was leaving soon? Should I have done anything differently? Which hug was our last hug?

Not long after facing grief in this way, I awoke to Miss Kit dragging the lower half of her body toward me with great panic in her eyes, as if asking, "Why won't my body work? What has happened to me?" She had suffered a blood clot. While I honored the possibility of her healing, I attended to her steady decline.

Then one day, I brought Kit out into the garden. Her eyes and nose were a little crusty. Gently, I washed her face. I breathed deeply. The air was clean and fresh. My mind and heart stilled. I knew that very soon I may need to help her go. If she needed help, I would indeed be there for her. With this delicate thought in mind, I placed her on my lap. For now, we would enjoy the breeze.

As I stroked her, she turned her face up to me. Her eyes began to turn round and black. In this moment mixed with both confusion and percolating loss, a tender wave of awe came over me. My eyes filled with tears. She was leaving her body now.

This truth washed over me, and her spirit lifted. All I could voice was "Thank you." She had given me the gift of her passing, with me as present as possible.

Rescue

By Janet G. Nestor

Sadly, animal suffering is always present, and we accept some of it because the violence and lack of concern has become part of our culture. Gradually, I've come to understand that all animals are sentient, intelligent beings capable of the exact same love, fear, and pain experienced by human beings. Knowing this, I've become an animal advocate.

For years, my friend has rescued abandoned and feral cats that gather around the dumpster at a local fast-food restaurant. Once they're caught, she takes them to a veterinary hospital, has them treated for any illness they might have, makes sure they have the medicine they need, and sometimes has them spayed or neutered. Once the cats are healthy enough, she tries to find them a forever home or a foster home, or she takes them to a no-kill shelter. She does this from the goodness of her heart, doing her part to end animal suffering.

I rescued my Dalmatian, Petie, from a kill shelter when she was a terrified six-month-old puppy. Gradually, as she relaxed in her new surroundings, she became my companion and walking partner, my guard dog when I was home alone, and a permanent resident of my heart. Petie found a group of new friends at the recovery center where I worked. On the days she was with me, she welcomed the residents to my office, and played and walked around the grounds with them, adding joy to their lives and aiding them in their recovery.

My sweet boy Cozmo was born at a Yorkie rescue center. His mom was rescued from a puppy mill, and she too was adopted into a forever home. Today, Cozmo is a happy five-year-old rascal who barks too much, jumps as high as the rail fence in our back yard, runs like the wind, and loves to sit in the basket when I ride my bike. Most of all, he warms my heart with his sparkling eyes, his cuteness, and his unconditional love.

Together, with clear intention, we can end suffering for all mistreated, neglected, and abused animals, not just locally, but throughout the world.

Spring Green

By Joy Harris

There is nothing more rewarding than walking along a path in springtime and counting the shades of green. You'll find ten shades of green in the leaves, more than ten in the grass, and hundreds more in the stalks, stems, and vines of new growth in the spring.

When you stare into the buds and the new leaves on the trees and look at the blades of grass that are turning green, you cannot help but smile with all the new life. Fortunately, there is no shortage of spring bounty. There is abundance on the grape vines, strawberry plants, and blackberry bushes. And when the trees and plants bud and produce fruit, the vibrant colors multiply!

Counting the shades of green provides an opportunity to see hope. Look around you, and you will see a future filled with the knowing that the seeds you plant will produce the rewards that you get. Grins produce laughter, smiles produce hugs, and the love of nature produces hope. The signs of the wheel of the year – moving from new growth to full bloom and then to rest and hibernation of fall and winter – remind us of the seasons of our lives. That's Mother Nature.

Millions of flower buds pressed become aromatic oils and produce the fragrance of peppermint, eucalyptus, and sage. The lovely scent of roses, jasmine, and chamomile can move you to ecstasy. If you have ever seen vanilla or the tea tree plant (*melaleuca*) blooming and smelled those scents as you walk by, you know the beauty and scent of some of nature's most special gifts.

Everyone who raises a garden is temporarily in charge of a little bit of heaven that can be enjoyed by everyone who sees and smells a bouquet or enjoys green vegetables.

There is no end to the richness found on every garden path. Gardeners with a green thumb know there's no end to the butterfly bushes that can take over your garden. Goodness knows they can take over mine any time they want!

Max, the Generous Jack Russell

By Veronica Mather

Animals touch our lives in many ways. They perform heroic deeds, saving people from fires or drowning. Others detect cancer or work as rescue dogs or assistance companions. Some mothers feed babies from another species, demonstrating love without boundaries. There are animals who just make us laugh, brightening our day. And there are those who move us with their kindness and generosity of spirit, as our Jack Russell, Max, has done for me.

Max is terrified of thunderstorms. After trying various ways to ease his stress, we discovered that a drive in the ute with the radio playing works every time. Strapped into his harness, Max rests his front paws on the dash of the ute. He watches the wipers as they clear rain from the windscreen, and flashes of lightning light up the distant sky.

One stormy night, my husband, Dale, took Max for a calming drive. About an hour later, they returned...with another furry friend! Dale had observed a panicked terrier running down the road. He coaxed the little dog into the ute. Max isn't keen on strange dogs, particularly in his ute. But he was happy for our unexpected friend to share the ride home – and even "allowed" him to stay overnight until his family was found.

I was especially moved by Max's willingness to share because it wasn't something he normally liked to do – with his ute, his home, and especially his treats! Max simply adores treats, and whenever he doesn't finish one in a single sitting, he'll hide it down the back of the couch or place it parallel to the wall – because nobody will ever find it there!

One day while visiting my parent's farm, Max approached Smokey, Dad's sheep dog. He dropped something at her feet and walked away. I was stunned to see Smokey chewing one of Max's treats. For a little dog obsessed with his food, this was a generous and loving gesture.

I have always felt a strong connection with animals. My pets, along with wild animals that find their way into my world, hold a very special place in my heart.

Becoming Free

By John R. Fyfe

There was a bird who had lost his way. He had returned to his nest only to find that his tree had been cut and lay broken on the ground. His family was gone.

Months he stayed, hoping for their return. He flew around to where other birds lived. Some offered him a branch to sleep on. They even offered food, but he couldn't fit in.

Always, those families wanted him to conform to their ways, but he found this to be difficult, as he only wanted to be free. Yet when he was alone and free, he often felt sad. He missed his family.

He became worldly and traveled across the land, meeting up with many other birds. He began to see life differently, but not many cared to listen when he shared his experiences. Nobody gave him a branch when he spoke of change.

He lived with the mystical crows, busy sparrows, aggressive blue jays, chattering magpies, and a hardworking woodpecker. He even dared to befriend a wise owl. He became a chameleon, able to take on the characteristics of all. He had to laugh when he acted like a rowdy blue jay.

However, he slowly began to forget who he was, as he lost his individuality and power.

Disillusioned, he returned to his barren tree, but once there, memories of happier times brought only more sadness.

Hope was fading. He decided to leave his forest forever, to fly toward the mountains where the eagles lived. The only way out of this bleakness was to fly toward the sun.

He was afraid his heart wouldn't make the journey, that his transformation to Eagle consciousness would fail.

He was ready to fly off the mountain peak. He was afraid his tiny wings wouldn't be able to handle the strong air currents, yet he was determined to go home. Suddenly, he heard a call so familiar! Was it possible? His partner was singing to him. He answered her and saw his family flying behind their mother. They had found each other on the top of the mountain peak!

Puppy Love

By Jena Brown

When the housing market crashed, many families all over the country lost their homes. These losses led to many animals losing their families. It became fairly common for real-estate agents to find dogs and cats abandoned, with large buckets of water and food, locked inside an empty home.

I know many friends who adopted these lost pets – taking them into their homes and giving them love. One selfless woman took that act of kindness and love one step further when she found an abandoned puppy locked in an empty home.

The mother and the rest of the litter were nowhere to be found. He was too small to be without his mother, and my friend was afraid he would be put to sleep at the pound or a shelter. He was simply too much work for their already-strained resources.

So my friend took him in. She bought milk and bottle-fed him. She slept downstairs on the couch for weeks so that he could feed and go outside without waking the rest of the house. She also made sure he got the shots and medical care he needed.

My beautiful friend mothered this puppy, making sure he was healthy and giving him the love he needed. Her family also got involved: her kids played with him, began leash training, and helped begin potty training. Under their care, he went from scared and malnourished to thriving.

Incredibly, she did this knowing they couldn't keep him. They already had three dogs. One more just wasn't feasible. While they cared for this tiny puppy as if he were their own, she was interviewing potential parents to be sure he would be loved and cared for.

The day they said goodbye was heartbreaking. But she knew he was going to thrive in his new home.

Adopting a pet into your home – giving an unloved animal the love they deserve – is beautiful. But giving them that love even when you know they aren't yours to keep is absolutely amazing. By caring for that abandoned puppy, that loving foster mom reminded me that kindness and generosity really can be unconditional.

Sunflower Magic

By Ruthie Lewis

The one-year anniversary of losing my daughter, Christina Faith (who we called Tina), 10 days before her 21st birthday, was nearing and occupying many of my thoughts. I was simply trying to get through another day of living this life without her when I got a call from Pam, my dear friend who had been there for me every step of this excruciating journey. She said she was picking me up after she got off work.

"What…? Why…? Where…?"

My questions were answered with only, "We're going somewhere," in the familiar up-to-something tone.

This forced my smile. "Okay."

Riding to our mystery destination, I felt a bit giddy for the first time in a very long time. Our chuckles sprang spontaneously. As we drove down the back roads, I looked at her and said, "If you weren't my best friend, I would be very afraid." She laughed and slyly proceeded.

She said, "Look over there."

I saw nothing.

She pointed, "Look!"

Rounding a bend in the road, my eyes, heart, and entire being were awed by the sight of never-ending sunflowers. Gasping in wonder, tears sprang to my eyes. If ever I'd felt fairy dust, it was at this moment. I exited the car while Pam snapped pictures. The breeze carried the scents to me, and the heavens seemed to open up with the bright, breathtaking smile of my beautiful Tina. You see, she adored sunflowers. How could something as simple as sunflowers empower such magic as to reveal the golden treasure within such tragedy?

Pam and I frolicked, basking in reverence and giggling like little girls. "I want to build a tree house and live here," I said. I'd never seen a sunflower field; now it was forever emblazoned in a magical place within me.

Gazing back, driving away slowly, I told her with barren words how much this expansive and sunny experience meant to me. But to this day, I know she has no idea how this tiny goodness created healing magic for my sliced-open heart.

Kiaora the Brave

By Kris McLeod

When we looked our bundle of love in the eyes for the first time, we knew she would change our lives for the better. She was so sweet and smart, and she smelled amazing! Our little Kiaora brought the fun, the chaos, and the noise with her tail wagging and velvet ears flapping. (Oh yes, Kiaora is a Black Labrador.)

She is such a happy girl that you would never guess what she has been through – and what she inspires in others. Here is just one of her stories:

One year, just before Christmas, she became unwell, vomiting for no known reason. She spent several days in the vet hospital. They didn't find a cause, and as she had improved, she was sent home. Within hours, she was vomiting bile, and we rushed her to the animal emergency clinic. After x-rays and checks, we were sent home again. The next day, however, we were back in emergency. Finally, the ultrasound revealed a perforated bowel that was missed by two vets! They said it was amazing she had survived this long.

The first surgery went well, but her recovery was bumpy. We received a phone call at four o'clock on Christmas morning asking permission for some expensive interventions and a second surgery, as she was crashing. That day was long and full of tears. Our amazing friends and family joined us in sending love, Reiki, and prayers. And it worked; she was getting better!

We later found out that the surgeon who operated on her that day refused to charge us for his services, as he was so adamant that two vets misdiagnosing her was the reason she needed that extra surgery. What a generous, compassionate man to help her and us in that way.

We went from tube feeding and hourly support to an energetic, defy-all-the-odds happy, healthy doggy again. Her strength, love, and attitude have inspired us all. She is part of our family and reminds us daily of the goodness in life and to enjoy yourself every chance you get!

Showered with Love

By Lori Thomas

I'm supposed to be writing a story about goodness – something that somebody has done for me, or goodness that I have witnessed. Instead, I'm walking in the woods behind my house, standing on a narrow, unpaved path flanked on both sides by ferns, grasses, trees, and bushes. A small brook babbles along its way beyond the trees on my right. The sun shines down, creating a mist on the damp earth. Myriad birds sing and call to each other. The cicadas serenade the trees with their unique music.

In looking at the beauty surrounding me, what comes to me is the kindness, the generosity, and the selfless love that Earth gives to every single person every single day. She supplies the ground beneath our feet, no matter what we do to it. She gives us oxygen. She provides our food. She shows us what abundance is. And even in the asphalt jungles of Manhattan, her heart beats beneath the cement, beneath the subways, in the swampy substrate that comprises New York City.

No matter what we do, no matter how unkind we are to her, she just loves us back. She treats us with such loving kindness. Today, she has given me a cool place for my feet in the stream. She gives us water. No matter how we treat it, she always gives us more water. She gives us inexplicable beauty in the trees, the animals, the plants. She shows us what balance is. All we have to do is look around ourselves and focus on what she does for us every single day.

I'm so eternally grateful for her. My body comes from her. Everything that is found in my body is found in the earth. Without her, there's no me. Without her, there's no physical existence. Without her, there's no us.

So, today I honor the earth for her incredible kindness, her generosity, and her love that she showers on every single person on this planet...if we just know where to look to see it.

A Calico Named Ruby

By Janet Womack

I've been an animal lover since I was young, but cats have always held a special place in my heart. I somehow seem to attract them wherever I go.

One day, I was visiting my friend Debra in southeast Texas when a calico cat wandered onto her porch. I put some food out for her and asked if she could sleep with me that night. I'd been fostering kittens for a rescue in Las Vegas for a few years, but right now I wasn't in my own home.

Without pausing, Debra said yes.

That night as the cat lay next to me graciously purring, I suddenly felt her belly moving. This fur baby was going to have babies!

The next morning, I told Debra about kitty's belly rolling. Our nine-year-old granddaughters were excited to foster her and quickly named her "Sugarplum."

It was spring break, and they were coming to stay a week with us, six hours away. We made sure that Sugarplum had a safe haven while they were gone. When they returned home, Debra called to tell me that the kittens had been born: two Siamese mixes (one boy, one girl), a black-and-white boy, and an orange tabby girl.

Debra moved Sugarplum and her babies inside until they were ready to be weaned. Then she made another six-hour drive to bring them to me so that I could get them into a rescue.

We had recently moved across the U.S. and were renting a home from one of my best friends, Shelly. She, too, opened her home to these kitties until they could be adopted. The two boys, Raj and Perry, were adopted the first day, and I began working as an adoption counselor with the rescue. A few months later, Sugarplum (now renamed Ruby) and her two other babies, Bo and Lucy, found their forever homes.

Since then, many more rescue cats have left an impression on my heart and found loving homes. I'm blessed and grateful to be surrounded by compassionate friends who didn't hesitate to welcome the calico stray and her kittens.

Doggone Goodness

By Marla David

To most who knew me, I'm sure I must have been "that crazy dog lady." I was tending to eight dogs, each with their own special gifts and quirky habits. That's right...eight! And I received so much goodness from each of them through the years.

Now, it hasn't even been a year since I've watched the last of my fur babies die. Over the last 10 months, I've gone through this heartbreak five times. Most of the dogs were old, and you can probably say I was running a senior home for dogs.

Just like humans, dogs also get ill, both physically and mentally, and they have a way of letting you know when it's time. Poor Harley, my Heinz 57, looked at me with her cloudy eyes, making moaning sounds. What else could I do? In such pain, I had them put her out of her misery. Buddy's health had declined; Paws developed problems, too. The Shih Tzu brothers came together and died together, side by side. Then they had peace. Lucy, the Jack Russell Terrier, took ill. She developed seizures and was never the same after that. About four months later, she died right in my arms. It was just too much for her. Oh, how dogs pull at your heartstrings.

Of all the goodbyes I've said, though, perhaps the hardest was saying goodbye to Sunshine. I knew that Sunshine – my first Jack Russell Terrier and my RCA Victor dog – would leave me one day. Knowing that didn't make it any easier, though. When you love a pet as deeply as I loved my Sunshine, "easier" is not part of the equation. I just knew that Sunshine was my doggie soulmate. We clicked instantly, and she was always by my side. She was the matriarch of the pack and an intuitive. I buried her on what would have been her 20th birthday. I remembered how I would sing to her – "You are my Sunshine..." – while I held her tight, stroking her and feeling the softness of her ears. I still tear up every time I get to that one part – "Please don't take my Sunshine away." Sigh.

While it's heartbreaking to have said goodbye to each of these dogs, I'm grateful for the goodness that they all brought to my life. They will each live in my heart forever.

Rose Petals of Empowerment

By Carrie Kondor

Walking barefoot on the cool, open fields, I felt the soft ground under my feet. The evening was filled with the warm and vibrant hues fading into blues of the setting sun. It was the night of the full moon.

My Soul Sister and I had decided to create a blessing ceremony to celebrate our achievements and to untie the straps of untruths that wrapped around our beingness.

I was in awe of the magic around us: the shimmering and glistening lights of the fireflies, the sounds of the water trickling below, and the call of a nearby woodpecker.

After I laid out the brightly colored butterfly scarf and gathered the roses we had brought, we sat in lotus position across from each other.

As I softly rapped on the hoop drum and chanted ancient Sanskrit, I felt the soft winds blowing through my hair. In this stillness, I opened to divine love, liberating the emptiness, the longing that was within me. A deep calm enveloped me. Feeling into that powerful, uninhibited woman within me, the message was clear: *Let go and trust.*

Together, we moved soundlessly to collect the rose petals and showered them upon each other as we broadcasted our truths of what we no longer wanted to be burdened with. With the intention of letting go of what was holding me back, celebrating the triumph of remembering – and claiming – who I AM, I felt the raw sweetness of rebirth of life.

The ruby, pink, apricot, and white rose petals danced as we sprinkled them onto ourselves, rejoicing letting go of the past, releasing the challenges we had overcome, and freeing ourselves by saying goodbye to the grief of yesterday.

Today is a new start; how sweet it is to remember and honor who you are.

Dog Therapy

By Nathalie Rivett

When I was nine, a neighbor's Cocker Spaniel bit my face. Shocked and panicked, I screamed, "Mom! The dog bit me!" It definitely hurt, but the mental and emotional scar was far worse than the physical one!

From that moment on, I developed an irrational fear of dogs. The mere thought of a dog was debilitating. No matter the size or breed, I would feel in danger next to one. In my adult years, I realized I would require some therapeutic help to overcome this old fear.

Then, three years ago, a close friend adopted a cute seven-month-old stray female dog from a shelter. As soon as I met this shy puppy, I felt a gentle heart-opening shift within me. Amazingly, I instantly warmed up to her. Even more amazingly, when I found out she had a sister who also needed a new home, my heart said, "You could foster her!" Little did I know that this was the start of a love story and a healing journey for this rescue puppy and me.

My anxiety rose as I went to pick up my new puppy. She was thin and dirty, had kennel cough, and was infested with ticks, and her behavior showed signs of abuse. *What am I getting myself into?* I wondered. But the moment this adorable Australian Shepherd and Black Lab mix climbed into my car, my heart just melted.

Clearly, we were meant to be united for therapy! One day at a time, she's taught me trust, respect for dogs, and unconditional love. She has been the missing link that's allowed me to open my heart to forgiveness and goodness in my life. With love, patience, and compassion, Jazmine became strong and healthy – the perfect, happy, obedient family dog.

We nurture each other effortlessly, and gratefulness for her healing presence fills my heart every day. It often feels like Jazmine adopted *me*, and she is the best therapy I could have wished for!

Goodness Soothed My Aching Heart

By Nancy Merrill Justice

One of my dearest and most devoted longtime friends, Jeanette, was the first to arrive that morning – thoughtfully handing me a treasured Peet's cappuccino, which she knew would bring me comfort.

I have always appreciated and admired Jeanette for her strength of character and undying devotion to our friendship. Her unanticipated presence today touched my heart in an especially deep and profound way. Even her heart-of-gold husband, David, had come in support, even though he had to make pre-scheduled business calls outside in the warmth and humidity to avoid disturbing the gathering inside. Although I had told them not to make the long drive to attend (it was their wedding anniversary with a full day planned), my devoted friends stood by my side once again, supporting me with hearts full of goodness and love.

Shortly after Jeanette and David's arrival, my wonderful nephew, Adam stopped by. Next, my lovely friend and longtime healthcare consultant, Bruce, then veterinarian Dr. Jeni, followed by our sweetest and best-ever groomer of eight years, Shelle. These special souls rearranged their busy schedules with short notice and traveled long distances – each wanted to be present in genuine support. This was the day I had dreaded for many months, but my aching heart melted in gratitude as I looked at each of them gathered in the living room, pouring love all over Annie.

Although quite small for a Cocker Spaniel, Annie was a black beauty with the biggest of loving personalities. She had touched many lives during her 16 years, so it was not surprising when we all began sharing "Annie stories" that either made us laugh or that still amazed us. These shared memories cut through some of the heaviness of dread that permeated the air.

Through my heartache and impending grief, I had promised myself I would stay in appreciation – for the 16 wonderful years of loving, soulful companionship Annie had given me and for each of the loving family and friends who had come with their hearts of goodness to bid Annie farewell. Through goodness, Annie's sweet spirit rejoiced anew in Heaven.

Experiencing Calm
By Michelle R. Griffith

"You know why I like horses?" Gabe asked. "They don't make you guess."

Gabe has autism. He is finding words to express his experiences and exchanges with others. He is learning about frustration and calm.

"I know what he is thinking," Gabe continued. "He shows me with his body, and I get it. I know how to act back to him. I'm just here, and he is just here. I'm brushing, and he is calm. I know he doesn't like his back leg brushed because he swished his tail at me. People should be more like horses."

Gabe has confidence with the horse. He isn't confused or trying to make sense of a bunch of words and questions. He isn't being rushed or pressured to finish, and he finds words to describe what's happening. Gabe connects the word *calm* with the feeling in his own body and the body language of the horse.

"I know he is calm because one foot is tipped up on the toe and not standing flat. That means he doesn't want to run away. You know horses run away when they are frustrated."

The horse raised his head and pricked his ears forward as the breeze picked up.

"Now he hears something. I know this because his head is up and his ears are up," Gabe said. "But he is calm because his foot is still tipped up."

Gabe will continue to navigate the breeze of change as inputs and expectations get faster and bigger through his high-school years. He may get frustrated, act out, and be told to calm down. Since Gabe has experienced calm in his own body, he will have a realistic connection to the word *calm*. Given some space to process, Gabe will be able to access his simple exchange with a horse and his authentic experience of calm.

Furry Angels

By Tiffany Andersen

Do you believe in angels? I do. I believe that God sees and hears all; and when it matters most, he answers with furry angels.

I cried my eyes out one night knowing that it wouldn't be possible for me to have children. Newly married to the love of my life, I realized for the first time that I actually wanted a child; but between the life-altering accident at 15 and stage IV cancer at 34, I knew that children would never be. I would never peer into the eyes of a life I created in love. This heartbreaking realization almost became too much. My husband, coming in to see his beloved wife upset, gently said to me, "Honey, let's just get another puppy – you know, the kind you love so much – the little Chihuahuas. Let's get a black one that looks like Harley."

Everyone knows I love little dogs, but we already had three! How many furry animals did I need to make up for not having children? I didn't want another dog; I wanted a baby with skin, not fur. But Tony insisted: "Honey, all you need is a puppy. It will help." I said maybe, but I honestly had no plans to look for another animal.

Later that night, my phone rang. "Hi, Tiffany; it's Lisa. I'm sorry it's so late, but I found one of those dogs you love so much – you know, those little Chihuahuas? He's only about two months old, and we can't keep him here. Any chance you want him?"

Wow, I thought. *God, are you literally bringing me a puppy TONIGHT because you see how sad I am?* I told Lisa to bring him right over. Incredibly, he was a little black Chihuahua, just like Tony said I should get – the sweetest little puppy I have ever had – and he instantly removed the baby blues. That night – and every night thereafter – he cuddled into my neck to be safe with me, his new mommy.

Chopper is a custom-ordered angel that God dropped down from Heaven, and he could not be more perfect. He will always be proof to me that God delivers angels in all shapes and sizes, exactly when they are needed.

The Deep Kindness of a Cat

By Helen Ferrara

Early one Sunday morning, I was getting ready to hold a Chakradance workshop. Mocha, my cat, was awake, too. After having a drink, she walked up to me, so I paused what I was doing and bent down to stroke her. She was my Earth Angel, a 17-year-old brown Burmese who invariably joined me whenever I meditated, and curled up near me when I worked at my writing. She'd been getting frail, and I dreaded the thought of a last trip to the vet with her.

I'd barely touched her, when she looked up at me and meowed really loudly. For those familiar with Burmese cats, you'll know that their meowing is quite loud and distinctive, but if their needs are met, they don't meow much. Well, Mocha meowed much louder than ever before, and went on and on for a few minutes, like she was really telling me something. My overwhelming feeling was that she'd just told me she was going to pass away.

I took her into the back yard (it was the middle of October – spring in Australia), and she spent the morning lying a while in each of her favourite spots. I went to the Chakradance workshop and danced for her, not knowing if I would see her alive again.

But she waited for me to get back; she hadn't eaten anything the whole day, and by then she had stopped drinking, too. We sat together on the front verandah as the sun set. Then I put her in a soft basket and on our bed, where she curled up. My husband and daughters spent some time with her, too, and she purred when we stroked her – but it was so faint, it could barely be felt.

She stayed on the bed the whole night. At 5 a.m., I saw that her breathing had gone very light. She didn't wake, and I knew she wouldn't again.

By dying in her way, Mocha saved me from the fearful last trip to the vet.

Grey and Bearded, Kind and Giving

By Faye Rogers

There once was a small puppy with hairy legs who travelled all the way from Ireland to New Zealand. This puppy became a massive 110 kg Irish Wolfhound with a grey beard, hairy eyebrows, and personality to boot. People just loved him. Wherever he went he would find the right people to attach himself to, and they in return loved the attention he gave them. He would find youths who were without a home who needed solidity. He would find the elderly and quietly embrace them with love. He would find youngsters who were terrified of dogs, and he would charm them. He was also full of laughter, always up to antics, always wanting to please others through his comical ways. Strong-minded, determined, and incorrigible, Bran lived every minute as if it counted, making the most of every opportunity.

One of the people he adopted was Jay, a man who came to live with us at a time when he needed a good friend and somewhere to rest out of the storm of life. Bran and Jay became best buddies. When Jay was killed in a motorcycle accident, Bran was heartbroken. He refused to eat for weeks and would just lie there with mournful eyes.

We had trouble finding Jay's next of kin, as his mother refused to be responsible for his body to bury him. Luckily, an uncle stepped forward so that Jay could receive a proper send-off. Jay's funeral was massive, and his friends asked if Bran could lead the procession. Bran took this in stride, walking out front of over 1,000 motorcyclists, and led Jay to his final resting place.

Bran's verve returned, and it wasn't long before he was receiving appeals to come and hang out in some of Auckland's finest pubs and cafés as people were missing him. He had more to do, more people to charm, and more people to help, and he gladly gave his kindness to many.

Oreo the Cow

By Tessa Shaffer

On the Witmer Farm, there's peace among the animals. The chickens don't chase the bunnies and the cats don't chase the chickens, but each group does have its own pecking order. The largest cow on my stepdad's farm is a steer that's over 2,000 pounds, all black except for a wide white band around his belly and a small spot on his head. The neighbor kids call him "Oreo." Although there is a fence between Oreo and everyone else, my stepdad taught us to watch for threat displays, telling us stories of other bulls who had kicked out teeth. But there was something unique about Oreo, other than the patch of hair on his forehead that he would sometimes let me pet into a heart shape through the fence. Despite his blocky, muscular size, he has a softness in his eyes, where I sense a beautiful soul I call "Handsome One."

Often, when cows give birth, they go off alone over the hill where we can't see them. We started to notice Oreo sometimes standing alone on the crest of the hill. It was his signal to us that a new calf had arrived. He continued to do this for each birth, even standing alert outside the door of the barn one day when all the cows were accounted for in the field. When we went to investigate, there was a sheep inside the barn in labor. It was not only surprising that Oreo was so in tune, but his signal allowed us to assist animals who needed help delivering.

When Oreo's own mother had a calf, it happened on the side of the hill where we could watch. Oreo held the other cattle back from interrupting while his mom licked her new baby. After she was done, Oreo slowly walked up to the calf and gave it a big lick, welcoming it into the family. For the first time ever, all the other cows formed a line to give kisses as well. He's created a kinder herd and has a permanent place on the farm helping birth and babysit calves.

People Are a Problem

By Marci Kobayashi

As the road curved around toward the bridge, I saw the orange tabby cat sunning himself on the bank. Though I walk through his territory often, I rarely see him. I feel lucky whenever I catch a glimpse of him napping in the bushes or patrolling the river bank. Today he was sitting in plain view. I presumptuously took this as an invitation to stop and visit.

When I sat down near him on the grass, I thought he might move away. Instead, he shifted his weight and continued looking out at the river. I started to feel bad. Maybe I was intruding. Maybe he was irritated. "People are a problem," I heard in my head. I agreed and imagined all the ways people must interfere with his life – the nosey walkers like me, the dog owners, the cyclists...*Crash!*

I whipped my head around. There was a young boy in the middle of the road trapped under his bicycle. He must have taken the corner a little too fast. I raced over to help him and was relieved when he stood up, shocked but uninjured. After a few words, the boy got back on his bicycle and pedaled away.

With the excitement over, I looked back to my spot in the grass. The cat was gone, so I continued my walk, thinking about the boy. His accident reminded me of years ago when I, too, had crashed my bicycle. A nice lady had stopped to ask if I was okay. A thought popped into my head: "People are nice, you know." I chuckled to myself and hoped the cat had been watching me with the boy. Maybe he would understand that sometimes people are nice. I looked up. The cat WAS watching. Had he been following me? He sat there facing the road. Facing me!

Then I got it. My exchange with the boy was not to show the tabby cat that people were nice. It was to remind *me*. I bowed my head and thanked him. All the way home I chanted, "People are nice, you know! People are nice."

Tucker's Gift

By Trena Anderson

It began on a blustery, freezing cold February morning. As my daughter, Jordyne, and I walked through the front door of a horse sale, we noticed a strategically placed cardboard box with a sign that read "FREE PUPPIES."

Over the next 12 years with our family, Tucker shared many moments of gratitude and spontaneity, tears of joy, laughter, and heartfelt licks. He served as an overwhelming source of comfort even in the darkest moments, when his nurturance through a simple touch of his tongue would dissipate the tears and remind you that you are never alone. He was our family's "Walmart Greeter," an instigator, and an avid hunter. To him, being in joy was of utmost value. His zest for life also showed up in his love for food — his exuberant display of how everything tasted wonderful.

More than anything, Tucker taught us through his willingness to be present with every moment. Even in our last hours together, with his tired body and diminished eyesight, he showed a readiness to greet the unknown, just as he had always invited every new moment, every new guest, and every experience. This moment, too, was accompanied by a knowing that another "new" was occurring. His spirit exuded a sense of calm and complete relaxation.

Tucker's openness to free himself of the old body that no longer worked for him allowed me to acknowledge how much we, as humans, hang on to things, relationships, and thoughts that no longer work for us, rather than making a simple choice to let go and begin again. Tucker showed that he knew there was no "end."

Tucker, I thank you for allowing me to witness where I've limited myself or gotten caught up in what I had perceived as hard moments. Thank you for your gift of trust and the ease and joy that you showed me is truly available in every moment. Thank you for the growth and expansion that, even in your final moments here, you offered me in consciousness and connection. I'm so grateful. You continue to touch the lives of many.

From My Hands to My Heart
By Nora Rose

My mother had the wisdom to know that planting a garden was the best way to bring the feeling of family to any given situation.

In the final years of her life, she had trouble walking due to congestive heart failure and couldn't see very well because of her diabetes, so I brought the garden inside. Together, in large pots we put fresh soil and planted basil in one and tomatoes in the other and then set them in the sunroom. Each day, she could water the plants.

The tomatoes grew, but the sweet basil grew wild! The beautiful green, elongated, heart-shaped leaves that curled on the end had a strong, sweet, minty smell that filled the room when they were picked. This was an essential ingredient in Italian cooking. My mother put the basil in pasta, on pizza, and mixed into salads with tomatoes, olive oil, pepper, and sea salt. It was our time to talk, cook together, and enjoy a delicious meal.

I was heartbroken when my mother passed. When summer arrived, as a way to process my grief, I prepared a garden outside in her honor.

In the glorious hot sun, the dog and I gathered gloves, a shovel, the wheelbarrow, and a rake, and we got to work. All of a sudden, I heard voices and slamming doors. The dog began to bark. I walked over to a driveway filled with cars. My dearest friends and neighbors, with unbelievable kindness, showed up in my yard with plants and tools to help with the garden. My daughters smiled. As we kneeled and put our hands in the dirt, many stories were shared. Some were about my mother, their mothers, and the joys and tears of being a mother, daughter, sister, aunt, and friend. I am so grateful for their generosity.

The garden will always be part of the yard, shared from generation to generation. It is alive and well and always reminds me of my mother.

And to this day, the indoor basil plant is still growing wild!

Goodness Abounds, Even in Death

By Claire Chew

One Sunday 14 years ago, I was sent to pick up a rescued pup and bring her back to the adoption fair where I was volunteering. I wasn't planning on bringing her home, but there she was, the sweetest canine soul with the most loving eyes that could melt the hearts of strangers. If eyes are windows to our souls, hers were extraordinary – a perfect match to her name, Lulu.

Lulu had an inviting spirit about her. Her patience was unwavering and steadfast. You would never find her demanding love or food. Her strategy was to wait for a morsel to drop from the table or to lie strategically with her legs up for a belly rub. Graceful and patient, part Border Collie, part Kuan Yin, she knew exactly when love was needed. On our daily walks, she offered her love freely. When someone in the family was feeling sad, she was right there, putting her head in their lap.

After her 13th birthday, her health began to decline. One week before Christmas, she had a stroke. Reaching for food became challenging, yet she kept trying. Even after her legs grew weak, her grace and dignity remained intact. She would stand at the back door, until one of us could help her down the three steps to the back yard so she could do her "business." Then she had another stroke right after her 14th birthday.

She continued to persevere. On good days, she would go about to greet others on our daily walk, sharing her love. Then a cough appeared, and it turned into respiratory failure. Even as her breath became shallow and labored, she still offered her head in my lap for love. She wanted to make sure we were okay. With dignity and grace, she kept her heart available through her last breath.

In her absence, there is a great void, yet Lulu continues to remind me to keep my heart open to love, giving everyone the benefit of the doubt and offering love to those who need it. May her goodness prevail.

An Autumn Walk

By Joy Harris

Loving the colors of the fall leaves on the trees comes to me naturally. My mother and grandmother loved the oranges, russets, and burgundies of the colorful leaves as well.

One afternoon, we decided to take a walk to look at the turning leaves. After a long way, we came upon an old woman hanging wash on a rope clothesline. She had done it a thousand times before – probably every week of her adult life. She hung the laundry in a single, gentle move – one that she had done so many times, she could do it in her sleep. We thought she must be bored, so we asked her if she would take a walk with us to see the fall leaves and to break away from her drudgery. She made excuses not to take a walk in the middle of the day with so much laundry to hang.

So we hung laundry with her and found there was something therapeutic about the rhythmic dance of hanging it on the line. We soon moved in an assembly-line style of cooperation and hung the rest of the clothes from the basket with ease.

We were determined to get her to realize that she deserved to take a break, to see how awesome it would be to walk among the autumn leaves before the north wind blew them all away. The woman agreed to take a walk but not until the all the laundry was hung on the line. Then she produced two more baskets full and told us that all the lines would be full by the time the laundry was hung.

We found ourselves in a meditative state, using smooth movements of hanging laundry and seeing it flapping in the breeze. Once the woman discovered that we enjoyed hanging the laundry, she took off on a walk and left us with a half basket left to hang.

I hope she enjoyed her walk; we continued ours as soon as we'd finished hanging the remaining laundry. The leaves were never prettier than on that day.

Yoga Nidra Prayer Mascots

By Cynthia Lee Horn

I love creating sacred time with others – bringing like-minded and diverse people together in creative ways, like a conductor of a symphony! In one of my past careers, as a 911 dispatcher, I loved coordinating EMS, fire fighters, and police – it was like choreographing a dance. During another time in my life, I hosted a monthly "Great Soul Gathering" in my home. We'd all enjoy great conversation over a potluck dinner, then I'd guide us through some gentle living-room yoga and light meditation. In whatever form it takes, I love to co-create with willing souls, feeling the goodness of the group's collective energy ripple out and touch lives. "For where two or more are gathered..."

But when others aren't available to play and co-create with me, I sometimes feel disappointed. So when I'm without human companionship, as is often the case during my assignments as a professional pet sitter, I often rally the pets in! They're usually quite willing to join me for yoga or to sit close while I work on creative projects. That's exactly what happened this morning.

I'm currently pet sitting two dogs: a Great Dane named Joey and a Parti Standard Poodle named Talbot. My clients live in a quiet area near the mountains in the far north part of Peoria, Arizona – a beautiful spot for yoga nidra! So, early this morning, I set myself up outside on the double lounge under the stars and moon and began my prayer and yoga nidra time. Both pets were settled in a distance away. Shortly after I began, though, Joey came over and rested her chin directly on mine, breathing with me. Later, midway through, I opened my eyes to see that Talbot had moved right next to me, attentively standing guard like a royal sentry.

My flower essence teacher and mentor for 10 years, Lila Devi, has pointed out that some animals are actually altruistic; I agree! Truly, it's almost as though, at times, pets are able to cross the line between instinct and intuition. They are deeply sensitive, spiritual beings, and I'm honored to create "symphonies" with them!

Be the Good

By Davalynn Kim

I was in a dark place. Everyday battles had left me feeling unarmed against an army of Alzheimer's and cancers. The simple beauty of life escaped me. I had never been one for self-pity, but I was adrift in a sea of anguish, and my boat was sinking fast. Something had to give, and that "something" had to be me.

Ultimately, what made the difference wasn't my young son making a 360-degree turn in his behavior or the random financial gifts that came during a time of need. It wasn't the work-from-home position that surfaced a week after I fell to my knees praying for a solution. Yes, I did feel blessed that my father's cancer was cured and the progress of my mother's dementia slowed, but those blessings were not what brought me back. It was the everyday wonders of Creation.

I began bird watching. Their colors and songs captivate me. The way they share the bounty at the feeder, uncaring if they are of the same feather, mesmerizes me. I whistle the perky tune of the white-throated sparrow and delight at their response. Birds supply such a magical symphony for our lives. They sing of His Goodness.

I began caring for flowers. An abundance of blooms grace my surroundings. I speak to them and they flourish. Isn't their transformation from a simple seed miraculous? His Masterpiece is a living work of art. I have a slice of Paradise in my own back yard. Oh, there is nothing quite like the sweet smell of the mandevilla wafting lazily on a balmy summer breeze! Botanical beauty symbolizes the ability to transform from something small and plain into something greater, something sensational!

From a rose-colored moon in a cerulean sky, to the towering pines, to the ten thousand types of feathered friends taking flight, evidence of goodness surrounds us every day. We are each a Light of the world entrusted to care for His Works. We are all inherently good. When we are having trouble seeing the good, it is simply time to *be* the good, and our eyes will open anew.

An Angel for Our Animals

By Alison Ellison

Ken, a retired police officer, has dedicated his time, attention, and resources to caring for animals that have no one else to care for them. He runs a local SPCA chapter and has made this program his life's mission.

What makes Ken so extraordinary is his way of making sure the animals always come first. There is a vigorous training program for volunteers, which Ken runs himself. Ken personally meets every family who is interested in adopting a pet. When an animal is sick, Ken will stay at the shelter throughout the night, knowing there is no staff member on duty. On Christmas morning, Ken hand delivers goodies to each and every dog, cat, rabbit, and bird that may not have a home on Christmas Day.

Ken has a no-nonsense approach and, by his own admission, isn't overly affectionate with the humans in his world. Rather, his whole focus is on the animals. When you ask him how and why he is such an advocate, he will unapologetically tell you that he considers himself the voice and the protector of those that have no voice and have no other protection.

While his manner with people can seem abrupt and short, it is quickly evident that he fully chooses to expend his patience, gentleness, and kindness with the animals. He kneels down to look each and every new potential adoptee in the eye, soothing them with soft, kind words. Sadie, a parrot, lived on Ken's shoulder for three weeks until she found a home. You see, unless Sadie was on Ken's shoulder, she would frantically pull out her feathers.

Ken lives his life with his higher calling at the forefront. His own personal GPS system is guided by the knowledge that every day and in every way, he is living in full authenticity and bold goodness of what matters most without succumbing to pressure from others to do or be any certain way. He personifies strength, humility, and presence, and he is a haven for any animal needing a home.

Blessings to all our animal caregivers!

Gift of the Garden Light

By Michelle Smith Mufarreh

The day my tuxedo cat Mitts died, the sun was shining just perfectly through the windows, illuminating a shiny spot on my studio floor.

I was scheduled to work that day. And work for me meant flying away. I had been off for weeks, and this was my first day back. Mitts had been sick for many months. I didn't know this would be the day she would move out of her body.

I had been talking with her for some time about leaving. I told her I would help her if needed. I also suggested that she could walk out of her body into the sunlight whenever she felt ready. She loved being outdoors, and we had spent many hours in the garden together. So I showed her pictures in my mind of the sun shining onto the grass and into the flower beds and an image of her stepping out of her body into that garden light. I sensed that this light would aptly lead her from her tired body to the freedom and lightness of spirit.

She wasn't ready yet, though. Healing was taking place between her and my other cats. Mitts had been a defiant loner. But the past few months had brought opportunity for all of them to make peace with her.

So this morning when my Mitts greeted me and moved gingerly toward me and that patch of light on the studio floor, I just sat down. I drew her close and said, "Mitts, this would be a perfect day to go. You can do it. See the sunlight there for you." I hesitated just a bit and then checked my heart. The guidance was there. I should keep a normal schedule just as we had been doing throughout her illness.

I left then with tender acceptance. While grieving, a part of me cheered her on toward this crossing journey. I hugged my husband goodbye and told him to check on her very soon. She would likely be leaving today.

With the perfect and timely beckoning of nature's light, she did...before I was even off the ground.

Have Some of Both
By Michelle R. Griffith

Looking to the west tonight at dusk, the lovely blue sky is still visible. It is a bold canvas for white, fluffy clouds and intermittent rain clouds. The rain clouds are dark gray and heavy with condensation, dripping tiny streams of teardrops not quite making it to the ground.

I scan the horizon to the east, looking for a rainbow – nothing at the moment. As I turn back to the west, the sun is splitting through the mix of clouds sprouting golden rays of light high up through the white, fluffy tops, like a graphic rendition of sunshine rays on a breakfast logo. In the same cloud, I can see the heavy trails of rain sneaking toward the green spring earth. It smells like rain. It looks like the gaze of Mother Nature shining with rays of light from one eye and winking tears from the other.

Mother Nature is offering me a glimpse of her wisdom about all or nothing. My human perspective often leads me down a path of polarity to the garden of either/or. It taunts me in times of change and polarizing political landscape. It nags me to choose a side. My human perspective tells me I can't have both.

In stark contrast, this beautiful look into the eyes of Mother Nature reminds me that sometimes it *can* be both. Most of the things we hold as opposite that create polarization are really just elements of the same thing. The sky today has all the elements for sun, clouds, and rain in the same space, with the same ingredients, just in different proportions.

Thank you, Mother Nature, for showing me an alternative to my human path of polarity. I realize that following along the twisted path of either/or is not necessary. The sun and the rain are both at home with the blue-sky backdrop. In this time of us-versus-them polarity, I choose to listen more and tune in to what might happen if the choice is actually to have some of both.

Blessed by a Butterfly

By Pauline Hosie Robinson

Sunlight sparkled on the water as I approached the bay. Weighed down by a heavy heart, I knew it was time to surrender my pain. Gently, I cupped my hands and offered my despair to the Universe. Breathing deeply, I focused on the aliveness around me. As the weight of despair lifted from my shoulders, I noticed a beautiful butterfly on the grass. Turquoise wings folded, she rested without movement. Believing her to be dying, I gave thanks to the Butterfly Nation for the joy they bring to our world.

To my surprise and delight, the blue triangle butterfly flew onto my arm. Expecting her to fly away at any moment, I stood quietly. After a short while, I realized the butterfly was not in a hurry to leave. Overjoyed, I spoke gently to her, thanking her for sharing her delicate beauty with me. Those glorious turquoise wings remained closed.

Knowing I needed to return home, I asked the butterfly if she wished to accompany me. Believing this delicate creature was offering me the gift of healing, I walked home with her on my arm. Once home, I sat in my lounge in silent gratitude. Within the silence, I remembered that it was the same day at this exact time a week ago that I had received the sad news of a Facebook friend's passing.

Part of a loving group with a deep soul connection, I logged on to chat with those online. Mentioning our friend's passing and my delightful butterfly visitor, it soon became clear that many in the group had shared a butterfly connection with our departed friend. Content to stay on my arm as I typed, my beautiful companion added magic to each moment as we shared tender messages online.

Hours later as I signed off, my butterfly opened her wings and flew to the door of my office. Surprised and delighted to see her fly, I jumped up quickly to open the door for her. As she flew away, I gave thanks for her gift of kindness and the message she reinforced that day: *Goodness abounds in our world in so many ways.*

Chapter 6
Kindness at Work & School

There's an unfortunate stereotype of unsympathetic bosses who don't care about their employees' happiness or well-being. (If you've ever seen the movie *Office Space*, you probably remember Gary Cole's character, Bill Lumbergh, who nonchalantly told a Monday-Friday employee just before 5 p.m. on Friday: "Yeeaahh…I'm gonna need you to go ahead and come in tomorrow…oh, and I almost forgot: I'm also going to need you to go ahead and come in on Sunday, too.") Yes, mean bosses do exist (we've certainly had a few!), but so do ones who care about their employees, do everything they can to improve their work experience, and even go above and beyond to help them in their personal lives. (Fortunately, we've had bosses like this, too!)

The same goes for co-workers, teachers, students, and mentors in every field. Despite the occasional "bad apple," we've found that the good people far outweigh the bad (or occasionally insensitive) ones in any job, school, or professional relationship. And we're so glad that we get to shine a light on some of these big-hearted bosses, marvelous mentors, caring clients and co-workers, and spreaders of goodness in schools, offices, and homes around the world.

In this chapter, you'll find accounts of colleagues coming together to help a co-worker in a time of need, clients who taught and inspired their mentors, and bosses who gave much more than a paycheck. We hope these stories touch your heart, put a smile on your face, and remind you that school and work don't necessarily have to be places of toil and suffering – they can provide endless opportunities for sharing goodness!

How Was Your Game?

By Dan Teck

I actually liked my first few years of school. The classes were fun, and the teachers were nice, guiding us through the unfamiliar yet intriguing terrain of letters, words, numbers, and ideas. Somewhere along the line, however, I began to see teachers as adversaries whose primary goal was to keep you in line, quash any form of self-expression, and enforce the school-wide ban *on joie de vivre* (and gum). In this new world order, it was us against them.

There were exceptions, however – most notably my cello teacher, Mr. Sophos. From the first moment I began lessons (in sixth grade), he made me feel more welcome than any other teacher had done. With his orange velour V-neck shirts, quintessentially Greek curly gray hair, and genuinely warm smile, he immediately put me at ease. Somewhere in the back of my mind, though, I feared that the other shoe would drop and he'd eventually reveal himself as "one of *Them.*" After all, he was still technically a *teacher* and, therefore, someone to be wary of.

Eventually, a conflict did arise: my Little League baseball championship game fell on the same day as my cello lesson. But Mr. Sophos was very understanding and was happy to reschedule. The night after the game, though, he called me at home. I was worried that, upon reflection, he'd become upset about me missing my lesson and would chastise me for not having my priorities straight. What he said, however, caught me by surprise: "How was your game?" I offered the briefest-possible summary and then launched into a preemptive explanation of how I was still keeping up with my cello exercises, learning my practice pieces, working on my bowing techniques…but he cut me off. "That's fine. I just wanted to know how your game went," he said cheerfully.

In that moment, a gestalt shift in my brain revealed a new reality: a *teacher* cared about me. Not me-as-student but me-as-person – simply *me*. He had no ulterior motive. There was no "us against them" – it was just *us*.

Today, I can't remember who won that game or what cello pieces I was learning at the time, but I do remember that feeling of being cared about. And all it took was a simple question – "How was your game?" – that conveyed a simple yet life-changing statement: *I care about you.*

Help from a Generous Heart

By Lori Thiessen

It started with a pre-dawn phone call from my young-adult son, who was temporarily living away from home. His car had just broken down on the freeway. He was standing alone beside it, traffic whizzing by, asking what to do next.

I tried to stay calm as I directed him to call a tow truck and get the car towed to the service garage near his place. After a few more words of encouragement, I hung up, then wrung my hands in despair. I had no idea how we were going to pay for the tow truck or what to do about repairs.

Work that day was equally chaotic. I struggled to keep the tears back. Things were busy, though, so I had to keep going. Late in the day, I needed to go down to the front reception for something, and as I walked past our senior admin lady, she smiled brightly and asked how I was. I'd been avoiding eye contact with everyone else, but I had to look at her when she spoke to me. I didn't say anything, but she saw on my face that there was a big problem. Nobody else was around, so I blurted out the whole story. She handed me a Kleenex, then directly asked me, "How much money do you need?" I wasn't sure I heard her correctly, but she repeated herself, then explained her belief that God had given her resources so she could help others.

Her reassuring voice and matter-of-fact, let's-just-get-this-taken-care-of manner settled my frantic thoughts. I went back to my office and tried to accomplish something in the bit of time left in the day. Within a few minutes of the business closing, she was in my office, cheque in hand.

"Here you go," she stated. "Now, you just don't say anything. Use that for what you need, and don't even think of paying me back."

With deep gratitude, I accepted the money – amazed at the gift and the goodness that abounds in our world.

When the Client Becomes the Mentor

By Maureen Hollmeyer

As a social worker for over 15 years, I would like to thank each one of my clients and their families for allowing me into their lives during their most delicate and fragile times. While I hope I have taught them something during our time together, I can say with absolute certainty that *they* have taught *me* some of the most valuable lessons of my life.

The homeless have taught me that we can still be happy without material belongings, as long as we have love in our heart. Nobody can take that away. Also, that everybody is only one catastrophe away from being homeless.

The mentally ill have taught me that it's not a choice but a physical condition that can be stabilized with medications. I have witnessed many people who, once they received help, transformed their lives and accomplished what they had once thought to be impossible.

The elderly have taught me that they are, as the saying goes, "old and wise." While working with them, I have learned manners, respect, kindness, laughter, and genuine love. They have lived a life we will never know, and they have lessons to pass on to the next generation.

The abused and neglected children have taught me that a child will always seek love from their parents, no matter how awful the situation. Some children spend years chasing this dream, even when the parents are unaware because of their own deep issues and pain. Sometimes it's safer and healthier to make your friends your family.

The victims of domestic violence have taught me courage. It is possible to untangle the web of an abuser's control and anger. It can be tricky, but it *can* be done. Those who have survived give others hope, and I admire their persistence in establishing a better life.

The at-risk teenagers have taught me that they need only one mentor to care about their future and well-being. They are a product of their environment and just need a little guidance and stability. When encouraged, through the heart and with love, they can succeed.

I have become a better person through my clients and what they have taught me. My career has opened my heart and mind. My only hope is that I have been able to make an impact on their lives, too.

Flying on the Wings of Kindness

By Eva Muserelli

It was Monday morning and, as usual, I was busy at my desk when my phone rang. "Mom, I just found out I'm being deployed this weekend."

"Again?" I said. "You've only been back six months!" My son is in the Air Force and had already been deployed almost back-to-back to Iraq and Afghanistan. Thankfully, he'd made it home safely (aside from a few concussions and some minor injuries).

"I have to see you before I leave," he said. After a recent house remodel, money was tight, but I told him not to worry – I would be there...even though I wasn't sure how I was going to make it happen.

I hung up the phone, walked into my boss's office, and told him I needed time off the following day to visit my son before he left for Afghanistan for yet another year. Without hesitation, my boss said yes, but he didn't stop there. He handed me his credit card and told me to book my flight and take as much time as I needed; after all, it was the least he could do to thank my son for his service to our country. My eyes filled with tears, and my heart was overjoyed. His kindness allowed me to see my son for a few days and give him the love only a mother can (not to mention his favorite home-cooked meals), which is exactly what he needed as a send-off.

I am grateful that my son made it home safely again. And I am thankful for my boss's kindness. Could I have visited my son without his help? Yes, with some financial stress, but his kindness afforded me peace of mind. For a natural-born giver like myself, his kindness allowed me to open myself up to receiving. After all, that is what life is meant to be: a cycle of giving and receiving. I will never forget that moment of kindness.

God's Ace

By Brian Monahan

Early in my career, I ran a small audio-visual operation at a hotel 60 miles from my company's headquarters. At our events, it was not uncommon to fill clients' last-minute requests, such as needing a pair of wireless microphones around 6:00 p.m. That's where this story begins.

Steve Donahue, a co-worker I had never met, was nominated to bring the equipment from company headquarters. "Hi, Brian – great to meet you!" Steve said with a big smile. His face was puffy, he had a very noticeable limp, and his fingers were severely bent – but his smile was unstoppable. I had expected to be greeted by someone disgruntled, especially after being asked at the last minute to drive 60 miles in rush-hour traffic. Instead, I was amazed by the man I met. He looked to be physically in pain, but his demeanor was pure joy.

I came to learn that Steve had a significant case of arthritis that was destroying his body – but not his spirit. Steve was the company's "Ace" when it came to customer service: the first to grab the heaviest equipment and the first to greet the customer. If there was a project that needed something extra, Steve was on the job.

Steve and I collaborated on many projects in the 20 years that followed, including one that required travel and a massive load-in. Our customer shared his concern about Steve pushing it too hard. I explained that Steve didn't want our pity or worry, and that his can-do attitude was the thing keeping him alive. He would not let us take that away from him. That evening, in the privacy of the hotel room we shared, Steve loaded up his legs with ice bags. It was a rare behind-the-scenes glimpse, and suddenly, I was the one who was concerned. Still, the following morning, it was all smiles as we hit the show floor together.

Steve left his body last year, but his spirit and smile live on. I now realize he was God's "Ace."

Keys from the Heart

By Kimberly Hutt

In 1996, my husband and I purchased an old fixer-upper home. With love, sweat, tears, and persistence, we transformed that old house into a warm and welcoming home! Before long, family gatherings and special occasions filled the rooms with an energetic signature of love that was almost palpable...and often commented on by visitors. We had achieved our goal of resurrecting the old soul of this beautiful home — our job was complete!

Eventually, however, we made the difficult decision to sell it. Within weeks, we had multiple offers over asking price, and we accepted a purchase agreement. In the meantime, we found what we thought was the small hobby farm of our dreams. We started the process of due diligence, arranged financing, and placed an offer. It seemed like all our ducks were in a row.

Two days before our purchase was scheduled to be completed, however, our financing fell through and we were forced to abandon the contract. We now faced a real dilemma: We could go through with the sale of our house, which would leave us with nowhere to live; or we could back out of the deal, which would mean that we'd forego the money from the sale but would at least have a roof over our heads!

We decided to take a leap of faith and go through with the sale. This meant that we'd soon be moving out — unsure of where we would go — no home and no ideas!

Two weeks before moving day, we received a surprise visit from a couple whose home we were renovating. The woman handed me the keys and said, "I changed the sheets on the bed — you are staying together!" Not only did this kind couple let us stay in their house while we renovated it (and for as long as we needed, until we found a house of our own!), they also allowed us to stay in their beautiful cottage for a month during Christmas.

This couple will never know the extent of relief, gratitude, and love they shared that day...but *I* do!

Pursue Your Passion

By Robin Chellis

When I was around eight years old, I saw an artist drawing caricatures of people at a fair. I was intrigued with how he could capture someone's likeness so quickly. When I stopped to chat with him, he shared some tips and gave me some paper to try it for myself. I wasn't that good, but he told me "anyone can make art" and to keep practicing. I went home and set it aside. Occasionally, I would look at those drawings and practice…thinking I wanted to be an artist. Until one day I forgot about it.

Fast-forward to my first class in college: art. I remembered that moment from when I was little, and right then I decided to major in art. I had not practiced or done much art, but I loved every part of it: the color, the movement, the design, the power...the creativity of it all. Applying to art school, I felt a bit apprehensive as I didn't think I was great at drawing. But one of the teachers, who later became my favorite, said something similar to what the caricature artist had told me: "Everyone is creative, and anyone can create art." That helped me to pursue my passion. I went on to receive an art scholarship and get my bachelor's degree in visual art.

At first, life took me in a different direction. I became an energy healer. However, art was always there for me in the background, and I knew that one day art would also become a big part of my work. I had to be patient because I could feel there was a very specific type of art that wanted to come out. Some days I wondered if it ever would. And one day it did! Now I create beautiful energetic art that elicits a visceral reaction in others, and I LOVE doing it. I'm grateful for those people who made a positive impact on my life with a few simple encouraging words. They helped to cultivate my passion and make my dream a reality.

An Angel Named Joy

By Irene E. Bradford

In October 1989, I arrived in Stowe, Vermont, transitioning from a career in banking and financial planning in Boston to become a psychologist. I was applying to graduate programs when I met Joy in an aerobics class. She and her husband had retired to Stowe years earlier. I learned that she had practiced Jungian dream analysis and taught workshops at the C. G. Jung Institute in New York City prior to retiring. I asked her out for coffee to learn more about this vibrant woman and her psychology practice.

When we met for coffee, Joy arrived with a large shopping bag full of books on Jungian and depth psychology. Our mentorship began that day. She taught me how to remember and record my dreams and offered to interpret my dreams when next we met. I couldn't believe I was sitting with an angel!

I read ferociously, and each week Joy analyzed my dreams. She gave hours of her time and charged me virtually nothing. She said I would mentor another when the opportunity arose. And I did.

The crucible of our relationship provided the experiential learning of how to be a mentor/coach/therapist. She coaxed my underdeveloped intuition and creativity to the fore, steadily leading me inward to find my own answers through dreams, associations to symbols, and rich discussions. Foundationally, she believed that our truth is within. She would not take credit or even compliments for my epiphanies and healing, reminding me of *my* discovery. She guided me away from outer answers and validation to finding answers within. She weaned me from overusing my mind, teaching the wisdom of the heart.

I spent only nine months in Stowe, yet I continued to work with Joy over the phone throughout graduate school. We remain friends to this day. Joy gave me the courage to let go of attitudes, beliefs, and behaviors that did not belong to me. She guided me to choose new beliefs and attitudes consciously. She taught me wisdom for a lifetime simply out of the goodness of her heart. Her mentorship and generosity live on in my work and my life.

Public Display of Affection

By Heather Wiest

Leaning against the chain-link fence, my high-school sweetheart and I held each other close and shared a tender kiss. During this blissful embrace, Mr. Sheets, my guidance counselor, gently tapped me on the shoulder and stated, "No P.D.A. at school. I want to make sure we don't make any babies around here." He smiled, patting my back. "Now get to class."

Mr. Sheets always looked after me, making sure I stayed on track. At least once a week, he intentionally found me on campus to have a chat. He knew I lived with friends as an independent teen, and he aspired for me to graduate, pursue college, and thrive as a successful adult. This man truly cared for me, and I soon considered him my mentor. He encouraged me to dream big, challenged me to work hard, and motivated me through our weekly conversations. In an affirmative voice, he always responded to my requests, "Let me see what I can do." Mr. Sheets consistently modeled a healthy public display of affection. I trusted he always had my back.

During my senior year of high school, I surprisingly placed in the top 1% of my class! With the help of my counselor and mentor, I was awarded a full scholarship to a private university I had hoped to attend. Four years later, I graduated from this college with honors, obtained an amazing job as a high-school social worker, and began my graduate studies.

Mr. Sheets loved, served, and inspired me. And my life purpose has been to love, serve, and inspire those in my path. My soul swells in gratitude and joy for his tremendous influence upon my life! Full circle moments synchronize as I allow myself to be an instrument of Divine love and kindness, just as Mr. Sheets demonstrated for me.

Who has inspired you? And who do you inspire? We all make a difference. Never underestimate the power of one. One person. One smile. One word. One dream. One challenge. One percent. One public display of affection.

Taking Time to Check In

By Joanne Angel Barry Colon

In September 2016, one of my clients moved into a nursing home. I'd been seeing him for one-on-one rehabilitation training and Reiki for six years, and our intention was for me to continue his training and Reiki. However, scheduling became a challenge, and the nursing home was not open to independent trainers coming in.

After a few weeks of not seeing my client, I started missing him, so I paid him a visit. When I saw him, I was so excited; I felt as though my entire body was glowing. We sat down and talked for a bit, then his nurse came in. He introduced us, and I asked her if it would be okay to administer Reiki healing on him. The nurse said, "Of course!" It made me so happy to be able to help him in this way.

After that day, I made a commitment to myself that I would check in on him every other week to administer Reiki healing. Each time I saw him, I noticed my own energy shifting. I was extremely joyful and felt so much love from him – his smile was so big, which made *my* smile even bigger!

Most visits, I would bring him a gift – such as a crystal or gem, or an article or book I'd written – leaving him with something to remind him of our time together.

At the end of each visit, I felt uplifted and blissful – my heart was always filled with so much love. I would tell him how much I appreciated our time together, and he always called me his angel. Yet *he* was really *my* angel! Although my intention was to help make my client/friend feel better, I always walked out feeling better than when I'd walked in.

Thank goodness that goodness abounds!

Everyone Is Someone's Special Someone

By Melisa Archer

Do you ever have a moment that changes how you look at things? I recently had one.

While scrolling Facebook, I noticed a former co-worker's update. I reached out to touch base. Throughout our text conversation, Lynne revealed to me she had been working at the retirement home where my Nana had lived until she passed away last year. I asked, "Did you know my Nana?" Lynne asked what her name was, and I replied, "May."

Lynne paused. "Yes, I remember May. She had a bandage on her forehead." Learning that Lynne had spent time with my Nana, I momentarily lost my breath, and my heart skipped a beat. Lynne shared that they would wave to each other every day as she was leaving work. Once May passed, Lynne stopped exiting by the table where May used to sit in her wheelchair. Lynne contemplated if she should be connecting like this with residents because it was emotionally very hard for her once they passed.

Lynne was surprised to learn that May was my Nana, and she told me what a wonderful lady she was. Lynne reminisced about the time I had given her a chance at management years ago, telling me how much she had appreciated this opportunity, then reflected on positive memories we'd had throughout our years of working together.

My eyes welled up with tears, and emotions ran high as I realized that the extra attention I'd invested in developing Lynne as she was building her career had now gone full circle – from my caring for Lynne, to Lynne caring for my Nana, and my Nana caring for me. It was very overwhelming. I also realized that if everyone could just take a few minutes a day to be extra special to someone, this world would be such a better place because everybody is somebody's special someone. Nana was my special someone.

What an amazing gift! I went from a state of grieving the loss of my Nana to overflowing with gratefulness. I was so comforted, knowing I am part of a circle of love and joy that defies space and time.

Compassion Blooms to So Much More

By Jamie Lynn Thompson

Listening to Mrs. O. talk animatedly at kindergarten orientation, I could see and hear her excitement and her love for her new students – even before she met them. She spoke about a number of students in the class, including a disabled girl named Teri Anne. Mrs. O. proceeded to say, with tears in her eyes, "If all I teach the students this year is compassion, I have done my job." But I could tell she was a bit apprehensive about the year ahead, not knowing what to expect.

Right from the very beginning of the school year, however, the students embraced Teri Anne as one of them. They were taught the best ways to help her. I remember my son coming home one day so excited because he got to be Teri Anne's helper that day and push her wheelchair. As the school year continued, students even argued over who was helping Teri Anne each day.

On the last day of school, the school put on a track meet for the elementary students. Each student chose three events to participate in. Teri Anne was no exception. One student pushed her down the track, and she was all smiles.

Over the years, the class and the school as a whole continued to include Teri Anne in all school events, from chorus and band to prom and graduation. The girls didn't forget to invite Teri Anne to birthday parties either. The class included Teri Anne in everything, and she loves them all. You can see her light up when a classmate approaches her to say hello.

Year after year, the teachers told Teri Anne's mom that Teri Anne taught things in the classroom that they couldn't. A job well done, Mrs. O. and all the school staff. Compassion bloomed to so much more.

A Moment Can Change Everything

By Nicole Donovan-Wells

There are pivotal moments in life that can drastically alter our course if we choose to awaken to the magic that lives all around us. My 42nd birthday was one of those moments.

Six months earlier, I had made a decision to leave a 10-year career as a midwife. This decision shocked many and appeared to be the absolute wrong choice to almost everyone around me.

Yet a nagging whisper from deep within my gut told me it was time. My nervous system was suffering deeply. I struggled with anxiety, panic attacks, and depression that came crashing like high tidal waves, constantly trying to rip me into their current.

So I left it all behind to do my own healing work and began birthing a business supporting women who were longing to transform and rebirth their lives.

During that time, I had been feeling a pull toward a program called Chakredy by Alexis Saloutos, which connects chakra and organ energies to facilitate the path to healing on physical, mental, emotional, and spiritual levels. The program gripped my heart and wouldn't let go.

At the time, as a new business owner, finances needed to be delegated elsewhere, preventing me from signing up for the program. Instead, I entered every contest Alexis ran and showed up to every free informational call about the program.

My 42nd birthday arrived shortly after, and I received a message from Alexis asking if I was still interested in the program. You can probably guess my answer: "Yes! Of course I am. Here is why I haven't signed up yet…"

She messaged me back to tell me she wanted to gift me the program out of the goodness of her heart. No expectations. No payback needed. It was mine if I wanted it.

That was a moment when everything came together. My experience as a midwife deepened as I learned to energetically midwife women through the transitions of everyday life in this way. That moment changed everything for me and how I am able to offer my gifts to the world.

Programming in Poetry

By Cindy Smiczek

High school is tough: the racing hormones, the stressful pressures, the ever-present confusion about the future, and of course, the teachers and all those tests! Let's just say, the struggle is real. For me, though, there was a bright spot of kindness that shone through.

It was 1986, and I was a junior. Computers were showing up more in homes and in schools, and I decided that I needed to learn about programming. Mr. Murphy was going to be my BASIC programming teacher, and I knew it would be tough. Around the school, a familiar phrase was, "It's not fair; he's such a *hard* teacher!"

Mr. Murphy was as I expected: demanding, kind, and a bit sarcastic. "I apologize for the simplicity of this test," was his most infamous saying before beginning a grueling 60-minute exam. The class started as a full classroom of 20 kids. Within four weeks, most had dropped the class. For the five of us who remained, *inputting, sequencing,* and *looping* became well-known terms as we learned to survive the class.

Halfway into the semester, Mr. Murphy realized I was dating David, a student he had known for a couple of years. One day, while Mr. Murphy and I were talking, he abruptly said, "Follow me." He and I left the class of four other students behind and went to the library. He searched for a while and then pulled out Elizabeth Barrett Browning's *Sonnets from the Portuguese,* a book of poetry on love. "Have you read it?" he asked. I told him no, I hadn't, feeling a bit flabbergasted at the situation. "Go check it out," he said. "I'll meet you back in class."

Did he know I was taking creative writing, or could he tell how in love I was? Or perhaps he just thought I would like it. Which I did. A lot.

This moment was a recognition of my uniqueness. A positive nudge to believe that I deserve what I want. Because of Mr. Murphy's kindness, I continue to live this positivity within myself, as well as reflect it to those around me.

A Gentle Wall

By Valerie R. Vestal

It was nearing the end of the workweek, and I felt both blessed and a bit defeated. I am grateful to have a career as a Psychiatric Nurse Practitioner that allows me to use my personal strengths to connect with others and inspire hope. I am aware that many people go a lifetime without finding a career that fits. Nonetheless, after this particular week, I was also feeling defeated. I seemed to have had a run of patients who were hard to please.

I was eager to discuss the week's cases with my supervising physician. I looked forward to receiving his clinical judgment and wisdom. He never ceased to amaze me! No matter how busy he was – traveling to lectures or managing his own patients – he still seemed to have a sense of what was going on with each of his providers, and today was no different. He sensed that I was personalizing feelings of rejection from a couple of clients whom I couldn't seem to please. In his infinite wisdom, he said, "You need to build a wall, and what should the wall be made of?"

In my attempt to impress such an accomplished man with my own good wisdom, I responded, "The wall should be made of steel."

This was not the answer he had in mind, but there was no harsh rebuke; he simply stated, "A pillow." He explained: "A pillow will allow you to be gentle, yet you can block out the harsh words that cause us to take things personally."

At that moment, I learned that providing help and healing is more than graduating from an Ivy League school and studying with world-renowned scholars. My supervising physician has done both of these, but he also realizes that goodness is not taught in a book; it is lived.

Two and a half years later, goodness continues to abound, as I've been able to share this same simple lesson with families in crisis who try to build those steel walls to protect themselves from the harsh realities they are struggling with, forgetting that they need to maintain contact with those realities to navigate them successfully.

Praise Behind My Back

By Lateefah Shaheed

I sat nervously at my first Success Team meeting, where I was acting as both facilitator and participant in a group of four. We were starting our second and final team-building exercise, entitled "Praise Behind Your Back."

Each woman gets the chance to sit in the hot seat with her chair and body turned away from the group. Although she hears everything being said about her, she cannot respond. Her only job is to sit and listen while the rest of the group describes her assets behind her back. Absolutely no criticism is allowed.

I hesitated to facilitate this exercise among a group of strangers because I feared that the praise would sound superficial, such as "She obviously has good style. Look at her clothes, hair, and makeup."

Surprisingly, that's not what happened. I witnessed each woman being genuinely praised for her character traits rather than her physical traits. I heard these wonderful women describe each other as brave, free-spirited, creative, nurturing, powerful, kind, and loyal.

What an incredible gift to watch the transformation that occurred within each of these ladies upon hearing others talk about them in such a positive light!

When it was my turn to sit in the hot seat, I listened as others described me as inspirational, authentic, thorough, and caring. I felt mixed emotions as these generous and thoughtful women showered me with praise.

I have been taught that it is not polite to toot my own horn. So there is a part of me that craves praise while another part feels uncomfortable receiving it. I must learn to embrace my many shades of beauty, which includes both light and dark tints.

The following day, still feeling the ripple effects from this powerful exercise, I found myself pondering how different the world might be if each of us consciously chose to focus on the good instead of the bad in *every* person – stranger and non-stranger. My eyes sparkled as I marveled at the possibilities.

The Art of Receiving

By Daniel Nilon

Everything in nature flows – from wind and water to the spiral of the universe.

For a long time, I understood this concept of flow – including the idea that life too, as part of nature, should essentially flow. However, I was not *living* it. The biggest challenge I faced was that of feeling unmotivated and unrecognized for my work…until I realized the secret to unlocking flow: the art of receiving.

In early 2015, my partner and I attended a home-business event in Gold Coast, Australia, that changed the trajectory of our lives (and our business). It was also the place where something huge shifted for me. It was like a switch was turned on, where I stopped pushing towards goals and targets, feeling disappointed when I did not get results, and started finding alignment, attracting the right kind of work and clients towards me.

During this event, I met Ken Krell, who was the presenter. I really connected with his heart-based style of coaching and his high energy throughout the three days. He asked me to explain my "big why" in my life and business and to go home that night and write a page or more to really express it further. That night, I wrote down my goals, dreams, and ambitions. But most importantly, I really felt a great sense of gratitude for the entire experience, for Ken's pushing me to do the exercise, and for arriving at this turning point in my life. I felt blessed to have amazing mentors who guided me to follow my passions in life and showed me the way to do things – the *right* way.

For me, the art of receiving starts with becoming aware of what you already have and what is flowing to you right now. When you can see how far you have come, you stop feeling disappointed and start celebrating your life. Your heart opens up in gratitude. As your energy shifts, your heart expands further and you start receiving more of what you want in life. Positivity attracts more positive things from the universe, and suddenly you find the strength and support to go out and manifest your best life.

Finding True Abundance

By Ahana Lara

Goodness abounds. And it's not just in your personal life, but also in business. Working with my coaches, mentors, and other successful entrepreneurs on their projects and getting a behind-the-scenes look at how they work with success, I realized that the hidden gift is in being generous. The more you give, the more abundance is given to you. The secret to manifestation lies not just in mastering the art of receiving but also tapping into the science of giving.

I wanted to share a story of a consulting session I did with a holistic entrepreneur in Asia. She came to me with a request to look into her business challenges and the personal struggles she was facing in keeping her business going. However, she said that it was difficult for her to afford the consultation at the time. I decided to offer it to her anyway. Around the same time, my partner and I were looking to buy a gold ring as a gift to a family member on his 21st birthday. We were swamped with work and trying to finish off our projects (it was right before Christmas), and we just did not have the time or the resources to go hunting for the appropriate ring. We kept putting it off.

On the day of the appointment, my client came to the office with so much love and gratitude for what I had offered her. At the end of the session, she said, "If you don't mind, I may not be able to pay you from the business or pay you cash, but can I gift you one of my family's gold rings? Would you accept this as a token of my gratitude?" Believe it or not, it was the perfect ring and the perfect size for the person we were looking for. What are the chances of that happening?

True value is not in the money you charge for the service you provide. It's in the generosity that you exchange. When you truly wish for someone's happiness and want to contribute to it, you increase your value manifold. In return, you experience miracles!

Positive Energy

By Corina Y. Muro

I believe that when you give positive energy, you receive it back. When I was injured, however, it caused a major setback for me and my family and made it difficult to stay positive. But thanks to friends and family helping me through my hardship, I was able to maintain our household. Being a single mother, I had no time for a pity party – after a year it was time to get back to work! I reached out to agencies, seeking work as a caregiver, and it wasn't long before I was full time again.

The lady I was assigned to lived about 20 miles from my home, but it seemed like another world. I stopped at the 7-Eleven near her house, and people were so friendly – smiling and saying, "Good morning!" I found myself feeling calm and peaceful rather than being on guard and watching my back for safety.

I pulled up to the house just as my client and her daughter arrived home from the hospital. Both were so welcoming and appreciated my help so much; I felt more like their guest.

After my shift, they invited me to stay for dinner. While we talked, I saw that although the daughter was in a lot of pain herself, she was still caring for her mother. I told them I had lost my mother but wished I could be taking care of her now. The daughter said she had recently lost her sister and understood how I felt. "I was actually able to write about my sister in a book that was published," she said. Hearing this inspired me to ask how to write my own memoirs – something I've really wanted to do. Sitting and in pain, she was happy to share some insights with me. Then, I was offered a spot to write for her publisher's upcoming book!

That day showed me how a total stranger can reach out and care about how life is for others – and that staying positive really does bring people with goodness and kindness in their hearts.

The Greatest Gift

By Anne Bradley

My fifth-grade teacher, Mr. D., had a unique teaching style that fostered a lifelong love of learning in his students. Our favorite thing was the way he read books to us every single day, even though we thought we were too old for that. After reading a chapter from *Tom Sawyer*, he would lock the book away in his desk drawer. We would all beg for one more chapter, and he agreed only after we did a social studies or math lesson. We applied ourselves, and even enjoyed the other subjects, because he asked what we thought and listened like our opinions mattered.

Whenever the going got tough, he would pull out the desk keys and jingle them enticingly, and we would get back to the task at hand. Then out would come the book, and he would read to us some more.

I could hardly wait to get to school, and the day always ended too soon. I eagerly did my homework, looking forward to the next day of learning new things and hearing more of the book he was reading to us.

As a treat now and then, he would pull out a college book, such as calculus, and have us try just one little problem on the chalkboard. When we solved it, he would laugh and tell us we were as smart as college kids and how proud he was of us.

He stressed that the only thing we ever needed to learn was "how to learn." And with that "superpower," we could be, do, or have *anything*. He showed us how to use the library to look up whatever we wanted to know and taught us that knowledge could never be taken away.

I am ever grateful to Mr. D., who devoted his life to teaching grade school. I have thought often about this very special teacher and the huge impact he has had on my life. His goodness has spread far and wide through thousands of his students just like me. He gave us the greatest gift of all: he taught us how to learn.

A Well-Respected Man

By Catherine Laub

Although I didn't meet Richie until 1981, he offered me a job through my ex-husband after I was laid off in 1979. I was amazed that this president of a 900-employee company was so welcoming!

When I was pregnant with my first child and was preparing to go on leave, I was summoned to Richie's office. I was presented a large check, which I was told was a performance bonus. We later learned that this was a made-up program to help us financially.

Another time, we were looking for a home to rent and were short funds to pay the realtor. Once again, Richie came through and gave us the money. He did this one more time for us a couple of years later. He always did this type of thing for others. If an employee had a relative looking for a job, they were hired even if there wasn't a position for them at that time.

My ex-husband was hired after his car broke down close to the company and Richie stopped to help. The friend who was with my ex-husband was Richie's nephew, so he offered both of them jobs. My brother was also hired, right out of the Air Force; a few years later, his wife was hired, too. When my father could no longer drive his school bus because of a massive heart attack, Richie offered him a job.

My current husband, Tony, also worked there as a VP, but I didn't know him when I was employed there. Even now that Tony no longer works there, Richie remains a good friend of Tony's, and they still do business together.

Tony has told me many stories about how Richie has reached out to help others. For instance, if someone had car problems, Richie had them bring their car into the back, and he would physically help fix the car. When any employee's teenage kids were out of school in the summer, he always made sure they had some kind of work to do.

Many people are thankful for this wonderful man because he gave them hope when they had none.

Love Always Wins

By Michelle Goguen

I had been an art teacher in the NYC Catholic school system for 12 years when the public school across the street from where I lived had an opening for an art teacher. I knew that it might be rough, but nothing prepared me for this.

From the very start, it was tougher than tough. Students swore at each other, ran through the halls, got into fist fights, and disrespected every adult in the building. We were expected to endure it all and "be nice" and "don't play into their drama." Most of the children were lovely, but the ones who weren't were so determined to cause trouble that I simply didn't know what to do.

One boy in particular, a third-grader named Kyleek, seemed to love to cause me pain. He would hang on the table as I tried to teach, and all his buddies would follow. He was causing trouble all over the school.

One day, he ran out of the lunch room and slumped his body across from the art room. Sherrie (the school's security guard) and I went over to him to see if we could help. "What's wrong, Kyleek? You can't do this, Kyleek; you have to stay in the lunch room." Nothing. "How can I help you, Kyleek?" Nothing. Then Sherrie added, "And remember, Kyleek, that we love you." I was a little stunned by this but added my own "Oh, yeah...we do love you." To my utter surprise, Kyleek wrapped his arms around my stomach and hugged me tight.

Things changed after that. Kyleek was attentive in the art room, getting his buddies to be attentive, as well. All he needed was to know that he was loved. I told him every chance I got, and while I did not stay with public school in NYC, I will never forget how simply being loving changed the life of one troubled child. I am a better teacher, thanks to Sherrie, and a better person for having had this uplifting encounter with a little boy named Kyleek.

Goodness of a Conscious Conversation
By Carolyn McGee

My biggest growth opportunities are finding gifts in trusting my intuition. I believe that we learn what we are here to teach; and while I know that the more I trust my intuition, the better my life is, when that lesson comes from a mentor I worked with for over three years, it is not easy!

I invested many hours and dollars working with my mentor to market my business as an Intuitive Healer and Angel Communicator. I took an intensive class with her about being in our body versus being in our head, where one does not have the physical energy to make decisions using intuition. I loved feeling empowered on how I was using my intuition to guide my choices and teaching.

Then she made a statement about being skeptical that people can talk to angels. I immediately felt distressed and sick to my stomach. How could she publicly discount years of us working together?

I took a deep breath and felt into what my own intuition was telling me. I know who I am and what I can do. I do not need outside validation. So I knew that this was an opportunity for me to speak my truth, honor my feelings, and express vulnerability.

After class, I asked her for a conscious conversation. She listened, completely heard my words, and re-explained her intention. There are people who use outside energy for decisions or validation because they are not connected to their body, so they can't truly bring forth divine energy.

She agreed that she is skeptical, but she knows there are connections she cannot feel. She understood how her statement was not supportive to our relationship. We hugged and brainstormed ideas on how I could use this experience to help others.

The next day, she asked me to speak to the class about intuition and the value of being connected to our bodies. By me speaking my truth, I encouraged others to feel their power in their body and trust their intuition – and that is pure goodness!

My Students Are My Greatest Teachers

By Tanya Levy

Several years ago, one of my students gave me a poem she'd written about dementia. Her words really struck a nerve with me because I'd recently noticed my mom becoming confused — forgetting things I told her and sometimes even mixing me up with the nurses. This was not only unsettling but startling, given that my mother had always had a perfect memory. As I read the student's poem, I started to tear up, so I quickly left the classroom.

Later that day, I saw a gift box that another student had left for me outside my office door. I opened the box and found a tea light, a coffee-scented candle, and a package of tissue, as well as a note saying that she'd seen my tears and was giving me these gifts to help me after all I had done to help her. She told me that the items were to encourage me to take care of myself. For the second time that day my eyes filled with tears, but this time they were happy tears.

I was used to helping students feel witnessed — seen and heard. It was a surprise and a blessing to be witnessed in return. These gifts — and the kind words that went with them — gave me encouragement at a time when I needed it the most.

Over the coming days and month, I learned to go with the flow of my mom's memory lapses. Sometimes I would tell her, "Hey, Mom — it's me, your daughter, Tanya," and she would say, "So good to see you; I love you." I learned to live in the moment and be present with her. Her moments of confusion were short-lived and were often followed by beautiful chats where she asked about my life, my work, my husband, and her grandson.

My mom's goodness shone beyond any momentary confusion. She taught me that love does not need to remember; it just is. And my students' goodness helped to uplift me throughout my journey with my mom and beyond.

A Gift That Keeps on Giving

By Joy T. Barican

Coaching is my passion, and it shows in the results and the life-changing experiences of the people I've had the privilege to support and work with. However, setting up a business is no easy feat. Most of my work comes from word-of-mouth. To supplement these referrals, I've placed advertisements on social media but had never advertised in print media…until I received a pleasant surprise: an email from Bennett and Shirley Tesara inquiring if I would like my business featured in a magazine. This publication was to be distributed by an association that supports scholars and their alma maters.

The email went on to explain that, as alumni members, Bennett and Shirley and other fellow sponsors were given the option to publish their family photo with accompanying messages or commentary. These photos would provide a means of reconnecting everyone with their university friends, many of whom they had not seen for years. It was therefore understandable that there was a considerable advantage to having a photo.

In the case of Bennett and Shirley, however, they decided to offer me the space to advertise my business instead. This was a thoughtful and extremely generous offer, given that the ad will occupy half a page in the magazine, which will surely help towards giving my business the exposure it needs. It is truly a gift that keeps on giving. I may be the direct recipient, but many more will be helped by it.

Having known Bennett, Shirley, and their daughters for many years, I know that it is typical of them to always think of a higher purpose for every endeavour and decision they make. Receiving their kindness is uplifting and humbling.

Mr. Mickelson's Tall Girl

By Marci Kobayashi

Nicknames get imprinted and can be hard to remove. Therefore, it takes a special kind of person to call positive attention to the one trait in a child that wavers on both sides of strength and insecurity. My sixth-grade teacher, Mr. Mickelson, had a special knack for this, and I always wondered how he did it. Was it an intuitive hit, or did he choose the nicknames with intention?

I am 5'11" (179 cm) tall, which is well above average for the area where I was raised. In grade school, I was almost always the tallest in my class. My mother, also a tall woman, taught me to be proud of my height and to have good posture.

Despite my mother's training, I must have been feeling insecure when I got to 6th grade. That first day of school when Mr. Mickelson called me "Tall Girl," I was surprised and a little embarrassed. Then, I was secretly thrilled. All year, I stood a little taller every time he used it.

To me, having a nickname from Mr. Mickelson meant he recognized me. He saw me. I wasn't just some kid in the class. "Tall Girl" felt like my code name or a special talisman letting me know I was in the right place. It meant I belonged and that he was a trusted friend.

Now, many years later, I wonder if the other students cherish their nicknames as much as I cherish mine. I am a teacher now myself and marvel at Mr. Mickelson's gift. I realize that my nickname was probably an obvious choice, given my above-average height. And who knows, there may even have been a "Tall Girl" in every one of his classes. Whether the nickname was uniquely mine doesn't matter. What matters is that it was used with such love, and love is always something worth imprinting!

The Candy Man

By Tiffany Clay

"I have something for you," he said as he pressed a candy into my hand, like it was a secret. I smiled and dropped it into my bag.

"Do you like them?" he asked one day.

"Sure do!" I replied.

The candy itself is smooth and hard, the kind that lends itself well to sore throats – soothing, like the honey it's made from. "It's the best honey, Manuka," he assured me with a twinkle in his eye.

Giving me candy has become a ritual of sorts, an introduction to our Pilates sessions, often followed by a little storytelling – which we both know is a ruse to delay the unavoidable but necessary exercise routine that will keep the hips and core strong enough to yield another productive week of business meetings, tennis, and socializing.

Not unlike the old-fashioned custom of an apple for the teacher, this client brings me something every session. Always a candy, often accompanied by a book or a carefully clipped newspaper article, always shared with a knowing smile as he waits excitedly for my reaction.

Our discussions are fascinating, with me as the lone audience for the tales of his extraordinary life: a history of faraway places, exotic travel, shrewd business deals, and ghost stories (and maybe a little showing off, too).

He always goes out for lunch first. He delights in describing his favorite foods, which, truth be told, are mostly desserts – his favorite being rice pudding.

After a recent trip to Florida, he commented that he didn't like it much because it was "full of old people." I laughed. But I knew what he meant. Because, at 87, he's the youngest old person I've ever met. With no intention of getting old, he chooses to live like the 8-year-old he is inside, hearing aids in one pocket, candy in the other.

Now I have an overflowing bowl of candy in my cupboard, a collection from our many sessions together. And I'm finally able to see the goodness he shares with me: his incredible knowledge and experience, his kindness, and his zest for life. For that I am truly grateful.

Joy Is in My Heart

By Gunhild Lorenzen

"You must meet her," Clara urged me.

"I am very busy," I replied. I did not want to engage in holy talks about healing and consciousness. I was a rational woman, both feet on the ground and not ready to believe more than what I could see and touch.

"She is in Brussels just for one week," Clara insisted.

"All right then, make an appointment for me. But only because you are my friend." What could I lose besides some money?

That Thursday at noon, I rang the doorbell with the name I was given. "Gunhild here."

"Seventeenth floor. Come up, please."

The elevator took me to my destination. A woman with big glasses welcomed me into the room. "I am Joy. Please sit down." When she looked into my eyes, I softened. "Your parents belong to a different soul family. Let them go."

Sitting on the sofa in disbelief, my brain was whirling and somersaulting. Joy Messick touched my soul. "You are your worst enemy!" she kept on. "There is nothing wrong with you."

Direct words, and yet it felt as if I entered into a full bath of love. My judgments about life and especially about myself tumbled down. Some months later, Joy invited me to her home in Ann Arbor, Michigan. Together with other healers, I learned her method of "Resonance Healing," connecting Heaven and Earth in our bodies through conscious breathing. We discussed the Unified Field and learned that we come from light and go back to light.

Joy's message to us was simple but nonetheless powerful: "It is what it is, and it does what it does." Adding: "Let's enjoy the ride in our space suit until we have to give it back." She not only taught acceptance, discernment, and compassion, but also embodied it: "We are here to love."

Sitting around the table with like-minded people from all around the world – eating, laughing, and sharing deep insights – changed my life. I am forever grateful to Joy, who remained my friend and spiritual guide until her passing.

Daydream Believer

By Mike Monahan

In the summer of 1987, I was introduced to a man who was a real-life Wizard of Oz. Thousands of people over the years would travel not to Emerald City, but to Cincinnati, Ohio, in hopes of finding their dreams. The wizard we met went by the name of Jim Quinn, and he was the facilitator of a life-changing seminar.

If you remember in the *Wizard of Oz* movie, there were three characters who traveled with Dorothy to the Emerald City looking for something. The Scarecrow wanted a brain so he could think great thoughts. The Tin Man wanted a heart so he could give and receive love. And the Cowardly Lion wanted courage so he could face his fears. Dorothy, the Scarecrow, the Tin Man, and the Cowardly Lion wanted all these things so they could find freedom and live their dreams.

The people who traveled to Cincinnati to attend the seminar were looking for many of the same things. Some thought they weren't smart enough or had had their hearts broken and were afraid to love. Many were afraid to make decisions for fear that they might fail and face embarrassment. Some, like me, were looking for all three things: how to think, feel, and act in better ways!

Jim, the Wizard, taught us the secret: we would have to get back to our child-like behavior. As children, we had powerful imaginations. We had visions of imaginary friends or scary ghosts – all of whom seemed real. As we got older, we traded in our imagination for being reasonable.

Jim led us through a series of exercises helping us relearn the power of imagination. He told us to close our eyes and imagine the outcome we wanted as if it had already happened. He then told us to open our eyes and take appropriate action.

I followed his direction and changed my life completely. Just like in the movie when Dorothy closed her eyes, clicked her heels, and repeated, "There's no place like home," magically, what I imagined really did happen. Now, I'm a Daydream Believer teaching others to imagine. Imagine that!

A Final Wish

By Marie Spencer-Rowland

One day while I was working for a local radio station in my late teens, I took a call from a lady who was desperate for help. Her friend had a 16-year-old daughter who was terminally ill with cancer. In order to stay alive, this courageous girl had to have a platelet transfusion every day. Even with these transfusions, however, her health was rapidly declining, and it seemed that she didn't have much time remaining.

The girl's dying wish was to go and see Taz, the Tasmanian Devil from Looney Tunes, but her family had no money left to pay for this. This is why the lady called our radio station: to see if we could help pay for a car big enough to take the friend, her family, and all of her daughter's medical equipment to Movie World.

I managed to get hold of a limousine company that was able to book a car straight away. I made the payment and sorted out logistics, and the next day the entire family went to fulfill the girl's dream.

I had the day off that day, so I stopped into a shop that I knew sold the Taz toy, and I drove down to give it to her as a memento of her day.

The following day, I was back at the radio station and received another call, again from the family friend. She thanked me for what I had done and said that the entire family had had an amazing day. She said the smile on this young girl's face when she got to meet Taz was one she will never forget...

Sadly, however, during the night, this beautiful young woman had lost her fight and was no longer with us.

I cried for hours after that call (and, in fact, I still do when I think about it), but what makes me smile deep inside my heart is knowing that she got her wish. Thanks to that one friend making one call, a young girl's final dream came true, and she left this world at peace.

All Things Connect with Love

By Nadene Joy Hagen

Love exists in every living thing. Love has the power to heal and transform lives. It is much more magical than people realize. I'm living proof.

Not long ago, I discovered a lady's name by chance and instantly felt drawn to her. I listened to my inner voice and reached out, as I felt something big. Later, I found out that the feeling was love. It turns out she's one of the best-known healers on the planet and has the strongest connection to the divine that I've ever seen. She has a never-ending love for humanity and a deep belief in me. Working with her was often challenging. I felt like giving up when we were unleashing all the limits I had placed on myself, but she encouraged me to continue.

Since I have been in her presence, everything has aligned. She has taught me to break through all barriers with love. In a short period, I created my life-and-parenting coaching business, launched my website and Facebook page, and attracted soulmate clients from around the world.

In the near future, I'll be creating an intuitive online parenting course unlike any other. I have created two kids' camps and will be opening a new hands-on school next fall. I also have started writing a book on helping others find their purpose.

Most days, it feels like I am living in a dream. I have learned to receive all that the Universe has in store for me. I feel blessed to positively affect thousands – even millions – of people worldwide.

"All things connect with love." This quote is written by my earth angel, Ria Ray. Thank you, Ria, from the bottom of my heart. Sending all who read this much love, light, abundance, peace, and compassion for yourself and others. You, too, have the power to make a difference!

The Gift from Pastor S.

By Diane L. Keyes

Each Sunday, with six people sharing one bathroom, we put on our Sunday best and went to church. Every evening, at 6:00 sharp, we prayed over family dinners. I don't recall a single discussion about our faith. It was our faith, and that was it.

In parochial school, beyond religion classes, those being confirmed went to Pastor S. for catechism. This was where real discussions about our faith happened.

In Pastor S., we had the Greatest Religious Authority in the World. He appeared larger than life with a booming voice that often brought thunder into the silence of the sanctuary. A Force of Nature, yet he seemed approachable. I asked questions at every class: "Why? What kind of a God would expect…? If God is Love then why this hellfire and damnation?" I needed to understand these rules. Pastor S. was tolerant of my questions and did not say "just trust" like other teachers. Classes frequently went into overtime.

On my Confirmation Day, I was in the church kitchen, about to have a pink carnation corsage pinned onto my white robe, when Pastor S. entered and motioned that I follow. I obeyed, worrying every step of the way: *Oh, God! I'm not going to get confirmed! My parents will kill me! My godparents are in the sanctuary! They won't be giving me that confirmation ring! The Bible with my name engraved on it will be held back! What about the people who are coming for the confirmation party? Will they be turned away? Who will eat all that food my mother has prepared? Oh God, my life is over!*

Pastor S. asked me to step into the pantry, standing on the other side of a large stainless steel table. I said nothing and was most likely as white as the choir robe. He said, "You are the apple of my eye. Don't ever stop asking *why*."

I have no memory of anything else he may have said. I didn't even know what being the "apple of someone's eye" meant. What I did know was that I was still going to have my confirmation that day – the party was back on! I took a breath. Hopefully, I humbly answered, "Thank you."

Pastor S. gave me a gift that morning that served me well all my life.

Hannelore, My Angel
By Heather A. Dempsey

Over 20 years ago, I walked into a classroom where a tiny blonde woman greeted me with her soft German accent. Her presence was magnificent, and I was completely drawn to her.

As she taught the class about Reiki healing, I couldn't get over the way I felt. She created a safe, empowering, supportive space that most of us had never experienced before.

My passion for Reiki was so obvious, and she expected that I would be continuing to the advanced levels. When I explained that I couldn't afford it, she immediately invited me to attend the next level for free – and the next AND the next! She said she saw something in me and knew I would share the good she wished to see in the world.

I lovingly referred to her as "my angel" and, for the next few years, spent as much time as possible auditing her classes in order to gain the confidence to teach and create the same impact she had for so many.

We kept in touch, but less frequently with each passing year. In 2015, I was going through a difficult time and was trying to find ways to cope and heal. Then one morning while I was lying in bed, a reflection on my ceiling caught my eye. It was the shape of an angel – a PERFECT Christmas treetop angel! As I looked to discover what was causing this mysterious glow, I found that it was a reflection from the sun shining off of a meditation cassette she had given me that had been sitting on my windowsill for ages. Since this had never happened before, I felt that it was a sign of loving support from her. I reached out to tell her, only to learn that she had peacefully passed away a few days earlier. I was blown away! Even without her physical body, she had found a way to be my shining angel in a time of need, offering support, hope, and strength. That helped me find my passion for healing again, first for myself and now for my work with others.

I am forever grateful, Hannelore!

Touching Lives

By Vijaya Gowrisankar

While I've experienced so much kindness in my life – such as my friend's support when I lost my father and my classmates' support when I struggled with a speech impediment – two special "goodness heroes" stand out: Amma and Naveen.

I met Amma (Tamil for *Mother*) while living in her home in Chennai, which she had converted into a hostel. As the landlady, she provided boarding and food for 20 girls. After the girls left by 8 a.m. each day, the house transformed into a small-scale industry: local women came and stitched embroidery, made pickles, and cooked and packaged papad. In addition to paying them good daily wages, Amma taught these women – who had never been educated – to read and write, and she opened bank accounts for them. Amma could have chosen to rest during the day, but she wanted to uplift the women – which she did!

My other "goodness hero," Naveen, had been my colleague for a decade when he told me he was going to fund a school – a goal he accomplished when he started the Dil Se Education Foundation. Through his work, he met with the principal and teachers of the Ramchandrapuram School, where he learned that, among other difficulties, the school had no toilets! In addition to building toilets, Naveen spent two and half years repairing the school building and providing infrastructure. By the time he was done, the school was in such good condition that all the children in the village wanted to study there.

With all this success and recognition (including an award from the government of Telangana), Naveen was happy but not satisfied; he wanted a sustainable mechanism to expand on this beneficial work. He took strides to fulfill this mission through his foundation's website, which raises funds to help farmers, uplift women, and improve the quality of education in government schools.

Through their kind hearts and good work, Amma and Naveen have touched my own life so deeply, and I know they will continue spreading kindness and touching lives for years to come.

Goodness Abounds in Mentorship
By Nikki A. Creber

When I was going through the difficult stage of finding my entrepreneurial path, I found a business mentor who helped me see beyond the bounds of my everyday life – and, through this process, helped me see that goodness abounds:

Growing a relationship with a mentor is a special undertaking.

Originally, a mentor's toolkit reveals new thinking and new opportunities for mutual exchange.

Opening the door concealed behind the hanging tapestry is the mentor's job – that is, helping you discover the special magic you have to share with the world.

Daring you to think critically and to think beyond your self-imposed boundaries is part of their process.

Nuanced and complex, this relationship is purposeful as you stretch to the mentor's expectations and expand your own,

Effectively painting a different, bigger, better, and sometimes even scarier picture of possibilities.

Suppose my mentor was right?

Somehow, right before me was serendipity and synchronicity.

As I figured out how to manage my Parkinson's disease, I felt vulnerable.

Baffling though it seemed at first, I came to see that my experience perfectly aligned with working with others with Parkinson's.

Opportunity often comes dressed in work overalls, and a complete turnaround and restart is sometimes required.

Unveiling the gift is the work of a good mentor.

Not an everyday gift or a quick exchange, but one that is mutually beneficial in the long-term.

Demanding and caring, mentors stretch you, fueled by good intent.

Seasons give gifts, and families give gifts; yet when you receive the gift of wonderful mentorship, it touches you deeply, transforms your thinking, and opens your heart to goodness.

With gratitude to Eric Rubin for being an excellent mentor, seeding enduring goodness into my life.

Beautiful, Spacious Gift

By Joanne Angel Barry Colon

What a gift it is to be in this beautiful space that I call Fitness "R" Us – a place where I have been blessed to heal and transform hundreds of people's minds, bodies, and spirits. Each client is authentic and brings creativity, knowledge, patience, excitement, empowerment, and joy into my life.

I am celebrating 16 years and counting in this space. During that time, God has blessed me with two landlords who have kept my rent the same – an affordable flat rate that has helped me keep my own rates affordable. I am blessed that God and the Universe surrounds me with kindness, abundance, love, prosperity, wealth, fame, and continued success. I thank God and the Universe for choosing me for this spiritual path and life purpose: to transform many people's lives with movement, nutrition, and meditation. This beautiful space has brought so much goodness into my life

The expression "People come into your life for a season, a reason, or a lifetime" is very powerful for me. In 2011, I was introduced to a client who is a Reiki Master. He took on my service to help him lose weight and get heart healthy, and I worked with him for several months. During one of his sessions, he asked me to administer Reiki healing on his upper back. I told him I only had Level One Attunement, but he said that, energetically, I was already a Reiki Master. Within a few months, he gave me my Level Two Attunement, and three months later, he gave me my Reiki Master Attunement.

Since then, my life has transformed and so has my business. And it all started with the gift of my special healing space. I now offer personal training and mind, body, and spiritual transformations by applying Reiki as well as meditation, crystal healing, essential oils, Aroma Touch Technique, and Angel Card readings. I've also become a columnist for a local newspaper, written and published two books, and contributed to several others (including this one!).

I look forward to the blessings and success that shall unfold over the coming years.

Kindness to Self

By Lola Pittenger

On a warm evening, six months into my study-abroad experience in Rio de Janeiro, Brazil, in a small yoga studio off of central Ipanema's main avenue, I had my first consciously enlightening experience.

Hypothetically, it might sound easy to allow enlightening experiences when you're living in such a paradise, but the truth is, you bring your baggage with you no matter how far you travel. My baggage happened to be self-hatred. Not the outward kind of self-hatred that many humans suffer from, but more the internal-dialogue kind that constantly provided me with negative thoughts about myself.

So there I was, sitting in Easy Pose, facing a mirror, in a dark room, at about 7:00 p.m. It was the alternative to Savasana (or "Corpse Pose") for this particular class. Our instructor wanted us to face the mirror. We didn't have to open our eyes, but the mirror was there if we wanted to. She guided us to a peaceful place and encouraged us to listen to our hearts speak. I sat and I sat, knowing we had plenty of time. I kept my eyes closed, but eventually I began to raise my gaze. I met my eyes and actually became slightly startled. Something was changing but I didn't know what. Our instructor asked us to move as close to the mirror as possible.

Eyes opened, eyes closed, eyes opened, a small smile appeared on my lips. "I love you," said a voice. It was faint, but it was there.

"I love you," it repeated.

I was baffled, confused, startled, amazed. What was that? Who was that?

It was *me*. It was my heart!

I had never heard those words said to me *by* me ever before. I giggled. What joy! What beauty! "Thank you," I whispered. "I LOVE you." I actually mouthed the words this time – again and again. Silent tears ran down my face. My healing began.

I left yoga that night feeling a special peace in my heart that I had never felt before.

Courtney

By Melisa Archer

Courtney joined my Young Living Essential Oils team a few months ago. Although we never met in person, we seemed to chat every couple of weeks. Courtney shared that she had previously won a battle with breast cancer but was now back in the battle. A few weeks later, she called me very upset; her husband had died in her kitchen on Mother's Day.

Courtney's battle with cancer continued, with her mom by her side. Courtney had been in the hospital and had not changed her monthly oil order, yet she was so excited to receive the oil bottles. "I LOVE them," she told me. "I will just have more of the ones I know I like." I was in awe of her spirit as Courtney spoke with such passion and excitement, even though she had just lived through some very harsh weeks.

Just a few weeks later, Courtney passed. This was honestly the most tragic thing I'd ever heard of. I became aware that Courtney's monthly order processed on the day that she passed. After I contacted Young Living Essential Oils, they refunded her order amount, with sincere apologies for the loss of an "oily family member." Even though they refunded the credit card, they would still qualify her for a free diffuser and two oils. This news brought tears to my eyes. My hope was for Courtney's mom to receive this gift in the mail. I envisioned that the diffuser would be an unexpected surprise, to last many years, and the oils would bring her some comfort.

I was later blessed to share phone time with her mom, who is yet another amazing soul. Her mom spoke with courage, acceptance, and goodness. I could hear Courtney's son in the background, excitedly trying to get Grandma's attention as he wanted popcorn made. In an odd way, this brought me comfort – knowing that Courtney's children will be so deeply loved by her mom.

I'm happy to have had Courtney in my circle of friends, even though it had just been for a few short months. Courtney, you will be missed but not forgotten.

An Unexpected Angel

By Steph Walczak

In 2012, I studied abroad in Kenya, where I researched and wrote a 40-page paper on the maternal healthcare sector. This wouldn't have been possible without Anne.

Anne was a host for the members of our program who moved to the western town of Kisumu. Her job was to check in on us and assist in connecting us to locals. I thought we'd meet her once or twice during our four weeks there. Five years later, I still think about her kindness and generosity.

She quickly became a second mother to our little group of *mzungus* (the Swahili word for "white person" or "foreigner" – similar to *gringo* in Spanish). We all had different topics, we all needed local people to interview, and we all needed to visit different areas around Kisumu. Anne personally took us to where we needed to be – from the city center to the rural slums on the outskirts of town. She translated, bought gifts for our interviewees, brought us lunch, gave us advice, and answered all of our questions, no matter how ridiculous. And she asked for nothing in return.

The least we could do was invite her to the Thanksgiving dinner we were hosting. She found us a turkey and even prepared it herself! She also brought a dish to share, even after being asked not to, and spent the night laughing and lifting everyone up in her own subtle way that we were quickly growing used to.

As the weeks passed, we discovered a few things that made her all the more inspiring: she had a full-time job, was a single mother, and was HIV+. She volunteered often with several HIV+ support groups and other local non-profits. I truly do not understand how she was able to do it all and fight her illness at the same time.

Her perseverance and compassion were incomprehensible, but with everything she was going through, she never failed to put a smile on our faces. She taught me more than how to navigate the research field – she taught me that it's not only important to have compassion for others but to make sure to save some for yourself.

Sarah's Story

By Kimberly Brochu

"Let's go," Patty said.

Sarah hesitated, took her hand, and headed outside. As Sarah took a breath of fresh air, she felt life being drawn back into her body. They reminisced about Sarah's days as a librarian, about her family, and about her deep concern for her dying husband. Sarah had already forgotten how, only minutes earlier, she'd been banging on walls and screaming in frustration, feeling trapped within the walls that now housed her and a memory that was failing her.

Prior to her dementia, Sarah had been a vibrant, intelligent woman, always involved in community work – a true social butterfly who loved her job.

Now, despite the staff members' efforts, Sarah felt imprisoned and yearned to go home. Patty became her lifeline. Sarah connected with her gentle and kind energy; she felt something different from her, knowing on a deeper level that she could count on her, that Patty would meet her wherever she was emotionally and offer her a safe place to land in a world that was becoming unfamiliar and a body that was being taken over by anxiety.

As the Therapeutic Recreational Director, Patty spent her days working with residents with dementia. At times, she would develop a special connection with a resident that went beyond words. Patty began including Sarah in her errands around the facility: they made copies, delivered newspapers, and chatted with others. They became friends.

Each morning, Sarah would anxiously scurry into Patty's office asking for a suitcase. "I'm going home today," she'd say. Patty would simply hug her and offer to look for one.

Two years went by as the two friends handled busy work together, and Sarah's short-term memory loss became more and more severe. "There's my girl!" she'd call out when she no longer knew Patty's name but still recognized her loving soul.

Sarah is no longer with us, but the gift of bringing meaning and purpose back to Sarah's life, when she had lost so much, was something Patty felt honored to have been a part of.

Giving from the Heart

By Felicia D'Haiti

During the months of chemotherapy treatments for colon cancer, I became increasingly exhausted. My treatments occurred every other week, each one lasting three days. After the three days of treatment, it took me an additional three days to recover enough to go back to work. At work, I had limited duties but did my best to continue coordinating an academic program. I would go to work every day that I could. After all, we needed my income, so I kept going to work for as long as possible. Finally, in the last months of treatment, I couldn't manage any longer.

It was quite a stressful situation for us. I was not unemployed, yet I was not going to get paid. Between my surgery, recovery, and chemotherapy days over the last six months, I had used up all my leave from work. I had no idea what I would do.

Later, I discovered that my co-workers were looking out for me. Without my knowledge, a small group of teacher colleagues began to inquire about ways they could help me. They contacted the union and spoke with the principal. After they received approval, they began to pass around a list on which they signed up to donate hours of their own sick leave to my account.

In the end, the staff allotted me nearly two months of leave and helped me to appeal my case with the sick-leave bank to be granted another 30 days of leave. I was able to receive pay for the remainder of my treatment time. After I returned to work, I found out how much they had given and was overwhelmed with gratitude. Many of my colleagues gave as much as a week of their own leave to help me out. This and their other acts of kindness gave me a new appreciation for how people can come together to help someone – no matter how well they may or may not know that person – just from the goodness in their hearts.

Chapter 7
Community

W hen we lived in Jemez Pueblo, New Mexico, and worked at the K-8 charter school there, we had a close-up view of a very special community. The Jemez Indian tribe has lived in this village for many centuries, and they still maintain a great deal of their traditional culture. Some of their customs are private, but we were invited to observe the public ones, including their annual Feast Day, tribal dances, and other traditional ceremonies. Several families invited us to their homes, became close friends, and shared important pieces of their lives and their culture with us (including the occasional tribal secret that would inadvertently slip out).

While we won't reveal any Jemez secrets, it's certainly no secret that special communities of all kinds, all around the world, deepen our experience of life and goodness. And while some of these communities (such as the Jemez tribe) are based on family, heritage, and location, a community doesn't have to be a group of people living in one place – it could be an online community, an organization, or even a community of authors…such as those who contributed to this book!

In this chapter, you'll read about special communities from Arizona to Australia, from India to Botswana, in big cities and small towns all around the world. You'll be introduced to members of communities who supported one another during illness, financial struggles, and natural disasters and who were there to celebrate the good times together, too. The communities vary tremendously – including communities of bikers, the military, Bible-study groups, homeless people and those who help them, and online groups – but they all include members who are dedicated to uplifting one another and spreading goodness.

The Suncatcher

By Tara Leduc

As the train doors opened, he scanned their faces. Who would he approach next? He'd done this enough to realise it didn't matter. He'd learned that most people were willing.

He cleared his throat. "Excuse me, would you be willing to do something for someone who has cancer?" His eyes caught theirs. "Would you be willing to send love and healing to a stranger?"

He brandished the suncatcher, a simple string of beads with a crystal ball on the bottom. Usually it hung from the rearview mirror, refracting and reflecting light through her car. But he knew that it could do more than that. It could refract and reflect love, looping rainbows of healing around her.

He explained his mission: "Would you put love, healing, and best wishes into this? It's for someone who has cancer."

Nearly everyone stopped a minute. Nearly everyone had time to fill the suncatcher with love, hope, and dreams of good health. Nearly everyone had time to give a gift of positive intentions to a stranger.

Smiling gratitude, he offered the notebook next. "Maybe you'd like to write a message to her?"

With love! ... Hearts around the world are thinking of you! ... Be strong!

He brought the suncatcher to a primary school. The little ones understood right away. Fill a prism with the most important things – fun, happiness, and love – and that is what is reflected back. With a newly learned skill, they printed their names: Rowon, Malika, Abraham, Binu, Lillian, Aggrash, Taneen, Rose, Murphy, Yousif, Michael. A rainbow of children sent wishes for someone they didn't know.

After months of approaching strangers, friends, co-workers, and children, he gave her the notebook. He returned the suncatcher to her car. He explained why he needed to borrow it. "This is to heal you. People filled it with love. Kids filled it with play and fun. They wrote you notes, so you'd know they sent love."

Six years on, the suncatcher still hangs in her car, radiating rainbows of love, strength, and fun. It heals not only her, but anyone who catches the light as she drives by.

Unexpected Gifts

By Kimberly Hutt

Witnessing the early adventures of married life and young families always brings a mixed array of feelings for me: the memories of all those firsts, the growing pains and struggles of learning about each other and ourselves, and the connection and independence of learning to balance *yourself* with *us*!

One of the toughest challenges my husband and I faced as a young married couple was finding our way through work and money. We were just out of high school – I was working, and Bill was headed back to school full time. Money was tight, but we always managed to pay our bills and have the basics.

A few weeks before our first Christmas as a married couple, I received a phone call from a local church stating that I had won the first prize of a ticket draw: three huge boxes of groceries! I told them there must be some mistake, as I had not remembered purchasing a ticket. They assured me with confirmation of my info – yes, I was the winner, and I should come pick up my prize. I went gratefully to gather my winnings and thank them.

Years later, I realized that a beautiful soul I worked with had given my name and asked that we be recipients of the goodwill of the community! Every day for weeks, she'd heard me trying to figure out the puzzle, yet she never said a word! It was a much-needed and much-appreciated gesture.

Bill and I have been blessed with the kindness of gestures like this frequently. It wouldn't be unusual for our family members to stop by with a donation of funds, groceries, diapers, formula, and children's clothes – always at the exact time we could use them, always with so much selfless love and a willingness to share. It was a family tradition and was always appreciated and accepted with gratitude when it arrived.

To this day, I make a point of helping whenever I can and paying it forward – knowing that it's the thought and intention, not the size of the gift, that matters most.

Welcome Home

By Micheal Taylor

I was an Army solider on an 18-month tour in Iraq. During this tour, I took an R&R break back in the U.S. The first stop was the Dallas/Fort Worth Airport. As the plane load of 400 soldiers on a break from the war zone taxied to the gate, we passed through two airport fire trucks that showered the plane with water, just the beginning of our welcome home.

When we entered the airport, the entire terminal cheered and applauded until every uniformed soldier disembarked. Once we claimed our bags, we would go our separate ways to see our families.

I was the first to go through the door that separated us from the rest of the public. To my surprise, there were flags and banners and a crowd waiting for us. A line had formed to give us small gifts and to thank us. The crowd seemed immense and overwhelming. There were school children, their parents, veterans from previous wars, and many American civilians. I was overcome with emotion. "I can do this," I told myself. "Take a step and start with the first person."

The first person was a young boy around five years old. He looked at me nervously with a sense of awe on his face, not sure if I was a monster or a hero. We held each other's gaze until his mom prompted him, "Give it to him."

His face broke into the biggest smile as he handed me a small bag decorated with an American flag. He said, "Thank you for protecting us." In that instant I was transformed from a monster into a hero. I was home. It brought tears to my eyes and still does. I shook hands and received kindness from every person there.

That young boy's simple and pure act of kindness made the madness of war melt away and gave me the strength to return and finish my tour and ultimately do a second tour. That day I was able to embody why I did what I did. It was for that young boy.

Ceara's Village

By Annie Price

Over time, our society has raised its awareness and become more enlightened about people with physical or mental special needs. While there's always room for improvement, comparing how "disabled" children interacted in the 1970s (when I was in school) with today, we've certainly come a long way. Today, our society includes many people we might describe as "developmentally challenged," such as my 15-year-old daughter, Ceara.

When Ceara was first diagnosed with moderate autism at the age of three, I had to catch up fast, as I had little awareness of developmental delays. It was also necessary for me to get over the fact that I didn't like asking for help. During these past several years, I've needed – and asked for and received – support from many people in many areas.

It soon became clear that for Ceara to achieve her greatest potential, we would need all the help we could get – it would indeed "take a village." We gratefully received assistance from many therapists, school teachers, neighbors, members of our church, and others.

Ceara is now a freshman in high school, where she receives extra assistance and continues to make progress. She's definitely an energetic powerhouse, and her social skills remain a challenge – she can be blunt and often misunderstands social situations – so interacting with her requires extra patience and understanding. It helps that we are in a small district where many of the kids have known Ceara since early grade school.

I believe that not only is Ceara learning much, she is teaching much at the same time. Thanks to her, I've learned that there is an overall goodness in our community. I would sincerely like to thank the many therapists, school staff members, students, friends, family members, neighbors, community groups, and leaders who have in some way helped Ceara. They may not even know that they've made a difference, but they have.

It does take a village to help raise our children to their fullest and best potential, and we can *all* make a difference.

Unlocked

By Diana L. Hooker

Alexis had no idea what she would find when she unlocked the storage unit of a homeless man named Ray, just as she had no idea of the bond she would form with Ray while participating in a college service project serving ice cream at a transitional home three years earlier.

Coming to America with his family as a Cuban immigrant, Ray had spent most of his life in poverty. He followed his passions, playing music in a band and writing poems and comics, but a stable life was just beyond his reach. That did not keep Ray down, though, and he was a beam of light for many with his kindness and positive attitude.

When Ray recently passed away, he left all his belongings to Alexis and another homeless man named Chuck – everything that was important enough to this man who seemingly had nothing but nevertheless made arrangements for someone else to have what he did possess.

Opening the door to Ray's storage unit and seeing the collections of another person's life was surreal for Alexis. As it turns out, Ray was thrifty. Among all of his things, she found a duffle bag containing $2,000 cash, half of which was now hers. He had accumulated this money contributing stories to and selling copies of *The Contributor*, a local newspaper written and sold by the homeless community.

Inspired by her friendship with Ray, Alexis formed a partnership company called Unlocked. They employ homeless people to assist them in a transition off the streets and back into a stable society. Their ability to help others was made possible by their first capital investment from a homeless man's duffle bag. What Ray was able to save and build will help others in similar circumstances who need opportunities unlocked for them.

Beauty in Disaster

By Leslie P. Felton

Following Hurricane Matthew in October 2016, many families in and around our community of Greenville, North Carolina, were left with next to nothing. As a result of this natural disaster, I was out of work for two weeks and lost wages, but what I gained is priceless.

Within just days of this catastrophic event, our church became a distribution center through the Churches of Christ Disaster Relief non-profit organization. People came in droves. Some had lost food due to the power outages, some had minor damage to their homes, and some had homes completely destroyed. Yet from the ashes of catastrophe, beauty emerged. Local congregations and caring citizens came out to help those who had been impacted, and some who endured loss payed it forward after they had been helped.

One such person was Olivia, a young Latina mother. After she and her family (including a three-year-old son and a two-month-old baby) received assistance following the hurricane, Olivia returned day after day to make her own contributions – interpreting for us, unpacking boxes of supplies, and even bringing food to feed the volunteers (reminding me of the poor widow's offering from Luke 21:1-4).

Since Matthew, Olivia has brought many of her relatives to be a part of our congregation and has also opened her home to many of us. One time, my husband and I were invited to the family's modest home for a gathering where we were treated like royalty and served a tasty homemade meal. We experienced the goodness of the Lord through this great meal and fellowship, but it did not end there. Following our gathering, Olivia and her relatives said they wanted to prepare a meal for our entire congregation, which is over 100 members. They accepted no money or food donations to assist with their efforts. Following our Sunday church services, everyone was invited to experience this royal treatment. We even took home leftovers!

I am blessed to have these newly forged friendships from the ashes of Matthew. In my eyes, Hurricane Matthew has lived up to its name, gift of Yahweh (God). Sometimes it takes what people call a "disaster" to help us experience and appreciate the beauty that follows.

Grand Rapids of Love
By Heather Wiest

We began the cross-country adventure in our 1976 beige Ford Granada, my mom passed out drunk in the back seat. Dad was driving us from Southern Arizona to our new home in Michigan. However, I knew he wasn't staying with us this time. My parents had recently divorced, and my mom was choosing to live in Grand Rapids with Larry, her new boyfriend. As an eight-year-old gazing out the front-seat window, I wondered how life was going to change.

Larry's apartment seemed foreign, Mom continued her addictive patterns, and the Michigan autumn felt quite chilly to this desert native. In the midst of the upheaval, my new school provided a welcome refuge. During the snowy recess periods, the caring third-grade teacher patiently tutored me and raised my spirits with her smile.

Six weeks quickly passed, and Mom informed me that George, our neighbor in Arizona, would be flying in soon to drive us back to live with him. Confusing thoughts and feelings flooded me. On my last day at that Grand Rapids elementary school, the sweet teacher had each classmate create a unique goodbye card for me. I tightly clutched the brad-sealed manila envelope filled with genuine, colorful expressions of concern, sadness, hope, and love. This quiet, young girl wasn't used to being showered with attention and hugs. Teary-eyed, I walked outside to the school parking lot, opened the back door of the beige Granada, and began the long journey back to the Southwest.

The beautiful letters in that large manila envelope often encouraged my soul through the turbulent years to come. I would re-read them, remembering names and faces of Michigan acquaintances, all of whom made a permanent imprint upon my heart. Grand rapids of love flowed through me. Gratitude lifted my soul. Smiling, I somehow knew my future would overcome these challenging circumstances.

I wish I still had that well-worn manila envelope filled with goodbye cards. I long to personally thank each of the thoughtful creators. I hope they realize the tremendous impact of their expressions of kindness and continue to initiate waves of love.

The Grace of Giving and Receiving

By Tandy R. Elisala

Giving is proof of receiving. I have been fortunate enough to give my time and money to important causes. While in corporate America, I made it a point to know when someone on my team needed extra financial support. One of my best memories of giving occurred when I was 11 years old. The Shriners held an event and gave us $200 to sponsor kids. I was blown away when the kids I sponsored wanted things like socks, underwear, pencils, and paper. They were beaming from ear to ear when we got a Barbie and a basketball in addition to the necessities the kids "wanted."

This was such a humbling experience, and it was the first time in my life that I gave to those less fortunate. That experience stayed with me throughout my life. I regularly paid for military members' meals anonymously. Each year, our family sponsored one Christmas Angel per person. We volunteered for the homeless. We gave in so many ways. It never occurred to me that I wouldn't have money to share and spare…until I didn't.

When I went through cancer a fourth time, I had no insurance and no income. Every penny was accounted for. My adult kids worked and took care of the household. Having cancer was a lesson in truly learning to receive.

We were given food from people we knew and from those we didn't know. We received donations to help manage my healthcare expenses. I had many healer friends offer free sessions. I had friends paying for gas, food, and more. It was humbling, to say the least. I never anticipated I would be in a situation of needing financial assistance from others.

Now, my commitment to giving is stronger than ever. Having come full circle from having massive financial abundance to share to needing help for basic things to having more than enough to spare and share helps me appreciate the value and grace of giving and receiving.

Meatballs Made Me Cry

By Randy Bassett

Many of us have extended a helping hand as a member of a local organization or through a donation to a favourite charity. We do it for a variety of reasons, not the least of which is the feeling it gives us. We simply feel good when we give of our time and resources, making the community a better place.

But what happens when the tables turn? What goes on in our hearts and minds when we find ourselves in need and people extend to us? I found out when my daughter was born. Rather than the usual two- to three-day stay in the hospital after her birth, what started was a whirlwind that included many months in the hospital and an open-heart surgery at 13 days old.

It was then that the gentle touch of the community reached out to us. Aware of the challenges unfolding, friends, family, and strangers stepped forward to help us.

During this period, people perceived my wife and me as being very strong, but in reality, we were lost, seemingly disconnected from our emotions. The fast-moving vehicle we were on did not allow us to bring into focus the people around us as they were reaching out to us.

But then there was a moment of abundant clarity.

Just a few days after our daughter was born, a friend and her 12-year-old daughter came to visit. Knowing that we probably were not focusing on eating or making meals, she brought us a large bowl of meatballs. It seems I had dammed up a wall of emotional energy waiting to be discharged because that friendly hand touching us at just the right time made me break into tears.

I have never forgotten that moment. It was symbolic of the warmth of the community cradling us in our time of need. I realized that these people were also hurting, and I discovered that by reaching out, it gave these wonderful friends an opportunity to heal as well.

I also realized that meatballs do not need to be spicy to make me cry.

Big Men, Big Hearts

By Julie Jones

I live in a small southern town where, a few weeks before each Christmas, members of a motorcycle club come to the local hospital to share gifts and treats for children who are admitted for treatment during the holidays. They arrive in a wave – hundreds of men, women, and children (they even have a police escort!) with trailers and truck beds full of holiday goodies for the kids. As they turn the corner to enter the hospital property, they rev their loud motors, to the delight of the many folks who have come out to watch their grand entrance.

This year, I am one of the nurses assisting the group as they make their rounds and visit the children. I have to say, I had some preconceived notions – I imagined them showing up on their large, loud motorcycles, wearing leather jackets, covered with tattoos – and I am not disappointed.

I introduce myself, and off we head immediately to the pediatric units. We start with the cancer patients. In and out of rooms we go. I watch in silence as the group hands out treats and gifts and spends a few moments talking to the kids and their families.

We arrive at the end of the hallway, and three large men go into a room where a pale, young girl is lying still. The visitors walk to the edge of the bed and, as if on cue, kneel at her side. One tenderly holds her hand; another gently holds her feet while the other one places a hand on her shoulder, talking gently and encouraging her, praying for her and her family. It is a moment of tenderness and loving kindness that overwhelms me.

I notice tears falling gently down my face, and I turn away. The tears are sacred and remind me that my heart is still able to stretch and open. I quietly wipe the tears from my face, remembering how precious and fragile life is – and, if you notice it, goodness abounds.

Breath of Gratitude

By Chris Anderson

Kindness, whether experienced through grand gestures or in subtle moments, has the power to influence our hearts and change our lives.

At 30 I was married, living in a sleepy one-light town. I had adapted well to a quiet way of life, so radically different from the mega cities that I had grown up in. The church community provided a support system I had not previously known, and though my knowledge of religion was limited, I learned that God's knowledge of me was not such a mystery. A kindness shared at a kitchen table made that evident and forever changed my life.

A small group of women, our ages spanning from early 20s to late 70s, had gathered to study the Book of Ruth at one woman's modest home. She served warm banana bread and coffee after the study, and during conversation I admitted my fear of dying and the judgment that surely awaited me in Heaven. Only kind eyes witnessed my confession, yet I felt laid bare and vulnerable, my deepest fears out for everyone to know. Then a gentle hand reached over and took my own.

Each woman had something to say to me. I listened as they lovingly explained that there is no judgment in Heaven, that I would do well to forgive myself and let go of my fears. As their message sank in, I felt a mighty wave crash over me and take my breath away. I stood and sprinted for the door, stepping outside and gasping the deepest breath I had ever taken. It was the first fear-free breath I had ever felt, and I gasped for it again and again, hungrily. Safety and gratitude radiated through me from the inside out.

I sat at that kitchen table nearly 20 years ago. Like everyone, I have faced adversity, experienced sorrow, and had my share of regrets. In challenging moments, I remember the wave of surrender I felt that day and take a deep breath, feeling it as it fills my body with peace and gratitude.

Tornado Strong

By Jamie Lynn Thompson

It was a beautiful, sunny day on Sunday of Memorial Day weekend. Enjoying the day with friends outside, we had no idea that this was the calm before the storm. Then, just like that, the sirens started blaring. We all looked to the sky to see nothing happening.

With the sirens wailing, we headed inside to check the weather on the news, only to find that there was no cable to watch. My cell phone rang; my father was calling from Arizona to make sure my family was all right. He informed me that a tornado had just touched down, and almost half of my hometown was no longer there.

Shortly thereafter, there was no cell phone reception either.

Utter destruction could be seen for miles; not much was left standing. It was determined that an EF5 tornado, three-quarters of a mile wide with winds up to 205 mph, had ripped through the small town. Everyone here was in complete shock.

Nearby towns' volunteer emergency services poured into town to help. As they assessed the damage and checked on each home to see if people were all right or needed help, they were greeted by looks of utter despair mixed with appreciation for surviving.

But the assistance wasn't limited to emergency services. To everyone's amazement, help came pouring in from all over to assist in salvaging through the rubble to find anything they could of what was left of the homes. For months, the help kept coming. Schools brought in busloads of students and other people to help with the cleanup.

It was so overwhelming to witness the wreckage that was once a community. However, little by little, piece by piece, the many helping hands of family, friends, neighbors, and strangers brought the town hope. The outpouring of support was amazing to see.

The town has now rebuilt, stronger than ever – Tornado Strong!

Oh, Holey Sight

By Sheila Jenkins

Early one morning as my daughter took her kids to the bus stop, she noticed the little boy. It was the same little boy she had watched board the bus with her kids over the past 72 days. This particular boy (accompanied by his sister and cousin) was easy to spot because he always had on the same pair of pants with holes in them. Not the kind of ripped jeans that are in style now but real holes. This would be her last day of remaining silent, even if that meant stepping on the parent's toes.

She made a single Facebook post that very morning about the little boy with holey pants. What happened next was something very beautiful to witness. One by one, the comments and private messages started coming in from all over town as well as the surrounding towns asking what size the little boy wore. Over the next couple of weeks so many people came and donated clothes, not just for him but for his sister and cousin, too. My son-in-law's boss donated money to buy them all new clothes as Christmas was just around the corner.

My daughter was overwhelmed by the outpouring of love, goodness, and charity for this little child and his family. She drove into the nearest city to buy them the nicest clothes she could find and wrap them up as Christmas presents. She took all the donated clothes to his house and gave them to the parents. She handed the children their presents when they got off the bus, and their faces lit up.

We may never know the circumstances of another in need, but what we do know is that we can make a difference by just stepping up and stepping in.

One mother and a single Facebook post brought an entire community together to help a little boy and his family...and show that, indeed, goodness still abounds.

Praise You

By Noelle Adamo

Tears glistened on our smiling faces in the November-dark, lamplit parking lot. We were dancing, about 70 of us, to celebrate my husband's 60th birthday with a surprise flashmob. Marc was shining while we spun around him and wove in and out of each other. To say it was purely joyful wouldn't be true. But it was full of a piercing surrender to life.

A month earlier, a teen, Maya, who was exceptionally close to us, had unexpectedly taken her life. She had been a big sister to our children and a treasure to her family and friends. Our world was shaken, and we were overcome with enormous sorrow. Thoughts of celebrating Marc's milestone birthday dissolved in the wake of this encompassing loss.

But then a friend gently suggested we do something collectively to honor Marc, to recognize the preciousness of his life in the midst of our grief, to acknowledge both in our hearts. Though it seemed impossible to dance, when the idea for the flashmob emerged, I smiled. Marc had been saying that without Maya it was essential we "do it double" – live with kindness and fun, like Maya, plus extra. This was a chance to experience his medicine, and hers.

So here we were, breathing in the web of loved ones who rigged the sound system, helped choose the song, orchestrated the surprise, and in our connectedness, affirmed that it was not only possible to dance, it was *necessary*. "Praise You" kept playing. As Marc embraced each friend, a beautiful woman came forward – Maya's mother, Elise. Courageous in this time of raw heartbreak, she was also willing to dance this song with us. It was a blessing beyond compare.

These expressions of love helped us discover how praise comes wrapped with grief, the foil twisted on both ends, and waits to be opened and savored. It requires more than a small craving and collaborators who want the same – a lived experience of pain and joy, loss and life that positions us in awe. We cannot do it alone.

An American Dream

By Hue Anh Nguyen

It had been over two years since our family of 10 arrived at Palawan Refugee Camp in the Philippines, accompanied by over 40 additional townspeople. Families were immigrating to North America and Europe. My parents were favoring America, but although we had a family sponsor, we were denied. We were accepted to several other countries but were encouraged to immigrate to Australia. After two years, finally our miracle arrived: Father Kerry Crowley – a Catholic Parish Priest in Cairns, Australia – provided us with an opportunity to not only live in Cairns but to flourish in this new environment. Finally, a place to call home!

We boarded the airplane (the first time ever for all of us) and had a short transit to Manila, Philippines. On June 13, 1983, after two weeks in Manila, we embarked on a 2,744-mile, eight-hour flight to Australia.

Cairns is warm and tropical, a lot like Vietnam. When we stepped off the plane, however, it was a chilly 6°C (43°F), and we had no winter clothes! We were cold, exhausted, and very unsure of what the future might bring. But we felt incredibly warmed by the open arms and smiling faces that greeted us, including the local Vietnamese who came to welcome us. Ten minutes later, we arrived at a two-story, four-bedroom house that was four times the size of our home in Vietnam – and fully furnished with toys, bikes, and everything we needed!

After 12 years in Australia, I graduated with a Bachelor of Science degree in Nursing and opted for a traveling position – a great opportunity to meet so many people with such diverse personal and professional backgrounds. My employer was able to procure a contract for me in England, a dream come true. In August 1996, my dream continued as I met my future husband, a Vietnamese American living in the U.S. and traveling through England. And so my parents' dream of their children living in America was realized!

When I reflect on these experiences, I'm reminded to stay hopeful, remain positive, and never stop dreaming – despite sadness and unfortunate circumstances – because miracles really do happen! I will always be grateful for our friends at the Cairns Parish and everyone who helped make our dreams come true.

All Is Not Lost

By Terry Corrao

The oppressive August heat descended heavily during my morning walk to the subway. I was going to work at Manhattan's James Beard House, a culinary mecca for chefs, where I interned as a kitchen assistant. That day I had volunteered to work a 12-hour shift, assisting the guest chef and his team from a prestigious American hotel. His five-course dinner with wine pairings for 100 guests had been months in the planning.

Around 4:30 p.m., the chef invited our team to take a break in the outdoor garden. We were chatting with the chef when we were stopped short – the intense city sounds had mysteriously gone dead. Then we discovered that the kitchen lights and refrigerators were out. Panicked, we ran to the front of the house. Passersby said the traffic lights were out and subway trains were stalled in the tunnels. Word soon arrived: a blackout had hit the East Coast grid.

Crushed that his night was in ruins, the chef opened the refrigerator and began disposing of perishable goods. Suddenly, the house manager appeared in the kitchen and said, "Wait, do not throw anything away! We are going into emergency mode. We will feed the staff from St. Vincent's Hospital across the street. Most of them will not be able to go home for some time, so we will give them dinner."

With that directive, the kitchen fell into military formation and quickly readied the meal. The gas stoves still worked, allowing the chef to heat the entrees and side dishes. Soon, hundreds of stressed hospital workers began forming a line at the townhouse door. As they made their way through the kitchen, their eyes grew wide with wonderment at the buffet of exquisite hors d'oeuvres, entrées, vegetables, and desserts. Seeing their faces light up and hearing their sighs of pleasure with each bite was the most heartwarming experience any cook can hope for. Even though it was a night nobody had anticipated, it became a most memorable one for all.

Our Miracle Man
By Tammy Foster

It is said that it takes a village to raise a child. Our village was given the opportunity to help by one pebble dropped in our lake of humanity.

A new couple, far from home, were driving to work, one following the other, when the young man pulled out into oncoming traffic and was crushed. His young, newly pregnant wife, observed this surreal experience and then acted out of instinct to get the help her husband needed. With the many angels around them, he was rushed to the hospital.

The news we received gave little hope as his family rushed from Arizona to Utah to be by his side. That is when our community came together. Prayer chains were started immediately; through Facebook and emails, we were kept abreast of his recovery. A GoFundMe campaign was set up and reached people all over the world. People were touched and gave generously in any way they could. Through community sites and friends sharing on Facebook (reaching 27,625 followers), other fundraisers began in local restaurants, at the stockyard, and in small businesses selling t-shirts and jewelry.

After days of uncertainty, the young man finally woke from his coma, saw his wife, and could not believe he was actually married to the most beautiful woman in the world.

It was a perilous time even after this precious discovery, and we all waited, feeling helpless, holding our breath for more signs of his recovery. These came in small steps, but each was celebrated as a gigantic leap toward his new life. He went through a year of intense therapy to relearn who he was, who his family was, and how to begin life again.

He not only returned to college but graduated this year – a dream that we never imagined, but hoped, would be fulfilled. Even after three years, the village still holds this small, growing family in our hearts and prayers. This experience showed us that it does take a village to thrive in our world, and we have our Miracle Man to remind us of the power of prayer and the village.

Just in Time

By Mikaela Che'lean Hicks

In the summer of 2000, I was a 34-year-old, recently separated mother of two. Struggling to cope with this new status in my life, I was shocked when a sudden illness and trip to the ER ended with a diagnosis of stage III colon cancer. Considering my treatment options with no family nearby for support and so many things on my plate, I felt completely overwhelmed. I consider myself a Christian and prayed a lot during that time. Even so, I don't think I really had any expectations of receiving a "miracle."

I received a call during my first week of treatment from a group of ladies who attended First Christian Church, which many of my co-workers attended. They had heard that I needed prayer. They also quickly arranged a meal schedule and began bringing meals to the house daily. Then my car broke down! Two days later, I went to the mailbox and found a note with money to fix the car and help with a few bills.

Each time I began to feel hopeless, a small note of support or a little help would show up in my life. During my surgeries, my mom flew down to help. The pastor showed up and prayed with me. He also sat with my mom during the procedure and the long hours of recovery.

Miracles showed up in small ways each day from people I didn't even know. The outpouring of love toward me and my daughters changed my life. Small acts of kindness deepened my faith in faith. I discovered my miracle through the collective power of each gesture.

Seventeen years later, I am cancer free. The proud mother of two strong young women and a beautiful granddaughter, my life is full. The experience of receiving such unconditional support helped me heal then and continues to inspire my love of supporting others. I look forward to being someone's "miracle."

Superheroes

By Aphrodite Mirisis

Goodness is a simple word, but those who embody it are the real superheroes of the world.

Three and a half years ago, my world was pulled out from under me when my husband passed away suddenly. My body became a hollow shell; I became a robot, empty of emotion, empty of grief. I had no tears to cry. But my brain went into overdrive. I kept wondering: *How can I clear the turmoil clogging my brain and make sense of my life again?*

And then, like superheroes, my family and friends came to the rescue. Armed with goodness, they helped me in ways I never could have imagined possible. They offered me their hands to hold, their ears to listen, their smiles to lead me back to sensibility, and their ideas to open my mind and guide me through the cloud of blindness. They surrounded me with love and listened to me as I tried to make sense of my life. They offered suggestions. They kept me company at times when I could not stand to be by myself. But most of all, my two boys – my rocks – helped me the most. Together we talked about things that concerned us – our finances, our ability to survive our loss – and together we brainstormed. They gave me fresh ideas on how to conquer the challenges in front of us.

Through the goodness of individuals around me, I found my way out of the darkness. And over time, I was finally able to grieve, cleanse my spirit, and re-enter the world of the living.

Goodness, I learned, is one of the most healing powers we hold within ourselves. Not only can it help us within, but it can help those without. It lifts, it nourishes, and it saves, and it does this ever so quietly, like flowers reviving after a long, hard winter. It warms us and gives us strength.

Many think that superheroes do not exist, but in my eyes they are all around us, armed with goodness and ready to save those who need saving.

Transitions

By Charlene Williams

Have you ever come to a place in your life where you thought you'd made the right decision but then started to seriously doubt yourself? I experienced this after I pulled myself and my five children out of a cult religion, left an abusive man, and attempted to pick up the shattered pieces of our lives while still trying to maintain some sense of normalcy and fun for the kids. Because of my decision, people I had thought were my friends weren't allowed to speak to me yet were actively (behind my back) trying to recruit my kids. The kids were confused – missing the way our family used to be and the church that had become such a central point in our lives.

On top of all this, my part-time job didn't supply nearly enough to cover expenses, and groceries were always the first thing to be cut back. My children never knew that, twice a week after I got them off to school, I would stand in line at the food bank to gratefully accept a few extra bags of food for my family. Christmas was just around the corner, and I felt so inadequate, fragile, and scared.

Part of me was questioning God – wanting reassurance that my kids and I would be all right, that God really was there and loved us and would help me provide for my family. Then, two things happened that reaffirmed my faith: First, my therapist's organization called and asked if the kids and I could come in. I assumed it was in regard to family counseling, but when we got there, my kids were directed to a pile of gifts for them for Christmas! They were so excited to open their new toys and each got a coat for winter! I also received a special gift: a hand-stitched quilt! I was so moved by the generosity of spirit exhibited to my family. A few days later, I was in the kitchen and saw a woman from the church walk past my front door and get into her car. I was puzzled, so I went and opened the door…and found three bags full of groceries! While I brought them into the house, sobbing in gratitude, a loud voice said, "Those are man's laws, not my laws."

After my racing heart slowed to a normal beat, I realized that I'd been shown that I was not alone and that there were people with good hearts and good intentions who would take a risk to bless someone else.

Dumela

By Lauren Bear

It was spring in the Kalahari desert, and things were just starting to come back to life. I couldn't tell if the short desert trees were dead or just dormant. The dusty red sand reminded me of New Mexico.

Botswana's landscape may have been striking, but it wasn't easy to get around in. I was farther out of town than I'd expected, and traveling anywhere was a challenge for me. It was a kilometer, maybe more, in the hot sun to where you could catch a taxi.

When I heard from Samara, I was afraid I would have to cancel. We'd been talking for months about a tattoo, but I told her that I had no idea how I would get to her studio. Her response – "I'll pick you up" – was a delightful surprise!

Over the coming weeks, my interactions with Samara turned into episodes of her waiting patiently for me…and being central to some of my best experiences. I decided I needed to be closer to town, so I moved to stay with Ryan, who knows Samara.

My first night at Ryan's, Samara picked me up to have dinner. I ended up with a terrible migraine, and Samara was like a mother caring for me. I felt safe and looked after. When she took me back to Ryan's, the path to the house was lit with gentle lights strung in a mulberry tree. It was magical.

At Ryan's, there were stories, lovely gatherings, many cups of bush tea, and people who treated me like an old friend. Ryan felt like he was my brother, and he introduced me to my new "sister," Anah.

Ryan also introduced me to Mma Modisa's street-food. Anah took me to a gorgeous garden, and we all shared evenings of quiet conversation. We watched a movie projected onto a sheet in Ryan's organic garden with the sounds of chickens behind us.

Kindness and looking out for each other seem woven into the fabric of life in Botswana. The typical greeting there is *Dumela*, which means "I see you; I believe in you." Ubuntu is a philosophy of kindness, and I found it in Botswana.

Bubbly Blessings

By Michael Brewer

I am a Front Office Manager at a beach resort in Australia. I love my job because I have the opportunity to meet so many beautiful people. I do everything I can to ensure that our guests enjoy their stay at the resort.

I recently received a call from Mary, a woman who wanted to purchase a bottle of champagne for one of our guests. Mary explained that her daughter-in-law, Michelle, was having a brief holiday before starting chemotherapy the next week. This would be her last opportunity for quite some time to have a drink. My wife and sister are breast cancer survivors. I told Mary that I would not charge her because of my understanding of what Michelle was going to face in the coming months. When Michelle checked out, she thanked me for the champagne, and I wished her all the best in her upcoming battle.

A few days later, I was checking our online reviews. Michelle had written a wonderful review, complimenting my empathy and amazing service. Michelle wrote in part, "Michael went above and beyond and refused to charge for it, and sent it to us off his own back due to his experience with cancer. Absolutely amazing!" Reviews like these really make my job worthwhile.

I decided to post Michelle's review on my Facebook page. The positive message spread around the world. I was touched again by many wonderful comments. One in particular really touched my heart. It said "Because you and Ann [my wife] are fantastic, beautiful people, so many of us are blessed to have met you."

I was already happy to offer a small gesture of goodwill for someone facing such a daunting challenge, but to see the appreciation and love return to me made the whole experience even better. By adding their own goodness through their kind words, Michelle and my friends allowed the goodness to ripple across the world, providing a blessing of love and gratitude to all.

We all have the opportunity to spread a little goodness to make a positive difference in the lives of others.

Light Outshines the Darkness
By Kelli Adkins

It was like a bad dream. My life had changed forever in an instant. I felt trapped – full of guilt, shame, embarrassment, and fear. *How did this happen to me?* I wondered.

Just two days earlier, I experienced domestic violence that triggered a cascade of chronic pain, dementia, traumatic brain injury, and spinal cord damage. I was still covered in bruises, and my life felt like it had fallen apart.

At that time, I was working at the VA Hospital as a nurse. No one knew the truth, only that I had fallen severely ill. However, when my co-workers found out I was in need, they quickly jumped to the rescue by serving our family. They put together a much-needed fundraiser for mounting medical expenses and donated 400 hours of their own paid time off. That meant that I was paid for four full months despite not being able to work.

They also took turns bringing us food – an ongoing act of kindness they kept up for nearly a year! During that time, my co-workers were sometimes the only people I would see all week, providing me with a bright light in a very dark world. And after a year, many of them even came to help me move when I decided to leave the failed marriage.

Even though each co-worker may have felt they did a seemingly small act of service, it added up! Due to their kindness, I was able to feed my family, keep our home, pay our bills, and have much-needed surgeries. But most of all, their acts showed me that there was still hope and light in this world.

Opening to Receive Love

By Erin Fritts

Through a local church, I was recently invited to join a group of women entrepreneurs on a spiritual "I Am" journey. A year earlier, I would have said no right away, but I had been connecting with my purpose and a power greater than me, and something was gently telling me that this journey would be a good idea. Before I could overthink it, I committed.

On the morning of our first meeting, I could feel the nerves and tension rising in my body. As we all sat down together, the first question was to share our religious backgrounds. Oh no! Fears and memories came flooding back from years ago when I was accusingly asked by a friend's mother, "Why don't you go to church?" I was too young to understand how to answer. I remember feeling the hot embarrassment and wishing I could disappear. I felt I didn't belong. I wasn't good enough.

Here I was now as an adult, sitting in a circle of devout women, and I was going to have to say that I don't attend church once again. My throat constricted, and I instantly felt the beads of sweat forming! *Deep breaths*, I told myself. *That was years ago. These women aren't going to judge me that way...or will they?*

They did not – quite the opposite, in fact: I was welcomed with open arms, literally! This amazing group of women quickly created a safe and powerful container for sharing and growth. I was even acknowledged for stepping out of my comfort zone, giving me that little extra support and appreciation I wasn't giving myself.

The love, acceptance, and uninhibited sharing I experienced forever changed me. I felt a powerful shift, a steady confidence and faith. I didn't recognize this as a turning point in my life until months later. I integrated their love on a cellular level, the way in which you don't even remember how it used to feel. Amazing things happen when we come together and raise up one another.

Goodness Abounds...Even on Facebook

By Alisa Auger

I remember the moment like it was yesterday. After spending hours journaling about all of my repressed pain and really allowing myself to feel those forgotten feelings, after years of being comfortably numb, I found self-love and deep gratitude. I was truly thankful for all my past experiences that had led me to this place. I saw myself. And it was in this moment that I awakened to my new reality – the one where the Universe bestowed gifts upon me that I couldn't explain.

I started to hear the music – songs floating down from above in complete and finished form – the words, the melodies, both beautiful and inspiring. It was magical for me to witness, even though it was all happening to me! It was almost unbelievable.

After hundreds of songs flowed through me, it was time to start sharing. I had a knowing that these songs weren't just for me. I felt compelled to share...so I started simply. I recorded myself singing my song "The Inner Child Knocks" and posted it in a Facebook group. I had no expectations and just followed my inspiration. Little did I know how much one comment, from someone I didn't even know, would mean to me.

She said, "You speak for me!"

I was taken aback. I felt the enormous impact of her statement. It was just the confirmation I needed to truly believe in the importance of sharing my creativity. It was no longer just about me and my own self-expression but rather an understanding and connection with others. It wasn't long after that I found myself in a professional recording studio.

I unleashed my creative voice in a big way, and I discovered that my voice matters, just as yours does, too! It's vital that we express ourselves; for many, creativity is the perfect vehicle. Explore, create, and celebrate. Share your voice with the world...because your voice truly matters. Even if you're just sharing a generous comment on a Facebook post, you may never know the impact that you have.

We Are One.

Dancing in Istanbul

By Sarah Atkinson

These days, my favorite way to connect with others is through folk dancing. I live in Turkey, a country with rich and varied folk dance traditions. When I first moved here, it was summer. By the pier, where the ferry takes foot passengers from the Asian part of Istanbul to the European side (the city straddles two continents), I would often encounter a group of young people dancing in a line or a large circle. They danced to the sound of a single kemanche, a simple stringed instrument that hails from Turkey's Black Sea coast, usually played by an elderly man. The style of the dance dictates that the dancers huddle close together, shoulder to shoulder, with hands clasped behind them. They move as a fluid unit, as a wave.

From first sight I was intrigued, and I wanted to learn more about these dances. My wonder spurred me to investigate, and eventually I found an organization where enthusiasts of such dances can learn and practice these and other regional dances.

In addition to lessons, I started regularly attending weekend events, often by myself. At first I felt shy, awkward, but I felt compelled to be there. I rarely approached anyone, although I am by nature quite outgoing. This was clearly an established community, with people bound by a common love of music and dance. In the beginning, I mostly observed. I would arrive, get a beer, and hold up the wall until I built up the courage to try a dance.

Gradually, I became a part of the community. I got to know people; they welcomed me in, were patient and encouraging. I've now learned many of the dances. I love how it feels to join hands and feel the pulse and hum of the supportive and dynamic energy that flows from joyous body to joyous body. It's a powerful way of communicating and connecting with others that doesn't involve language and its requisite liabilities.

Life here is not so easy nowadays; the political situation is dire. The dancing helps us get through it.

It Takes a Village

By Shari Sorbo

It's been said, "It takes a village." This is a true statement, especially when it comes to growing in consciousness.

Over the past several years, I have been blessed to be able to participate in a two-year program that licenses practitioners to become teachers and facilitators in their field of consciousness studies. This program ended this past month with all seven students taking their oral panels and passing with flying colors.

As I look back on the past years, there have been many people who contributed to the growth of these individuals, and these contributors were not without their own challenges and growth as well. It was wonderful to be able to participate and step in when needed and also to be able to sit and observe when that was needed.

What I began to see was that not only were we able to nurse along seven individuals into their brilliance, we as a team nursed each other as well. When we started this journey, we began as separate individuals with one goal in mind: graduation. Gradually, as the months and years progressed, we became a "village" of elders together raising "children."

During graduation, I noticed how bonded this class had become – bonded as a class, yes, but also bonded as a *village* and now as a new group of people experiencing their brilliance! This graduating class merged into the body of elders, making their way into serving a new class.

Yes, it takes a village, and a beautiful village it is!

Asking for Help

By Taryn Pyle

Life had gotten out of control. I was in constant pain, my husband had been hospitalized three times over the past five years, and we were drowning in debt. And just when I thought I'd already hit rock bottom, I tripped and broke my femur, forcing me to spend three months in a rehab facility. On top of extensive, daily physical therapy, I was trying to keep up with work. My husband was struggling to keep the house together on his own, and I was struggling to walk. It all felt hopeless.

I had always been a very proud woman, intent on never asking for help, but I just couldn't keep it all together anymore. I finally reached out to my younger sister and her husband. They sat down with me and my husband, and we shared all the bad and the ugly of what our lives looked like. We were embarrassed, but they were kind, respectful, and honest. They gently guided us through some very tough decisions, provided alternatives to the "no-way-out" perspective we'd been tied to, and relieved a lot of the pressure that had been building for so long.

With help from them and other family members, we remodeled our house, sold it, downsized to a one-level apartment, found loving homes for our foster pets, paid off all our bills, corrected our taxes, and started to get out of debt. Friends also came out of the woodwork to help us through this challenging time. There was a friend who built a ramp for me to get up into my house, a realtor who sent her husband to our house to rake leaves and prepare the house for sale, and a friend who brought us fresh meals. There was a woman who came by every day just to walk our dogs, an organizer who helped us sort through three floors of our house to decide what to take and what to give up, and friends who showed up to pack it all up and help us move.

It pains me to think about how long we suffered without asking for help. But when I finally let go of my pride, shared my situation honestly, and reached out to others, goodness came out full force! Today, we are close to debt free, and my load is lighter in so many ways. I have less to worry about and more to love about my life. I've learned to love others as greatly as I was loved and to pay it forward, as others did for me. Most of all, I've learned that it's okay to ask for help.

Making Magic

By Robin OK

For the past six years, I have served in the role of Visionary and Coordinator for the annual Creative Collaborative Retreat in Cincinnati, Ohio, where I live. I can honestly say that it is my favorite weekend of the year. Each one is different, with its own theme and its own unique collection of women who choose to attend. Yet the healing, the love, the powerful positive energy, and the enduring impact consistently and continually astound me.

Magic happens when we come together in community with the intention of nurturing ourselves – mind, body, and spirit. What kind of magic, you ask? That would be indescribable. And unplannable. The kind that takes us all by surprise. The kind that happens simply because of who shows up – the stories, the experiences, and the willingness.

At these retreats, we gather in circles, large and small, centered on connection and play. The focus is on creative exchange – heart to heart, spirit to spirit. The intention is to simply *be*. The effect is profound.

The first year, one woman reveled in the weekend and has often gushed, "Honey, that weekend changed my life! This space you create is so important. Everyone deserves to have this." She was so grateful that she has anonymously donated funds, making it possible for other women who could not afford it to attend. Over the years, her generosity has sponsored magic in the lives of many women. One of those recipients had been a caregiver for her ailing father for years and was able to participate in the retreat soon after he passed away. After years of isolation and sacrifice, she found profound friendship and re-awakened her natural creative spirit. As a result, she found the courage to write her father's story – a trilogy of books, the first two of which are now published. (Can you say "Magic"?)

I have had the honor of holding the space where grace and love manifest. In this process, I have borne witness to transformation and healing. The ripple effect of goodness makes my heart swell with gratitude. I offer my thanks to those who generously provide opportunities for others – *this* is creative collaboration...aka MAGIC!

Light a Lamp

By Pratibha Badurkar

"Wish you a very happy Diwali," I said, smiling at the man behind the shop counter.

I was there shopping for gifts for Diwali, a five-day festival of light that we Indians celebrate each autumn. During this holiday, we light lamps all around that celebrate the victory of light over darkness. Diwali also symbolizes wealth, prosperity, and abundance and is also celebrated as New Year. The time leading up to this holiday is always a season for shopping, as there is a tradition of exchanging gifts with friends, relatives, and loved ones with wishes for Diwali.

Because of all the extra shopping during this season, people who work in the shops often work longer hours, spending more time away from home and family, in order to better serve their customers. When I saw the man working at the shop counter, I felt that I must show my gratitude, even though he was a total stranger.

For a moment, he didn't realize that I was speaking to him, but when he did, his face lit up with a beautiful smile and his eyes glowed with happiness. He replied, "Thank you, *didi* [sis]. Wish you happy Diwali, too."

Feeling the happiness in his broad smile and warm words was a beautiful gift to me in that moment. Soon, however, the gift multiplied. I heard people all around the shop wishing each other happy Diwali, as if the store had been converted into a huge get-together of friends. All the faces were shining with beautiful smiles, as if a line of lit-up lamps were shining all over the store. I was filled with a feeling of joy, prosperity, and abundant happiness that I'd never experienced before.

This experience reminded me of Buddha's saying: "If you light a lamp for someone else, it will also brighten your path." Indeed, the small seed of a smile grows into a great tree of goodness, spreading its branches all around us.

Generous Souls

By Kimberly Hutt

Living in a small community has so many blessings – being able to personally witness so much kindness and love is inspiring and uplifting. Much of our community functions on the kindness and generosity of the people who reside here and call this lovely little area home. Volunteers contribute many hours in many areas of expertise. Many are involved in everyday functioning of daily life:

Hospital volunteers share time manning the visitor desk and the gift store, assisting people with locating loved ones, and escorting people to and from appointments.

Hospice volunteers assist terminally ill patients and provide relief for caregivers and family members. Day Hospice provides much-needed social time and a chance to get out of the house for many people. Staff and volunteers create a welcoming and wonderful space for self-care, comfort, and companionship.

We have three fire stations, all manned by volunteers and kindhearted souls who sacrifice time, sleep, and pay to assist in emergency situations. (This week has been a very busy one for many of them!) Their families selflessly take the risks and pray that they all return safely from each call.

Many organizations – such as the Lions Clubs, American Legion, and 100 Women Who Care – create amazing opportunities for social connection and community growth. They also lead huge fundraisers that generate tens of thousands of dollars for deserving charities.

Local churches and food banks ensure that no family goes without. Volunteers organize and assist in these generous activities year round.

Local high-school students volunteer community hours to receive their diplomas, gathering those hours with pure hearts and open minds.

We also have a huge organized soccer program that sees up to 600 kids and families gather each Saturday morning for fun and exercise – all hosted and run by volunteers.

I am very proud of this small community and all the love, light, and generosity that is exchanged here – and I've learned that home is as beautiful as you make it!

Chapter 8
Giving Back

As we write this, many natural disasters are occurring in our world — from hurricanes and flooding to earthquakes and fires. Seeing so many people and animals suffer is absolutely devastating. While these disasters are absolutely heartbreaking to witness, we're seeing people's hearts expand and goodness abound because of them. When faced with destruction such as this, we all tend to forget our differences and do whatever we can to help.

Because of these recent tragedies, we've learned about people and organizations who are really stepping up and making a difference, such as the many animal rescues and humanitarian efforts that are literally saving lives, or the man who turned his furniture store into a temporary shelter for those whose homes had been flooded, or the ordinary (who were truly *extraordinary*) people who opened their homes, their wallets, and their hearts to complete strangers. While of course we wish natural disasters never happened, we are glad that people continue to give when others are suffering. That's what goodness is all about.

We're also happy to know that it doesn't require such devastation for people to open their hearts to one another. For example, we knew a woman who bought one book and wrapped it up for each child at a charter school where we taught. She wanted to make sure each child knew they were thought about, which warmed our hearts. Another example of giving back is that we frequently see a woman picking up trash on the side of the road in our community, which we're so thankful for. On the pages that follow, you'll find many stories of others who give from their hearts. And it's our hope that your heart gets all warm and fuzzy while reading them. Ours definitely did.

Play Ball!

By Mauri Barnes

Shawn and I were among the volunteers helping to build a medical clinic in Kaugi Village, a mission that took us into the highlands of equatorial Kenya. It was his first trip overseas. He worked construction with young men from the village while I assisted at the free clinic set up in a church down the road. Each team member had filled their suitcase with donations for the village. He packed donated baseball equipment, enough to outfit a team.

It was the Meru County District Commissioner's dream to bring baseball to Kenya, and he was delighted to schedule a clinic for Shawn to coach the local schools' teams. Sharing years of training in baseball was easy, yet nothing prepared Shawn for the reality of these village teams. For some of the young students, he was the first white-skinned person they had ever seen. He knelt as they lined up to touch his skin and long golden hair before running away giggling.

The school's sports field sloped down the mountainside. The upper edge of the field was lined with the entire student body. The commissioner, his bodyguards, the principal, and our friends Ruth and Ben stood close by, smiling and ready to help. Cell phones recorded the demonstrations. The baseball teams shyly gathered to show their skills. Many were barefoot. They played with a hand-carved wooden bat and a single shredding baseball. Not being familiar with the game, they swung wildly at every pitch, gleefully chasing balls down the steep slopes of the outfield. They had never watched baseball on TV. They didn't have TV or electricity or money to buy baseball equipment.

Shawn handed out treasures from his bag to the players, each of them so excited to learn how to swing a real bat and catch a ball wearing a glove. The principal translated instructions into Kimeru, and teachers helped students learn by watching and mimicking. We joined in, laughing and helping the boys learn to play the game.

Shawn's gift of baseball equipment and coaching helped those boys develop their game, earning them baseball scholarships and acceptance onto international teams. And a man's dream became a reality.

With Tragedy Came Purpose

By Farahana Surya Namaskar

"Earthquake Devastates Nepal, Killing More Than 1,900" (*New York Times*). "More than 1,800 dead as magnitude 7.8 quake rocks Nepal" (*USA Today*). "Nepal earthquake: Death toll climbs above 4,800" (*CNN.com*). These are just a few headlines after the April 2015 Nepal earthquake that shattered the lives of thousands of individuals and families. Among the thousands who witnessed the tragedy is a 65-year-old female survivor.

She had flown to Kathmandu, Nepal, a few days earlier on a spiritual retreat. It was her first visit to the country. She was mesmerized and in complete awe of the beauty of the Himalayan Mountains and the centuries of culture and traditions embodied by the people, temples, and spiritual centers. Her soul danced, and a serene peace embraced her in this foreign yet seemingly familiar land.

After two days of sightseeing and capturing images on her camera, she was sitting in meditation one morning at her hotel with a group of other women. As she got up from the meditation for a bathroom break, she suddenly felt the ground beneath her shaking violently, throwing her a few feet into the air. The pain from the impact as she hit the ground, pierced through her arthritic knees. The next three days felt like the longest of her life. Camped outside in cold, rainy weather, with continued aftershocks threatening their already disrupted peace, the woman and other guests at the resort desperately prayed for their lives – with no promise of ever returning home safely to their families.

By the grace of God, the woman was able to return home safely. However, this was not the end of her journey, rather, only the beginning. At 65 years old, she believed that a door had opened, revealing her divine life's purpose. She is now actively involved with helping to rebuild the lives of people in Nepal. She has been raising money and donating school supplies to children and families in Kathmandu and surrounding areas. She has made two trips back to Nepal since the earthquake, and she strives to involve other people in her mission as well. Her courage and determination at her age inspires me so much, and I am so proud to call her my mother.

Hugs and Haircuts

By Cynthia Lee Horn

It was a lovely afternoon. Momma and I were visiting in her bedroom – her "sanctuary," as she calls it. She lives in a private assisted-living home in Surprise, Arizona, close to our large family. We like to think God hand-picked this home for her – and for us! It has eased our hearts and minds to know how well she is cared for by the lovely people who touch her life daily – the very personable owner, her children, and even some of the other residents' families who visit.

Momma told me about one of the regular visitors – the wife of a gentleman living there – who cuts everybody's hair at the home and doesn't charge for it. *How nice of her,* I thought. *Haircuts can be pricey these days!* Feeling grateful for the kind, generous service this lady was offering – the bit of goodness she was adding to the world – I sent up a little thank-you and blessing to her and then let the thought go.

We continued our afternoon visit, creating moments and memories. Momma was sitting in her recliner working on a needlepoint Christmas gift for a family friend, and I was sitting on her comfy twin bed when we heard a knock on the door. In walked a woman I'd never seen before, but I noticed how Momma's face lit up as soon as she saw her. She was an older woman with gentle mannerisms, a bright smile, kind eyes, and a darling silver-gray haircut. The woman said she was just coming in to check if Momma still wanted to go to church with her in the morning. I thought how nice it was that my mother had a support team and opportunities for a full and meaningful life!

Then I made the connection. "Are you the one who cuts everybody's hair here?" I asked her. She said yes, and I thanked her for her service.

She humbly and joyously replied, "Well, God gave me this gift and talent, and it's my duty to share it. All I ask for is a hug in return."

We all smiled and collectively enjoyed sharing this sweet moment of goodness.

God Stepped In

By Teresa Velardi

I have the honor and privilege of being part of a church that has a heart for community outreach. We've filled thousands of backpacks, donated large sums of money to shelters and resource centers, and most recently, donated a massive number of diapers to local organizations helping families in need.

When "Diaper Duty" was announced, the goal was to collect 100,000 diapers. The church family faithfully stepped up with over 126,000 diapers collected! But that was only the beginning!

Matt, who was a relatively new church attendee, learned about the diaper project. While driving home one day, a neighbor's dog ran out in front of Matt's car. Unable to stop in time, he hit the dog. Fortunately, the dog was not seriously injured; even more fortunately, Matt is a veterinarian. He and his neighbor went to his office where Matt treated the dog and sent him home.

During a follow-up visit, Matt mentioned the church "Diaper Duty" project. As it turns out, the dog's owner is an executive at Proctor and Gamble. Because of that conversation, P&G decided to join the efforts of the church by donating a 53-foot tractor-trailer filled with diapers and baby wipes. That generous donation added 180,000 diapers to the total!

The project ultimately yielded over 300,000 diapers, which were then donated to many organizations helping young families in northeastern Pennsylvania.

Whenever I think of how this unfolded, I can honestly say that only God could have orchestrated it. Had Matt not run into that dog, then he would have never met...well, you get the picture. Something good comes out of every situation, so be grateful for everything.

When we step up, that's when God steps in!

Be generous. Improve lives. Change hearts.

An Upward Spiral
By Barbara Toller

"What lies behind us and what lies before us are tiny matters compared to what lies within us." - Ralph Waldo Emerson

Modern neuroscience tells us that the brain can rewire old internal response patterns relating to trauma and establish new, healthier coping behaviors. A sense of belonging, connection to others, and being seen, understood, and accepted all build feelings of safety and trust leading to self-esteem and resilience.

My friend Paige is a living example of this theory. When her parents divorced, she was raised by her mom. Her dad – a prominent trial attorney who suffered from mental illness – was unpredictable and verbally abusive and was briefly sentenced to jail. The family spun out of control, and her siblings battled many demons, including drugs, mental illness, and crime.

It took Paige years to understand the toll her upbringing had on her. She had feelings of worthlessness, fear, and vulnerability. Over time, she learned from her mom that helping others can build inner strength and enhance self-worth. Together, they volunteered at homeless kitchens and opened their doors to host international students. Paige wanted to pass on the skills she learned that helped her become the confident, secure woman she is today. For this reason, she dedicated her adult life to empowering others. Her children carried on the tradition, and when they grew old enough for independence, Paige started the Youth Ambassadors Program.

This non-profit program gives teenagers in underserved communities in Kansas and Missouri the tools and resources to overcome early childhood trauma. Students are prepared for success through mentorship, skill development, and character building. They're given a voice through the publication of their writings, documentaries, and photography to educate others on the issues affecting youth today.

Paige says she will never have the "empty-nest syndrome" because she loves every Youth Ambassador as one of her own. She is so proud of the thousands of students who have broken the cycle of addiction, violence, and fear and are "rewired" as resilient and empowered members of society.

The Kindness of an Unsung Hero

By Tracey Swainson

While growing up, Pete heard stories from his grandfather, a tall, lovely farmer who fought in a battle a very long way from home. Following in the footsteps of men before him, his father chose to serve in the Second World War, and then his older brother followed the men before him to Vietnam.

The importance of serving his country was instilled in this young man from a very young age. He learned to respect the men and women who go to war, never knowing if they'll return.

Naturally, when he came of age, he chose to follow in the footsteps of those who walked before him.

As he came through the ranks of the New Zealand Army and eventually retired, Pete realized he had friends who had passed away, buried with their loved ones in public cemeteries. Years ago, it was custom that soldiers were not to have their partners buried with them in military cemeteries, so many chose to be laid to rest with their families in public cemeteries.

Pete knew that his grandfather was placed in a public cemetery, and it was then that he realized he had a new purpose, a new reason to serve, giving him a deep sense of duty that filled his heart with joy.

It's now his personal quest to serve those soldiers laid to rest in public cemeteries. He has a profound understanding that he was so lucky to have served his country and yet never had to fight in a war like so many before him. He now takes this on as a duty of service, to honor all those soldiers before him.

Each year on the afternoon of Anzac Day, out of the public eye, Pete goes from cemetery to cemetery, cleaning grave sites and laying a poppy wrapped in a sprig of rosemary to honor those who have served and passed before him.

What a privilege it is to know this unsung hero who, in his own way, continues to serve his country with honor.

Loving Choices

By Linsey Fischer

I remember being a little girl, not understanding what it meant to see a truck full of animals go by on the highway. I thought the animals were going to the farm or to a pet store.

Later on in life, I realized they were what I was eating on my plate. However, I still didn't give much thought to what these animals went through, until I became vegetarian. That's when I started to read, research, and understand the things I had been consuming and how each product is made. It was then I discovered what it meant to be a vegan and why people choose to go this route.

What is a vegan?

A vegan is a person who does not consume animal products. I used to think this was extreme, but my mind has changed since I discovered that the food vegans eat is delicious and the choice to go vegan is made for such beautiful reasons.

Some make the choice as an act of self-care (for the health benefits). Some make the choice out of love for the planet (fighting against climate change). Some do it for their love of animals (for the ethical treatment of animals). The list goes on, but the core reason is based on one commonality: love. How could I argue with that?

Not everyone can commit to being a vegan, and some may choose not to. It's about what is right for you. What I have found is that there are many people who don't understand the choice. I have heard people say that vegans think they are better than others. I believe that this misconception is due to not understanding the message.

Vegans do not think they are above anyone. They are simply trying to better themselves, educate others, help the planet, and (most importantly, in my opinion) fight for the ethical treatment of animals – all things I wish I'd been aware of earlier in life.

Being a vegan or a vegetarian is about making a conscious decision to make loving choices, and that is a beautiful thing.

An Earth Angel Among Us

By Patricia LeBlanc

Once, at a major event where I volunteered, a life-changing course was being offered. One of the women there badly wanted to take this course, which she knew would allow her to go to the next level and create the life that she truly desired. The only problem was that she couldn't afford to pay for it. She tried to find a way but was having no luck – and began to grow quite frustrated.

On the last day of the event, someone who saw her full potential stepped up and paid for her to take the course. At first, he didn't want her to know that he paid for it, so he asked us to present her with the welcome kit that came with the course. When the lead trainer presented her with the welcome kit – and explained that it had been anonymously donated to her – the woman's face was priceless. She could not believe that a stranger would pay for the course she wanted. She started to cry, and she kept saying, "Thank you! Thank you!" She also wanted to know who paid for her course as she wanted to thank them.

Eventually, the man who'd donated the course came forward. She gave him a big hug and said, "Thank you! You've changed my life, and I don't know how I can ever repay you."

He replied, "When you go to the course, give it 100%, and when you leave, apply it to your life." He also told her to pay it forward when the opportunity presents itself.

You see, he was now financially free, but that had not always been the case. He had someone help him when he needed it, and he saw this as his opportunity to pay it forward.

I am so blessed that I got to witness this magical moment. It was nice to see someone who was in a position to help another person do so. This day gave me hope that goodness does exist.

A Fighting Chance

By Rev. Shelia Prance

In 2013, a group from a small rural town traveled to Haiti on a mission trip. While there, one of the team members saw a young boy with a large tumor on the side of his face. She took his picture and wrote down his name and address.

After the mission team arrived back in the United States, this lady started researching what medical options were available. She learned of a local university that provides medical services on an international basis free of charge. Through this program, she was able to obtain a medical visa for the boy. Arrangements were made for him, his mother, and a translator to travel to the community.

When the boy was examined in the hospital, the doctors found a life-threatening tumor obstructing his mouth and nose. Fortunately, the tumor was non-cancerous and was successfully removed.

During the period of convalescence, the three visitors from Haiti were guests in the home of the lady and her family. She provided food, housing, and transportation to and from the hospital for the boy's numerous doctor visits. They lived with her family until the medical team released the boy to return to his home in Haiti.

Two years later, however, the tumor returned and spread toward his brain. Again, he flew to the U.S., where the doctors removed the tumor and a large portion of the roof of his mouth. This procedure was followed by reconstructive surgery and dental work, which an orthodontist performed at a reduced cost.

In 2016, the boy was granted legal immigration with special juvenile status (which is valid for 10 years from the date of approval). He is currently enrolled in a local school, where he is learning English as a second language and is very popular – partly due to his soccer skills!

Thanks largely to one woman's kindness, this young man now has a fighting chance for life.

People Helping People

By Shannon L. Brokaw

I've recently noticed a deeper anger brewing within many people. Any time I was online reading the news of the day, it was followed by a barrage of vitriol that I didn't care to engage in.

I started to wonder if humankind was still alive and well. If so, where was the *humanity*?

With these thoughts in mind, I headed to a local park where I walked my dog. While there, I noticed many "tunnel people" – a community of people who had come here to Vegas, the city of broken dreams, full of hopes and aspirations – now just trying to eke out a meager living in this precarious labyrinth of uncertainty.

Immediately, I knew what I needed to do. I ran to the local grocery store and grabbed whatever was the special of the day – followed by glares of being that cheapskate. Utensils in hand, I headed home to divide what I had: socks, lotions, shampoos, first aid, food items, and anything else that I thought would be needed. I packed the "blessing kits" and shoved them into the back of my truck.

Back at the park, I ran into a few ladies who had brought clothes and prepared dinners for the community of homeless at our doorsteps. There was no ego. No "who did what." No snaps for Instagram or Facebook. It was just pure, unconditional giving.

That rush, that feeling, that *love* – breaking all political and social boundaries – *that* was what I needed. I discovered the piece of community that I had needed to quell my restless soul.

To see it in action – to see people helping people – reassured me that, no matter what, all was right in the world. All was well…and always would be.

Philanthropy

By Carly Melnick

Webster's dictionary defines *philanthropy* as "a love for humanity, to care for and nourish the people around you, no matter their situation." Since I was a young girl, I was always encouraged to practice philanthropy – to give time and money for the benefit of others. In this area, I've been heavily impacted by some of the top philanthropists in central Florida: my grandparents, Cynthia C. and William E. Perry.

In one act of philanthropy in 2004, my grandparents donated the Perry Pavilion in the Dr. Phillips Hospital in Orlando, Florida. They had seen that it wasn't unusual for family members of patients to sleep in waiting areas or hallways at a hospital. Often, these visitors are from out of town, can't afford a hotel room, or are afraid to leave their loved one. The Perry Pavilion provides a beautiful suite area, kitchen, study, and kids' play area connected to the hospital. I also donated my toys for the children staying in the pavilion and spent time as a volunteer.

The Perry Pavilion is just one example of philanthropy from my grandparents. If someone is in need, they are willing to help, no matter the circumstances. For example, they donated the first computer lab to my school to make sure we were getting the best education experience possible. They also give to Shepherd's Hope, Camp Boggy Creek, and many other charities. As 1 Thessalonians 3:12 says, "And may the Lord make your love for one another and for all people grow and overflow, just as our love for you overflows."

I'm truly blessed by the impact of my grandparents' philanthropy. I aspire to be like them in all that I do. They are a great image of Christ and His love for His people; they witness to everyone around them and touch peoples' lives. Giving is very important to me, and I look forward to making philanthropy a bigger part of my life.

Divine Communion

By Charlene Kussner

"Do good anyway." - St. Mother Teresa

This is a phrase that gets used quite a bit in our family; in fact, it's our motto. These words (from Mother Teresa's poem "Anyway") state that people may not understand what you do, they may even try to take your good away from you, but we should do good anyway. In the end, what we do and who we are is only between us and that power and presence that we call God, Universe, or Spirit.

This way of being was reflected to me once by a dear friend. It's something that has stayed with me, a reminder of being selfless, giving, and immediate. My dear friend Kat was wearing a lovely vibrant green-beaded bracelet one night when we went out to dinner. I commented on how beautiful it was, and without any hesitation, she removed it and placed it on my wrist. This seemingly small moment impacted me in a great way. In that moment, Kat reflected the purity of heart in giving of oneself to another.

This act of kindness stayed with me. It transformed me. It challenged me to "do good anyway." It instilled a willingness to respond immediately, even in situations where I might be unsure. Thanks to this experience, I moved into a greater expression of myself and a more loving experience for others. I now remember to listen to that inner whisper and to act without hesitation. I realize that every act of kindness, no matter how great or small it appears, impacts someone or something, and it does change the world. And I know that in "doing good anyway," I help to create a better place.

We are all engaged in this life together; this is our Divine Communion. As we walk considerately on this planet, we are part of this Divine Communion, this circle of life. As we love, we are loved. As we serve, we are served. As we do good, goodness indeed abounds!

Seva

By Ayeesha S. Kanji

The word *seva* is Gujarati for the intention to volunteer. Anyone who volunteers their time is performing seva.

While working in the not-for-profit sector, I witnessed volunteerism at a level that allowed me to embrace the goodness of humanity around me. The foundation supported World Partnership Walk every year in the USA and Canada, supporting international development to alleviate global poverty. Within Ontario, Canada, I managed volunteer teams for each city.

In preparation for an event in Toronto, with a projected attendance of over 45,000 attendees, the volunteer team of about 150 people set up in one day (as they did in London and Kitchener/Waterloo as well). This included food, entertainment, technology, interactive activities for kids, opening ceremonies, and volunteer activities. It amazed me to see volunteers with that much passion come together for a cause they believed in. As I worked with the volunteers and developed relationships with them, it dawned on me what we all have in common – a passion for world peace, happiness, and giving gratitude back to the world for the betterment of humanity.

Ever since I was old enough to understand the concept of volunteerism, my parents and my brother always instilled in me why it was important to give back knowledge, to give back time, and to give back goodness from a place of gratitude. Volunteerism comes from a place of genuine gratitude in caring about the happiness and well-being of humanity.

The examples of volunteerism are endless. It is not limited to an event, a cause, or a formal program. It can be as simple as picking up someone else's trash that they left behind or even just walking an elderly person along the road so they feel safe. It is pointless to overthink goodness or to feel that we have to search far and wide for it; it can be found right under our noses!

Volunteerism is an expression of goodness and passion for a cause – a humble act that comes from the heart, where goodness begins.

Miracle from Heaven

By Ruby Mabry

He was born with hydrocephalus – excessive buildup of fluid in the cavities of the brain, which causes an unusually large head. At a young age, he had surgery to insert a shunt in his head to relieve the pressure on the brain. The doctors told his parents he would not live past the tender age of 13.

Growing up, he was raised just like his other siblings. He was not given special treatment from his parents, who wanted him to be productive in life instead of hindered due to his condition. As he grew older, both legs were broken and he had to wear a special medical shoe with a metal bar across the middle with an adjustment dial.

As he went through his school years, he was often made fun of by the kids. People can be very hurtful with their taunts and their snares. One time, while walking home from school, one of his classmates sicced his dog on him. Because of a condition he was born with, and no fault of his own, he was being ridiculed and harassed.

Due to complications with his shunt, he has had five surgeries to his head, and he is in debilitating pain daily. Nonetheless, he is very social and has a contagious personality. For as long as I've known him, he has done community work and has always given back. He plays the piano for churches and sings solos. He also does prison ministry.

Battling his own medical issues, he has remained strong by prayer and his faith. He definitely gives for the sake of giving, not recognition. My hope is that this story brings inspiration to someone who has lost hope and wants to give up. Despite his health issues, this young man did not let his condition break him. He defeated the odds, and today, at 52 years old, he remains a compassionate, loving soul and an inspiration to all he comes in contact with.

Sweet Nectar to My Soul

By Courtney Long

The hot Arizona sun blazed down upon me as I put one foot in front of the other. Thousands of other walkers and I marched forward on a mission to eradicate breast cancer. We walked 60 miles in three days, spurred on by encouragement and donations from our friends and family. Although no one in my life had breast cancer at the time, my friend Helena inspired me to walk through her dedication to this important cause.

Even as an avid exerciser who had trained diligently for this walk, I was not prepared for the pure exhaustion that set in by the second day. *What did I get myself into?* I wondered. *Was I crazy to do this walk?* I had just fueled up at a rest station with water, electrolytes, and a snack, but my body and spirit still felt weary and depleted.

Up ahead, several community members had created a cheering station with balloons and encouraging posters. As I approached the cheering station, a little girl reached out her arm to me. I stopped and bent down, and she placed a sticker on my t-shirt. Reading my name tag, she said "Good job, Courtney," in the sweetest, softest voice.

Suddenly, I forgot how tired my body felt. The soreness in my feet disappeared. Tears streamed down my face, and a surge of energy flowed through my body. The little girl's loving words were like sweet nectar to my soul.

Although she was a stranger who I would likely never see again, she placed an imprint on my heart that will last forever. Like an angel, she reassured me and gave me just the boost I needed to keep going. Thanks to the kindness of the human spirit, the rest of the walk was a breeze!

I silently thanked my friend Helena for inspiring me to walk. I realized that even when I feel defeated or afraid, I can accomplish anything with kindness and love. With love, anything is possible.

In memory of my friend Helena, who later died of breast cancer.
Her generous spirit lives on.

Hungering to Make a Difference

By Nicole Schiener Manary

I am blessed to know two incredibly compassionate people who went from noticing a growing number of people asking for money in their own neighbourhood to deciding to spread goodness weekly. Prior to launching their Kitchener Vegan Paper Bag Movement in the fall of 2015, my brother-in-law, Collin, would sit and talk with the people near his street for hours. He realized that what they hungered for most was a sense of connection – of being seen and feeling like they mattered. Lisa, his wife, told me that Collin arrived home one day with no shoes; he had given them to a man who had none.

While Collin and Lisa had donated to their local food bank and sponsored a child overseas, they felt disconnected from the people they were helping. Their hearts longed to do something that would make a bigger impact. Lisa stumbled upon a link to the Paper Bag Movement in New York City on the "Bite Size Vegan" blog. Within hours, a Facebook group had been created as the couple made plans for their first trip to the local City Hall to help nourish the bellies and hearts of their neighbours.

I was so inspired by their courage and kindness as Lisa described that first awkward Saturday afternoon on a cool fall day when they arrived. They didn't know where to go or what the need would be or how they would be received. But they showed up and found another group that provides hot vegan lunches weekly. The couple have formed rich connections with many "regulars" over the past year and a half. Their weekly act of generosity began with 10 bags that first week and grew to 54 in their fourth week, which included giving to a man who had nothing for his child's birthday party.

More than 3,500 bags later, Collin and Lisa have been unwavering in their commitment and are overwhelmed by the outpouring of support they have gotten from family, friends (especially Andrea), co-workers, and local businesses. It seems they are not the only ones hungering to make a difference.

Kindness in Tragedy

By Niki Meadows

With such an overwhelming amount of negativity in the media, it can be difficult to see that good things happen in the world. Sometimes kindness goes unnoticed; other times, it just doesn't get the same platform as its negative counterpart. Yet goodness is present every day. Everyday heroes who walk among us and kindness in all forms help ensure that negativity remains a small portion of what happens in the world. Even in the midst of tragic events, kindness can be found if we look for it.

One example of this recently came to my attention when my mom sent me an article about a woman who had been killed in a car accident. My mom said the woman had worked at her office. My heart sank, even though I didn't know her. As I read the story and continued to the comments section, I saw that my best friend said she witnessed it. I immediately sent her a message to check on her. I couldn't imagine the emotional distress she was experiencing after witnessing such a tragic event. I cried as she told me about the accident and how she tended to the woman and held her son.

It's not every day that we know what happens behind the scenes of a story we see on the news. We don't always hear of the help or kindness in the middle of tragedy. While we didn't know this woman, she's had a huge impact on our lives. We're currently looking into ways to keep Prachi Gupta's memory alive through road-safety awareness in our local community. My friend has even been inspired to discover how she's meant to dedicate her life of service to others. As Mahatma Gandhi once said, "Be the change you wish to see in the world." It's up to each one of us to be the kindness we want to see.

The world lost a wonderful young woman. We'll do our best to make it a better place for the son she left behind.

Holy Chaos

By Patricia Downing

My husband and I are sitting at a round table with a blue tablecloth, linen napkins, and a flower centerpiece. We've just met the other seven people sharing the table with us. Conversations have begun as people pass the large salad bowl and basket of freshly baked rolls. Sounds of greetings and laughter from other tables fill the large room, as strangers and friends come together to share food and fellowship.

Soon, our waitress brings a platter of chicken and serves each of us, then leaves the rest on the table for those who want more. A bowl of fresh seasonal vegetables is passed around, and soon we're all enjoying this meal prepared by a professional chef and a team of volunteers.

Located in the Haywood Street Church in Asheville, North Carolina, this is the Downtown Welcome Table, where all are welcome, free of charge, every Wednesday for a midday meal or Sunday evening for dinner. Around us are homeless and others living on the fringes of society – and some, like ourselves, who choose to be part of this amazing gathering.

In the adjacent room, others wait for the next seating while drinking coffee or tea, getting haircuts, or just enjoying the camaraderie in a place that feels safe and welcoming. Some have selected needed items from the clothing closet, and a few are waiting for an acupuncture treatment, made possible by the local acupuncture college.

I would later learn that a large team of volunteers – many of whom are homeless themselves – makes all this happen: setting up, cooking, serving, clearing, dish-washing, and caring for the community garden out back that supplies flowers and vegetables for our table.

Pastor Brian Combs says he sought out the homeless. He wanted to create a place where everyone feels welcome – no exceptions. He tells them they are all children of God and are loved unconditionally. As I look around the room, I see my brothers and sisters, showing up in all colors, shapes, and sizes, and drinking in that love.

Some call this "Holy chaos." I call it love in action.

I'll Stand by You

By Danielle Redmond

Nothing made sense anymore. Since my beloved partner Pedro's sudden death, I found myself sinking into deep depression. It had been weeks since I'd left the house, but in that tender moment, I put my furry four-legged companion first, mustering the energy to walk to nearby Turtle Lake, where Pedro and I had spent many blissful hours as he strummed beautiful chords on his Spanish guitar.

Just a few months earlier, while swimming in a lake together on holiday in Mexico, Pedro took his last breath and dove under, never to resurface alive. He was 37 years old.

So here I was – back at home, by the lake, sobbing. I arrived at our spot, the picnic table, which was newly graffitied. The artwork was loaded with significance: a Mexican Day of the Dead skull with a wispy, cloudy spirit emerging from it. Feeling his presence, the song lyrics "I'll stand by you, won't let nobody hurt you" roared in my head for hours as I stared out at the lake, tears streaming, mesmerised by the beauty and synchronicity of life. For the first time in months, I felt at peace, connected with myself, with Pedro, and with the springtime nature surrounding me. At that moment, I found it impossible to ignore that I was not alone – life goes on and is indeed beautiful.

When I returned home, I looked up the song and stumbled upon a video dedicated to raising awareness to children orphaned by HIV in Africa. Overpowered with emotion, I signed up to volunteer in an orphanage dedicated to their care.

Overcome with inspiration, I sold most of my possessions and bought a one-way ticket to Africa. Upon my arrival at the orphanage, I saw the orphans' smiling faces, and my depression lifted. They have so much love to give, and I have so much love to share with the world. A better perspective of life emerged. I am now able to savour the present moment, appreciate this precious life, and live in love more fully.

I remind myself that regardless of sorrow, tragedy, loss, and things not going as planned, it is a perfect universe.

When the Beatitudes Came to Life

By Thomas E. Uharriet

For less than renting an apartment, I bought a travel trailer and set off for a year-long road trip. It would be a great savings and an adventure!

Months later, the friend who had sold the trailer to me suddenly had nowhere to live. I invited her to join me for a while. We settled in at an RV park in Roswell, New Mexico, for the snowy winter. Weeks later, while I was away, she stole the trailer. My home was gone.

With my belongings in the stolen trailer and not enough gas to drive to a warm climate, I was in trouble. My trailer was well stocked with food, blankets, and clothes. But it was gone.

Imagine my relief that a homeless shelter took me in that night! They provided a warm bed and daily meals followed by Bible lessons. Although I had spent most of my life immersed in that book, in recent years I was more focused on scriptures of other religions. Returning to the New Testament was joyous, adding lasting value to my homeless experience.

After filling in to lead the Bible study, I soon became the shelter's primary teacher. In my 14-week stay, I mostly focused on the Beatitudes and on related chapters. They came alive to us.

Having searched other spiritual traditions, I internalized Jesus' words in a broader context than I had understood them before. His brilliant message flowed miraculously to all there hungering for spiritual comfort. It was so transformative to that group of people in need that it became the basis of my book, *The Beatitudes and Heart-Based Happiness.*

The Rivers of Life Outreach homeless shelter not only gave me a warm bed and daily meals when I desperately needed them, but also re-centered me in the joy of extending love to others. By all that they provided, I became less concerned about my own struggles while reaching out with words of peace to those struggling alongside me. We all loved and supported each other. Thank you, Rivers of Life!

Volunteering Makes a Difference

By Teresa Velardi

The Ronald McDonald House (RMH) is a home away from home for families with seriously ill children. Occasionally, I volunteer to cook a meal for people staying there.

Christmas was just around the corner, so a friend and I went to RMH to bake cookies. There were a couple of kids staying there with their parents, excited to help. We sang carols and talked about the arrival of Santa in a couple of days. They were having fun despite their brother, who had suffered life-threatening injuries in an accident, being in a nearby hospital.

My friend and I did the best we could to engage the kids in decorating the cookies. We had a good time together, making the most of a very stressful situation. Once I got home, I realized I'd left my bracelet on the counter. I called the house to let them know I would be there the next day to pick it up.

When I arrived back at RMH, I was greeted by the mother of the boy who had been in the accident. "I'm so grateful you were here yesterday," she said. "My son had a wonderful time with you. You girls took his mind off of his brother and the critical situation at hand. It was the highlight of his Christmas. His brother passed away last night, and the joyous time he spent with you made a real difference. I can't thank you enough."

With tears in my eyes, I hugged her and expressed my condolences for her loss. She handed me my bracelet, engraved with, *With God, all things are possible.* God had made it possible for me bring joy to quell sadness.

Volunteering is an act of kindness. Always be kind. You never know what's going on behind the smile of another.

The Power of One – Pass It On

By Nora Rose

One cold January evening, my friend got lost while driving on Lower Wacker Drive in downtown Chicago. It's called "Lower" because it is underground. This dimly lit street is darker than aboveground streets but also a little warmer.

Just as my friend made a U-turn, her eyes moved along the sidewalk. Up against the wall were blankets, bags, pillows, shopping carts, and people – homeless people. One pushed a cart, trying to find his spot; the others were lined up next to each other with only their blankets and the clothes on their backs, ready to settle down for a cold night's sleep on the concrete!

My friend wondered: *Where did all these people come from? What happened in their lives to get them here in the middle of a very cold winter?* She felt grateful to climb into a warm bed and wondered how she could help.

The next day, she packed snacks and made sandwiches. She put the food into a bag to bring on her way to work. As she passed a homeless man sitting in the snow, bundled in a coat and blanket, she handed him the bag of food. His expressionless eyes looked at her as he muttered, "Thank you."

"You're welcome," she said with a good feeling. Tomorrow she would bring clothing.

Another evening, she went on a dinner date. Usually she left half her meal on the plate to be taken away. This time she asked for a take-out box and a soup to go. As she and her date walked down the street she searched the sidewalk and doorways. She found a homeless person huddled in an entrance way. She walked up to him, handed him the food, and kept walking.

In class, she asked her professor where she could donate her professional legal services. Her professor guided her to such a place. She learned so much from this experience, and her time and talents were put to good use.

A Reason to Smile

By Mauri Barnes

I knew when packing for our medical mission that we would have to take everything we needed to operate on children born with cleft lips and palates.

We traveled over 24 hours to reach our destination high in the northern Andes mountains of Peru. When we arrived in the city of Huanuco late at night, it was shocking to drive past the families camped outside of the hospital's gates, waiting for our team to arrive. The line extended for blocks. Some families had been waiting there for weeks, praying that their child could have the operation that would change their life.

The next morning, when we began to triage patients, I noticed a teenager standing taller than the rest. He covered his lower face with the grimy sleeve of his sweater, his eyes searching my face. I smiled at him. His arm lowered, revealing the gaping hole in his face where his nose and upper lip had never joined together and his teeth had grown into the defect.

I could not imagine this boy's life, growing up in an isolated mountain village, his family ostracized because of his appearance. In the United States, infants have corrective surgery during the first few months of life. We don't notice because they look normal. The operation takes a couple of hours, and the change is miraculous.

My heart was filled with joy, being a part of this medical team, making a difference in the lives of others. It was a grueling week. We operated on as many patients as we could. Three surgical teams worked compassionately and tirelessly with local nurses by our side.

We had just operated on the teenage boy. Waking up in the recovery room, he asked a question. We thought he was asking "How do I look?"

"*Muy guapo* – very handsome," we gushed.

He shook his head. "He wants to know if he looks normal," said our translator. A nurse took off, returning with a large mirror she'd removed from the bathroom wall. The mirror reflected his thumbs up and beaming face encircled by all of our smiling tears.

The Miracle of the Multiplying Food

By Rhonda Lee

When I was a teenager, my parents did mission work for a community that was about an hour away from our home. Being a shy outsider, I was an easy target for bullying, and those years were some of the hardest of my life. However, in the midst of all the strife, I witnessed a miracle that has stayed with me always. I learned at an early age the value of unity and focus on the greater good.

One year, our little organization decided to undertake an incredibly large project for such a small area: providing a Christmas meal, presents, and groceries for over 150 people in need in the surrounding area. Almost every day, a handful of us would hit up businesses in surrounding counties to ask for help and donations. We ended up with boxes of groceries as well as bags of presents, which we carefully wrapped for the people we were sponsoring. The one thing we did not have a lot of was food to prepare for the Christmas meal, so we decided that we would just give each sponsored person only one plate of food and that those of us who volunteered would not eat anything. We would only serve.

When the big day arrived, volunteers brought in the sponsored individuals for us to feed and shower with gifts. We gave generous servings of food and realized that we still had plenty. Next, we started piling plates full of food for everyone to take home. Still, the food did not budge. It simply seemed to multiply! We just could not believe our eyes as we loaded down plate after plate. We ended up having so much food that all of the volunteers got to eat a meal *and* take home leftovers!

My lesson from this momentous occasion is that when people come together and put aside their differences, miracles can and will happen. Love, focus, and dedication to service can transcend strife, transform everything in its path to pure love, and yes, even multiply food!

Chapter 9
Goodness from Beyond

S ome things in life just can't be explained with the human mind, and receiving goodness from beyond our world is one of them. Whether it takes the form of a loved one sending signs from the other side to let you know they're still with you, or it shows up as a sign directly from God, the universe, or your angels, helping you remember that you're never alone, goodness truly is all around us. We love knowing that loving kindness doesn't have to take place only here on Earth; it can take place in our entire universe – reaching far beyond our imagination and landing right in the center of our soul.

We've certainly experienced goosebump-inducing goodness from beyond, and each time it happens, we feel extremely blessed. When our beloved dog-ter, Xena, passed away in 2013, we immediately began receiving signs from her that she was still protecting and loving us. Her spirit always seemed to show up with a message when we most needed it, which warmed our hearts and helped us heal from our grief. We have also received signs and messages from our human loved ones who have passed on, as well as our angels. These experiences have opened our hearts and made us more excited than ever to live in such a magical universe that's truly filled with endless possibility.

The pieces in this chapter each share an experience of goodness that came from the other side or was somehow divinely inspired – where people were in the right place at the right time. It's our hope that they help each of us see that goodness can come in many forms, and sometimes it shows up in the most unexpected – yet completely magical – ways.

A Flock of Angels

By Annalene Hart

One autumn day in 1989, my mother's friend called to ask if we could watch her grandchildren, who lived just up the road from us. Normally I would have accompanied my mother for this neighborhood jaunt, but on that day, I uncharacteristically decided to blow-dry my hair after a shower, so my mother headed off alone.

There had been intermittent rainfall, so the roads were quite slippery. Perhaps because of the rain, my mother became disoriented and concluded she was definitely lost. Starting to feel agitated and panicky about getting to her friend's place in time, she sped up and the car swerved out of control and went over a cliff!

As my mother (Helena) plummeted, she heard these words: "Helena, you know we always take care of you!" Rather than panicking about her dire situation, she felt a deep peace envelop her…even as she heard the shattering of glass all around her as the windshield and windows blew out from the impact of the fall. Miraculously, the car landed on an old barbed-wire fence, clinging to the top of a tree, which caught her like a net under a trapeze artist.

She assessed the situation and found that her only injury was a scrape on her hand from the jagged glass while getting out of the car.

In survival mode, she eased herself down an embankment and clawed her way up to the roadside (which entailed using her brute strength, grabbing tree branches and foliage to hoist herself up the hill – quite a feat for a 5'2" woman wearing Hush Puppies with no traction)!

Once she reached the side of the road, she flagged down the car of a compassionate couple who drove her home. When my mother got home and told me her harrowing experience, she started shaking uncontrollably as the reality of what she had endured began to sink in.

It was God's goodness – and probably a flock of angels – that protected my precious mother that fateful day. Thanks to this miracle, we were blessed with another 26 years together on Earth.

French Toast Ghost

By Sarah Huffer

It had only been a few hours since I'd left the nursing home. I couldn't sleep, but I lay in bed cuddled next to my two-year-old daughter. The creaking of the stairs told me that my aunt was entering the room. She put her hand on my back and said, "I'm so sorry, honey. She's gone. Just now." I already knew. I could feel the piece of my heart break away before she told me. I squeezed my daughter tighter to my chest, applying pressure to my new pain.

I felt like I might shatter wide open with grief and just lie there forever. I couldn't breathe. I couldn't swallow. There was a sharpness in my throat that traveled to the back of my head; it felt like someone was strangling me. Tears burned my eyes. Without waking my daughter, I inched out of bed. I needed coffee, or a cigarette, or a shower, or whiskey. Most of all, I needed my mom to still be alive.

For the first time in months, the house was quiet. I sank into the couch, taking up the whole thing. The itchy material scratched my skin. A family friend walked into the room and asked, "What can I do? When was the last time you ate anything?" I didn't know the answer to either question. "What would your mom have made for breakfast?"

"French toast and sausage," I said. "She would let my syrup spill over the bread and onto the sausage links." He disappeared. I needed to arrange the funeral. Find her chiffon dress. Go through her pictures. What is it like to die? It must be better than losing someone.

He appeared with a heaping plate. I wasn't hungry. I hadn't been for a while. Maybe I could move the food around to make it look like I ate. After all his hard work, I decided to take a bite. And there she was. I'd found her in my plate of French toast. The imperfect toast on everyday bread reminded me of my mother. The powdered sugar conjured my childhood. The butter tasted like Sunday mornings. The plate was familiar; the silverware was hers. Somehow, she was there. He'd brought my mom back to life for a few minutes. I will never forget this kindness. My mother loved to cook, and I imagine she whispered the recipe in his ear. He showed the way through, just by making breakfast. He directed me to the truth: that she is everywhere, even in French toast.

Parking Lot Miracle

By Gretchen Oehler Hogg

Working in a newborn nursery, we behold daily miracles. Anyone witnessing birth or giving birth knows how miraculous this is. However, despite all the fertility and medical enhancements, there remains a variety of challenges such as maternal age or a myriad of other issues leaving families still desperately wanting children.

One day, our head nurse expressed her joy of finding love in her later years but lamented about having missed her childbearing years; she had desperately wanted children but had given up her dream. She commented about loving her job where she nurtured and cared for newborns and found tremendous joy in this, yet she still longed for her own child. I shared my belief that children come to us in a variety of ways, and if they're meant to be a part of our soul family on this earth, our souls will find a way to unite.

One day, we received a call that a woman was in our hospital parking lot with an imminent birth occurring. Our head nurse responded with all the appropriate equipment and staff to manage this situation and ran down to assist. There was a teenage woman and her mother in a car with the baby destined to arrive at any moment. There was no time to move the young woman into the hospital, so the baby was successfully birthed right then and there!

Both the young mother and baby were later deemed to be healthy. However, this young woman had already decided to put her baby up for adoption but only if she could find the perfect family. She instantly recognized the soul connection with this head nurse, and the serendipitous nature of her parking lot miracle birth confirmed this. She begged the head nurse to consider adopting her baby. The mother and birth mother agreed that they received the sign they had been looking for!

The adoption was eventually legalized with birth mother visitations – an extended soul family united. Divine synchronicity and goodness abounding in mysterious ways.

Peter's Gaze
By John R. Fyfe

As Peter, a vibrant 70-year-old, waited for his heart bypass surgery, he wondered whether he would make it. His fatigue and shortness of breath had worsened, but his wife, Helen, had much hope.

After Peter's surgery, his heart stopped for 12 minutes, and he remained in a coma for six months. His soul, however, was very much alive. While clinically dead, he heard an echoing heartbeat sound and was encompassed by white light. Vague, dream-like faces smiled at him with welcoming arms. He felt compelled to go to them but suddenly was pulled into another realm, one in which he flew over bright blue seas, florescent green meadows, and brilliant white-peaked mountains.

In this realm, an angel came to Peter, taking the form of a young girl. She had luminous dark-blue eyes that made her glow. He felt he had known her forever. When they were not together, he felt desperately alone, lost in a vacuum of endless time, where everything was vague, gray, and empty.

In this vortex, Peter heard a murmur of voices as unknowingly he re-entered the three-dimensional world. Helen and his daughter Tracy were talking to him by his bedside. He felt torn and confused, for he desperately longed to be back in the realm where he could soar in the heavens with his spiritual companion. He missed her. He had felt blissful when they had traveled together. It felt like life had been a dream and this dream-state was life. But when he heard the words "Peter! Peter!" loud and clear, he opened his eyes and saw his wife. However, he felt he had left someone behind.

Each day, Peter's health improved. He was determined to go home, especially when he learned that his 40-year-old daughter had recently given birth. Unbelievably, Tracy had found out she was pregnant the same day as Peter's surgery and never had the chance to tell him.

On his first day home, Peter held his beautiful granddaughter. Her angelic dark-blue eyes gazed at him, her radiance transfixing him. Peter's heart opened in a way he could never have imagined, and his own gaze went deeper, affecting everyone around him. His love became infectious. This beautiful baby was an old soul, and she and Peter had known each other for many lifetimes.

Goodness from Beyond the Veil

By Nancy Merrill Justice

After the heartbreaking loss of another child, my mother did her best to accept and come to terms with the reality that two of her three children, along with her husband, had passed. At 90, losses in life are inevitable but never easy. And with each passing day, time allows one's mind to wander – to ponder the circumstances surrounding those losses and the "what ifs" that often give way to feelings of guilt. Although she did not often speak of those thoughts that haunted her, this recent loss seemed to weigh more heavily on her heart than the others.

When my dad and brother were alive, we three would comment amongst ourselves at how much my sister, Carol, and my mother were alike. They were similar in looks, and they both were overtly friendly and had unparalleled "gifts of gab" that were foreign to my dad, my brother, and me. And, as so often is the case with similar personalities, they often set off fireworks of irritation and angst between themselves – and those fireworks lasted until the day of Carol's passing.

Religion was one area of distinction, however, although both considered themselves Christians. Carol was devout and incorporated church, choir, and Bible studies heavily into her daily life. Mom was not a churchgoer but lived by the rules of The Ten Commandments. However, her ability to recite a religious prayer, even if her life depended on it, was nil.

So when my mother recently shared her "morning dream" with me, I was as moved as she was. "I have not been sleeping well," she said. "I feel so bad, and I keep thinking of all the things I didn't do for Carol. Then yesterday morning I awoke, but it felt like a dream. I was reciting The Lord's Prayer, over and over – but I don't know the words to that prayer! Then I felt a peacefulness flow through my body. I think Carol came to tell me all was forgiven!"

This "morning dream" completely released my mother from guilt and worry – a gift of goodness from beyond the veil.

When God Steps In, Miracles Happen

By Rani St. Pucchi

Never stop believing in hope, because miracles happen every day.

A few years ago, I found myself on the floor of my living room, unable to move from sheer exhaustion, feeling miserable and alone.

Through a series of strange and unexpected events, all my relationships had suddenly collapsed, work was losing its meaning, and I felt deeply misunderstood, unloved, and lonely.

For so long, I had kept going like a robot that goes through the motions – accomplishing tasks, smiling, and serving others, all the while never allowing myself to dwell on my misfortunes or mourn my losses.

That day was a wake-up call. Something changed.

I decided to shift my perspective and see what my life would be like if I stopped beating myself up over "not being good enough" and accepted the fact that I needed to step away from my business, even if just for a short while.

Having made the decision, I was lost as to how I could accomplish this Herculean task. Who could I call for help with the numerous things that needed to be put to bed before I took this sabbatical?

Walking into my retail salon early the next morning, I closed the door behind me and sat with my head in my hands. I felt numb. All of a sudden, I heard a knock on the door. Looking up, I saw a smiling face and a hand waving at me. There was Ellen, an acquaintance I had met briefly through a friend, here to deliver some dresses I had loaned for a photo shoot. I unlocked the door.

"You're not your bubbly self, Rani; what's up?" Ellen said. That's all I needed. I broke down and cried, pouring out the recent turn of events and the struggles I was facing. Ellen listened quietly, then went to the back and brought back two cups of tea. She hugged me and squeezed my hand. "You're not alone. I'm here to help."

God had sent her, a near-stranger, into my life as an anchor, to help me with what was to come. It was as if God were present, comforting me in my hour of need.

Indeed, God works in mysterious ways. Through Him, goodness abounds.

A Team of Life-Saving Angels

By Melisa Archer

Energy work often takes up my day, but today spirit was insisting that I go to the local coffee shop, NOW! In my car, while at the stoplight, the truck on the other side did not move when they got a green arrow. The lady in the car behind the truck jumped out of her car and ran up to the window of the truck, where she saw the man slumped over the steering wheel.

My light turned green. Shaken up, I pulled off the road onto a driveway. I immediately called a pastor, and we prayed for the man. I could see angels working on the scene.

The lady broke the passenger-side window, unlocked the door, put the vehicle in park, and aided in getting the man out of the vehicle and onto the road. She began CPR. Just then, a fire truck happened to turn onto the road. It stopped, and the emergency unit used the defibrillator paddles on him. Firefighters then loaded the gentleman onto the back of the pick-up truck that had been in the traffic. The entire process only took about five minutes. At the hospital, an emergency helicopter flew the man to a bigger hospital.

It was amazing to witness all of these seemingly random people who worked with little verbal communication to save this man's life. I later found out that the woman in the car behind the truck was an off-duty paramedic, the fire truck had just left a safety inspection, and the medevac helicopter had just dropped someone off and was therefore able to take care of the man immediately. If one of those people and events had not happened at just the right time, there most likely would have been a different outcome. As it was, the man recovered…and my faith was further strengthened.

Sometimes when it is not your time to pass, you can live through some very crazy situations. However, if you are guided outside of your comfort zone to help others, please help without hesitation. You may be utilized as an Earth Angel who may affect many interwoven lives, maybe even your own!

Jesus Loves You

By Lupe Ramirez Peterkin

It was April, and activities requiring my full attention to detail mounted as the end of the school year quickly approached. Being the office manager at a high school, I felt guilty for being out sick so much, but the tension on the back of my head, along with extreme anxiety, was debilitating.

Waking up in this condition felt bittersweet. In spite of my physical discomfort, I invocated, "Thank you, Lord, for another day." I picked up my inspirational quote cards and thought, *Okay, Lord, what do I need to know?*

The card I picked read *Be not afraid, only believe.* I took a shower and left for work, still pondering these words during my commute.

As I got to work, the palpitations, body aches, and pressure on my chest grew worse. My body and mind felt so disconnected that I felt like I was losing my mind. I left work (again) and staggered to my car.

As I approached the freeway, I began to weep and asked Jesus to help me feel better. Just then, I changed directions and drove to my chiropractor's office. I pleaded with the receptionist for a quick tune-up with the chiropractor because my tension headache was throwing me over the edge. The adjustment gave me immediate relief.

As I left the office, I received a call from my doctor stating that my sonogram taken the day before was normal and that the lab work identified menopause. Finally, I knew what was going on with me! My wonderful body was talking to me in ten different ways, pointing to hormonal imbalance, and I had been panicking instead of praying.

Since I was on the other side of town, I drove down a street that I don't frequent, where I saw a gray-haired man on the side of the road holding a sign that read *Jesus loves you.* The sun's warmth washed over me in that moment. Simultaneously, I beamed and cried. The messages from Jesus sent assurance and a reminder to love myself every day and trust his divine love.

God's Gift

By Saundra Lee

On March 30, 2016, while visiting Sedona, AZ, our family took a Sunset Bus Tour to the Grand Canyon. It was a very cold day, and as we drove through snow flurries, our driver pointed out snow falling 100 miles away over the canyon.

About an hour into our two-hour trip back to Sedona, it started snowing again, which was very pretty at first. Then our driver, Dave, announced that it was sticking to the road. Very soon, my grandson told me to look at the windshield. We were at 7,000 feet, headed to 8,000 feet, and it was already a complete whiteout. All you could see was the heavy snow falling on the windshield and nothing beyond.

Almost apologetic for this unexpected snow, Dave announced that his priority was "safety first" as he carefully steered the bus away from the snowy shoulder. The road was straight, and he traveled it every day, but we knew he couldn't see past the windshield. We told Dave that we were praying for him, and he was quick to say thank you.

I closed my eyes to pray, and when I opened them and looked at the windshield, the wipers were off and the road was perfectly clear. No sign of snow!

In Dave's next announcement, he said that it had quit snowing much sooner than he'd expected. We were at 8,000 feet nearing Flagstaff, AZ. After Flagstaff, there were many hairpin curves coming out of the mountains, and the road was perfectly clear the rest of the way!

When Dave made his next announcement, he said, "I can't say I wasn't sweating. This was a first for me, and I've been making this trip for 10 years. I was surprised when it stopped."

Prayers were answered!

The next day, my daughter read on the tour company's website that Dave was cited as the best driver/tour guide they had. Would God have it any other way?

Kindness from the Other Side

By Claire Chew

Ten years ago, the same week I found out I was pregnant, my mother committed suicide. By that point in my life, loss was not new to me. I'd had decades of experience leading up to this – beginning when I was seven and we left our home in Hong Kong for San Francisco after being told I was going on "vacation." Loss and abandonment set the stage for more ups and downs with my parents throughout my childhood and teen years. Eleven years later, I jubilantly left home for college, only to return six months later diagnosed with stage IV cancer. Given an 11% chance of survival, the overachiever in me persevered, graduated from college, and did everything I was expected to as a first-generation immigrant. On paper, everything looked great, but I felt numb inside. I always believed it was the same with my mother but had no way to know for sure.

As my own child grew, I found myself thinking about my mother more often. There were things I wished I could have asked her – things one doesn't usually think of before becoming a mother. Although we had healed our relationship before her death, there was so much more I wanted to know.

Then one day in the fall of 2011, I received a call from a new friend – a school teacher who was building her practice as a medium. She told me that while she was driving to school that morning, my mother appeared to her at a stoplight and demanded that she give me a reading! (Mind you, we'd only spoken a few times before this, and I had never given her *any* information about my mother's death.) During the reading, she shared information from my mother that I hadn't told anyone. What a download! She relayed how my mother was sorry for the conflicts we had while I was growing up, how she was proud of me, and how she wished for me to continue doing what I was focused on at the time. The unexpected kindness my friend showed while she held a space for me brought so much healing.

I still carry in my heart the priceless gift I received that day, and I've made it a mission – in my coaching practice (helping others through major transitions) and in my life – to pay forward this kindness and love.

Angels on Earth

By Suzanne Fortino

By the age of seven, I had already suffered atrocities that many people never experience in their lifetime. I bore witness to and was a victim of many traumas that wounded my spirit and left scars on my soul. My family offered me no religion or faith to aid my wounded spirit.

On August 18, 1976, my babysitter took me to a Billy Graham festival called Mission San Diego – a message of happiness. While attending, I was introduced to an extraordinary couple. Most of the details about them have faded over time, but I still remember that their souls were filled with faithfulness and love.

We visited often after that remarkable day. The couple would come pick me up from my home (after meeting my mom, of course) and take me to SeaWorld, picnics, the zoo, or to buy clothing. I still think about them often, and although I don't remember their faces or what we talked about, I still recall the love, compassion, and faithfulness they showed me and how it made me feel.

I believe that these angels were sent to me by God. They were two human beings doing God's work. Even though they could not stop the traumas I went through and continued to suffer throughout my life, they gave me strength and encouragement – the tools I needed for survival. And they taught me the most valuable lessons: faithfulness and love.

Since that time in 1976, I've met many angels who have encouraged me on my healing journey, and I look forward to meeting more. I had always hoped to someday reconnect with the two angels so I could thank them. For now, however, I will have to be content thanking them with my words and my heart.

Angels are on Earth; they walk among us doing God's good work, and I keep my heart and eyes open for them. My scars are healing, I feel blessed, and I thank God and my guardian angels daily for my life. Without the traumas – and angels to teach me faithfulness and influence me – I would not be who I am today.

Witnessing Divine Guidance

By Phoebe Fazio

I am forever grateful for the two men who appeared out of nowhere to assist my husband when he fainted while holding on to a parking meter on a busy sidewalk in downtown San Francisco, my hands lovingly protecting him from the cold, hard pavement.

This story could be about those Earth Angels who hailed the emergency vehicle and took his vital signs, monitoring him as help arrived. And yet the story expands as we pan the camera back for the bigger picture, rewinding the scene just a bit.

With our two very young children by my side, my parents walking briskly out of earshot half a block ahead of us, I heard my husband's frantic call from behind. He was bent over, trying to catch his breath, calling for me to stop.

Before turning to him, I sent our tender, shy, three- and seven-year-old lights-of-my-life to catch up with their grandparents. It amazes me to think about what had to happen for these quiet, not-from-the-city young children to get their fast-moving grandparents' attention!

As I check in and ask my guides and angels now, some 17 years later, I can see the gentle souls who conspired to assist and carry us with kind, loving gestures through the angels on the streets of San Francisco: a tender tap on my mother and father's shoulders so they knew to turn around to see their grandchildren hurrying to tell them something, the caring person who gestured back up the street to where the incident took place, and the Divine protection that swooped in, swirling and hovering over this entire scene.

This event was a precursor to bigger, even more challenging, life-changing experiences to come, experiences that would shape me deeply in becoming the sensitive healer and channel I am today – although, at that time, I barely acknowledged that angels existed, let alone that they were always among us.

We are all protected by a higher power, larger than the kind deeds we witness, showing us the way to our purpose here on Earth.

Manifesting the Holy Spirit

By Tiffany Andersen

Have you ever seen the Holy Spirit with your own eyes? I believe I have.

Often, times of suffering can bring about beauty in life, like when a child recovers from a life-threatening disease. The parents kiss their child and give thanks to the angels of love for bringing them back to life. But does the spirit only come during the hardships of life? I don't think so. I think it is always there if we call on it with the right state of mind.

One such time in my life, I cried out to God, seeking explanations for the beautiful miracles I have seen. Could they really have been magnificently orchestrated from the angels in flight? Desperate for answers, with tear-filled eyes I reached for the Book of Life to inspire me. I stepped out in faith, trusting I would hear something to help me believe. I walked out to the gardens where I know the spirit lives, but before I could even get to my special place to read, I froze with fear. Something in a cloud formation appeared in my line of sight from above. Fearing that it was killer bees, I gripped my Bible and prepared to run back inside. As the swarm got closer, I could suddenly see beautiful white wings—a pure and holy host of white butterflies swirling around me. They fluttered above, just within my reach. They danced around me in a circle, freezing time and space where the Holy Spirit was singing magic to me. The winds they created tingled my skin, bringing the spirit's peace into every ounce of my being. I then knew the truth: that miracles in life happen because there are angels that protect us from the other side.

As the beauty of the spirit passed with the last white butterfly kissing goodbye, I knew that I didn't even need to read a word from the Bible, for the message was clear – the spirit is real and can truly be seen with human eyes.

You Can See Me Now

By Kimberly A. Elliott

Why am I here? What makes me angry? What brings me joy?

It was the last day of a six-day leadership retreat and time to get real with peeling back the layers that allow me to hide in plain sight. What leader doesn't aspire to be a dynamic coach, a master of introspection, a model of positivity? Uh…"Change is good. You go can first!"

In reality, I was fully prepared to follow in the footsteps of so many leaders…and boldly go right on deceiving myself! I can tell you why I am here: I believe in purpose and aligning our lives with our passions. I can tell you what brings me joy: I am inspired by creativity and wonder. I love the sparkle in a child's eyes…that hint of hope, and the sentimental smiles of seniors…blessed with remembrance.

The safeguard I embraced, however, as my answer to what makes me angry was the tipping point. The truth wasn't the one in my head – "hopelessness in others" – but instead, the one my heart revealed: "hopelessness in myself."

From my earliest memories of my father's untimely death, my mother's inescapable widowhood (twice), and my brother's and my missing dads, to my failed attempts at martyrdom through marriage and my unwelcomed intervention efforts in the lives of my grown children, I consistently wrestle with not knowing enough, not giving enough, and simply not *being* enough. Enough!!!

What I learned at the retreat, and throughout my life, is that what makes me angry also reveals my true self-interest. It is my guide to consistently moving forward.

God's thoughts toward me will always give me hope and a future. I have also learned that power is the ability to act, the ability to achieve purpose. So, although I alone may sometimes still feel as though I'm not enough, the power within me is omnipotent. I no longer need the mask that hid my tears – while I told others not to cry. You can see me now, confidently facing both failure and fear, proclaiming…*hope in God is fierce!*

A Shifting of Consciousness

By Cheryl Lawrence

In the beginning, God created Heaven and Earth. Each child is truly a child of the Universe, for each has the entire Universe within. Many have chosen this time to live on Earth to participate in a great awakening, an ascension. The reason many have chosen to be present at this time is to help bring about Light across the planet.

Earth has endured many years of darkness, and it is time to open your heart to love, compassion, joy, happiness, fun, abundance, health, success, acceptance, and many other higher vibrational energies.

You are a perfect being in the eyes of the beholder, God/Creator. Each is created equally, all of significance. Each has the right to choose, the right to use free will. Each can contribute to the wellness and happiness of the whole.

Open your hearts, dear ones, to more love and light. By inviting more of these higher vibrations into your life, you create this for others, allowing all to move forward with grace and ease. This is a time of great change and truth, a time for awakening from a deep slumber.

As each chooses to help create a better world, you will begin to see changes…many positive changes. Let us not dwell on what we perceive to be bad, but let us imagine and co-create a world of peace and glory for all who reside in, on, and around Earth.

(Channeled by Archangel Raphael and supported by other healing angels)

Frere Andre and the Umbrella

By Cydney Mar

Some years ago, I lived on top of a wee mountain called Westmount. It was a quiet, special neighborhood filled with mature trees, curving roadways, and gorgeous homes. If you walked up the street by the forest for a short block, you'd find yourself on the back street leading to the St. Joseph Oratory. I would often take my dogs up to the nearby church, above which my saint, Frere Andre, had lived.

One particularly rainy day, I grabbed my favorite black-and-white polka-dotted umbrella and headed up the street, intending to go pray on Frere Andre's tomb in the church's crypt, a special place where I went for loving, quiet time in hopes of finding peace. The church was built into the mountain, and I needed to descend a few floors to where his tomb was tucked behind the smoky, intensely warm Votive Chapel. The old stone walls curved around, making me feel held and safe.

I leaned my umbrella against a wall, stepped to the black marble tomb, and prayed. While I prayed, I heard others arriving and coins being dropped into the metal coffers on the sides of the tomb. I finished my prayers and reached down to get my umbrella, but it was gone!

I raced up the stairs, searching for the person who had stolen my umbrella. I was angry and upset, especially to lose my umbrella while I was praying! And then I distinctly heard Frere Andre chuckling at me. "You don't need that umbrella, child, " I heard him say. "You'll be fine without it. Don't worry so."

As I burst out of the heavy back doors of the church into the fresh air, I realized that he was right – the skies had cleared, and the sun shone brightly on my face. I did not need my umbrella; the Divine was going to make sure that the sun shone down upon me.

Butterflies from Heaven
By Debby Spitzig

I stood at her bedside, heartbroken, wondering how I would survive the pain of not having her in my life. Although she lay in a coma, I whispered that I couldn't get through this without her, my dearest Aunt Jo. I told her how much I loved her and asked her to send me a sign so I'd know she was still with me. Then I gave her a hug and walked away, knowing I would never again hear "Hi, babe!" as she greeted me with a love that lit up her face – a welcome that wrapped around my heart like one of her famous bear hugs.

After her funeral, my cousins gifted me the beautiful silver butterfly their mom had picked to wear on that day. This touching gesture reflected the love we all shared; my heart healed a little.

My grief was soul deep, like the bond we shared. Her unconditional love and faith in me had always been a comfort. If ever there was a time I needed her with me, this was it. She was my soft place to fall, but now I was alone…until the butterflies appeared. They were everywhere! My aunt had heard my wish and was there to comfort me and ease my pain, as she had always been.

They say that signs from Heaven stand out and seem out of place; often they appear when you are thinking of your loved one. It's true! You can feel they are meant for you. There were times I tested this truth by asking her for a butterfly so I'd know she was there. Amazingly, she always came through, sometimes within minutes. Once, while watching TV, in the next scene there was a butterfly on a couch pillow!

The comfort of those butterflies from Heaven helped me through my grief. She still sends them, just not as often. She was there when I needed her most, and now we are both at peace knowing that our love for each other is truly never-ending.

Birthing into the Beyond

By Chireya K. Fox

There is something mysterious about the Birthing Cave in Sedona. In it, you wonder whether the semi-spherical area in the red rock is a natural phenomenon or something carved by ancient heroes. Looking up, it appears that Mother Earth is opening her legs to let a mythical child spring forth.

My sons and I were in the Birthing Cave on December 22, 2012 – celebrating the powerful "day in between time" of the end of the previous Mayan Calendar cycle – when my father, George, visited me there. It was not an ordinary visit. His physical body was in a hospital in Virginia, and I did not know that this would be his last day.

In my childhood, my father and mother struggled with negative thinking, overeating, and alcoholism. They did their best, but the difficulties were palpable to my brothers and me. In his wisdom, my father undertook the 12 Steps process and made amends to each of us for hurts he felt he had caused. He apologized to me for emotional abuse. I had already been on a personal healing path, yet this moment of loving kindness, humility, recognition of the hurt, and caring for me touched me deeply.

When my father visited me etherically in the Birthing Cave that day, he stood in front of me, looked at me, and then dropped his gaze to two stones, one in each hand. Looking into my eyes with a sense of revelation, he said, "These are not me."

I replied, "That's right; those are not you," and he proceeded to put the stones down. He had realized that he is Spirit – not his body, not his mind.

Later that day, I felt an energy leaving the top of my head. George had transitioned, much sooner than I had anticipated. While part of me grieves not having been with him in the physical that day, I also wonder if this was not the more profound, the more perfect, departure embrace.

George, I appreciate your kindness, your humility, and your willingness to work your stuff. And I'm so grateful for our final visit.

Gifts from Heaven

By Tessa Wuyts

On November 11, 2015, while I was seven months pregnant, I lost my baby girl. I never thought I could get over the loss of my beautiful princess. But there was another little miracle who also needed Mommy – her seven-year-old big brother.

I had seen the bond between big brother and his little baby sis. He had seen a picture of her and felt her in Mommy's tummy, yet the love between them was beyond comprehension!

While I was lying awake one night, I thought about how many little children and parents have to go through this very same experience, and I had an idea: I wrote a children's story to help little children and their parents. It isn't published yet, but I believe strongly that this little magical story WILL help!

I can't imagine my life without children, and ever since I was a child, I wanted to help and educate little children. During my life, I thought I could never ever accomplish this, but my little girl – our beautiful princess – pushed Mommy to follow her dream.

It makes me very happy to help children and people of all ages all around the world. I believe that my baby girl came to her mommy because Mommy had lost her true self. But I promised my baby girl that her loss wasn't for nothing and that *we* would make the world a better place. And I *will* keep my promise to my little miracles!

My miracles are gifts from Heaven…and so are *you*. However bad life seems to be, never stop believing and looking for the blessings. There *is* more, and that more is *you*! YOU create miracles!

Now please listen to the song "This I Promise You" by 'N Sync – and know that this I promise *you*: Goodness abounds within you!

Spirit Provides

By Teresa Madrone Sinay

It happened so fast that I jumped right out of this dimension. I awakened. Suddenly, I was aware of so much more around me than one typically experiences with their five senses alone. I met Mother Earth, spoke to star beings, and greeted separated aspects of myself. It was the end of duality, and time to come home.

For me, this experience was beautiful, incredible, and wondrous…in the beginning. Then it became confusing and overwhelming. I couldn't find balance between realities. How was it possible to be in so many places at once?

For those around me, it was terrifying. Where was Teresa? Could her sanity be recovered? They did the only thing they knew: They called medical professionals. I ended up in a mental ward. Three times.

I was on a spiritual journey of remembering aspects of myself from multiple dimensions. If this happened to me within an indigenous tribe, it might be deemed the birth of a healer. But this was the Western world. And in it, one who responds to such realities is deemed "crazy." An experience like this carries with it many terms: psychotic break, bipolar disorder, schizophrenia. Recommended treatments included medication, group therapy, and counseling. But I needed support for a spiritual awakening.

My family gathered around me in unconditional love. They gave me sanctuary in their home, making sure I was fed and safe. They established medical leave for me at work so my job was protected. And they arranged support that included facilities where patients maintained dignity. Shamans and mystic healers who I found online provided support by listening and validating. A psychiatric nurse showed up "serendipitously" who had a metaphysical background. She met me "on call" at my house and offered follow-up sessions that helped reintegrate my otherworldly experiences with my "this-reality" self.

In my lightning-speed awakening from within deeply asleep America, I needed a soft landing of kindness and grace. Spirit provided, in the form of loved ones, lightworkers, and support professionals who acknowledged and addressed my true need.

An Angel Watching Over Her

By Darlene Gaetz

I didn't always believe in angels, but after what happened six years ago, I do now.

For many years, our family lived in a very cold, dry area in the North, but we had recently moved to a coastal city. I was born on the coast, so it was like coming home. I felt like I could breathe! My skin was happy, and I had no more sinus issues. But something else was also happening that took many talks with my spiritual friend to finally uncover and accept.

While we were living in the North, our teenage daughter had the opportunity to spend a year in South America on a school exchange. When it was time for her return, we were so excited to have her home, and we made plans to welcome her at the airport surrounded by all her family and friends.

We were tracking her flights and noticed there was a delay. She was able to call and tell us that there was a storm and she was going to have to spend the night at the airport, behind security. Of course we were upset, but we suggested she get on Skype with us so she felt like she wasn't alone.

She found a cozy little area where she could lie down with her computer and bag, and we stayed with her on Skype until she felt like she was tired enough to sleep.

The next morning, we got a call from her that all was well and she was boarding the plane to come home.

We met her at the airport with all her friends and family. We shed happy tears and were so glad to have her physically with us again.

She told us later that after we had hung up on Skype, she slept, but awoke during the night to a man with scraggly hair lying close to her, but she didn't feel threatened, so she went back to sleep. When she awoke again, he was gone.

I look back now and think, *I have no doubt that was a long-haired hippie angel!*

What You Give, You Receive

By Manpreet Komal

I went through a major health crisis a week before I was planning to move to Ibiza, Spain, to write my book. What I didn't know was that the book was going to write me.

A month later, I got a call from my doctor's nurse saying that I was going to be okay. I was excited that I was going to gain strength and be able to move to Ibiza. But right then, I got another call from a friend saying that my best friend had been diagnosed with leukemia.

Although I was still healing and recovering, I became her caretaker. I was so concerned about her health. She was suffering, and it hurt me to see her in so much pain. I recited mantras and prayed to find peace, ease, and stillness inside myself. The doctor even gave me anxiety medicine so that I could fall asleep at night so my health wouldn't get worse. I was also going through a difficult job at the time. To state it simply, the year had been hell.

One day while reciting prayers, I felt a presence in my hands. Tears flowed through me to feel that level of love from God and to know that it was with me. Then another day, I saw the same presence in the eyes of my friend's picture. I knew immediately that she would be healed. Not only that, I intuitively heard an answer to a question I had been struggling with regarding my job.

As I look back now, I can see that God existed within each of us during those times. Anything is possible with the power of God. Have faith always and go beyond the egoic needs of material things. When we stay true to God, God returns in unexpected ways. In my case, God was working through me and noticed my pain in addition to my friend's and had mercy on both of us.

Growing Vines of Goodness

By Amy Lloyd

I read recently, "Tragedy strikes; goodness grows slowly." As I contemplate the vine of goodness, I see that it has indeed grown slowly but steadily throughout these past years.

On May 15, 1997, I stood on a hotel balcony, 16 floors up, knowing that, with my impending divorce, tragedy had struck. I had lost everything, including everybody I had ever loved, everything I had ever believed to be true, and all I thought I knew about myself. My husband, my three children, my parents and siblings, my home, my reputation, my *self* – GONE.

As I gripped the protective, rusty, wrought-iron railing, it flashed through my mind that this was much more than I could bear. I could end it. Maybe that would be for the best. Maybe nothing could grow for me again. I took a deep breath and made a firm choice. I would not take my own life, no matter how difficult circumstances became. I would stay, I would fight, I would become, I would never give up, I would learn, I would pay attention, I would take responsibility, and I would live my life fully, making the best choices possible based on what I wanted in life…LONG TERM.

I knew I was not going to make it if I did not find goodness in this world, so I asked God to begin growing something new within me. I now believe that this is what saved me. Not just once or every now and then, but every day over the past 20+ years, this vine of goodness has grown, becoming stronger as I cultivate and celebrate it. I follow very simple caretaking instructions: open your eyes, open your heart, set your intention, and allow every tiny thing – each new bud, unexpected bloom, heart-shaped leaf – to be enough for this moment.

Years ago, I stopped asking *Why me?* Yet, as I write today, I know that THIS is the why! – to be able to tell you, with absolute certainty: The vine grows wild with low-hanging fruit for all to harvest! There is much more goodness in this world than any other thing you will ever find!

Bella Angel Cards

By Angie Carter

It's been three years since my angel got her wings. Bella was only 19 months old when she passed away suddenly. The day after losing my daughter, I went into shock and almost died, too. When I stopped breathing, my family drove me towards the hospital to meet the ambulance on the highway. The paramedics were able to resuscitate me before we arrived at the hospital.

I wanted to do something special for Bella's birthday that year. A local band showed their goodness by writing a song for me. They also wanted to hold a fundraiser for a memorial park bench in Bella's honour. For the fundraiser, I created random acts of kindness cards with an image of Bella as an angel on the front. I asked others to use these cards by doing random acts of kindness in memory of Bella. I continue to share these cards whenever opportunities arise.

The emergency services team was especially good to us when we tragically lost Bella. As a small token of appreciation, when an EMS vehicle is behind me in any drive-through, I always pay for their order. A few weeks ago, I was ordering my morning coffee and there was an ambulance behind me. I paid for their order and left two angel cards for them.

A week later, my sister (a nurse) was transferring a patient by ambulance. The paramedic with her in the ambulance commented on her "Bella" tattoo. He pulled out a Bella Angel Card from his wallet and told my sister that I paid for his coffee a week earlier. He then told her that he was in the ambulance who came for me. This was one of the paramedics who saved my life!

I've mailed Bella Angel Cards all over the world to people, and others have told me about many miracles that have come from sharing them. I believe that spreading love and kindness in Bella's memory allows her to help make the world a better place. In this way, she continues to spread goodness. It also feels great to do kind things for others, and you just never know who you might touch!

His Divine Timing

By Karen Ciran-Barnes

A few years ago, I was struggling in all aspects of my life. I felt lost, unsure of the person I had become. I had achieved "The American Dream" – the husband, kids, house, and career – yet I was not fulfilled in the least. I had such deep-seated pain in my soul because I was struggling for years, fighting against my truth. I used many forms of coping mechanisms to "hush" the voice of my soul – from food and gambling to prescription drugs and alcohol. I was hiding who I was. I carried so much pain and no longer wanted to live.

I'd heard people talk about hitting rock bottom, and now I knew what it felt like. I hit the bottom of the lonely well at full speed – and sat there in complete darkness, ready to leave this planet. I was so tired of struggling to survive and just wanted the pain to be over. I prayed to go home.

My prayer was answered – not in the way I expected but through the help of Karen. I'd heard about Karen years before, but we had never met. My husband had told me that she was an extremely gifted healer and channel; however, I was skeptical…until we met. My husband invited her to Arizona for a visit, and Karen and I hit it off immediately.

When she walked into our home, she went from room to room to cleanse the negative energy. She located ordinary-looking objects in our home that she knew held special significance to me. Right away, my soul *knew* – her connection with my mom (who had passed on), the Angelic realm, and her Guides on the other side – all of this was indeed *real!*

Karen has been instrumental in my journey and continues to mentor me daily in sharing my gifts with the world. I am SO grateful for her love and friendship! I told my husband he didn't find her again by accident. "She wasn't sent here for you," I said. "She was sent here for *me!*" Thanks to Our Creator and His Divine Intervention, Karen helped my soul break free. She lit my candle from hers, and now I share that same spark to light others.

The Universe Sends Nothing but Angels

By Michelle Anne Gould

I once met a real-life angel who reached out and pulled me out of the darkness. But I let him go…and found myself engulfed deeper in darkness – sometimes sinking, sometimes swimming, occasionally coming up to gasp for breath before submerging again.

Relying on my inner compass, I turned to unseen angels by my side. I preferred that world to the numb and crumbling one in front of my eyes.

My angelic team and my thirst for knowledge led me on a quest for deeper truth, purpose, and meaning to life. On some level, I began searching for more real-life angels, those with whom I felt a sense of connection and comfort – a sense of Home.

As my days drifted in and out, directionless but hopeful, I became addicted to fixing myself. That stopped when I heard another real angel's voice that actually got through and bypassed my ego, despite all my barriers and armour.

I accessed my own way back to feeling alive and purposeful, a journey that included many bumps and bruises. Each time I pulled out the white flag, my angel was by my side, walking with me, saying the right words I needed to hear in those moments.

This soul's kindness centered and renewed me. Guided by this divine being, I deepened my own connection to Spirit and dove deep into my soul, finding love and peace through stillness. I discovered more ways to be more Me. I know in my heart that the Universe wants us all to experience the goodness of life and of one another.

Recently, my angelic team humorously placed a (faux) diamond in my new home. It reminds me that each of us is like a diamond; even if we're covered with layers of grime, goodness always surrounds us. Perhaps every being is an angel and each encounter is sacred. Yes, even those that have hurt or betrayed you – some polished diamonds, some still quite rough – each offers treasures and lessons. The small exchange of smiles with a stranger or a seemingly tiny act of kindness can cause ripples of love.

The Universe sends nothing but angels.

The Goodness of Everyday Life

By Helen Ferrara

There appears to be a fundamental goodness intrinsic to life. What has brought me to believe this, at the age of 55, is the way things have changed for the better all the times I've asked for help – sometimes through prayer, when I've felt desperate and at the end of my tether. When I reach out to this source of goodness and ask for a "benevolent outcome," solutions unfold – from the seemingly banal (such as finding a parking spot) to the serious and profound (such as the healing of a person or a situation for the highest good of all involved).

Some may call this benevolent force Goodness, Love, God, Spirit, the Universe, Beloved…or other names, depending on their beliefs and affiliations. No matter what I've called it, this hasn't seemed to affect it or its presence in life. I can barely comprehend how vast and unconditional this goodness is if I but call on it; whereas if I don't, I'm left to my own devices. It's my choice, but there's never any rancour there – I may give up on it as I'm totally free to, but it never gives up on me. If I choose to listen, I recognise it as the most beautiful voice within me.

It may be invisible, but we can be part of it, just as some say angels are, and it connects us all (if we want) in a whole huge collective of goodness. It is mother, father, brother, sister, friend, and teacher. I'm often brought to tears and to laughter at the sheer wonder of it. More and more, I've felt called by it to live deeper than I have been, by trusting and being all I can be. The feeling of answering that call is amazing; it's as if I can trust myself to fly, knowing I'll be safely held if ever I fall or falter. There's no coercion or threat of punishment; that's the realm of man-made religions. I feel as if I'm a young child to it, always beloved.

Fade to Black

By Marla David

I was on top of the world. Wisps of clouds lay below, like pieces of a torn pillow scattering the sky. Various hues of white contrasted the expanse of blue in each direction I looked. I suddenly became aware that, although I was strapped in a seat in a tin can floating through the sky, I was not just viewing it. I was part of it. I was having an out-of-body experience.

Below me lay many wonders – the mountains and the expanse of the land. I was in a state of awe and totally in the moment. I was not attached to anything, but floating among the clouds, somehow being supported by an invisible force. I was inside and part of the clouds, as I traveled down and directly through them, an up-close-and-personal first-time experience. But then, it is always the first time, as the sky is ephemeral, and ever changing.

Pure, as it was at the dawn of creation, I thought that there surely was goodness. Then for a moment, I thought I could have been in Heaven. I wondered how that could be, then looked at the still-bright sun in the sky before me, squinted, and smiled.

Every glance out the little window brought a new view, as in the blink of an eye, the sky morphed completely. The sun continued to descend on the horizon, and the canvas before me began to change, bringing a new palette. The vivid colors melded together, staining the tops and sides of some clouds but leaving the rest pristine white. The brighter shades dulled, just as the autumn leaves do – they begin brightly, then fade, dry out, and get darker. It is the way of things, of the patterns and cycles of life itself.

Totally immersed in the beautiful banquet before me, I thought of a line from the 23rd psalm – "You prepare a table before me..." – and then it came to mind: there is God. There really is!

Fade to black.

Winks from God

By Katie Cox Jackson

When I choose to be aware and conscious of life around me, I can't help but notice the random acts of kindness that occur daily. Some acts are modest, while others are extraordinary. I call the miraculous ones "winks from God." Reflecting on a particularly challenging time in my life, I recall several significant examples of kindheartedness that profoundly impacted my life.

One such instance occurred on a cold Sunday morning. Through tears of worry, I shared with my AA group that I was broke and didn't have money to buy juice for my children. After the meeting, I received hugs, love, and emotional support. An older gentleman gently hugged me and put something in my coat pocket. Minutes later, another man did the same thing. After getting in my car, I pulled $20 out of one pocket and $60 out of the other. Tears of gratitude poured down my face. Thank you, God!

Later that week, I received a call from the church secretary. She said it was Market Day pick-up and there were boxes of food for me. I explained that I hadn't placed an order. She assured me that this was my order. I stopped by that afternoon and brought home enough groceries to feed us for weeks. My heart was overflowing with gratitude. To this day, I don't know who provided for us. Only God!

As Christmastime approached, there were no funds for gifts. I didn't know what I was going to do for my four-year-old son who was expecting a visit from Santa. One evening, I received a call from an acquaintance. She was clearing out toys that her daughter had outgrown and asked if I'd be interested in anything. I joyfully visited her and left with a blue bike and other cool toys. That Christmas morning was filled with excitement and wonder. God is good!

Whether a great gift of generosity or a simple smile from a passerby, acts of kindness, compassion, and love are ever-present. Take note of how often God works through others to touch your life. Appreciate the winks from God!

Angels Watching over Me

By Cynthia Starborn

One afternoon, my neighbor invited me into his apartment and told me, in a low voice, some unsettling news: his stamp collection had recently been stolen, with no sign of forced entry, and he suspected that someone in management was responsible. I felt a chill and knew that I could not continue to ignore the red flags that I, too, had been picking up about this apartment complex. I gave my 30-day notice, started searching for a new place, and soon signed a lease for a beautiful new apartment that would be available in exactly 30 days.

While grateful that a new home had appeared so easily, I started to feel very uneasy in my old apartment at night while waiting out those 30 days before I could move. Suspicious characters were hanging around the building, watching everyone go in and out, and a part of me wished I could move right away.

One night, as I was lying awake in my bed, I suddenly called out, "God, if you're there, I need you right now." I had grown up Catholic but had gotten disillusioned and drifted away from religious faith. Yet in this challenging time, I found myself opening back up to the potential of a benevolent Power far greater than the shadows around me.

As soon as I reached out for divine assistance, four angels promptly appeared in my apartment – huge, strong angels who, unlike the harp-playing cherubs I had often seen depicted in art, looked like they belonged on a football field. I felt their wings brush against my cheek, and then each angel went to a different corner of my apartment and stood guard, in a force field of white light. Once the angels were watching over all four corners of my home, I felt a deep sense of peace and slept like a baby all through the night.

The next morning, I knew that no matter how dark it gets in our lives, the angels are always happy to come shine their light – as long as we are willing to reach out and ask.

Chapter 10
Everyday Goodness

This book contains true stories of enormous acts of kindness: founding a charity, moving halfway around the world to help those in need, or donating thousands of dollars to improve other people's lives. These monumental good deeds are certainly worth celebrating – as you well know if you've been fortunate enough to have given, received, or even witnessed one.

But goodness doesn't always have to come in grand, bold, or expensive packages. Sometimes it takes quieter, subtler forms that often only last a moment and don't cost a thing. Each of us experiences goodness every day – usually in simple but still important ways: a friendly cashier at the supermarket, a kind person holding a door open for someone, or just a smile from a stranger. Sometimes these small gestures can lift your mood or even change your whole outlook on life, and sometimes they simply make you feel a bit better in that moment…which is also wonderful!

In this chapter, you'll read many examples of everyday goodness. You'll find goodness shown by people while doing their everyday jobs as a waitress, a repairman, a bus driver, and even a traffic cop! You'll read about people experiencing goodness during everyday activities such as shopping, writing, and meditating. You'll see people find goodness through getting a much-needed ride from a friend, listening to music together, or just looking at the photos on their refrigerator.

Life is made up of moments, and small moments of everyday goodness can add up to a good life! We hope these stories contribute – in small, large, minor, or profound ways – to *your* life of goodness.

My Refrigerator Door

By Amanda Roggemann

How many times do we pass by something that we might glance at but not really take it in?

I for one am guilty.

I was having one of those fabulous days – a party with me, myself and I – when out of the blue, Ms. Pity showed up. From elation to gloom and doom in a second! Feeling down and parched, I decided to get something cold to drink in hopes of refreshing myself back to at least a glimmer of joy.

Proceeding to the kitchen, I found myself completely stopped as I glanced toward the refrigerator. Standing there in stillness, my eyes began to scan the front of my refrigerator door.

As I began to focus more deeply on the door, memories came flowing back into my awareness. There before me, looking right at me, were birth announcements, movie receipts, save-the-dates for weddings, and numerous postcards and other pictures: family, friends, pets, places I'd been, foreign-exchange students I'd taken into my home who became part of the family…what a collage of my life!

As I took in all these wonderful memories, ever so gently I could feel Ms. Pity slipping away. A big smile started to form on my face, and I could feel my heart bursting with love and gratitude as that glimmer of joy was singing once again in my soul.

No wonder Ms. Pity had to leave – because Ms. Goodness came in and was kind enough to help me remember how my life abounds in goodness and love. All I needed to do was look on the front of my refrigerator door!

I have often found my most profound answers in life in the smallest of books (not to say therapists haven't helped, too), but never did I think I would find them on my refrigerator door!

The Baby and the Bus Driver

By Jerri Eddington

I was a 19-year-old pregnant college junior at The Ohio State University, majoring in Elementary Education. My son, Marcus, was born on spring break. In order to student teach the next school year, I needed to take three classes that weren't offered in the summer, which meant returning to college when Marcus was only 10 days old!

I did not have a car or a babysitter nearby. My mother was already babysitting my nephew, Ryan, on the other side of town. She agreed to watch Marcus for 10 weeks during spring quarter. Now I just needed to figure out how to get Marcus there!

My first class started at 8:30. I decided to investigate our city bus schedule and determined we could catch the 6:33 bus, which would give me enough time to make my first class. Soon we met our bus driver, A. J. Miller. I remember seeing his nameplate in the window. He wore a blue baseball cap and had a welcoming smile. Forty-five minutes later, we arrived at the stop where my mom was waiting. Mom got on the bus as I got off. I crossed the street to catch another bus downtown so I could transfer to a third bus to take me to OSU.

A. J. continued to drive west, taking Mom and Marcus toward my sister Rose's house. Mom would push Marcus in his umbrella stroller two blocks to Rose's house. Before long, Rose would leave to catch her bus downtown, which was also driven by A. J.

Marcus and I rode with A. J. for the entire spring quarter. We lived three blocks from our bus stop. If I was running a little late, A. J. would inch his bus along as I was flying down the street with my book bag and diaper bag, pushing the umbrella stroller. On rainy days, he would stop on my sister's street (not a regular stop) to let Mom and Marcus off a block closer to Rose's house.

Today, Marcus is a true advocate for public transportation, which he's been using ever since he was 10 days old!

All That Jazz

By Rebekah Bernard

"I will always remember this moment," Charlie said as he simultaneously smiled and shed tears while observing his husband, Jack, convey a deep sense of peace.

Days earlier, Jack had been admitted into hospice inpatient care. As his cancer progressed, he openly expressed his existential distress and engaged in life review – exploring forgiveness in an effort to obtain a sense of closure and readiness to transition. Charlie lovingly sat bedside and actively supported Jack's process, including seeking assistance from me (the spiritual counselor) and honoring Jack's Jewish faith through religious traditions and the presence of Rabbi Rachel.

Jack slowly became unable to respond verbally, and we all began to search for a sense of peace within him. Charlie, Rabbi Rachel, and I gathered around Jack's bed and explored his joys in life. We soon discovered he was a fan of musicals and were able to find a handful of musical soundtracks in the facility, among them the musical *Chicago*. We played the *Chicago* CD, and when the song "All That Jazz" played, we watched true goodness emerge.

His furrowed brow and tense body, which indicated discomfort, transformed into a relaxed face and calm demeanor. Jack began rhythmically toe tapping, his eyebrows danced to the music, and a small smile appeared. Mindfully observing this sacred nonverbal communication illustrated how important this present moment was. We could all feel the goodness in that moment, abounding the perceived darkness of the dying experience. There was now a lightness in the room. Jack emanated peace, and so did Charlie. The power of music offered a gateway for this precious harmony. Whether the song evoked a positive memory or became a theoretical representation of Jack's dying experience didn't matter. This music brought some light into the world.

Through my hospice experience, I have learned that goodness happens when people allow themselves to be vulnerable and accept the goodness already in their heart. I, too, will always remember this moment. Even in the darkest situations, may we notice how goodness abounds.

Simple Kindness
By Fiona Louise

It warms my heart to know that every day, somewhere in the world, someone is right now receiving an act of kindness from a stranger. A new mum and an elderly widower have just received a hot meal from a neighbour, a door has been held open for someone carrying bags, and a smile has brightened the day of someone feeling lonely. These little moments have such a profound ripple effect.

I am honoured to be part of this positive movement, seeking out and sharing stories that encourage us to pay it forward, celebrating the examples of humanity, altruism, and hope that happen every single day, everywhere. The more we focus on these random acts of kindness, the more peace and love we will experience in our daily lives, and the more hope and positivity will manifest in the lives of others.

I've noticed a recent surge in community initiatives that seek to connect, unite, and uplift – for instance, the local couple who've started a book- and produce-swapping project in which people donate fresh fruit and vegetables from their garden or books they no longer want, and others are encouraged to take what they need with the intention of giving something away themselves when they can.

Another kindness-based initiative is a café that's open to the general public each day, then provides free evening meals and service to the homeless, offering not just a hot meal and a warm environment to shelter them from the cold for a couple of hours but also the dignity, respect, and kindness they deserve.

An act of kindness doesn't always have to be a major undertaking, however. For instance, despite her physical pain, a friend of mine always engages her cashiers in conversation, using their name read off their name badge. It would be easy to just pay for the goods and walk away, but this small act of kindness shows the cashier respect and genuine human connection.

It is so simple to act with kindness, and it need not cost you anything; just sharing and sending out positive vibes with a peaceful heart has an effect. The more we feel and think loving thoughts, the more loving our world becomes.

Kindness in Edgemere Park

By Cara M. Rosch & Alex Biholar

"Hi, my name's Groom. I lost my bride, but I'm still Groom," said the old man with a whistle through his teeth.

Groom, a long-time resident of the neighborhood we moved to, had seen many people move in and out of the neighborhood over the more than five decades he and his wife had lived there. At first pass, he could come across as a bit stubborn, crotchety, and a tad eccentric. Over the course of the next few months, however, Groom would walk down the street to visit with us, and we began to see through that stubborn exterior and learn about a man who lived a full life filled with equal parts adventure, loss, and love.

At 92 years of age, life was getting harder for this man who had worked his entire life to make sure he and his family were cared for. Time had taken its toll on his body, and Groom found it increasingly difficult to take care of his home and himself. But he was stubborn and refused to ask for help from anyone.

Every so often, however, we saw a lady who lived down the street stop by Groom's house with a package. She would take a seat next to him on the patio and patiently talk to him about his day, his plans, and the letters he was still writing on his old typewriter to Congress and the president.

Over time, we noticed that it wasn't just every so often that she would stop by; it was every day. We found out that she prepared a meal for Groom each day and delivered it along with some kind words. She had voluntarily taken it upon herself to look after her old neighbor who was unable to keep up with all the small demands of preparing a meal or keeping medical appointments. She expected nothing in return, and she continued her daily deliveries until he left the neighborhood to live in an assisted-care facility that she personally vetted with him.

For us, it was an inspiring act of kindness to observe each and every day. For her, this was a small act of kindness repeated daily. But for Groom, it was much more. She set an example without even noticing that we were watching and learning how to care.

Finding Goodness

By Karen Wythe

Each day, we experience untold counts of goodness that are mostly taken for granted. The simple "God bless you" when someone sneezes. The husband who brings coffee to his wife in the morning. The co-worker who brings doughnuts or special treats into work. The step-parent who helps raise a spouse's children as their own. The kind crossing guard who smiles at passing strangers daily. The teacher who goes the extra mile for a student. Throughout my life, I've experienced countless acts of goodness, including many from my friends and family.

There is the caring truthfulness of my longtime friend Marifran, who is faithful to our weekly accountability call. She is a compassionate, listening ear and coaching voice who shines with goodness. Her volunteerism and dedication to charitable organizations such as The Hunger Project sings of goodness.

Then there was my dad – "Al Pal, the Practical TV Man" – who waived the charges for his customers who couldn't afford to pay. He had many others on an honor system for their debt, allowing them to pay when they could.

As a child, I also remember many acts of pure goodness from my mother, Charmaine, exemplified when she helped a neighbor who had suddenly lost her husband. When this newly single mom with six kids to feed, clothe, and house needed to have the gas and electric turned back on, my mother offered to pay. Through her compassion and generosity, the family's financial burden was reduced.

I also learned about goodness from my Grandma Ollie, a great Legionnaire and civic volunteer. She taught me how to fix dolls to donate to the sick kids. In the process, she taught me the importance of doing good just for the sake of goodness – with a spirit of compassion and without expectation, judgment, or concern for recognition or reward.

We can find countless measures of kindness – genuine, pure, and selfless acts of true goodness – if we only open our eyes to them. Yes, there is an infinite amount of goodness in this world if we just look.

A Love Story

By Benjamin Bush

Love stories always seems to be crowd pleasers, so maybe that's why I chose to write about the story I'm going to tell today. It all begins in the sacred space of a mother's womb – a place of unbelievable creation, inspiration, and a love so unbelievably pure and potent, it's tangible. Our little star bathes in this sacred space. Eventually this little star, like every little star, will emerge groomed, cultivated, and ready for life on Earth. Completely surrendered to the hands of the world and whatever magic may lie therein, the little child is born.

Love has created an all-encompassing space in this infant's heart. Without judgment, the infant experiences the raw beauty hidden in every aspect of life – a notion utterly incomprehensible to the reasonable mind, yet totally enthralling to the inner senses. Such an awareness easily passes into the infant's unfiltered conscious mind as a place of refuge and sanctuary.

As our child grows, calling to mind even the memory of this state becomes harder and harder as the modern world surrounds him. Though the mind may have become akin to the outer world, the inner child of our now-grown human lives on, dancing in the same sacred space it has always known. In our star's greatest challenge, he suddenly remembers the space he once knew so well. He can feel the knocking of his inner child whispering a sacred presence. The desires and stories of the modern world he once identified with melt away, and he's left with a raw experience of life once again. How familiar and simple this space feels.

This story is dedicated to the unfathomable love that held me in my mother's womb and is held in the wombs of mothers around the world. Our future is in your hands, heads, and hearts. You are alive, awake, and inspired with the elements of time and space.

My story of goodness starts at birth. I am just grateful to be alive and of service, right here and right now.

Kindness Counts

By Kim Wright

Waiters. Servers. We interact with these people almost every day. Those of us who have held these positions understand the stress involved in working with the general public. As customers, we're quick to complain or even withhold tips when our service isn't perfect, but do we take the time to notice the people who serve us?

As I traveled last week, I had the opportunity to witness two situations that increased my appreciation for these hardworking people.

One afternoon, I stopped at a mountain restaurant to use their internet and grab a quick bite to eat. The place was packed, and I could hear good-natured laughter and general camaraderie around me. I was about to belly up to the bar with my laptop when a young woman appeared with her toned and tattooed arms loaded with plates. Smiling, she nimbly gestured over her shoulder at the lone two-top as she turned and unloaded her cargo. I sat down and watched her multi-task like a pro, clearing off a table on her way to the kitchen, dropping off more food, and quickly returning to me with a glass of water, silverware, and a menu. Her smile and kindness – and her calm competence – made a huge difference in my world.

The next morning, I entered another small-town eatery with some friends. The tiny restaurant's sole server greeted and seated us. In contrast to the day before, this gal seemed stressed. It was only 7:30. As we sat down, two parties of four entered. A loud table of eight sat to our left and two single gentlemen to our right. The poor waitress looked like a deer in headlights. After we had waited 10 minutes for our coffee, she finally brought it. Another group had just come in and didn't notice or care that she was the only server there. As she looked around frantically, I caught her eye, smiled, and told her to hang in there. I saw that my small gesture affected her. She thanked me, straightened up, and went back to her daunting tasks with a little more confidence. I felt a connection with this woman, and I felt good.

Kindness matters. Take the time to notice. Take the time to care.

The Enchanted Hour

By Tiffany Andersen

It's a magical place and time. Daylight is almost past, and the birds have come home to nest, singing a song to their little ones and putting them to rest. It's the enchanted hour of peace, when so much beauty in life is seen — a moment in time when one can slow down and hear the secrets from beyond, secrets that reveal the vision that comes in the early night, providing sights of beauty and hope to continue in this life.

For one hour of the day, there is rest in a place of power, capturing the inspiration just waiting to take flight. It's a gift from above. It's my duty to use it wisely, letting the beautiful ones sing a song of peace to me, so I may pass it back to those who need to see the beauty that comes during the storms of life.

If you look hard enough, you can find your enchanted hour of peace somewhere before the night shades put you to sleep. But you must look with open eyes of love. Remove the veil that chokes out your sight with pain and misery and keeps you from winning the good fight. Find your hour, and you too will find the power. You're worth the time to rest for a minute or two or three…renewing your soul and grounding your mind. Breathe in the beauty and find the healing power, give thanks to God above, listen, and seek pure knowledge of love.

My wish for you is that you find peace, that the gentle wind that blows kisses on your skin reminds you of the beauty in life. It's always there for the taking, but you must start waking to feel the magnificent power that comes from the enchanted hour.

Sparks of Love
By Sarah Auger

"Kindness is the language which the deaf can hear and the blind can see." - Mark Twain

Acts of kindness heal, inspire, and connect every living being. Through each good act, light and "sparks of love" are sent out into the universe. A simple smile can change the course of someone's day, even if this exchange lasts only a second or two.

When I have been touched by unconditional acts of kindness, any illusion of separation has vanished and all I could feel was love. As I reflect on the generous deeds of others, both received and witnessed, I notice how the feeling of love is everlasting.

I would like to briefly share three different acts of generosity that I have either witnessed or directly experienced:

Once, while taking a certification course in Arizona, an issue at the hotel I was staying in forced me to relocate to the nearest available room, which was 35 minutes away! When I described this situation to the lady sitting next to me at the course, she offered to pick me up and take me back each day. The same lady continues to give unconditionally to me, as she gifted me with this exact spot in the book! Thank you!

The second act of generosity is one that I didn't experience firsthand but which, nonetheless, moved me deeply: When my friend became pregnant unexpectedly – and was about to become a single mom – her uncle offered to pay for daycare for her child until the child could enter kindergarten.

Acts of kindness come from pets, too! My dog, Primo, always licks my tears when I am crying.

When looking at commonalities in these experiences, I see that others have been willing to give of themselves. Sometimes they have offered their light through tangible items, while other times it was through their own unique expression and gifts. I have learned that in order for me to fully receive these "sparks of love," I need to be open and aware each day. When I receive with an open heart, I can feel the blessings flowing to me.

I'm Not Alone

By Cynthia Lee Horn

It's a sweet, soulful Arizona afternoon, and I've set aside some time for writing. I'm sitting here by myself, but I'm not alone. I have many decades of memories – family, friends, teachers, mentors, and pet-sitting "fur clients" – a menagerie of "Creative Muses of Goodness" gifting me with the joys of their creative spirits and coloring my writing…and my life!

Energies beyond the physical are here cheering me on, celebrating our camaraderie, and softening the sting and the sorrow of recent tragedies here in the USA and throughout our planet. As I write, my heart begins to melt into the memories sprinkled through time, and I move from sadness into gratitude.

Memories from my New England childhood flow to the surface and create a gentle softening in my heart: Moments of color in the midst of the chaos of a large family. A rich garden. A menagerie of fur friends. Musical instruments. The beauty of nature. Picking berries. Finding peace in the stillness of the woods. Lying on the grass with my mother as she combed through the clover with painstaking devotion. The joy of finding the lucky four-leafed ones! Layers of life, layers of love.

Creative and caring connections so deeply color my heart – my life. A personal care package or thoughtful gift sent from a friend lifts my heart. A Soul Portrait painting arrives in the mail at just the right moment, revealing so much more than I can see. A video call with my grandgirls. A touching pet-sitting moment. A dear friend or family member creating time in their day for a loving connection, conversation, or prayer. Artful ways of being, of living.

Life would be cold and gray, stark and sad, without the colors of memory, the beauty of connection, the loving energies that wrap me in layers of kindness and allow me to move forward. I am deeply touched by the bounty of goodness and grace in my life! The Great Creator truly shines through all.

Nothing But More Goodness

By Rael Hall

I am always asking my clients to reconsider how they label and interpret those challenging situations in life that trigger us into bouts of unhelpful frustration, stress, anxiety, and self-judgment. Most people see these challenges as negative events, but it is my passion to show people how they often bring the opportunity of valuable life lessons or powerful messages that can empower us into new and better ways of walking in the world. Little did I realize that, on this day, *I* would be the one needing a reminder to see things in a better way, a way filled with only goodness.

I was on my way to an appointment with a new client, excited to help someone to empower themselves in new ways. Realizing that it was already warm outside and that I would need water before my appointment, I pulled into Starbucks to get a cold drink.

Oh no! I thought as I looked into my rearview mirror and saw the flashing lights of an officer pulling me over. I immediately started grumbling to myself: *Urrrgghh! What did I do wrong? I haven't had a ticket in years!*

The officer explained that my right turn was illegal and asked for my license. I realized that I left my purse at home – no license! The officer was firm but kind, and issued me a ticket. I could have seen that there was big goodness here – he let me continue to my appointment; he could have towed my car and written me a stronger ticket – but I was too busy grumbling over this ticket. To me at the time, it simply meant more expenses that I didn't need.

Later, I met a past client for dinner. When I told her about the incident, she reminded me of the concepts I taught her – that there are life messages in challenging situations and there is nothing but goodness abounding. I am so proud of my client! She and the officer became my teachers/mentors, presenting another way to see more goodness and reminding me that my only challenge is my incorrect perception. My awareness is more clear now; I have even more trust for abundance of goodness (Godness) for everyone.

Goodness Is Always Waiting for You

By Jennifer Larkin

Seeing the good takes courage and an unrelenting willingness to look into the deep recesses within – those places where subtle internal judgments reside. If left unchecked, these judgments often make seeing the good impossible.

Allowing goodness to abound is a lifelong endeavor. It's the path of spiritual champions and lion-hearted heroes. Yet for fearless warriors with their eye set on the ultimate prize – the conscious awakening of humanity – there is no choice but to see beyond external reality into the goodness within each soul regardless of the circumstances.

As this piece was being written, a series of horrific events took place in the UK in rapid succession. The terror attacks in Manchester, London Bridge, and Westminster, and then the towering inferno of Grenfell Tower. Having lived in the UK for most of the last two decades, these incidents pierced my heart. Sometimes it is so very hard to find the good.

Yet, in truth, within every incident there is divinely orchestrated wisdom, and within every perpetrator there exists a wounded lost soul doing their best to survive in a messy world.

In the last few years, I've used breathwork in my daily practice to shift into an evolved state of consciousness. It has become one of the most profound and expansive tools enabling me to expand beyond everything I once was. Research shows that specific breathing patterns are strongly correlated with specific emotional states. Conversely, this same research reveals that physical, psychological, and emotional states can be transformed simply by altering the breath. We are always in charge if we allow ourselves this degree of personal power.

Goodness always abounds, even if it appears imperceptible. Look more closely today and go within – it's always there waiting for you. And don't forget to breathe.

It's the "Little Things"

By L. A. Reeves

My life changed when my baby was born. The high of parenting quickly turned to exhaustion and worry. I returned to work, and my life became a regimen of routines that dictated my every waking moment. My days were full, but I was not. Everything was rushed, and I had no time to notice (let alone *embrace*) joy or grace.

On one particular day, I was right on schedule. I had left the house *on time*, dropped Zoey off at daycare *on time*, and was well on my way to getting to work *on time*. Then it happened. The cars around me swerved and frantically braked. I was in the middle, the unlucky one – my car was destroyed at both ends, and I quietly lay cradled by wreckage.

I found myself in an otherworldly place, vaguely familiar and full of beautiful sights, sounds, and a mighty but gentle Presence. All the joy and grace I had thought I lost were not only remembered but now were part of me, beads of loving light that danced through me. The Presence guided me to look closer at each tiny light. They were memories – *my* memories.

A stranger's hello in an elevator when I was feeling low. Someone who stopped to hold a door for me as I rushed. A shiny penny lying on the sidewalk waiting just for me. Zoey smiling at me when my back was turned. My mother saying a silent prayer for me, unbeknownst to me. There had been so many "Little Things" in my life that had shown me what joy and grace truly were.

I wondered where all the "Big Things" were. My valedictorian speech given flawlessly? The sporting events I won? The promotions at work? Instantly, I knew: it is the "Little Things" in life that matter most. The "Little Things" pile upon each other and lift us up in gratitude for noticing. They complete our life, if we let them.

I awoke and healed from that accident…appreciating all the "Little Things" along the way.

A Fabric of Small Kindnesses

By Sarah Atkinson

We sit at a small outdoor café in Taksim, an urban pedestrian area in Istanbul. Perched on low stools, we sip tea from tiny glasses. A young girl approaches – maybe eight years old – hawking packages of tissues. This is her trade. She might be Roma ("Gypsy," as they are often called) or perhaps her family has fled war in Afghanistan or Syria.

Her wavy hair is tangled, her clothes well worn. None of us needs tissues, but we greet her warmly and she hangs around. My friend Özgür draws her into his arms, gives her a thorough squeeze, musses her hair, speaks to her in soft, teasing tones. His affection towards this young stranger is easy and natural.

He releases her, and she comes over to me. She fancies the clip in my hair. She gestures that I should give it to her. It's a cheap plastic clip, and I can easily get another. I fix it into her unruly black hair.

She lives on the street. When I see young girls like this, especially when it's late at night, I wonder how long she has – how long before she's assaulted, raped, or sold, or ends up pregnant with an abusive partner. She is vulnerable, and it's hard to witness. I feel powerless. There are many like her in this city. As wars rage in neighboring countries, their numbers increase.

There are endless things to be scared, angry, and frustrated about. Endless. If I started listing them I might never stop.

But every day I see expressions between strangers of easy kindness, simple warmth, love. These weave the fabric of a world I want to inhabit, a fabric of strong but delicate threads. I can't say whether these kindnesses outweigh the brutalities – that's not a useful calculation; all I know is that they flow.

Maybe conflict and war are inevitable. Humans are beasts when desperate. But one thing I know for sure: despite the fear and hatred and danger that are always close at hand, love wants to flow from us. And it does. Thank goodness it does.

The Roller Coaster of Goodness

By Sabinah Adewole

You cannot always be a receiver of goodness; however, you can always be a *giver* of goodness. I consider myself very fortunate when I am able to be a giver, as well as when I find myself in the position of receiving the goodness of God. In either case, I've found that goodness often involves many ups and downs…like a roller coaster!

I experienced a roller coaster of goodness following my redundancy. I found myself nearly hitting rock bottom, and I asked God for a miracle. My faith guided my thought processes and my footsteps. I started by believing in that miracle, even though I had not yet received it. I also spent several months searching for a job and attending countless interviews. During this time, just as I recalled how I would not be paid in the third month, I came across a bond I had purchased over 20 years earlier. I was able to relinquish it, and that tied me over until I found a new job.

Another blessing in my life is my husband, who has been a friend, a loving partner, and the first man to be a true rock in my life since I lost my dad when I was four. When I turned 50 this year, I felt scared and didn't know what the future would hold for me (again, that roller-coaster feeling!), but my husband surprised me with a party, which turned out to be a big event in my house. Two weeks later, we went on a cruise with a group of friends. I am ever so grateful for having a husband who has been everything to me.

I truly believe that goodness abounds; to experience it, we need to give (without any ulterior motive), count our blessings (even before they show up in our lives), and leave our hearts open to receive from God (even when we don't know what the future holds). In fact, sometimes, the feeling of *not knowing* is what pushes us out of our comfort zone, opens us to experience all the pleasure that God has in store for us, and allows us to enjoy the roller coaster of goodness!

Goodness Abounds in Everyday Folk

By Lisa Hawkins

I've spent months trying to work out what to say.

My initial reaction when I first heard what this book was all about was, "Hmm…that'll be tricky." As an observer throughout my life, I've really struggled to see the goodness in a lot of people. It's not that I haven't tried or given people the benefit of the doubt, but sometimes not even rose-coloured glasses can disguise the way some people choose to treat each other and the pain that is caused.

Don't get me wrong; I've also seen amazing people do wonderful things. But I wanted to write about something that affected me deeply – something that *really* meant something to me.

So I stopped thinking about it, knowing that one day something perfect would come up. I'd witness the thing that would help me to see and express that goodness does abound.

And then I saw it…as plain as day, right under my nose: *Goodness abounds in the unsung heroes all around us!*

Goodness abounds in the people who stick by us through thick and thin. People who support us and show us grace and integrity. People who keep serving others, regardless of what happens to themselves. People who pick up the pieces and take responsibility for those who choose to look away. People who take responsibility even if it's not theirs to take. People who value compassion, understanding, support, resilience, and love.

Thank you to all the unsung heroes, the everyday folk: the mothers, the fathers, the worker bees, the caregivers, the people who work behind the scenes. They don't do what they do to get noticed or rewarded; they do it because they care, because they want to see a better world – not just for those they love but for everybody.

Thank you to these everyday heroes and their innate ability to show compassion and understanding. They are the glue that holds us together. Where would we be without them?

Goodness abounds in them.

An Abundance of Love

By V. Krishna Lakkineni

It's important to know the purpose of life, to find the right path. We never know for certain whether we are on the right path, however; only destiny will guide you there. But when you enjoy the journey, there is always an abundance of joy, empathy, kindness, compassion, and love. I always felt that these are the important elements that nourish our soul. Just like the water, fire, air, earth, and space, which help us live abundantly, we need the "soul elements" to live a life of fulfillment.

All of the soul elements are vital to us, but the most important of them all is *love* – love for one another and love for humanity. Love is an emotion that hurts when you are apart and blooms when you are together. It can lead to vengefulness when you are selfish or hurt by someone. It can also lead to joy and fulfillment when you share an abundance of love with an open heart. It is the one emotion that can control all the other emotions and all the other soul elements.

The first time I felt love was in my mother's womb. Upon delivery from a familiar world to an unknown world, I felt the touch of someone. When my mother took me closer to her chest, I felt warmth, love, joy, and many other emotions I couldn't understand. I felt safe.

Over the years, I've felt an abundance of love and the other soul elements in many life situations. They've nourished my soul in every possible way. Every time I was sad, the soul elements healed me and helped me understand the meaning of life.

I am still on the journey to fulfillment, but I live with abundance. I understand that we are just tiny particles in the universe, guided through this life's journey by an abundance of soul elements. And I understand that life is not just about living for oneself. The first instance of this in my life was when my mother took a great risk to give birth to another being. Dedicating my life to the abundance of others always leads me on the right path – a life filled with an abundance of joy, happiness, and love.

Goodness Equals Rightful Living

By Marihet Hammann

I was at a crossroads, and I decided that it was time to honestly look at my life and ask myself: *Am I living up to my full potential in all areas? Is my life filled with abounding goodness?*

With these questions in mind, I set the intention to pay attention to goodness in my life throughout the year. It did not take long before I became aware of incidents of goodness – inspiring me towards rightful living and reminding me that goodness abounds all around me:

My local radio station gathered tons of animal feed to assist farmers during the drought; their intervention reminded me that we have the right to love and be loved.

My deaf friend was persistent in getting our government to add sign language as an official language; her persistence reminded me that we have the right to speak and be heard.

My mentor stood at the United Nations as an ambassador against violence to women and children, using her visual art to inspire; her courage reminded me that we have the right to see and be seen.

One of my clients sponsored a local village's children to attend school for the year; her generosity reminded me that we have the right to know, learn, and understand.

Another client allowed a student at her school to participate in a program that she had dismally failed, yet through this act of kindness and against all odds, this same student graduated and returned to the school as a motivational speaker; this client's kind heart reminded me that we have the right to acknowledge and be acknowledged.

These rights and the abounding goodness I witnessed had such a profound effect on my living that I decided to create a world where kindness is the currency, love is the answer, and soulful business is the economy. I declare that, with so much goodness in my life, I'll colour, create, and nourish goodness as inspiration for others to share their own goodness while reclaiming their beauty, brilliance, and bravery through rightful living. I am rolling out the red carpet in honour of those who have given my body, heart, mind, and soul a soft place to land while I explored my rightful living. From my colourful soul to yours: thank you.

High Vibrations of Unconditional Love

By Mimi Quick

One brisk morning while walking outside to get my exercise, I suddenly felt a glorious feeling wash over me. It was beautiful, unlike anything else I have experienced in this world. It was like my near-death experiences but not quite. What happened was that I felt God Source, The All, communicating with me through everything: the sun's rays, the breeze, the leaves, the trees, all of it, all at once.

It was the best and most amazing connectedness I have ever felt. Everything was speaking to me at the same time. The breeze spoke to me of freedom and how to be at ease in life. The tree shared stories of standing tall in my truth and growing roots to stay grounded as I do my spiritual work on this plane. The leaves shared the letting-go process with me, and the little ants on the ground told me I was a gentle giant in their world and not to forget the little ones.

I heard beautiful sounds and felt like I was in a space of love. I could go in and out of that place; when I felt like I was pulling away, I entered the space more to enjoy all the love it was sharing with me.

I know beyond a shadow of a doubt that the universe speaks to us. Everything has a voice, and it is the most amazing thing I have experienced. To know that this unconditional love is all around us at all times is a gift I treasure beyond anything, and I wanted to share it with you, too, through this simple exercise:

Close your eyes. Feel into your own body. Allow the feelings of unconditional love to rise up within you. Stay in that unconditional-love vibration for as long as you can – 30 seconds, five minutes, or more. Now open your eyes and just allow the universe to speak to you and feel the amazing feelings that come along with it. Do this every morning to activate loving connection.

Open Your Heart to Joy

By Moni Rodriguez

Every single day, we have the opportunity to look at life and our daily situations from very different angles. We have the power to choose what we want to experience and what we want to live. I believe that as human beings we are capable of creating immense joy and happiness for ourselves and everyone around us.

I recently faced a very unpleasant situation that turned out to be a great lesson. My online bank account got compromised. The scammers transferred all my money into another account while I was away on a spiritual retreat. By the time I noticed, it was too late – all the money was gone.

At first, I was panicked and really disappointed that someone could do that. Shortly afterward, though, I decided that I wouldn't allow this situation to rob me of my inner peace.

I shared the experience with some close friends and instantly got back all my hope and light. Immediately, people started calling to support me, offering me money, and sharing loving words. The whole experience became a blessing because it allowed me to see how much love I had around me, and I felt truly grateful. I chose love over fear. I decided to forgive the scammers and send them my blessings instead of anger.

Even in despair, we can choose how we want to feel about the situation. In truth, what we are at the core of our human essence is just pure love. Anything else is not real; so to me, the goodness of humanity is always present as long as I choose love over anything else.

Despite any darkness that might want to take over, we must remember that we are true love manifested in a human body. If we do that for ourselves, we impact others with our simple presence; and eventually, we can change our reality and ultimately shift the reality in our world.

There is so much good to experience that we just need to make a decision right here, right now. Deciding to love unconditionally is our ultimate choice – allowing us to experience real freedom and manifest pure joy.

Loving Kindness

By Nikki Ackerman

Some cultures believe that when we sit and meditate on a positive outcome – such as peace and love – this will permeate throughout the world as a wave influencing change. We have seen a lot of fighting and tragedies in the United States and all around the world. On a smaller scale, there are people struggling with conflict or negativity on a personal level. I, too, have dealt with discord at times. But rather than allowing inner and outer strife to throw me into a downward spiral, my negative experiences have motivated me to find peace within myself.

I started meditating on a daily basis seven months ago. One guided meditation that I love is *Metta Bhavana*, which is also known as Loving Kindness meditation. It teaches us that every person wants to be happy, well, and free from suffering. Practicing this meditation has helped me feel centered and find peace and forgiveness. This has opened my heart to be a better person and more understanding toward others. It has also assisted me in developing better boundaries and becoming more observant and less reactive.

I felt compelled to introduce the Loving Kindness meditation at my office. There is a sense of paying it forward by guiding others to cultivate this practice. When we wish ourselves happiness, wellness, and freedom from suffering, we become skillful and begin emulating these characteristics.

The practice of *Metta Bhavana* continues to extend loving kindness out to the world. One by one, we take the time to call to mind someone we love or feel close to, a neutral person or acquaintance, someone we may have some contention or difficulty with, those in the community, and then to all identified individuals as a group.

I encourage you to take the time throughout each week to wish yourself and others happiness, wellness, and freedom from suffering. May this practice fill you and the world with peace, love, and happiness. From my heart, I wish you happiness. I wish you well. I wish you freedom from suffering.

The Art of Being Courageous

By Shari Sorbo

The beloved Mr. Rogers once asked, "How do we make goodness attractive?" He spoke of serving others by bringing courage to their lives and allowing that service to inform everything we do.

Let's take a look at the word *courage*. It originates from the Latin word *cor*, which means *heart*. So, originally, courage meant to speak your mind by telling people what is in your heart, which in some cases means being vulnerable and dropping our masks.

We all wear masks. We've learned to put them on in order to survive in the world and hide our vulnerability. We wear them as a badge of courage that shows others how we've survived in a world that may at times seem harsh and cruel. We wear them – and sometimes get caught up in them – in many areas of our lives: family, work, health, politics, spirituality, religion, or even while performing simple tasks such as going out to the store.

It takes courage to expose ourselves to friends, family, or strangers – to allow our masks to come down and speak from our hearts. After all, revealing the person beneath the mask may bring about unwanted consequences: we may lose friends, jobs, or perhaps even a community we once were part of. We may find that we are the lone voice of dissention that needs to be spoken in order to effect change.

But when we find the courage to drop our masks and speak our truth – even in a world that tells us not to let our guard down – we bring courage to others. By showing up in our authentic truth, our kindness, and our vulnerability, we set an example of courage – goodness of the heart.

I'm so thankful for all the people who have the courage to live authentically and share their goodness.

Seeing Goodness

By Karen Wythe

Years ago, at 2:00 on a cold winter's night, I was fast asleep when the phone rang. The voice on the other end of the phone, my brother's girlfriend, said, "Karen, I'm stranded. Can you come get me?"

Without thinking, I said, "Yes, I'll be right there." I went and picked her up, dropped her off at her home, returned home, and went back to bed, never to think of it again. Well, at least not until many, many, many years later.

By that point, she and I had become good friends, but we never mentioned that late-night phone call until one day, completely out of the blue, she said to me, "I really want to thank you for that night that you came and picked me up." I strained my brain to remember, but I couldn't think of it. She reminded me and said, "What you don't know is that nobody else would do it. You made me realize I'm not alone. I really felt loved and cared about. I've never forgotten it because it changed my life. I can't thank you enough for that night."

This was a big surprise for me. The goodness of that thank-you showed me how a simple act can have a great impact on someone's life. We don't always know how actions we take affect others. I never imagined that something I did without thinking and that meant little to me could mean so much to someone. It has made me much more aware of how I choose to respond to others. I am forever grateful that I made the right choice when I answered the phone that night.

It has also taught me about goodness. Goodness is not just an action. It is also how an action is perceived by a person. In this case, my action was simply a natural response, so for me there was no goodness in it. However, my friend experienced goodness. The action held deep meaning for her. In turn, her thank-you was an expression of goodness to me. It remains a gift of insight into seeing goodness.

The Power of Kindness

By Pauline Hosie Robinson

"No act of kindness however small is ever wasted." - Aesop

Every kind word or deed expands our hearts beyond what we imagine love to be. In my life, I've been blessed by so many acts of goodness that have expanded my compassion and deepened my appreciation of others. Here are just three of the many examples of kindness I've experienced in my life:

As a military child, generosity of spirit abounded in my life. With no extended family, we supported each other. My most powerful memory at six years old was of arriving at night with my three siblings to a house with no electricity and no furniture. My father was devastated that the system had messed up so badly. Before long, however, neighbors arrived with candles, cots, pillows, blankets, hot food, and a heater to warm my mother and six-week-old sister.

Kindness is always a blessing, even when it's not directed at us personally, as I learned from this story I heard about a woman named Linda who bought a lovely orchid for an elderly friend who was anxious about her upcoming surgery. Linda's friend told her later how much courage the beautiful orchid had given her and how, during her convalescence, its beauty inspired her each day.

Kindness can expand our hearts, give us hope and courage, and even help to heal our deepest grief. Four days before my husband died in tragic circumstances, he presented me with a beautiful red rose. The rose, once a symbol of love, became a reminder of pain and loss. Invisible to me in its vase, I did not notice that it was no longer there. Unbeknown to me, my son and his fiancée had taken it. To my surprise and delight, the rose was gifted to me in a beautiful golden frame. The red rose, given with such joy, once again became a symbol of beauty and love. Loving kindness was able to crack open the pain I held in my heart, and I was able to transmute that pain into love.

Kindness creates a rainbow bridge enabling love to flow. Like a pebble in a pond, a kind deed expands in the heart of another and leaves a permanent imprint on the soul.

A Cloudy Day Filled with Sunshine
By Kris Martin

The cool, overcast summer day began with an early-morning walk to the local Starbucks, where I was greeted with a broad grin and eyes that sparkled, with a voice to match. "What can I get for you this morning?" a nearby barista asked as she looked up and gave me a smile. I sipped the hot latte and pondered my upcoming morning full of errands.

I was unfamiliar with my first stop, a flooring warehouse, so I asked a gentleman for help. He said, "Follow me!" As we walked, he explained the process and products needed to renew the luster of my aged kitchen counter. At the checkout, I overheard one customer, with obvious expertise, sharing his knowledge freely with a woman who had questions about her current project. The cashier in my line was graciously helping a man with limited English make a purchase with his company's credit card.

At my next stop, I assumed that the busy parking lot would mean long checkout lines. But as I finished my shopping and made my way to the register, to my surprise, the lines were nonexistent! Instead of lines, I was greeted by yet another warm smile and friendly voice. "Hello there! Did you find everything you were looking for?"

"Yes, I did. Thank you!" As I finished paying, I was moved to say, "You have a beautiful smile!"

Throughout the rest of my morning errands – from picking up my repaired shoes to getting helpful advice from the drug-store pharmacist and having someone point out the sweetest watermelon at the market – I was met with affable people.

Finally, I found myself at the post office where a 7-Eleven employee from next door, who was mailing a package, offered to bring lunch to the postman.

On my way home, I questioned where all the angst was today that I had seen on the news the night before. It dawned on me that I had never looked for it and therefore had never found it.

Conclusion

We created this book to remind us all that, despite how it may appear at times, our world is filled with goodness. As we read the hundreds of examples of loving kindness described by the authors – from major, life-changing gifts to small gestures that lifted someone's spirits – we felt our own spirits lifted. We hope you've also been uplifted, moved, awed, and delighted by these stories, and we hope you're more convinced than ever that goodness truly abounds.

We also created this book in order to *expand* the goodness in the world! We believe that energy flows where attention goes and that by giving our attention (and energy and positive emotions) to the goodness described in this book, not only are we saying "Thank you" to the universe, we're also saying, "More like that, please."

If you enjoyed this book and would like to help spread the goodness it contains, please share it with your friends and family (or co-workers or complete strangers)! We would also be grateful if you left a positive review for us on Amazon, which will help this book's uplifting messages reach even more people. And we would love for you to join us on our Facebook page, where you can share your favorite pieces, connect with the authors, and be part of our wonderfully loving and soulful community: www.facebook.com/365bookseries.

We hope that reading this book has been a positive experience, inspiring you to turn on your own "goodness radar" – to look for (and find and celebrate) even more examples of goodness in your own life and in the world around you. We believe that as you do this, you'll start to notice goodness more and more!

Hugs, love, and gratitude,

Jodi and Dan

Contributor Biographies

O ver 275 authors contributed to this book with the hopes that sharing their stories of goodness would help everyone who reads them see how we're all surrounded by so much loving kindness.

The co-authors come from many different walks of life from many parts of the world. The common thread that links each of us is our desire to share our words and to inspire others by doing so. That's all, and that's everything.

As you read through each author's biography on the pages that follow, you'll find some who are already bestselling authors and others who are sharing their words in print for the first time, which is such an exciting moment!

It's our hope that you'll enjoy meeting them all through their photos and biographies and that you'll reach out to those you resonate with and let them know how much their pieces moved you. What a gift that will be for them to receive!

About the Editors

Jodi Chapman and Dan Teck are a husband-and-wife team who loves living soulfully and joyfully. Since 2005, they've been living their dream of writing books and creating products that inspire others to connect with their soul and live fully and passionately.

Jodi has a BA in English/Technical Editing and Sociology, and Dan has a BA in Religious Studies and an MFA in Creative Writing. Together, they have over 30 years of experience with editing and publishing and have sold approximately 50,000 books. They have written over 20 books, eight ecourses, and more than 1,000 blog posts/articles.

Jodi is an award-winning blogger at www.jodichapman.com and the author of *Soul Bursts* and the upcoming *A Year of Silence*. Dan is the author of the personal-growth blog *Halfway up the Mountain* (www.halfwayupthemountain.com) and the book *Rewrite Your Story*. They are the co-creators of the bestselling *Soulful Journals Series* and the *365 Book Series* as well as *Your Soulful Book*, a heart-centered writing program.

They live on the Oregon coast with their sweet cats. They enjoy hanging out at the beach and working, creating, and playing together.

They feel truly blessed to be able to spend each day together, doing what they love. It's their hearts' desire that their books and products bring joy to everyone they reach.

About the Contributors

Nikki Ackerman is a holistic business owner and a Master in Usui Holy Fire® Reiki and Karuna Holy Fire® Reiki. She recognizes the rewards are very beneficial for mind, body, and spirit wellness. Her desire is to provide others with peace and balance through a soulful and holistic approach to self-care and well-being.

Noelle Adamo is a writer who enjoys living the rural upstate New York life and keeping a house full of family and friends. She serves on the Board of Directors for the Maya Gold Foundation (www.mayagoldfoundation.org) and is passionate about helping youth thrive.

Sabinah Adewole studied English Literature and Social Work and has an MSc in Applied Psychology, focusing on understanding human behaviour. She is an international bestselling author, and this is her fourth anthology. Her first book is *Seven Years of Bondage*. She enjoys yoga, Pilates, cycling, writing, and reading novels.

Kelli Adkins, RN, is the CEO of Every Day Living LLC. She wears many hats: mom, speaker, author, coach, and chronic illness survivor. She continues to feed her own light so that she can light the way for others wanting to walk a similar path. www.Everydaylivingwithkelli.com

Tiffany Andersen is a medical aesthetician with 20+ years' experience, stage IV cancer survivor, and victim of a major car accident. She turned tragedy into triumph, which is described in her award-winning memoir, *Finding Faith*. On a quest for elements to repair the body, she developed the toxin-free skincare line, Gavée Gold. www.gaveegold.com

Chris Anderson, Gentleheart Therapies LLC Founder, is an international bestselling author, nurse, and educator who helps individuals and families experiencing end-of-life transitions. She provides empowering workshops for caregivers and helps families honor their loved ones with Gentleheart Memorial Cards. www.1gentleheart.com

Lara Anderson is published in *Chicken Soup for the Child's Soul*, *The Pacific Review* (where she received an award), and a poetry and photography book entitled *An Echo from a Cliff*. She also has published 30 short stories in elementary standardized school textbooks.

Trena Anderson is an animal communicator, Gestalt Coach, body practitioner, and intuitive facilitator. Her sessions gift clients – people and animals – with the psychic awareness, physical support, and consciousness required to move beyond life's limitations into what is truly possible. www.ConnectingInSpirit.com

Melisa Archer, National Trainer for Tesla Wellness Energy, is certified in Pulsated Electromagnetic Frequencies, BIO Frequencies, Reiki 3, Raindrop Therapy, Vitaflex, essential oils, rejuvenation facials, Emotion Code, and Dolphin Neurostim. Her ability to see and feel energies benefits the clients' sessions. www.TeslaWellnessEnergy.com

Katrina Hokule'a Ariel is an old-soul rebel, a musician, a tree-hugging yogini who swears a lot, and the author of *Yoga for Dragon Riders* (non-fiction) and *Wild Horse Heart* (contemporary romance). Find her music, books, and blog at www.KatrinaAriel.com.

Sarah Atkinson is a musician, teacher, and traveller, originally from Canada and currently living in Istanbul, Turkey. Her favourite forms of play include folk dancing and folk music, learning languages, listening deeply, and celebrating the beautiful differences between us as we find the common threads that connect us.

Alisa Auger, The Creativity Muse, uses the healing power of sound and words to help visionaries express their magic and make their mark on the world. She teaches mindset reset, magical manifesting techniques, and how to become a deliberate creator in life. www.alisaauger.com

Sarah Auger is a spiritual seeker who is always eager to learn and offer love. As a counselor, coach, Reiki practitioner, meditation instructor, and angel-card reader, she dedicates herself to helping others step into their own power and light. www.sarahmckay.com

Pratibha Badurkar, Spiritual Coach, Guide, and Healer, is a channel of the Divine in transforming thousands of lives with spiritual coaching and healing. Her mission is to reach people across the globe and to spread happiness and peace through different healing modalities.

Joy T. Barican is a life coach who is passionate in assisting you to make meaningful, exciting, and viable choices for yourself based on your individual values, personal strengths, and beliefs. When results matter, contact her via email: jbarican@hotmail.com.

Nora T. Barican loves life and shares her smile, truth, and gratitude. Having a solicitor for a father and teacher for a mother, her various interests were encouraged. Her passion for singing has seen her participate in Messiah and Chorus Oz with Sydney Philharmonia Choirs for 20 years at the Sydney Opera House.

Mauri Barnes has always been a free spirit, volunteering and helping those in need. Living on the Gulf Coast of Florida with her rescued dogs and cats is her kind of happiness. She loves sharing her stories here and is grateful for the opportunity to commemorate a friend, Jim Whelpley.

Judy Basaraba spent most of her life working and volunteering for non-profit organizations, empowering people with disabilities through education and employment. After retiring, she gained certification in floral design, TESL, Reiki, and Rahanni Celestial Healing. She feels blessed to continue to empower people to live their best life.

Randy Bassett is a successful businessman, co-founder of the charitable organization Opening Hearts, published writer, and proud father and husband. He also recently launched a new blog called *A View From the Edge* (www.randybassett.com/viewfromtheedge), addressing mental health issues for teens and adults.

Susan Bassett ("Positively Sue") is determined, energetic, focused, and dynamic. She has a passion and calling for uplifting and motivating people. Her inspiring talks help people face and overcome emotional blocks and rise above challenges. www.positivelysue.com

Keyon Bayani is a lover and student of life. She is not into labels or defining who she is by her formal qualifications or work. She believes that if you follow and honour your own personal truth, and you're kind, you are living your purpose. www.keyonbayani.com

Lauren Bear specializes in Meditation as Medicine through her studies at home and abroad. Using a foundation of Buddhism, Taoism, Traditional Thai and Chinese Medicine, plus Chemistry and Physics, she integrates ancient traditions with modern science. www.laurenbear.com

Kimberly Beer operates a working ranch with her family as well as a successful business where she helps entrepreneurs learn to effectively market their businesses. She is also a professional photographer and writer. Catch up with her at www.KimberlyBeer.com.

Rebekah Bernard, LMHC, NCC, has been a student of interdisciplinary spirituality for over 17 years and is fulfilled with her work as a spiritual counselor through hospice care. She teaches, speaks, counsels, and writes about living a love-centered, mindful existence and is grateful to her loved ones and co-workers for remaining her lifelong teachers.

Tahira Bharmal is a success coach, entrepreneur, and writer. She believes in living a life you love and aims to inspire others to live their life authentically through her writing and coaching. "Everything we seek lies within us – all our answers are inside of us; we just need to look deep inside!"

Bevan Bird is an international speaker, author, and partnership broker known as "The Soul 2 Soul Connector." He connects visionary thought leaders with each other, soul to soul, to create the best outcome. He is all about heart and smart. Connect with him at www.Soul2SoulConnector.com.

Tamra Blankenship focuses on helping people unlock pain and discomfort through her unique approach to truth, transparency, and support. She has the courage to be vulnerable without attachment, be present, be intentional with communication, and transcend uncomfortable situations into the gifts that are hidden in every experience.

Cathie Bliss, MBA, cultivated a career in international business for two decades. When her daughter developed severe special needs in the 1990s, she reoriented to the healing arts, becoming a Certified LifeLine Practitioner and Intuitive Astrologer. Visit www.CathieBliss.com for her heart-centered offerings.

Kimber Bowers is a Mind-Body Wellness Practitioner, speaker, and author whose mission is to serve as a reflection of the Love that IS, allowing others to discover it within their own realities and within their own souls, facilitating a joy-filled existence. www.lovinglighthw.com

Irene E. Bradford, PhD, is an executive coach and licensed psychologist who works with clients seeking to express more of who they are in the workplace and life in general. www.irenebradford.com

Anne Bradley has always been a writer of one kind or another. Her recent transition from authoring software to memoirs is a welcome and delightful lifestyle change. She loves meeting and hanging out with her readers and author friends at www.facebook.com/annebradleyauthor.

Michael Brewer is living his life purpose of love and service. He loves ducks, horses, body surfing, and walks on Park Beach. He lives each moment of each day in heartfelt gratitude.

Kimberly Brochu's holistic certifications and life experiences are the foundation for her writing and guiding others through personal transformation. She and her husband reside in Massachusetts, where they devote themselves to their five children, their Holistic Center, real estate business, and each other. www.facebook.com/KimberlyABrochu

Shannon L. Brokaw is a writer, yogi, and Usui Reiki practitioner who loves the outdoors. She is a seeker of anything that makes her laugh in life and puts a smile on her face. *La Dolce Vita!* www.welliesandwhisky.com

Jena Brown is a blogger and aspiring author. When she isn't reading, she is reviewing books and writing her first novel. She believes that books are magical and dreams are meant to be pursued. Come talk books at www.jenabrownwrites.com.

Lydia Burchell is a speaker, coach, and alchemist. She passionately helps women wanting to make a difference in the world to speak their message in a way that motivates others to take action for causes such as cleaning up the oceans, creating world peace, or bringing more kindness into the world. www.lydiaburchell.com

Benjamin Bush's wholehearted dedication to service is his biggest cause for action. He is grateful to have an abundance of work in the meditation and mindfulness arena. He sees his work as his passion and is proud to consistently bring authenticity to the corporate table. www.BenjaminBush.com

Christine Callahan-Oke is an empowerment coach, mom, inspirational writer, and positive thinker. Through coaching, writing, and facilitating online group adventures, she offers practical tips and wisdom to help people uncover their inner treasures, find the beauty in everyday moments, and shine their light brightly. www.YourInspiredLife.ca

Barbara "Bobbie" Carr is a mother, grandmother, and author who enjoys gardening, choral singing, tennis, and reading. She truly believes in the power and grace of the Spirit in her life. She lives in New Jersey with her husband, Pat.

Cheryl Carrigan is a full-fledged peacock who loves to live her life in vivid 3D color and is inspired/guided by the Angels. She is an inspirational author, speaker, and mentor, a spiritual teacher, angel-card reader, and psychic/medium. www.cherylcarrigan.com

Angie Carter is a grieving mother and inspirational writer who began writing as a way to cope with the sudden loss of her 19-month-old daughter, Bella. Her blog, *A Mother's Journey Through Grief* (www.angiecarter.ca), is dedicated to Bella's memory. Her writing offers perspectives and encouragement to parents worldwide.

Crystal M. Cathell is an international author whose work appears in several Amazon bestsellers. The co-founder of Ever Expanding Life, she is also a Reiki Master, Certified TESL instructor, and the Editorial Director for Authors Without Boundaries. Connect with her at www.EverExpandingLife.com.

Karen Ceballos has lived and worked happily in Mexico for the past 47 years. She began her spiritual search in the early '90s and is grateful for the teachers who pointed the way to opening her heart. She shares her experiences joyfully with others, always deepening in her discovery.

Robin Chellis is an energy healer and energetic artist. She uses frequencies of light and love to bring awareness and shifts. Her work raises your vibration to activate deeper love, joy, creativity, peace, and more… awakening your true being. Experience her work at www.RobinChellis.com.

Katie Keck Chenoweth, MA.Ed., LMBT, CHt, a pioneer in wellness, has degrees in training and health and certifications in massage and hypnotherapy. Being an artist, she has the unique ability to fuse art, massage, and past-life regression into radical healing. She can be found offering tranquil touch and meditation on the NC coast.

Claire Chew kicked stage IV cancer's butt at 19 and now can be found coaching, teaching, cooking, and practicing spiritual psychology. Her favorite mantra is "Let love be your bottom line." She knows her time here is short and empowers women to live fully. www.clairechew.com

Karen Ciran-Barnes inspires, encourages, and empowers people to live healthy, happy, and free. Experienced in scores of disciplines with countless tools, she is a heart-based entrepreneur, spiritual warrior, wife, mom, and nani whose passion is to enlighten people in mind, body, and soul. www.dowhatlightsyouup.com

Tiffany Clay is a Wellness Coach who specializes in helping women get lean and healthy. She addresses mindset as the key to overcoming self-sabotage and promotes a balanced approach to exercise, nutrition, and self-care to help women lose weight and keep it off for good. www.yourfithealthylife.com

Lisa Rachel Cohen, author of *Grace is Born* and *My Grace is Born Companion* is the CEO of Sparkle Press LLC and InSparkle Media. You can join her on her sacred mission to embrace the heart and grasp the hand of every woman, child, and man at www.InSparkleMedia.com.

Joanne Angel Barry Colon has been blessed with a beautiful daughter, is the business owner of Fitness "R" Us, and is a personal trainer, nutrition coach, Reiki/crystal healer, and speaker. She is the author and publisher of *Healing Within Meditation* and *The Power To Release Weight*. www.fitnessrus.org

Keyra Conlinn is a coach, an educator, and an author who strives to motivate people to step out of their comfort zones, step beyond linguistic and cultural barriers, and step into new experiences and new lives by raising their personal and cultural awareness. You can find her at www.keyraconlinn.com.

Terry Corrao is a writer, photographer, and cooking instructor who shares her passion for life through storytelling, images, and food. She is the author of the photography book *Father Daughter*, a 2017 Benjamin Franklin Book Award winner. She lives in Tuscaloosa, Alabama. www.terrycorrao.com

Nikki A. Creber is a Parkinson's Coach and Consultant. Her own Parkinson's journey revealed her true audacious life mission: helping those with Parkinson's dispel depression, grief, anxiety, and apathy; take conscious control; and design their own better ways to live and thrive every day. www.theparkinsonsheroclub.com

Dianna Robinson Curren is an ambassador of love and kindness whose passion is to bring hope to the hopeless and love to those who feel unloved. She believes she can change the world with a smile or a random act of kindness. Her accreditations and spiritual gifts come from God. www.facebook.com/sunshinesouls17

Kathy Damas is a Master Certified Health Coach Candidate, happily alchemizing her lifelong interests in wellness and experiences as a biologist with her sense of curiosity and gift of encouragement. A late-blooming runner, she's also a grateful co-adventurer with her husband of 28 years. www.BeLightHealth.com

Marla David is a life coach, speaker, writer, and co-author of four #1 international bestsellers. This retired stay-at-home mom has three grown daughters and a granddaughter. She enjoys time with family and friends, her dogs, traveling, arts, and music. She is living her life of passion and is an advocate for nature and animals.

Patty Davis is a prayer chaplain at Unity of Auburn in Northern California and is a devoted wife, mother, and spiritual seeker. She loves doing artwork at imagePathways Creative Arts Studio in Newcastle, California. Her mission as an artist is to empower others to realize their self-worth through creativity.

Netta de Beer is the creator of the successful wedding-events company Delicious and Delightful, which began in 2010. Her great passion is writing poetry for a local newspaper. She enjoys playing with unsaid words and mixed feelings.

Kathy DeFinis is a mother, grandmother, spiritual seeker, energy healer, massage practitioner, essential oil enthusiast, basket weaver, quilter, and crafter.

Heather A. Dempsey, CCH, is a coach whose eclectic style assists individuals to find more joy and fulfillment by combining the LOA, Reiki, sound therapy, yoga, crystal healing, Emotion & Body Code, aromatherapy, and flower essences. It is inspired by her work with John Assaraf, Jack Canfield, and Byron Katie. www.hs-hp.com

Crysti Deusterman was a sales rep for years before changing paths. She had children later in life, and now spends some of her time advocating for dyslexia and education reform. Much of her time is spent learning from her children. This is her second opportunity to be a collaborative author.

Robyn Dewar leads a fulfilled life in an expanding community of empowered love-lifters. She is grateful for her wellness family network and celebrates each day committed to a beautiful state. She happily resides in Haileybury, Ontario, with her husband, Shawn, and their two daughters. www.robyndewar.com

Felicia D'Haiti is a Feng Shui and Soul Coach/Teacher who guides clients in shifting their perspectives and environments to move beyond perfectionism, fear, and self-imposed limitations. She is an author and educator who lives in Maryland with her husband and four children. www.feliciadhaiti.com

Ruth Donald is a strategist, coach, and educator. She works with individuals and enterprises from across the world, helping them to connect at the heart. Her number-one priority in life is seeing the love in every situation. www.ruthdonald.com.au

Nicole Donovan-Wells, Midwife of the Soul, Energy Worker, and Ritual Creatrix, is the catalyst to discovering your life's purpose, claiming the life you long to live, and connecting to your truest self. She offers one-on-one sessions, courses, group programs, and retreats. www.earthsoulmedicine.com

Patricia Downing is co-founder of Living with Kindness, an online community whose purpose is to recruit kindness ambassadors who inspire each other to practice kindness and help create a more compassionate world in which people join together to find creative solutions that work for everyone. www.livingwithkindness.com

Kimberly DuBoise is a poet who loves to inspire with words. When not writing, she is probably reading, cooking, or walking. She lives in the Midwest with her husband. You can find her book and blog at www.kimberlyduboise.com.

Dr. Jerri Eddington is the creator of Energy Connections and the co-creator of Lighten Up and Thrive, a sacred vision of sharing our expertise and wisdom as transformational Soul Coaches®. Be sure to check out her new book, *Work It Out Together!*, on Amazon. www.LightenUpandThrive.com

Denise Edelstein, Pockets of Joy Success Coach and Mindset Expert, helps heart-centred women start and FAST-track their online business, harnessing the power of "Pockets of Joy" so they can make a difference in the world. Join her Facebook group, "Women Who Dare to Be More" here: www.bit.ly/WWDMore.

Tandy R. Elisala is a cancer thriver coach who helps those affected by cancer lead their healing from within so they are empowered to live life on their terms and be aligned with their big, bold legacy. She is a radio show host, multiple bestselling author, four-time cancer thriver, and mom. www.tandyelisala.com

Kimberly A. Elliott is a believer in passionate living. She is committed to investing her time, energy, and resources in encouraging others to love lavishly, learn limitlessly, and laugh loudly...every chance you get! She enjoys reading, writing, world travel, and the amazing beauties God has given her in her children and grandchildren!

Alison Ellison, a soulful simplicity strategist, writes and teaches ways to shift from living a busy, stressed-out life-style into creating an authentic, stress-less soul-style. Her Life Simplified program shares ways to let go of the chaos of a hectic life and adopt a soulfully simple life. www.moresoulplease.com

Michelle Evans is an energy healer/teacher, spiritual guide, and transformational speaker. She is passionate about the self-love and soul-connection journey. She works with healers who are plagued with doubt in their abilities and helps them obtain unshakable confidence in their gifts. www.rocksolidlove.ca

Phoebe Fazio has been transforming people's lives through a unique form of healing called Sound Washing®. Using her voice, she channels vibrational messages from the Divine. As a Reiki Master of five years, her true essence radiates when sharing her gifts with others. Learn more at www.phoebefazio.com.

Leslie P. Felton is a speech pathologist at a public school. She has an MS degree from Alabama A&M University. She has been married 28 years and has two musically gifted children. Her most valuable assets are her faith in God and the love of family and friends. She resides in Greenville, NC.

Helen Ferrara, PhD, is passionate about the world we live in, believes that we are all creative, and has experienced that the broadening of one's perspective strengthens personal transformation. She fosters creativity and is a mentor who assists the nurturing of self-knowledge and authentic expression. www.creativenurture.com.au

Linsey Fischer discovered her love for journalism while writing for her hometown newspaper. She went on to study Broadcast Journalism, gaining experience in editing, reporting, hosting, anchoring, producing, and script writing in both radio and television. She's a #1 bestselling author in the *Empowering Women to Succeed* book *Bounce*.

Meredith Fjelsted is a Nationally Certified Health Coach and founder of Dream2bhealthy. She is a professional speaker and healthy-lifestyle expert who loves being outdoors, gardening, dogs, going on mission trips, and living healthy. She lives in Minnesota with her husband, Scott; two stepsons, Colin and Aidan; and two dogs.

Scott Fjelsted has been a Certified Personal Trainer since 1998 and is the author of *ForeverFitU: Making Fitness a Lifestyle that Lasts a Lifetime.* He is committed to the wellness of his clients, community, and home. He lives in Minnesota with his wife, Meredith, and two sons, Colin and Aidan.

Kim Brazier Flatland is a bestselling author, coach, speaker, and mindset momma. She has guided hundreds of women through her workshops and coaching. Her passion is helping women embrace their true spirit while gaining confidence in themselves by building on a foundation of self-love. www.loveyoursoulself.com

Gigi Florez is a lifelong spiritual seeker. She is committed to helping others along their journey and continuously growing with her own. It's her passion for learning and understanding that fuels her ability to explore one's fullest potential. She is a Reiki Master Usui, a distance healer, a fairy card reader, and an intuitive artist.

Suzanne Fortino currently resides in Idaho and is a mother of five and grandmother of two. She often finds herself wandering the Northwest, visiting friends and family. She's passionate about the path she's chosen, spreading healing love and light to all she encounters on life's healing journey. www.healingjourney.com

Tammy Foster has dedicated 30 years to public education in Arizona. She has raised three sons who have all grown to be outstanding young men, sharing their gifts with the world to make it a better place. She has a daughter-in-love and a beautiful granddaughter who enrich her life.

Chireya K. Fox, Visionary Coach, Transformational Catalyst, and #1 Bestselling Author, has dedicated her life to the awakening of higher consciousness and vibrational healing. Her #1 bestselling book *Fall In Love with the Beloved Within: Source Speaks* is available on Amazon, along with three other titles. www.Chireya.com

Erin Fritts, OTR/L, CHC, is a transformational life and health coach with a background in occupational therapy. She is the founder and owner of Simplify and Balance Wellness Coaching. She would love to help you create your dream life by building your connection with your inner knowing. http://simplifyandbalance.com

John R. Fyfe is a Vedic Astrologer and world traveler who studied in India, bringing together the modalities of Reconnection, Palmistry, and DNA activation. He is a published author of *The Meaning of Fyfe*, *Molly's Missing*, *The System's Approach to Vedic Astrology*, and *In the Palm of Your Hand*, an introduction to palmistry.

Darlene Gaetz is a wife, mother, best friend, and successful entrepreneur who lives on Vancouver Island, Canada. Effervescent and generous, she loves to inspire other women to create a life they want and deserve by having more wealth and wellness in their lives. www.darlenegaetz.com

Tammy Gamester is a healer and Intuitive Life Coach, using Reiki, crystals, aromatherapy, and coaching in her healing work. Her specialty is working with people who have suffered loss in their life. She lives in Tempe, Arizona, with her husband and father. www.bluebutterflyinspirations.com

B. J. Garcia is an author and inspirational teacher. She lives Austin, Texas, and loves sharing with others all the many strands of interest and wisdom she has collected and moved through in her personal journey for truth. Her deep love is teaching and sharing the Enneagram and Gene Keys. www.bjgarcia.com

Laura Garrett, RScP, lives in Menifee, CA, and is a licensed Spiritual Practitioner. She wrote the children's book *There Are All Kinds of Families* (scheduled to be published and available soon). She raised four children and has five grandchildren. For fun, she enjoys time with family, gardening, taking photos, and painting.

Michelle Goguen is an artist, teacher, psychic, and shaman. She has been teaching art to inner-city children for the past 13 years and is an expert in the Soulmate/Twin Flame concept. As an artist, she works with light and reflection, broken and shattered glass. www.michellegoguen.com

Ray Goodenough, CCHTA, is a recovered alcoholic, Clinical Hypnotherapist, licensed Neurolinguistic Programmer, and certified instructor of the Enneagram. He worked with adjudicated youth for 27 years. Now semi-retired, he has co-authored, with his daughter, a memoir transmitting love and forgiveness. www.Paralleljourneys.net

Padma Gordon is a Spiritual Counselor, movement educator, women's group leader, and devoted mother who guides people to connect to their bodies and hearts through mindfulness practice and soulful conversation. She teaches people how to embrace life and respond authentically so that they can thrive. www.padmagordon.com

Michelle Anne Gould, Founder of Abundant Spirit Education and Creator of SoulMagic™, supports people who are committed to enhancing their lives by unlocking abundance, wellbeing, and freedom from within. She is passionate about awakening people to their unique infinite magic and creating a life they love.

Vijaya Gowrisankar has released four books of poems: *Inspire, Reflect, Explore,* and *Savour – Art and Poetry Meet.* Her pieces have been published in *Silver Birch Press, Nancy Drew Anthology, Poetry Marathon 2016 Anthology, Sometimes Anyway: Pride in Poetry Volume II, Forwardian, Triadae Magazine, iWrite India,* and *Dystenium Online.* www.vijayagowrisankar.wordpress.com

Michelle R. Griffith is an author, advocate, and intuitive. As a lifelong learner, she follows where her curiosity leads and leads others to follow their curiosity. She uses a mix of modalities to support clients seeking functional balance in the business of life. www.MichelleRGriffith.com

Nadene Joy Hagen has a gift for increasing harmony and awareness in the world. She is an accomplished parenting and life coach and jewelry designer. A mother of four and former geologist, she has founded a new hands-on school, Star Elite Academy. She was born and raised in Regina, Saskatchewan, Canada. www.NadeneJoy.com

Rael Hall, Life Success Strategist, offers hope for women ready to dump their stress, anxiety, anger, and trauma quickly and shift into attraction for more abundance, confidence, and body wellness. Her holistic methods are fast, easy, and fun! She is available for both private sessions and corporate wellness events. www.RaelHall.com

Marihet Hammann is a seeker of the creative and the colourful. It's her core belief that our innate creativity is the key to healing our hearts, reconnecting to our true selves, and sharing our gifts with the world. She writes books, holds workshops and retreats, and shares her own creative journey to inspire you on yours. www.marihethammann

Joy Harris, Success Coach, assists women in defining success on their own terms. Her passion is to help women write, publish, and promote their work. She is a certified energy healer and uses techniques of meditation and writing exercises to achieve happiness. www.JoysWritersOasis.com

Annalene Hart is an Enchanted Living Life Coach, poet, and visionary artist who creates soul paintings. She has inspired her clients to pursue and realize their dreams. She conducts individualized Magical Child sessions to help activate the participant's innate creativity and imagination. www.mydivineenchantedlife.wordpress.com

Lisa Hawkins is a homeopath and healer who supports people who are struggling with a crisis in health or in life, often when no one else understands. She listens, helps clients work through their issues, and holds a loving space for them to reconnect with themselves and heal. www.theenergyevolution.co.nz

Ellouise Heather is an accredited Master Coach. She uses her own combination of coaching, intuition, heart connection, and mysticism to help sensitive, heart-centred women break free from judgment and the shackles of "should" to reconnect with and share their gifts with the world. www.ellouiseheather.com

Chadi Hemaidan has been working in the field of helping others as a personal support worker for 20 years. In 1981, he first volunteered at a camp for blind and deaf kids. He enjoys reading books, nature walks, and poems. He is pursuing his passion for writing.

Sharon Hickinbotham, Angel Intuitive Reader and International Bestselling Co-Author, is passionate about inspiring others to follow their heart and soul. She is a caring and sensitive empath whose abilities and love for helping others, animals, and nature drive her life purpose. www.facebook.com/PurpleReign444

Mikaela Che'lean Hicks has lived in Oklahoma for 19 years. By day, she helps people organizationally transform their homes, offices, and bodies. When she's not removing clutter, you can find her training for a marathon, working in her flower beds, or spending time with family. www.mikaelachelean.com

Karen Hill received her bachelor's degree in Human Services from Union Institute and University in 2009. She has extensive experience working with adults in residential drug and alcohol treatment. She recently became a first-time published co-author in the *365 Book Series* and is very excited to be on her journey.

Cindy Harpe Hively is a renowned intuitive healing coach and catalyst for women. Her life's passion and soul work is to help women experience a luscious, rhythmic life that's overflowing with love, joy, vibrant health, personal success, feminine mystery, spiritual connection, and prosperity. www.inherfullness.com

Jesse Hodgdon lives a varied, rich, and full life. Gratitude abounds for her most amazing life as wife, mom, LMT, Young Living Essential Oils distributor, mediator, and co-founder of Life Helpers. In 2016, she wrote and her husband illustrated their first book, *Now*. www.lifehelpers.life

Gretchen Oehler Hogg, BSN, CCHt, is a metaphysical hypnotherapist and Master Soul Coaching® practitioner. She helps people transform their lives by discovering their innermost truth and soul path. She's a co-creator of Lighten Up and Thrive: Joyful Living for Mind, Body, and Soul and Soul Journeys. www.LightenUpandThrive.com

Maureen Hollmeyer, LSW, is a Spiritual Life Coach who teaches others how to communicate with their angels through her Angels 101 Life Coaching Program. She designs angel décor and sells her treasures locally at Lucy & Ethel's Place in Cincinnati. She is a social worker and co-author, and she believes in divine intervention.

Sharyn Holmes is a writer, speaker, qualified youth mentor, and founder of Gutsy Girl. Her mission is to help women and girls lead brave, confident, wholehearted, and gutsy lives on their terms. She teaches women and girls how to cultivate the kind of confidence that makes the mountains shake.

Diana L. Hooker is an accountant, event speaker, and author. Inspired by the true stories of her friends and clients, she is following her passion to write an inspirational book titled *Living Your Greatness: How to Find Your Greatness in the Good, the Bad, and the Ugly.*

Cynthia Lee Horn is a professional pet caregiver and owner of Lotus House & Pet Sitting. She is a perennial student of life, yoga, wellness, and creativity. She is passionately crazy about her three Texas granddaughters, who affectionately know her as "Bo-Nana." Write to her at cynthia@wellnesswisdomandwealth.com.

Anne-Marie Hoyne is a fifth-generation Australian woman with Irish, English, Scottish, and German heritage. Nature is her constant teacher and guide, and she loves to dance, sing, read, and float in the ocean. She works as a celebrant, holistic coach, and facilitator of women's circles. www.coessence.com.au

Sarah Huffer resides in Cincinnati. She masters in perception, energy, and love with an authentic and emotional writing style. Check out her blog and follow her on social media. www.sarahhuffer.com

Kimberly Hutt is a Relaxation Therapist, Natural Health Consultant, and Intuitive Counsellor of Energy Therapies. She helps co-create sacred space where the essence of your soul and authentic voice of your spirit can be seen and heard. She travels across Canada as a guest speaker, facilitator, and instructor. www.soulyreconnected.com

Katie Cox Jackson's passion lies in helping others to live their very best life. Her body, mind, and spirit are fueled daily through spiritual practices, nutrition, fitness, and a passion for learning. She is grateful for the gift of an extraordinary life and embraces the "4F Life": Fervent, Fit, Focused, and Free. www.facebook.com/4katiecox

Kelly Jenkins is an author, mentor, ordained minister, and certified mind-body-spirit practitioner. At a young age, she realized she had a connection with angels, which influenced her sharing kindness with others and creating Caring Confetti, a campaign to spread kindness. kell@kelljenkins.com

Sheila Jenkins is the author of *The Day Before: Eternal Bonds into the Afterlife.* She is the mother of two daughters and grandmother of five. She is certified in Reiki 1. One day she hopes to help others process their grief. She can be found at www.sheilamjenkins.com.

Shayelee Johnson is down to earth and a natural comedienne. She loves to spend her time walking on the beach and soaking in nature. She is the mother of two beautiful children, has a huge heart, and sees the true potential and positivity in every situation.

Julie Jones is a nurse, researcher, aromatherapist, energy practitioner, health and wellness coach, inspirational speaker, and author. Her supportive coaching with small steps inspires and empowers people to move from sick care to health care – restoring balance for wellness. www.restoretobalance.com

Nancy Merrill Justice is an author, entrepreneur, and Certified Awakening Dynamics Theta Practitioner. With 25 years of succeeding in business and overcoming personal health challenges, she helps people to heal and learn techniques to maintain a "mindset of happiness" and manifest their heart's desires. www.nancyjustice.com

Surabhi Kalsi is a Heal Your Life® Coach, #1 bestselling author, and Master Teacher (Angels) with the Diana Cooper Foundation. Her work focuses on personal development and inner wellness by using practical spirituality, creativity, and transformational coaching. She teaches ways to thrive at work and relationships. www.surabhi-kalsi.com

Ayeesha S. Kanji, Career Coach and Professional Development Trainer, is passionate about travelling, dance, and writing. Living between the USA and Canada, she enjoys writing poems and blogs and inspiring others to believe in what they want.

Donna H. Kater is the bestselling author of *TurboCharged Vision Boards for the Digital Age*; *I'm Still Alive, Now What?!?* – *How to Survive and Thrive After a Life-Changing Event*; and *Handbook for the Compassionate Ones* – *Helping Professionals and Caregivers: Seven Habits to Stay Energized, Motivated, and Sane*. www.LiveWithBoldness.com

Jenna Kelland is certified in holistic nutrition and has a PhD in Adult Education. As owner of Spark Wellness, she helps women emerging from burnout to have balanced, energized lives. A self-employed mom of three, she recognizes self-care as essential for her success and her family's well-being. www.sparkwellness.ca

Diane L. Keyes, Administrator for the Center for Spiritual Living Temecula Valley, Bookstore Manager, and Unity Chaplain, is the author of *The Women of AngelFire* series. Her next book, *The Universal Woman: A Spiritual Feminist*, continues the work of Ann Meyer, DD, co-founder of Teaching of the Inner Christ.

Davalynn Kim is a dedicated mother, daughter, sister, and friend. She enjoys reading, writing, painting, and bird watching. She loves dogs, cats, horses, and a beautiful brisk winter day. She believes in love at first sight. She believes in doing things that make the soul sing.

Elizabeth R. Kipp, Health Facilitator in Stress and Chronic Pain Management, successfully recovered from chronic pain. She guides you into greater health, more ease, and peace. Founder of www.Elizabeth-Kipp.com, she is experienced in stress management, calming anxiety, and resolving conflict.

Marci Kobayashi, a long-term resident of Tokyo, is a business coach, web designer, and intuitive. When she is not helping clients come out with their woo, she loves discovering spirit in all shapes and forms and blogging about her life in Japan. www.marcikobayashi.com

Ingrid Koivukangas is an award-winning environmental artist, writer, teacher, flower farmer, and creator of the *Eco Heart Oracle* and *Alchemy Flower Fairy Oracle*. Visit her website for courses, virtual retreats, and booking intuitive readings. Eco retreats are held at Alchemy Farm on Salt Spring Island, BC. www.ingridkoivukangas.com

Manpreet Komal is a speaker, coach, and co-author of two international bestselling books, *HALO: Lighting up Heaven on Earth* and *365 Life Shifts*. She writes on a daily basis on her Magic is Everywhere Facebook page to inspire others through words. www.manpreetkomal.org

Carrie Kondor, MEd, owner of Caria, is a certified holistic practitioner of sound coding, Aufstellung, breathwork, and health coaching. Through her writing, workshops, meditations, and private sessions, she empowers clients to unlock their truest potential, free their minds of negative distractions, and tap into their divine creativity.

Marifran Korb is a relationship coach who has been married for 48 years. She has authored four books, including *Breaking Through Concrete: The Gift of Having Mentally Ill Parents* and *Thriving in Partnership Beyond Depression: A True Love Story*. She is a former English teacher and youth director. www.SoulfulSolutions.com

Charlene Kussner, RScP, is a mother, wife, and businesswoman. She is an intuitive spiritual coach and healer who moves with fierce grace and endeavors to empower others through prayer and guidance in living their unique individual bliss. www.fiercegrace.us

Debbie Labinski, Intuitive Angel Communicator, Speaker, and Author, instantly connects with her clients to create a safe place to explore feelings of hope and heartfelt answers, giving them the guidance they need to create positive adjustments in their lives. She is dedicated to empowering others to believe in their own intuitive abilities.

V. Krishna Lakkineni is an Amazon bestselling author, public speaker, and CEO at the digital marketing agency ROI Media Works. He believes in giving and sharing knowledge and loves mentoring new entrepreneurs. His interests range from artificial intelligence in marketing, chatbots, and cryptocurrency, to volunteering for nonprofits.

Ahana Lara is a Business Abundance Coach, author, and co-creator of ASP (A Simple Path) programs. She uses her experience in entrepreneurship, digital marketing, coaching, and journalism to take her clients through a journey of empowerment and growing a six-figure business with purpose. www.ahanaanddaniel.com

Jennifer Larkin is an entrepreneur offering a wide range of health and wellness initiatives, including life-altering healing remedies, delicious raw enzyme-rich food, meditation courses, personal-empowerment retreats, consciousness-raising workshops, and private coaching programs through Healing Light Center.

Destrie Sweet Larrabee, MEd, lives in Ohio with her wonderful family and cats. She enjoys following her peaceful life path, living close to Lake Erie in a city that celebrates community in a Solstice Circle amphitheater carved into the cliffs of Lake Erie, traveling, and learning.

Beth Larsen is a sought-after success coach and the founder of the Business, Bliss, and Balance Blueprint™, her signature program that helps ambitious, driven women achieve the financial, spiritual, and healthy lifestyle they desire AND deserve! www.bethlarsencoaching.com

Catherine Laub, Your Turquoise Angel Guide, hosts *Spiritual Destinations* podcast; is a psychic, spiritual guide, and nine-time bestselling inspirational author; and speaks on topics regarding depression, anxiety, and health issues similar to her own through her campaign "Brighten Your Day With Turquoise."

Cheryl Lawrence is a child of light, of the Divine pure light. She is an open channel and chooses to serve humanity with her gifts. We enjoy assisting her in all that she does. She is learning that she is an author and will be publishing more in the future. Please welcome her! (Channeled 6/30/2017 from Archangel Raphael)

Sarah Lawrence is a Brit abroad on the Kansas prairie. For seven years, she has been giving Akashic Records readings to clients – a type of intuitive and energetic reading that connects us with our inner wisdom. Find out more about her work at www.MomOnASpiritualJourney.com.

Kenneth I. Laws II has been on a spiritual path to understand the unexplainable, his awakening, after a series of life-altering events that occurred in his life in 2013. It was not until then that he started to understand the meaning of oneness with all, accepting all with no judgment. www.simplyindescribable.com

Tara Leduc is a storyteller, speaker, and certified International Ambassador for Peace. She is the producer of the Inner Peace Summit series and the founder of 1 Minute of World Peace. For the full version of the suncatcher story, please visit: www.taraleduc.com/suncatcher-heal with-intention.

Patricia LeBlanc empowers spiritual entrepreneurs to create the life that they desire. Her unique approach helps you shift your energy and subconscious programming and helps you disconnect from any patterns and beliefs that are holding you back and keeping you stuck in lack and fear. www.patleblanc.com

Rhonda Lee, MAEd, is the creator of Spirit Mist Smokeless Smudge. She is a Reiki Master, keynote speaker on stress management, and Laughter Yoga leader. She empowers others to take charge of their energy through various modalities. She chooses the path of love to guide her business and life. www.infusionoflife.com

Saundra Lee is a retired State and National Certified Business Education Teacher. She is a Reiki Master and incorporates meditation and the practice of Tai Chi in her daily life. She also advocates the use of Energy Medicine and Yoga to enhance health and inner strength.

Tanya Levy is a counselor in a community college and an inspirational photographer. She has worked in the human-services field for 25 years. She is a strong and passionate advocate for the healing power of each individual's own learning journey. www.facebook.com/heartladyinspiration

Ruthie Lewis is an author, life coach, and speaker. Her soul was shaken in an avalanche of tragedies, and her only lifeline was the light that dwelled within. Excavating the tiniest spark from the rubble, she was freed from a life of have to/supposed to. Her passion is now contagious, brighter than any firefly's glow! www.RuthieLewis.com

Amy Lloyd is a singer, poet, writer, and speaker who has been sharing her personal, creative inspiration since 2008, beginning with a newsletter, *Songs from the Valley,* a daily poetry blog, *Life Acoustic & Amplified,* and a weekly awareness blog, *The Oracles Compass.* www.songsfromthevalley.com

Courtney Long, MSW, LC, CHt, ATP®, is an angel communicator, life-purpose intuitive, fairy expert, author, and speaker. She inspires adults, teens, and kids to joyfully activate the angels' assistance, open their intuition, and discover their purpose and gifts. www.CourtneyLongAngels.com

Denny Long is an avid golfer who migrates between Michigan and Florida. As an entrepreneur of 40 years, his businesses have included a 27-hole golf course, a cable company, and a television station. He brings humor to everything he does. He is the father of Courtney Long, a contributing author in this book.

Gunhild Lorenzen, MA, Dip Psych, Art-, Gestalt-, and Transpersonal Therapist, is the author of *21 Soul Questions to Empower and Transform Your Life with Creativity* as well as short stories and poems. She is an artist and life coach who facilitates workshops on creativity, spirituality, and dreams. www.gunhildlorenzen.com

Fiona Louise, Nutritional & Natural Therapist, Author, Educator, and Marketing Guru, is currently developing programs to help you live with purpose. Discover her bestselling book collaborations and musings here: www.fiona-louise.com.

Ruby Mabry is a bestselling author, CEO of mental health facilities, and empowerment coach. She is the founder of Live on Purpose Movement, where she unites, inspires, and empowers women to live their true purpose in life, business, and personally. www.rubymabry.com

J. Scott MacMillan is a father, entrepreneur, filmmaker, blogger, and change agent psychology graduate. As a spiritual seeker, he employs daily meditation and mindfulness as his true guide. He enjoys meditation, photography, videography, writing, music, and anything outdoors. www.bethechangeuwant.net

Nicole Schiener Manary has been "playing with words" since she was a child. She aims to inspire others with peace, hope, and joy. Her poetry and articles blend lessons and blessings from conscious parenting with clinical wisdom. Her writing has been featured in *Holistic Parent Magazine* and *Elephant Journal.* www.facebook.com/peaceandpossiblity

Cydney Mar, Former National Level Figure Skater, International Fashion Designer, and Wellness Enthusiast, can be found in Montreal, QC, Canada, tending her wee menagerie of Jack (the mini Schnauzer) and Chuk (her Blue Bird of Happiness) and chasing after her wellness clients to drink more water! www.cydneymarwellness.com

Kim Marks is a Soul Coach who helps you transform into alignment with your soul. From manifesting a new goal to understanding and moving through the depths of grief, she helps you to reconnect to your internal abundance. Learn more about her and how she can help you here: www.KimMarksCoaching.com.

Anita D. Marshall is a Soul Awareness Coach and Soul Plan Practitioner/Teacher. After discovering her life purpose during soul-guided travels, she created *A Journey Into Soul* – a sacred space for sharing insights and providing resources to empower others to deepen their own soul connection. www.ajourneyintosoul.com

Kris Martin is a creative teacher with an adventurous love of life and the author of *Love Speaks*. She enjoys inspiring others to unwind their personal suffering through sharing experiences from her own direct introspection and her years of studying the Enneagram and the Gene Keys.

Lori Kilgour Martin is an angelic counselor and musical theatre artist from Canada. She is a co-author in *365 Days of Angel Prayers*, and this is her fourth contribution in the *365 Book Series*. She feels honored to walk in divine service. Visit Lori at www.diamondheartangel.com.

Vicki Ann Martinelli, Authentic, No B.S., Spiritual Life Coach, is a successful insurance broker by day and a hardworking Reiki Master, ordained minister, mind-body-spirit practitioner/teacher, and Certified Angel Intuitive Card Reader by night. She helps others recognize their blessings in the midst of blame.

Veronica Mather is a writer and keen photographer. She is passionate about animal welfare and shares her life with her husband, Dale; four rescued sheep; and two high-spirited dogs, Max and Blaze.

Charissa May-Riley is a fitness instructor who helps people find wellness through exercise and essential oils. She is a wife and mother of two beautiful boys. This Kentucky native enjoys music, reading, studying new subjects, and being outside. www.mydoterra.com/charissamayriley

Kristy Carr McAdams shares from her "spiritual tool belt" to show people how to discover their personal gifts. She's a mama, smile purveyor, psychic/medium, artist, Certified Angel Practitioner (ACP), Reiki/IET Practitioner, sound healing facilitator, mandala/art facilitator, author, and hugger extraordinaire. www.EnergyOfAngels.com

Kellie McGarry is a wife, mother, and yoga lover. She is a Certified Health Coach, a Certified Nidra Instructor, and a Certified Reiki 1 and 2 Therapist who specializes in body image and mindful living. She enjoys sharing her story of eating disorder recovery. www.kelliemcgarry.com

Carolyn McGee empowers women who have abandoned themselves to reconnect with their inner wisdom, enhance their intuition, and trust their divine messages so that they live guided by spirit with clarity, joy, purpose, ease, and grace. www.carolynmcgee.com

Victoria McGee is a writer focused on spiritual healing following trauma. Her blog, *Still Beloved*, has thousands of followers worldwide. She lives in southern California with her husband and a menagerie of dogs and cats. She practices Reiki and performs comedy improvisation – two different forms of healing! www.stillbeloved.com

Margaretta McIlvaine is the founder of the Bridge Between the Worlds Retreat Center in VA. She combined her formal training at the Barbara Brennen School of Healing with numerous modalities and developed Transformational Healing Systems. She has been in private practice for 20 years.

Jenny McKaig is CEO, writer, and coach at JennyMcKaig.com; international bestselling author and senior editor of *Empowering Women to Succeed*; and a certified Awakening Coach. She helps authors craft international bestselling books. She loves yoga; surfing; her husband, Shawn; their daughter, Liberty; and their child-on-the-way.

Trish McKinnley, The SASSI Goddess, is a bestselling author, human dynamic expert, and fairy godmother. She has helped countless people transform their lives via her podcasts, writings, workshops, and private sessions. To discover your Sassi Goddess, please visit www.thesassigoddess.com.

Kris McLeod wants to live in a world where people love their lives and are open-hearted, compassionate, and kind. And quirky. And where they laugh a lot. She helps lovely people with life, health, and business, and lives in Australia with her husband and gorgeous fur-kids. www.enjoymentrevolution.com

Niki Meadows is a Worthiness Ambassador™ who empowers women to live the fulfilling lives they're worthy of. She recently released a book detailing the process she used to overcome a 17-year battle with depression. www.nikimeadows.com

Carly Melnick is a young writer of 18 years who comes from the town of Windermere, Florida. She is a graduate of The First Academy, a Christian school where she learned her writing and character skills. Her inspiration comes from her family and friends who always encourage her to give 110%.

Giuliana Melo aspires to inspire. She loves life, God, and her family. She spends her days spreading love and light and helping others heal. She is a cancer survivor who is passionate about medicine, non-traditional healing, and angel therapy. She has been married for 30 years and has one 19-year-old son. www.giulianamelo.com

Cornelia Merk is an author, educator, holistic health practitioner, and personal trainer with an extensive background in the study of human potential, the body-mind connection, and the body's self-healing capacity. She works internationally, helping people discover and use their innate healing potential. www.corneliamerk.com

Haley Ryane Meushaw brings highly valuable answers – directed by spirit – to those seeking direction with physical, mental, and emotional well-being. Oneness sessions are amazing and enjoyable and activate your body's natural healing processes. Her business is NEON Living-Novel Energy 4 Oneness Now. www.neon4living.com

Aphrodite Mirisis is an administrative assistant in Midtown Manhattan and lives in Queens, New York. In her spare time, she enjoys photography, sketching, painting, and gardening. She has self-published two children's books: *This Is My House* and *The Best of Both Worlds*.

Brian Monahan, a heart-based thought leader in the audio-visual and event industry, is a passionate purveyor of delight. He is the author of *Customer Delight 365: A Daily Inspirational for Customer Service Professionals*. He believes that delight is in the heart of the beholder. Visit him at www.BrianMonahan.me.

Mike Monahan is the owner of ThinkMonahan, LLC. A 30-year experienced facilitator, business coach, author, and speaker, he has written four books. (His bestseller, *From the Jungle to the Boardroom*, debuted at #1 in *Inc. Magazine*.) He works from his homes in Cincinnati, Ohio, and Seminole, Florida, coaching, writing, and speaking.

Carisa Montooth, Dating Coach, Speaker, and Healer, shows successful women how to attract and date marriage-minded men without self-sabotage. She helps women energetically heal their subconscious blocks to love and navigate the dating world with ease, grace, and confidence. www.carisamontooth.com

Sonya L. Moore is an entrepreneur. She owns Moore Planning & Consulting LLC and co-founded two other organizations. She loves breathing life into new ideas, reading, writing, and being with family. She lives in Cincinnati, Ohio, with her husband, Craig, and teenagers, Craig II and Shanoah. www.sonyalmoore.com

Tere Moore is a woman of the world and modern-day scribe (court reporter); a student of philosophy, mysticism, and indigenous cultures; a musician, artist, and writer; creator of Terra Quest (a mini vision-quest experience); mother of two fine sons and grandmother to five grandsons; and owner of a wonderful life.

Michelle Smith Mufarreh is a copywriter for businesses that provide holistic products and services for animal companions and their people. She has also lived abroad and enjoyed connecting with people near and far for more than 20 years as a flight attendant. www.michellesmithmufarreh.com

Corina Y. Muro was born in Paramount, CA, and is the older of two siblings. After high school, her mother became ill, and she became her caretaker. In 2002, she studied at Los Angeles City College, in pursuit of her passion. Today she works with families, providing the best care possible for their loved ones.

Eva Muserelli is a Lightwork Gladiator™ who combines her intuition with her unique integration of modalities to facilitate and support physical, spiritual, and emotional balance and well-being. www.EvaRayofLight.com

Reema Sharma Nagwan holds degrees in Commerce and Law and a post-graduate diploma in Company Secretaryship. Living in Australia and now working full time as a compliance professional, she juggles her kids, household, and passion for literature. Her hobbies are baking delicacies and grooving to her favourite mix.

Farahana Surya Namaskar is a published author and motivational speaker. She strives to help others find meaning and purpose in their life. Her faith in God reminds her that everything happens *for* us, not *to* us. Her purpose is to help people discover their potential and divine life purpose.

Lucy V. Nefstead lives in northern Wisconsin with her dog, Sam. She is a retired English, Speech, and Theatre teacher who is co-chair of an animal rescue, president of retired teachers, on Wisconsin's board of directors, and serves on state committees. Spirituality is an integral part of her life.

Janet G. Nestor is a Licensed Professional Counselor and Diplomate in Comprehensive Energy Psychology. She is co-developer of Radiant Energies Balance, a mindfulness-based energy psychology that encourages nervous-system balance. This technique assists individuals with chronic illness and injuries to achieve the ability to move forward in their lives.

Hue Anh Nguyen is an intuitive healer and coach with 20 years of experience using her own unique, restorative process that corrects reverse polarity to create a life in balance. She has provided transformational healing for thousands of people by detecting and releasing negative energies. www.polarity4harmony.com

Daniel Nilon is a business coach who comes from a science background experimenting with the science of energy. He utilized online business strategies to build a global business around his passion. Currently he coaches through www.ahanaanddaniel.com, helping other innovators monetize their ideas and create a heart-based business.

Robin OK is a writer and Creative Collaboration Coach. She empowers people to see their creative dreams through to completion. She founded Laugh & Dream Creative Coaching, where she leads Laughter Yoga and Active Dreaming. She is a visionary for the Creative Collaborative ReTREAT. www.creativecollaborativeretreats.com

Cyvilstre Rio Olami is an international freelancer and a relationship expert/therapist with years of experience. He was born in a suburb of Lagos, Nigeria, and enjoys writing and working with both local and international firms. www.facebook.com/cyvilstre.rioolamis

Wendyanne Pakulsky is passionate about reminding people that with every life shift comes an opportunity for growth and healing into new heights of awareness.

Lisa Anna Palmer is doing her part to make the world a better workplace by helping people to fully step into their leadership roles at work. Her upcoming book, *Light a Fire in Their Hearts*, will contain secrets that great leaders employ to inspire and engage others and make a positive impact.

Neelam Patel is a qualified Optometrist in Kent. As a Spiritual Life Coach, she integrates Soul Plan Reading, Soul Transformation Therapy, Theta Healing, and Oneness Blessings in her sessions. She enjoys travel, yoga, nature, and sharing food and fun with loved ones. www.heartcentredcoaching.co.uk

Shirani M. Pathak is a modern-day mystic and visionary in the field of psychotherapy. She is trailblazing the integration of psychotherapy and ancient healing practices to help people heal deep wounds they have carried for years or even lifetimes. To learn more, visit www.CenterforSoulfulRelationships.com.

Lupe Ramirez Peterkin remains strong in her spiritual path. She uses her experiences with God to inspire others. Time spent dancing, writing, and visiting New York keep her passion alive. She is writing her autobiography and shares her life's adventures with her husband, children, and grandsons.

Lola Pittenger is a holistic life coach, Reiki practitioner, and producer of her own essential oil skin-care line, Glow by Lola. After receiving her Master's in Bilingual Education, she discovered her love of teaching others how to heal themselves from within. See more at www.glowbylola.com.

Danielle Pomerleau, Intention Alchemist and Intuitive, is certified in the holistic modalities of Reiki, TMRT, and The Aroma Freedom Technique. She helps people quickly dissolve unresolved emotions and limiting beliefs associated with unconscious memories. Passions include Tribal Belly Dancing and her son. www.dpomerleau.weebly.com

Poppy Popowich believes in the power of possibility and was able to master her failures and inspire countless others to follow their dreams. She is an accomplished speaker, published author with *Chicken Soup for the Soul's* Jack Canfield, guest speaker at Zig Ziglar International, and founder of www.PoweredByPossible.com. Live your dream life!

Rev. Shelia Prance, PhD, has spent her career as an accounting professional. She has a Bachelor of Science degree in accounting and is an ordained minister with a MDiv and a PhD in Religious Studies. Her graduate degrees are based in Native American Spirituality.

Annie Price is a spiritual healer who uses heartfelt, intuitive guidance to empower others in their divine purpose and in living the joyful expression of their soul. She has a BA in Psychology and loves being the mom of three. www.SoulSoaring.com

Donna S. Priesmeyer is a media professional who enjoys many creative pursuits, including: gardening; traveling; writing; creating art; and spending time with her husband, family, friends and pets. She is the publisher of a spiritually based website featuring consciousness-raising, art, music, and literature: www.LightonLife.net.

Misty Proffitt-Thompson is a bestselling author, angel-card reader, mind/body/spirit practitioner, teacher, and speaker. She helps those who are struggling to find their purpose, feel validated, and obtain clarity. She is married and has four children and four grandchildren. www.mistymthompson.com

Taryn Pyle is a woman with a mission: to help women live life in love – in love with their body, their life *now*, and all that surrounds them. She can be found at www.worthherweight.com.

Mimi Quick is known as the "Prosperity Muse." She is a psychic business mentor and owner of the Spiritual Business Institute – a spiritual coaching and training company that empowers spirited entrepreneurs to create prosperous, aligned businesses and lives doing what they love. www.MimiQuick.com

Michelle Radomski is a book designer, graphic designer, mandala artist, and author. For 35 years she's created customized, inspiring designs for purpose-driven individuals and organizations. She creates "art with heart" designed to make words and work visible. Because, "if you want to serve, you first must be seen." www.OneVoiceCan.com

StacyLynn Rasmussen is a coach, artist, wife, and mother who loves to inspire and guide others to help them shine their light. She has an eye for patterns and obscurities. She was raised "on the road," traveling the country with her comedian parents. www.stacylynnphoenix.com

Danielle Redmond is a London-born Certified Nutritional Psychology Coach, supporting clients in overcoming challenges related to food/body. Brought up bilingual in Spain, she loves to travel. When she isn't researching the nutritional realm, she spends time in nature with her dog, Niki, and practises yoga. www.yumyumguru.com

L. A. Reeves was born into an Air Force family and moved often as a child. She enjoys traveling for fun as an adult. She has settled in Texas and is blessed to have a son, Ty. She is the author of the upcoming book *The Back Side of the Heart – Journeys from the Front Side to the Back Side of One's Heart*. She has her mom, a poet, to thank for her desire to write.

Jacine Rilea is a single parent who has worked many casual jobs and also run her own business as a chiropractor. She is currently building her approach to health, which she calls "Orchestree." She says, "I love being creative, working with nature, and designing work flows that connect." www.Orchestree.com.au

Nathalie Rivett focuses on the power of the heart and mind combined to empower her family and clients. She is a Certified Hypnotherapist, HeartMath Coach and Trainer, and Reiki Master. Her life purpose is to raise people's vibrational frequencies through her Healing Hypnotherapy and meditations. www.coherentheartmindwellness.com

Lisa "The Link" Rizzo is a businesswoman, mother, wife, and full-time spiritual medium. She lives in Toronto, Canada, with her wonderful husband and three children. She would love to share her gift with you and can be contacted here: lisathelink@gmail.com.

Pauline Hosie Robinson writes about self-healing through the eyes of love. In her autobiography, *Triumph of Joy*, she utilized nature to help her cope with her husband's PTSD. After her husband's traumatic death, a shaman empowered her to heal herself. To read her healing journey through the natural world, visit www.triumphofjoy.com.

Moni Rodriguez is a #1 international bestselling author, speaker, and coach who helps women around the world transform stress and overwhelm into greater peace, passion, and joy. She believes that when women shine their light and claim their inner power, they can change the world.

Faye Rogers is an animal communicator, visionary, writer, intuitive healer, and qualified teacher of the Diana Cooper School in Angels and Ascension. She works with animals and people to bring more harmony and awareness. She is passionate about humanity and empowering others. www.animalcommunication-newzealand.com

Amanda Roggemann is retired, lives in Smyrna, GA, and volunteers her time at her metaphysical church and bookstore/gift shop, sharing with others how life truly is an adventure worth living.

Cara M. Rosch and Alex Biholar met in the spring of 2012, quickly hit it off, and became fast friends. This dynamic duo was married in September 2017. Alex received his BS and MS from UT Dallas and works as a geophysicist. Cara received her BS from U of Iowa, completed her MBA, and works as a child life specialist.

Isabella Rose is a bestselling author, certified Angel Energy Healer, angel oracle card reader and messenger, aromatherapist, and student at Quantum University. She is an advocate for those with no voice. Her passions include art in various media, traveling, and spending time in nature and with loved ones. www.bellarosehealinghands.com

Nora Rose is the author of *Gabriel's Journey* and *Bentley's Week*. She is a speaker, coach, teacher with several degrees, and a Certified Canfield Trainer. She has inspired many to believe in themselves and their dreams. She enjoys traveling the world with her three daughters and playing with her dog. norarosebooks@gmail.com

Ellyn Rothstein has worked extensively in the music, entertainment, and advertising industries. She holds a degree as a Certified Holistic Health Counselor from The Institute for Integrative Nutrition. She is currently a Licensed Real Estate Salesperson in New York City and can be contacted at ellynrothstein11@gmail.com.

Richard Saenz has been a sports anchor in Phoenix, Arizona, since 2003. Born in McAllen, Texas, he graduated from Incarnate Word University in San Antonio. Over the last 20+ years, he has covered events like the Super Bowl and interviewed sports celebrities like LeBron James and Muhammad Ali.

Leslie Sann is an award-winning author who serves as a mentor, teacher, and coach. Since 1986 she has been helping people change the way they think about who they are and what they can do while supporting them in creating a life they love. www.living-bydesign.com

Lori Santo is an artist, poet, writer, storyteller, dreamweaver, soul-recovery artist, life coach, ancient priestess, highly sensitive being, creativity maven, lover of life, and spirit. She is on a mission to bring light to the darkest caverns of our existence through writing, artistry, and creative soul recovery.

Kyra Schaefer is the co-founder of the Holistic Speakers Guild (HSG) – a membership site for authors to get their message to the world through speaking. HSG offers speaker and business training. Here, authors can gain more exposure and mastermind with others just like them. www.holisticspeakersguild.com

Susan Elizabeth Schoemmell's journey as a seeker of her authentic self has led her to Hawaii, Czechoslovakia, Italy, Ireland, Scotland, and England – from the Haleakala Crater on Maui to Stonehenge in England. She is grateful for the blessings and chooses to be a light on the path for other seekers. www.sesangel.simplesite.com

Salome Schori is an energy healer and environmental scientist. Her passion is to assist others in healing and personal growth. She would love to help you let go of old grudges and find more peace with a forgiveness meditation: www.salomeschori.com/goodnessabounds.

Isla Selupucin is a mindful mother and intuitive empath. She is the creator of www.littlebeeandbutterfly.com, a website that journals her spiritual stories and connections. She lives in Turkey with the loves of her life: her daughter, Ceyda, and husband, Koray.

Tessa Shaffer is the award-winning author of *Heaven Has No Regrets*, a 2016 *Writer's Digest* Competition Award Winner and an Indie Excellence Book Awards Finalist. Her work has appeared in *GirlsLIFE Magazine*. You can find updates on her books and inspiration to live life with "No Regrets" at www.TessaShaffer.com.

Kathryn Shah is passionate about Eastern philosophy and loves to travel. She is a Reiki practitioner, intuitive reader, meditation practitioner, and international teacher. In 2008, she decided to follow her heart, leaving everything behind in the UK to fulfil her dream of living in Australia. www.kathrynshah.com

Lateefah Shaheed is a personal-growth facilitator, coach, writer, and spiritual mentor. She feels inspired to create world peace through inner peace. She holds a BS in Business Administration and an MA in Professional Development. She can be reached at www.Lateefah.xyz.

Pooja Shende is an entrepreneur, author, keynote speaker, emotional-intelligence and NLP practitioner, and a performance coach who had over 20 successful years in a corporate career. She is the author of *365 Days of Mindfulness: Quotes for Life* and a contributing bestselling author of two books in the *365 Book Series*. www.lotussoul9.com

Jo Shepherd walked the final section of the Camino at the age of 60 and wrote a highly practical book, *Walking the Camino for Newbies: A Guide to Making Your Way to Santiago de Compostela*, to help you create a Camino pilgrimage that really works for you. Available on Amazon.

Teresa Madrone Sinay has served as a public school teacher and principal since 1987. She considers herself an "all-American" career mom turned rogue spiritual seeker. She openly shares her awakening journey and supports others also on a path of discovering their full essence of self at www.womanawakened.com.

Cindy Smiczek is a 40-something scrapbooker and artist who enjoys documenting her multifaceted journey through life. With a childhood nickname of "Happyface," she attempts to carry this positivity with her throughout her adventures. She has recently taken an oath to create daily. She can be found on Instagram @cindypurplehappy.

Sharon G. Smith was born and raised in the Pacific Northwest (USA) and owned a healthcare uniform business for many years. She also lived in Japan but presently resides in Michigan. She blogs about her experiences and observations touching on culture, lifestyle, and the people around her. www.sharonswalkabout.com

Dr. Shari Sorbo, DD, DS, MAP, RScP, is a transformational counselor and writer who blends her psychological and spiritual approach in assisting people to discover their true joy and passion for living a heartfelt life. www.sharisorbo.com

H. Michelle Spaulding is an entrepreneur and a self-taught artist. She owns Crafty Diva Cottage, a business offering creativity consulting, art events, classes, and workshops in the fiber arts. She expresses her creativity through the fiber arts and storytelling. www.etsy.com/shop/CraftyDivaCottage

Kelly M. Spencer is a mindful life enthusiast who creates a healing space for her clients and readers through being a life coach, yoga teacher, and wellness writer. Her fun and light approach to life creates a dynamic energy for her retreats, workshops, keynote speaking events, and books. www.KellyMSpencer.com

Marie Spencer-Rowland is an EFT therapist and women's coach whose passion is helping women let go of the emotional scars of past trauma so they can live a life of freedom, happiness, and peacefulness. www.wholisticwomenswarrior.com

Lynn Spiro underwent a deep, personal transformation and is now living a life of love, light, and spiritual mindfulness. She is passionate about leading lost, confused women into their own light through teaching meditation, healing with crystals, interpretive creative arts, and sharing her journey through writing. www.lynnspiro.com

Debby Spitzig loves writing and is waiting for her first book, *Inspiring Birth Stories*, to be published. She teaches HypnoBirthing prenatal classes, for the baby cuddles. She keeps her angels close and her granddaughters closer. She is happily married and loves sarcasm and football. Go, Steelers!

Rani St. Pucchi is the founder and award-winning designer of the world-renowned bridal house St. Pucchi, a bestselling author, an image consultant, and a relationship expert. Her #1 bestselling books *Your Body, Your Style* and *The SoulMate Checklist* are now available on Amazon and at Barnes & Noble.

Cynthia Starborn is an inspirational author, teacher, and soul guide. She offers transformative classes and consultations, based on the Akashic Records, for adults and children. Fluent in French, Spanish, and English, she loves helping you transcend challenges and tap into the magic of life. www.CynthiaStarborn.com

Alison M. Stokes is a native of Dublin, Ireland. She is a professional astrologer and angel-card reader who combines her certified healing and counselling skills to treat clients on a holistic level. Being with animals is her passion, and she's looking to live by the sea. Contact her at: www.facebook.com/silversoultherapy.

Sally M. Sutton is a spiritual catalyst for those searching for answers. She guides them to recognize their inner voice and to seek answers from within so that they can discover a path of true love, peace, and joy, while stepping into their own unique power. www.SallyMSutton.com

Tracey Swainson is an energy healer who is passionate about helping women who've experienced the trauma of pregnancy loss. She brings healing to the spiritual and physical bodies through sacred, supportive sessions. The healing of her own pregnancy loss fully birthed her into this sacred work. www.traceyswainson.com

Joelle Rose Szlosek is a mystic, healer, and teacher who creates heart-centered sacred space for all to reconnect, remember, and embrace their authentic self. Combining numerology with divinely guided insight, she provides uplifting sessions, readings, and workshops to individuals, couples, and businesses. www.joelleroseszlosek.com

Kaori Takada, currently residing in Tokyo, is a Japanese Reiki practitioner and meditation facilitator. Continuing the quest for mindful living, she enjoys the magical power of music by playing the piano. She lives a nomadic life along with her husband, who is a diplomat.

Micheal "Mike" Taylor served 25 years in the U.S. Army, reaching the rank of Lieutenant Colonel. Upon retiring, he wrote a mission statement for his life and has since been pursuing it: to be a joyous, self-exploring, and healthy adventurer who lives in community and integrity.

Lori Thiessen lives in Alberta, Canada, where she works as an architectural tech during the day, moonlights as a writer, and is mom to five almost-grown-up kids. She is a certified NLP Practitioner, Toastmaster, and runner. www.couragefinder.com

Jamie Thomas is a young man exploring life and nature to discover his deepest calling. Becoming a well-known and beloved author is one of his greatest desires. He enjoys time with his friends, mother, and cats on the East Coast, pushing his edge – and always welcoming the return home.

Lori Thomas is a Spiritual Ecologist who uses wisdom from nature and insects to help you rediscover your childlike wonder in the natural world as you reconnect with yourself, others, and all of Nature's Kingdoms to create a world where we can all thrive. www.spiritualecologist.com

Rev. Jamie Lynn Thompson's passion is helping to empower and uplift others to let their "Sparkle Shine and Live Toadily Divine." She is a spiritual ambassador, faith healer, angel practitioner, reflexologist, and spiritual life coach. www.RevJamieLynn.com

Barbara Toller is a Certified Archetype Consultant from Kansas City. She enjoys being a volunteer for the Youth Ambassador Program and invites you to learn more about what makes this organization so successful by visiting their website: www.youthambassadorskc.org.

Shannon Townsend shows you how to tackle everything on your plate, without adding on more work, by seeing how all the pieces fit together. "It's all about seeing things from a 10,000 foot vantage point, understanding how it all breaks down, and enjoying the process." www.ShannonTownsendCoaching.com

Thomas E. Uharriet is most celebrated as the encoder of *The Memoirs of Billy Shears*, written from the perspective of the man who replaced Paul McCartney in the Beatles. He also brings transformational teachings to light from sacred ancient traditions that are now available at www.uharriet.com.

Teresa Velardi is a speaker, potter, author, and publisher who lives authentically and gratefully while making a difference for others. She says, "The one thing that is always constant is change." Her pottery illustrates transformation "from a ball of clay to a work of art." www.teresavelardi.com

Valerie R. Vestal is a Psychiatric Nurse Practitioner who passionately helps her clients achieve unique and individualized outcomes by reframing their thoughts. She guides them toward achieving confidence, hope, and a life that has meaning. vvestal@gmail.com

Steph Walczak is a Minnesota-grown, Denver-based aspiring writer, philanthropist, world traveler, budding foodie, nature lover, and cat mom who has been lucky enough to witness many acts of kindness all over the world. She hopes to emulate the positive people she surrounds herself with to make a difference in this world.

Heather Wiest is beyond blessed to love, serve, and inspire the community as a Registered Yoga Teacher, Reiki Master, and Licensed Clinical Social Worker. Her holistic yoga sessions are engaging and rejuvenating, leaving one feeling balanced and inspired. Restore your body. Renew your mind. Refresh your spirit. www.loveserveinspire.com

Ty Will grew up in Montana camping, fishing, and just having fun. She is the author of *The Female Veteran*.

Charlene Williams is a mother of five, and "Gramster/Mami" to nine! She is blessed to have these people in her life. Her thirst for knowledge of God, Angels, and Spirit has always been a huge part of who she is, and she sends light and love to all.

Ella Wilson, an apprentice monk in the tradition of Dunisha, has been living a minimalist life for three years while training in modern psychology, Eastern philosophy, and interfaith leadership. Her future aspirations include helping communities in need of food and shelter, while building bridges of peace between all of humanity.

Janet Womack is a Holistic Life Coach who's madly in love with cats, laughter, food, nature, and personal growth. She helps entrepreneurs merge life passions and business. An infertility survivor, she inspires and empowers women to live their lives on purpose and create a fulfilling life after loss. www.janetlwomack.com

Jody Wootton lives with heart-centered gratitude. She works as an outside travel agent for Heart Cruises, LLC ("Create memories by taking vacations") and as an Independent Consultant for Touchstone Crystal ("Add sparkly jewelry to your everyday"). www.touchstonecrystal.com/jw3

Kim Wright is creative, unconventional, and passionate about adventure, nature, family, and faith. God speaks to her through her passions, and sometimes an inspirational story is born that she has to share. She works, plays, laughs, and loves in Denver with the splendor of the Colorado Rockies just minutes away.

Tessa Wuyts chases her dream every day of helping children and their parents, which is her life purpose. "Chase your dream, follow your heart, and be the true miracle that you are!"

Karen Wythe is dedicated to living life with passion. She is a lifelong Spiritualist, ordained minister, Certified Medium, healer, Life Transformation Coach, workshop presenter, writer, and fiber artist. She enjoys traveling through life with her husband, best friend, and soulmate, Bill. www.enrichingliferesources.com/AboutKaren.php

Joan B. Zietlow, BSN, RN, AFMC, CHHC, AADP, MBA, is a functional medicine practitioner who helps others thrive through health optimization. She inspires and educates while dispelling myths. Her clients enjoy energy, joy, health, self-confidence, peace, and solutions to long-time health concerns. www.vibranthealthandhealing.com

Jenean Zunk believes that every woman deserves to live a life of confidence and courage – and that suffering with emotional overwhelm, depression, or anxiety is simply a disconnection from our own divinity. She helps women master their emotions and reclaim their innate power to transform their lives. www.namastelivingonline.com

Contributor Index

For your convenience, we have listed each contributor in alphabetical order by last name and have included the page number(s) of their piece(s). We hope that this makes finding your favorite co-authors easy!

Nikki Ackerman: 375

Noelle Adamo: 277

Sabinah Adewole: 369

Kelli Adkins: 286

Tiffany Andersen: 205, 334, 362

Chris Anderson: 274

Lara Anderson: 10

Trena Anderson: 210

Melisa Archer: 232, 259, 328

Katrina Ariel: 38

Sarah Atkinson: 289, 368

Alisa Auger: 288

Sarah Auger: 363

Pratibha Badurkar: 293

Joy T. Barican: 47, 157, 246

Nora T. Barican: 32, 115, 142

Mauri Barnes: 117, 184, 296, 318

Judy Basaraba: 6

Randy Bassett: 272

Susan Bassett: 55

Keyon Bayani: 123

Lauren Bear: 66, 101, 284

Kimberly Beer: 188

Rebekah Bernard: 354

Tahira Bharmal: 76

Alex Biholar: 358

Bevan Bird: 70

Tamra Blankenship: 175

Cathie Bliss: 64

Kimber Bowers: 162

Irene E. Bradford: 229

Anne Bradley: 241

Michael Brewer: 285

Kimberly Brochu: 9, 114, 261

Shannon L. Brokaw: 305

Jena Brown: 195

Lydia Burchell: 58

Benjamin Bush: 360

Christine Callahan-Oke: 116

Barbara "Bobbie" Carr: 87

Cheryl Carrigan: 15

Angie Carter: 345

Crystal M. Cathell: 28

Karen Ceballos: 135, 164

Jodi Chapman: 3, 110

Robin Chellis: 228

Katie Keck Chenoweth: 69, 95

Claire Chew: 212, 331

Karen Ciran-Barnes: 346

Tiffany Clay: 248

Lisa R. Cohen: 98

Joanne Angel Barry Colon: 231, 257

Keyra Conlinn: 57

Terry Corrao: 279

Nikki A. Creber: 256

Dianna Robinson Curren: 141

Kathy Damas: 14, 91

Marla David: 71, 200, 349

Patty Davis: 42

Netta de Beer: 143

Kathy DeFinis: 37

Heather A. Dempsey: 254

Crysti Deusterman: 65

Robyn Dewar: 149

Felicia D'Haiti: 262

Ruth Donald: 153

Nicole Donovan-Wells: 234

Patricia Downing: 313

Kimberly DuBoise: 22

Jerri Eddington: 355

Denise Edelstein: 49

Tandy Elisala: 271

Kimberly A. Elliott: 107, 335

Alison Ellison: 44, 68, 216

Michelle Evans: 121

Phoebe Fazio: 333

Leslie P. Felton: 269

Helen Ferrara: 124, 206, 348

Linsey Fischer: 302

Meredith Fjelsted: 23

Scott Fjelsted: 126

Kim Brazier Flatland: 88

Gigi Florez: 77

Suzanne Fortino: 332

Tammy Foster: 280

Chireya K. Fox: 339

Erin Fritts: 287

John R. Fyfe: 187, 194, 325

Darlene Gaetz: 342

Tammy Gamester: 81

B. J. Garcia: 56, 109

Laura Garrett: 132

Michelle Goguen: 243

Ray Goodenough: 131, 156

Padma Gordon: 41, 138

Michelle Anne Gould: 347

Vijaya Gowrisankar: 255

Michelle R. Griffith: 182, 204, 218

Nadene Joy Hagen: 166, 176, 252

Rael Hall: 365

Marihet Hammann: 372

Joy Harris: 192, 213

Annalene Hart: 322

Lisa Hawkins: 370

Ellouise Heather: 30

Chadi Hemaidan: 93

Sharon Hickinbotham: 46

Mikaela Che'lean Hicks: 281

Karen Hill: 168

Cindy Harpe Hively: 97

Jesse Hodgdon: 102

Gretchen Oehler Hogg: 324

Maureen Hollmeyer: 34, 112, 151, 224

Sharyn Holmes: 48

Diana L. Hooker: 29, 51, 268

Cynthia Lee Horn: 214, 298, 364

Anne-Marie Hoyne: 104

Sarah Huffer: 323

Kimberly Hutt: 227, 265, 294

Katie Cox Jackson: 350

Kelly Jenkins: 92, 178

Sheila Jenkins: 276

Shayelee Johnson: 79

Julie Jones: 273

Nancy Merrill Justice: 73, 203, 326

Surabhi Kalsi: 75

Ayeesha S. Kanji: 308

Donna H. Kater: 173

Jenna Kelland: 80, 180

Diane L. Keyes: 144, 253

Davalynn Kim: 215

Elizabeth R. Kipp: 13

Marci Kobayashi: 5, 209, 247

Ingrid Koivukangas: 125

Manpreet Komal: 343

Carrie Kondor: 201

Marifran Korb: 21

Charlene Kussner: 307

Debbie Labinski: 179

V. Krishna Lakkineni: 371

Ahana Lara: 239

Jennifer Larkin: 366

Destrie Larrabee: 50

Beth Larsen: 145

Catherine Laub: 74, 129, 242

Cheryl Lawrence: 336

Sarah Lawrence: 130

Kenneth I. Laws II: 84

Tara Leduc: 264

Patricia LeBlanc: 303

Rhonda Lee: 319

Saundra Lee: 330

Tanya Levy: 134, 155, 245

Ruthie Lewis: 196

Amy Lloyd: 344

Courtney Long: 310

Denny Long: 128

Gunhild Lorenzen: 105, 249

Fiona Louise: 357

Ruby Mabry: 309

J. Scott MacMillan: 136

Nicole Schiener Manary: 311

Cydney Mar: 337

Kim Marks: 133

Anita D. Marshall: 8, 53

Kris Martin: 379

Lori Kilgour Martin: 36

Vicki Ann Martinelli: 96

Veronica Mather: 193

Charissa May-Riley: 85

Kristy Carr McAdams: 72

Kellie McGarry: 139

Carolyn McGee: 244

Victoria McGee: 19

Margaretta McIlvaine: 25

Jenny McKaig: 31

Trish Mckinnley: 18

Kris McLeod: 197

Niki Meadows: 312

Carly Melnick: 306

Giuliana Melo: 113

Cornelia Merk: 16

Haley Ryane Meushaw: 174

Aphrodite Mirisis: 282

Brian Monahan: 226

Mike Monahan: 250

Carisa Montooth: 94

Sonya L. Moore: 63

Tere Moore: 86

Michelle Smith Mufarreh: 190, 217

Corina Y. Muro: 240

Eva Muserelli: 225

Reema Sharma Nagwan: 78

Farahana Surya Namaskar: 297

Lucy V. Nefstead: 163

Janet G. Nestor: 191

Hue Anh Nguyen: 278

Daniel Nilon: 238

Robin OK: 292

Cyvilstre Rio Olami: 152

Wendyanne Pakulsky: 172

Lisa Anna Palmer: 118

Neelam Patel: 100

Shirani M. Pathak: 154

Lupe Ramirez Peterkin: 329

Lola Pittenger: 258

Danielle Pomerleau: 7, 169

Poppy Popowich: 4

Shelia Prance: 304

Annie Price: 267

Donna S. Priesmeyer: 186

Misty Proffitt-Thompson: 89

Taryn Pyle: 291

Mimi Quick: 373

Michelle Radomski: 2

StacyLynn Rasmussen: 160

Danielle Redmond: 314

L.A. Reeves: 367

Jacine Rilea: 171

Nathalie Rivett: 202

Lisa Rizzo: 39

Pauline Hosie Robinson: 137, 219, 378

Moni Rodriguez: 374

Faye Rogers: 207

Amanda Roggemann: 354

Cara M. Rosch: 358

Isabella Rose: 26, 54, 62, 127

Nora Rose: 189, 211, 317

Ellyn Rothstein: 61

Richard Saenz: 67

Leslie Sann: 140

Lori Santo: 99

Kyra Schaefer: 183

Susan Elizabeth Schoemmell: 165

Salome Schori: 82

Isla Selupucin: 33

Tessa Shaffer: 208

Kathryn Shah: 43

Lateefah Shaheed: 237

Pooja Shende: 35

Jo Shepherd: 24

Teresa Madrone Sinay: 341

Cindy Smiczek: 235

Sharon G. Smith: 185

Shari Sorbo: 290, 376

H. Michelle Spaulding: 148

Kelly M. Spencer: 45

Marie Spencer-Rowland: 251

Lynn Spiro: 11, 150, 161

Debby Spitzig: 338

Rani St. Pucchi: 327

Cynthia Starborn: 351

Alison M. Stokes: 17

Sally M. Sutton: 40

Tracey Swainson: 301

Joelle Rose Szlosek: 20

Kaori Takada: 83

Micheal Taylor: 266

Dan Teck: 60, 222

Lori Thiessen: 122, 223

Jamie Thomas: 12, 147

Lori Thomas: 106, 119, 198

Jamie Lynn Thompson: 170, 233, 275

Barbara Toller: 300

Shannon Townsend: 103

Thomas E. Uharriet: 315

Teresa Velardi: 27, 299, 316

Valerie R. Vestal: 108, 236

Steph Walczak: 260

Heather Wiest: 230, 270

Ty Will: 146

Charlene Williams: 283

Ella Wilson: 167

Janet Womack: 199

Jody Wootton: 90

Kim Wright: 361

Tessa Wuyts: 340

Karen Wythe: 52, 359, 377

Joan B. Zietlow: 120

Jenean Zunk: 177

Acknowledgments

This is the fourth book in this special series, and we continue to be grateful to all of the contributors who bravely open their hearts and share their personal stories. It's not always an easy thing to do, and we appreciate their honesty and vulnerability.

Some of the co-authors have been part of this series from the very beginning, and others have joined us for the first time in this book. We want to thank each of them for trusting us with their words, for allowing us to share their stories, and for believing that together we really can make a positive difference in others' lives.

We are not only authors in a book but people in a community who care about and support one another. And we're truly grateful for each of them.

From Jodi: Dan showers me with so much goodness each and every day, and I'm always so grateful for him. From leaving a sweet note by my computer every morning so it's the first thing I'll see when I start the day, to rubbing my back while we fall asleep at night, and everything in between, I'm beyond blessed to have him in my life. With each year, each month, each day, and each minute that passes, I love him more completely than ever before. Dan, thank you for helping me know without a doubt that dreams really do come true. I truly hit the jackpot with you.

From Dan: Thank you to Jodi for being the embodiment of love and goodness, for showing me that you can have it all and that love can be easy, and for being my everything! I know that this book series, the community of authors and readers that's grown up around it, and everything we do all starts with your love, your heart, your talent, your creativity, your authenticity, your goodness. My life is infinitely richer and my heart is infinitely fuller because of you. Thank you for making our lives a love-filled adventure.

Lastly, we would like to thank you, the reader. Your loving emails and reviews mean the world to us. As a community, we all get to celebrate together each time someone's life is positively impacted by one of the stories. This is why we each do what we do. It's a writer's dream to know that our words mean something to someone else. So thank you so much to each of you who have reached out over the years and shared what these books mean to you. Thank you for believing in us, in this series, and in our vision of putting loving kindness into our world.

Other Books in This Series

This is the fourth book in our bestselling *365 Book Series*, and we would love to invite you to learn more about the books and join us as a contributing author, a reader, or both!

365 Ways to Connect with Your Soul

In this #1 international bestselling book, over 200 beautiful souls came together to share how they connect with their own souls with the hopes that it will help you connect with yours as well. It's a wonderful addition to your spiritual practice!

365 Moments of Grace

This #1 international bestselling book contains 365 personal stories of grace, miracles, and transformations from beautiful souls all around the world to show how magical our world is and how connected we truly are. Moments of grace are presents from the universe!

365 Life Shifts: Pivotal Moments That Changed Everything

In this #1 international bestseller, over 250 beautiful souls came together to share life shifts that they've experienced that opened up their world, inspired, uplifted, shook them to their core, got them back on track (or onto a new track altogether), and led them toward their true selves.

365 Soulful Messages: The Right Guidance at the Right Time

This upcoming book will share messages people received (a sign from the universe, a piece of divine guidance, or a seemingly commonplace conversation) that changed their lives forever. Available in 2019.

You can learn more about our current and upcoming books from this soulful series here: www.365bookseries.com.

An Invitation

If one of your dreams is to write a book that inspires others, then we hope you'll sign up for our program! In it, we include everything you'll need to write, finish, publish, and market your own book!

This program includes monthly live sessions, monthly workbooks, over 30 videos, one-on-one time, a private Facebook community, tons of advice from experts, and so much more! We support you during each step of your outer and inner journey of being a writer, offering concrete writing/marketing tools while guiding you through the emotional highs and lows that you'll experience throughout the process of bringing your soulful book to life.

You've already got the book inside you. Now it's time to get it out of you...and into the world. Now is the time to share your gift, answer your calling, and write your book! Your words matter. Your message matters. Your book matters! It can change the world, touch hearts, and inspire thousands...but only if you write it! If you're ready to bring your soulful book to life, we would be honored to support you on this life-changing journey! To learn more, visit www.yoursoulfulbook.com.

Made in the USA
Columbia, SC
17 December 2017